Teacher Reform in Indonesia

DIRECTIONS IN DEVELOPMENT
Human Development

Teacher Reform in Indonesia

The Role of Politics and Evidence in Policy Making

Mae Chu Chang, Sheldon Shaeffer, Samer Al-Samarrai, Andrew B. Ragatz, Joppe de Ree, and Ritchie Stevenson

THE WORLD BANK
Washington, D.C.

Contents

Boxes

Figures

Tables

Foreword

One of the noteworthy global achievements of the past two decades has been the remarkable increase in the number of children in school and completing the primary cycle. But this achievement has come with more challenges. Larger classes and higher pupil-teacher ratios and a more diverse, heterogeneous classroom of learners—speaking more local languages, from a wider range of socioeconomic backgrounds, with a greater range of abilities and disabilities—have made the task of the teacher in the classroom far more difficult. The task becomes even harder where education systems are unable to expand school facilities, produce more textbooks, and train more teachers (of sufficient quality) needed to match the higher enrollments. In many countries the result has been that many children are learning poorly, if at all. This fact has reinforced the need to focus more on quality—*beyond "schooling" (students in a classroom) to "learning" (what students learn and whether they learn how to keep on learning)*. And this requires systematic, comprehensive reforms of entire education systems and, accompanying those reforms, equally systematic and comprehensive policies.

Nowhere are such policies more needed than in regard to teachers. Teachers are the transmitters, by both word and deed, of what any nation wants its children to learn and how it wants them to live. Once recruited, they teach for decades, shaping the knowledge and skills of generations of children who pass through their classrooms. They account for a large percentage of all education sector budgets. Truly, the ultimate policy choices related to teacher management and development (from initial recruitment to preservice training, certification, induction and probation, and continuing professional development), as well as to teacher status and remuneration, are some of the most important decisions that any ministry of education must implement—and implement well.

But systematic documentation of teacher policies across countries, especially of well-performing education systems, is difficult to find. For this reason, the World Bank has embarked on a process to develop a Systems Approach for Better Education Results (SABER) on a range of important education policy areas, including on teachers. One of these efforts, SABER—Teachers, has been developed to analyze education systems according to eight core policy goals. These core policy goals were developed based on a review of international literature that documents their relevance for student or teacher performance, their possible prioritization for resource allocation, and their potential to be achieved through policy reforms. This program collects information on key teacher policy areas and then shares resulting analyses and other knowledge products to promote a more-informed dialogue around teacher policies and ultimately a more collaborative approach to improving the quality of teaching.

Over the past decade and more, Indonesia has embarked on a set of innovative education policies, including the decentralization of education service provision, the promotion of school-based management, the development of national quality standards, and the provision of annual operational grants to all primary and secondary schools. This book, *Teacher Reform in Indonesia: The Role of Politics and Evidence in Policy Making*, therefore, comes at a critical time. Against a backdrop of the broader set of policies, it examines the implementation of recent teacher policies, their impact on teachers and student outcomes, and the challenges and occasional failures in this implementation process. Critical to the teacher policies was the passage, in 2005, of the Teacher and Lecturer Law, which was meant to improve both the quality of teaching and the welfare of teachers. Its implementation these past eight years has revealed new challenges, as well as unexpected rewards and key lessons that can be used to improve Indonesia's dynamic education system. Evidence from an impact evaluation of critical components of this law and from detailed classroom observations of teaching and learning has also shed new light on the complexities of undertaking such comprehensive reforms.

In middle-income countries, innovative solutions and knowledge services that the World Bank can offer are increasingly in greater demand than financing. How to improve teacher quality and performance is a policy challenge that begs for new knowledge and practical solutions. This book aims to contribute to meeting this challenge. It is especially relevant to—and useful reading for—other countries contemplating teacher reforms similar to Indonesia's. It also demonstrates that the SABER—Teacher tools that have been used in this study can inform research, dialogue, and choices about better teacher management and development.

Elizabeth M. King
Education Director, The World Bank

Acknowledgments

Teacher Reform in Indonesia: The Role of Politics and Evidence in Policy Making is the result of seven years of collaborative effort between the Human Development Sector of the World Bank Indonesia country office and the Government of Indonesia. The Human Development Sector, led by Mae Chu Chang, produced over 50 independent background papers by Bank staff, government researchers, and international consultants, as well several major research projects including an impact evaluation and in-depth classroom observations. This synthesis report was prepared under the team leadership of Mae Chu Chang and included as members Samer Al-Samarrai, Andrew Ragatz, Joppe de Ree, Sheldon Shaeffer, and Ritchie Stevenson (co-authors) as well as Rina Arlianti, Susiana Iskandar, and Titie Hadiyati (contributors). Research assistance was provided by Shahnaz Arina, Megha Kapoor, Imam Setiawan, and Susie Sugiarti. Mary Anderson provided editorial support, and the graphic designer was Yvonne Armanto Ramali.

The production of this report, as well as the variety of research studies conducted over the past seven years on which the book is based, was generously supported by the Dutch Education Support Program (DESP) funded by the Government of the Kingdom of the Netherlands. The team is indebted to Arnold Vander Zanden (First Secretary Education, Royal Netherlands Embassy, Indonesia) for his strong support throughout the years for demand-driven and "just-in-time" policy work that has been carried out under DESP. Technical contributions from AusAID-supported consultants, Graham Dawson and John Bladen, are also acknowledged.

It should be noted that although inputs of various officials have been incorporated into the report, the policy recommendations in this document do not necessarily reflect the policies of the Government of Indonesia, the Government of the Kingdom of the Netherlands, or the World Bank.

The team of authors who produced this report is grateful to the officials and staff of the Ministry of Education and Culture for their overall support. Special thanks are in order to Fasli Jalal, former Vice Minister of Education, who was the visionary behind the Teacher Law that inspired this report and a key supporter of many of the teacher management studies that contributed to it. The current Minister of Education and Culture, Mohammad Nuh; Vice Minister of Education, Musliar Kasim; the Special Advisor to the Minister, Taufik Hanafi; the Head of the Board of Education and Culture, Human Resources Development and Quality Assurance for Education, Syawal Gultom; and the former Director General for Quality Improvement of Teacher and Education Personnel, Baedhowi, played major roles in using the evidence produced to improve the teacher regulations. The report also benefited greatly from the inputs of the Ministry of Religious Affairs, the National Development Planning Agency, the Ministry of State Administration Reform, the Ministry of Finance, and the Civil Service Agency, together with inputs of donor agencies that were received during various consultation meetings and policy forum discussions. Key government support came from the directors, the head of centers, and senior key staff of the Ministry responsible for teacher management, quality assurance, and teacher-related studies: Sumarna Suryapranata, Surya Dharma, Hendarman, Unifah Rosyidi, Abi Sujak, Muchlas Samani, Anah Suhaenah, Gogot Suharwoto, Maria Widiani, Poppy Puspitawati, Dian Wahyuni, Santi Ambarukmi, E. Nurzaman, Giri Suryaatmana, Ahmad Dasuki, Bambang Indriyanto, Nugaan Yulia Wardhani Siregar, Hari Setiadi, Burhanudin Tola, Yendri Wirda Burhan, Simon Sili Sabon, Rahmawati, Handayani Sumarno, Rumtini, Yaya Zakaria, and M.S. Sembiring.

Insightful comments from stakeholders were provided by Lilian Rahman (Gorontalo district), Sulistiyo (Chair of the Teacher Association of Republic of Indonesia, PGRI), Sahiri Hermawan (PGRI), Arief Rahman (Chair of the Indonesian National Commission for UNESCO), Heri Akhmadi (a member of Parliament), Anies Baswedan (Rector of Paramadina University and Chair of Indonesia Mengajar), Hetty Herawati (Principal of SD Taruna Bangsa), Sudarwan Danim and Anthony Crocker (consultants at the Board of Education and Culture, Human Resources Development and Quality Assurance for Education), Agus Supriatman (Head of the Education Office, Karawang District), Nanda Suhanda (a member of the Karawang District Parliament), Obang Nurbayu (Head of PGRI, Karawang District), and Nanang Muchlis (Chair, Board of Education, Karawang District).

The report was improved by detailed feedback from the following principal reviewers: F. Halsey Rogers, Venkatesh Sundararaman, and Helen J. Craig (World Bank); Molly Lee (formerly UNESCO); and Tom Lowrie (Charles Sturt University). Helpful comments were also received from William Wallace, James A. Brumby, and Yasuhiko Matsuda (World Bank). The report was prepared under the guidance of Luis Benveniste, Sector Manager, East Asia and Pacific Region, and the support of Stefan Koeberle (Country Director for Indonesia).

About the Authors and Contributors

Samer Al-Samarrai is a senior education economist in the East Asia and Pacific Region of the World Bank. He currently coordinates the research and analytical work of the education unit in Indonesia. Before joining the World Bank in 2011, he worked at UNESCO and coauthored the annual *Education For All Global Monitoring Report*. Between 2003 and 2008, he managed a governance project in Bangladesh that supported Ministry of Finance efforts to improve the financing and quality of service delivery in the health and education sectors. He has also been a research fellow at the Institute of Development Studies in the United Kingdom and has undertaken research and advisory work in many countries in Sub-Saharan Africa and South Asia. He has published widely on gender, finance, and governance issues in the education sector. He holds a PhD in economics from the University of Sussex.

Rina Arlianti worked for many years at the Indonesian Ministry of Education and Culture and was Head of Section in several sub-directorates in the Directorate of Technical and Vocational Education (DTVE). She later became Deputy Director for Student Development at the Directorate for Special Education and then was seconded by the Ministry to work as a curriculum specialist at SEAMEO VOCTECH in Brunei Darussalam for three years from 2001 to 2004. Since 2005 she has been working as an independent consultant for several different donors in basic education, higher education, technical vocation and educational training, and education management.

Mae Chu Chang used to head the Human Development Sector of the World Bank in Indonesia and was a lead education specialist at the World Bank for the past 15 years in different countries and regions. She has worked intensively to help governments develop comprehensive education reform strategies and provide technical advice and financial support in countries in the Middle East, East Asia, and South Asia. Dr. Chang also managed a research program that has produced numerous titles, covering a wide range of topics in education from early childhood development, basic education, and teacher development to higher education, skills development, and science and technology. Dr. Chang holds a PhD in education and a master's degree in psycholinguistics from Boston University.

Joppe de Ree holds a PhD in economics from Utrecht University, the Netherlands. He is an economist with the Education Unit of the Human Development Department in the East Asia and Pacific Region at the World Bank.

Titie Hadiyati is a project management specialist. She has worked on various World Bank projects in the Agriculture and Rural Development unit of the World Bank (1996–2001) and in the education sector for the past 12 years. Her extensive experience with the education sector has resulted in a keen interest to explore education policies, particularly in the areas of early childhood development and teacher management. Her educational background consists of civil engineering and education evaluation.

Susiana Iskandar is a senior education specialist in the East Asia and Pacific Region of the World Bank. She has been managing various education projects in Indonesia and Timor-Leste. Her particular interests and in-depth experiences are in the areas of early childhood development and teacher management. Before joining the World Bank in 1998, she worked as a secondary school teacher and planner at the regional office of the Ministry of Education and Culture in Indonesia. She holds a master's degree in education and sociology from Stanford University.

Andrew Ragatz is pursuing his D.Phil in education policy at the University of Oxford. Prior to returning to academia, he was an education specialist for four years in the Jakarta office of the World Bank. His passion for education and development blossomed while teaching in a remote village in El Salvador as a Peace Corps volunteer. He has worked on education policy issues in various other countries, including Cambodia, the Dominican Republic, and Japan. He holds a master's degree in public administration/international development (MPA/ID) from Harvard University.

Sheldon Shaeffer was Director of UNESCO's Asia and Pacific Regional Bureau for Education in Bangkok for over seven years, retiring at the end of 2008. He holds a PhD in comparative international education from Stanford University. He was also for 10 years the Director of Education and Population Programmes for the International Development Research Centre in Canada and later was a senior research fellow at the International Institute for Educational Planning (UNESCO) in Paris. Before moving to Bangkok with UNESCO, he was head of UNICEF's global education program in New York for three years.

Ritchie Stevenson is an international education specialist in teacher management from Australia. He has practiced as a teacher and held a number of senior executive positions in the New South Wales Department of Education and Training. He holds postgraduate degrees in education from the University of New England and the University of London. His wide experience in organizational development, needs analysis, school review, strategic planning, project evaluation, and personnel appraisal has been gained on tasks performed throughout Asia and Australia.

Abbreviations

ALT	Academic Learning Time
ASEAN	Association of Southeast Asian Nations
BERMUTU	Better Education through Reformed Management and Universal Teacher Upgrading
BOS	School Operational Assistance (*Bantuan Operasional Sekolah*) (grant to schools provided by the central government)
CTL	contextual teaching and learning
EFA	Education for All
EGRA	Early Grade Reading Assessment
GDP	gross domestic product
HYLITE	Hybrid Learning for Indonesian Teachers
MDG	Millennium Development Goal
MORA	Ministry of Religious Affairs
NAEP	National Assessment of Educational Progress
NUPTK	Unique Identifier for Educators and Education Personnel (*Nomor Unik Pendidik dan Tenaga Kependidikan*)
ODL	open and distance learning
OECD	Organisation for Economic Co-operation and Development
PE	political economy
PISA	Program for International Student Assessment
PNS	civil service (*Pegawai Negeri Sipil*)
RPL	recognition of prior learning
SABER	Systems Approach for Better Education Results
SBM	school-based management
SC	school committee
SIMPTK	Management Information System for Educators and Education Personnel (*Sistem Informasi Manajemen Pendidik dan Tenaga Kependidikan*)
TALIS	Teaching and Learning International Survey
TIMSS	Trends in International Mathematics and Science Study
UNESCO	United Nations Educational, Scientific, and Cultural Organization

Note: All dollar amounts are in U.S. dollars unless otherwise noted.

Overview

Background of Teacher Reform in Indonesia

In 2005 the Indonesian government approved a comprehensive Teacher and Lecturer Law that was meant to radically reform the nation's teacher management and development process. Its overall objective was to change the nature and enhance the quality of one of the largest and most complex education systems in the world. This book analyzes the educational and political economy context in which this law was formulated and implemented; describes the structures, strategies, and processes that arose from the law; and assesses its impact on both (a) teacher subject and pedagogical knowledge, classroom skills, and motivation, and (b) student outcomes.

With close to three million teachers—from kindergarten through academic and vocational secondary education; in public, private, and Islamic schools; and with both civil service and temporary, school-based contract status—Indonesia has one of the largest and most diverse cadres of teachers in the world. The critical role played by teachers in enhancing the quality of education is especially salient in this context. The evolving nature of its education system and the increasing, and increasingly complex, challenges facing individual teachers and the teaching profession as a whole are of immense importance. How the country is attempting to reform its teacher management and development system and strengthen the teacher education institutions and processes that produce its teachers—and the kind of impact this reform effort is having on the quality of education and on the outcomes of its learners—are therefore of great importance to the future development of the nation.

Managing teachers (individually, both in a classroom and throughout a career, and collectively as an entire cadre) is a difficult enough task. Ensuring that they progressively develop in their profession, from first recruitment to final retirement, only adds to the complexity of the challenge facing ministries of education around the world. Meeting this challenge successfully requires a comprehensive framework of teacher reform. This reform must be based on essential teacher standards and competencies and result in the structures, strategies, and processes required to ensure that these competencies are achieved, assessed, continuously improved on, and ultimately rewarded. It must also be supported by a political economy context that provides the financial and political support needed for it to succeed.

Most attempts to enhance the quality of teaching are piecemeal in fashion. The framework used in this book makes clear the need to develop a comprehensive approach to this process by assessing and improving all the essential components of a systematic teacher management and development system. These components include recruitment; preservice education; induction, mentoring, and probation; formal certification; continuing professional development; teacher performance appraisal; and ongoing career development.

Provisions and Objectives of the Teacher Law of 2005

The Teacher Law, as it is known, and the many ministerial regulations that arose from it, defined (a) the competencies required of teachers in four areas (pedagogic, personal, social, and professional); (b) their incorporation into national teacher standards; (c) the role of various ministry units and agencies in supporting teachers to reach these competencies; (d) the teacher certification process and the qualifications required for such certification; and (e) the conditions under which teachers could receive special and professional allowances. The law also raised important issues concerning teacher management and development for further consideration: continuing professional development and its link to promotion and salary increments, teacher performance appraisal, and the role of principals in instructional leadership. In other words, the Teacher Law provided a comprehensive package of reforms that established an ambitious agenda for improving the national education system.

Specifically, the 2005 law and the many presidential and ministerial regulations that govern its implementation have major components covering virtually all aspects of teacher management and development. These include the following:

- The core principle that teaching is a "profession"
- The requirement that all teachers must meet a minimum standard of a four-year degree before being certified and that all teachers should be formally certified after the four-year degree has been gained
- The reform of preservice teacher education institutions
- A mandatory 24-period (18-hour) per week workload required to gain and maintain certification
- A "special" area allowance to be paid to teachers in defined areas such as remote locations, border regions, and so forth
- Improved processes of in-school induction and probation
- A comprehensive system of teacher appraisal and public service salary increases
- A more systematic program of continuing professional development
- The merit-based appointment of principals and supervisors based on mastery of the four core competencies for educators

Reform Issues Addressed by This Volume

But these reforms—partly because they are so comprehensive and basic—proved not easy to put in place. Many political and economic factors delayed and even temporarily derailed the reform process, including early political tensions over the nature of competency assessment; the pressure to certify many teachers quickly (rather than carefully) and to focus on the number certified rather than the continuing post-certification support they would require; bureaucratic complexities and delays; battles over responsibilities among different agencies and between levels of the government; and other deleterious effects of the political and economic factors that can accompany decentralization.

In analyzing the above process of reform, this book focuses on several important issues:

- The nature of Indonesia's teaching profession—and its supporting structures and mechanisms—before and after the Teacher Law of 2005
- The triggers for the comprehensive reform of this profession and the political economy context in which the reform was developed and implemented
- An impact evaluation of a unique component of this reform: the automatic and unconditional doubling of teachers' income upon certification
- Two pioneering research activities that explored the impact of the reform both on teacher knowledge, skills, and behaviors and on student outcomes— including (a) a randomized control trial with data representing approximately 50 percent of the country's primary and junior secondary schools; and (b) a classroom-based, time-on-task analysis of 8th-grade mathematics teaching practices linked to student achievement in the Trends in International Mathematics and Science Study (TIMSS) studies of 2007 and 2011
- The (in)efficiencies derived from—and not yet resolved by—the reform in terms of the system's financing and the distribution of its teachers, especially in terms of the trade-offs policy makers face when a decision is made to significantly increase investment in education

This assessment is developed in several chapters that explain the relevance of the Indonesian teacher reform to other countries; outline the research and analysis methods used in the studies upon which the book is based; describe the political economy context, the status of the teaching profession, and the situation of Indonesian education before the reform; explain the key triggers for the reform; and identify the major components of the Teacher and Lecturer Law of 2005. The book also presents a definition of quality and describes the book's conceptual frameworks related to teacher quality and teacher management and development; describes the institutions, mechanisms, strategies, and processes derived from the laws and regulations supporting the teacher reform; examines the impact of the reform on teacher quality and student outcomes through the lens of a rigorous study, using a randomized control treatment design; looks inside the "black box" of teacher practice in a set of 8th-grade mathematics classrooms;

examines the financial and efficiency implications of reshaping the system postreform, especially in terms of the impact on teaching force composition, teacher distribution, teacher supply, and the education budget; and presents lessons learned and recommendations derived from the book's analyses.

These lessons and recommendations include the following:

- The doubling of teacher income has significantly increased the status of the teaching profession and attracted better candidates to apply to teacher training institutions.
- The mere fact of certification and the consequent doubling of teacher income have not achieved what was expected: better teaching and better learning by those who were paid double.
- No significant differences were apparent between certified and uncertified primary school teachers in terms of either competencies (subject knowledge and pedagogical skills) or student learning outcomes.
- The Ministry of Education and Culture needs to more carefully analyze the serious financial implications of the current teacher certification and remuneration process in regard not only to the sustainability of this process but also to the implications for financing other aspects of education expansion and quality improvement.
- A quality assurance framework needs to be put in place from the beginning of any reform process and should include the development of a cadre of principals and supervisors selected on merit; specifically trained for their work (both administrative and academic); deployed to where they are needed most; and focused on the essential teacher management and development tasks of induction, mentoring, probation, and ongoing teacher appraisal and improvement.

Introduction

Why Indonesia?

The critical role played by teachers in enhancing the quality of education is especially salient in a populous, geographically dispersed, and culturally diverse country such as Indonesia. The evolving nature of its education system and the increasing—and increasingly complex—challenges facing individual teachers and the teaching profession as a whole are of immense importance in Indonesia. Indonesia has one of the largest and most diverse cadres of teachers in the world, with close to four million teachers from kindergarten through academic and vocational secondary education; in public, private, and Islamic schools; and with both civil service and temporary, school-based contract status.[1] How the country is attempting to reform its teacher management and development system as well as the teacher education institutions and processes that produce its teachers—and the kind of impact this reform is having on the quality of education and on the outcomes of its learners—is therefore of great importance to the future development of the nation.

The Indonesian teacher reform was designed and is being implemented as a genuinely comprehensive program, not a piecemeal effort as many teacher improvement efforts are. From its beginning, it has therefore considered and attempted to incorporate all of the necessary stages of an effective teacher management and development process.

The seriousness of this effort is underlined by two important facts:

- The reform is embedded in law—the pioneering Teacher and Lecturer Law (hereafter called the Teacher Law) of 2005—which was both built upon an even more comprehensive Education Law of 2003 and extensively discussed by a wide range of stakeholders (ministry officials, parliamentarians, civil society representatives, and teacher associations) and ultimately adopted by the Indonesian Parliament.

- The financing of the reform has been made possible through funds derived from a constitutional mandate that requires the government to spend 20 percent of its budget for education. This has had serious implications for the percentage of that budget spent on teacher salaries and professional allowances. The reform calls for the provision of such an allowance equivalent to the base salary of all certified teachers—in essence, doubling (and in some cases tripling) the income of literally millions of teachers in Indonesia.

The importance of this reform is further underlined by the efforts made by the Ministry of Education and Culture,[2] supported by the World Bank, to examine (a) the quality of existing (prereform) and new (postreform) teachers in the system; (b) the promotion of higher standards and enhanced competencies for teachers through more effective processes of recruitment, teacher education, certification, remuneration and other incentives, ongoing professional development and support, and career promotion or progression; and (c) the impact of these actions on teacher behavior and knowledge, student achievement, and the financing and efficiency of the education system.

Thus, the World Bank team, with the Indonesian Ministry of National Education, designed and managed a wide range of research projects and program support activities that, taken together, tell the story of the design, implementation, and impact of this reform. The result, outlined in this publication, *Teacher Reform in Indonesia: The Role of Politics and Evidence in Policy Making*, is based on the premise that a multifaceted reform related to teacher development and management as comprehensive as that in Indonesia can inform countries elsewhere in the world seeking to improve their education systems and, ultimately, the outcomes of their teachers and students.

Contributions of This Volume

Of particular importance in regard to this book is its systematic basis in analysis and evidence. In addition to over 50 background reports, it presents the results from

- Two innovative, methodologically rigorous studies;
- An exploration of the political economy (PE) of the time, which strongly influenced the design and implementation of the reform; and
- An analysis of the tensions and trade-offs around policy making when education investments are significantly increased (for example, trade-offs between large teacher salary increases and investments in other system expansion and quality improvement strategies).

New Studies

In terms of the new studies, the book first reports results from a randomized controlled trial that aims to evaluate various impacts of Indonesia's teacher certification program and its subsequent doubling of teacher income. (Box I.1 describes the method used in this trial.) The explicit objective of this impact evaluation study is to assess the effect of this increase in teacher income on performance. And because this increase is not conditional on later performance improvement (of either the teachers or their students), the analysis will add to a

---

Box I.1 Design and Methods of the Teacher Certification Impact Evaluation Study

The discussion in chapter 4 includes evidence from a randomized controlled evaluation of Indonesia's teacher certification program. Such an evaluation has the explicit objective of estimating the causal effects of a program or intervention under minimal statistical assumptions. For the study, 240 public primary and 120 public junior secondary schools were sampled. All core subject teachers (n = 3,000) and all students (n = 90,000) were tested using a multiple-choice subject matter test. Teachers were also interviewed. The data are representative of 40 percent of the primary and junior secondary schools in Indonesia. Three rounds of data have been carried out: a baseline in November 2009, a midline in April 2011, and an endline in April 2012. This book presents findings from an analysis of the first two rounds of data collection. The final results, which include the analysis of endline data, are expected subsequent to this book's publication.

One-third of the schools were randomly selected into a treatment group; the remaining two-thirds became the control or comparison group. The random selection into treatment and control ensures that treatment schools are similar to control schools, on average, prior to the study's intervention. The study intervened by granting immediate access to the certification process for all teachers in treatment schools who prequalified for certification. Prequalified teachers in control schools were subject to the standard procedure. The number of certified teachers in control schools is consequently much lower, but not zero. The intervention created an artificial difference between treatment and control schools. If the certification process were to have any effects, differences would be observed between treatment and control schools within one or two years after the project's intervention.

Chapter 4 presents the effects of this intervention (teacher certification and the associated professional allowance) on teacher behavior and welfare and on student learning outcomes. For a more detailed discussion of the research design, see De Ree *et al*. (2012).

---

growing body of research that is investigating the effect of pay increases that are conditional on performance (Bruns, Filmer, and Patrinos 2011).

The second innovative study featured in the book examines, at the classroom level, the links among the teacher quality improvement reforms, changes in teaching practices, and student learning. This video study relates to the Indonesia Trends in International Mathematics and Science Study (TIMSS). It aims to clarify what takes place in the classroom through detailed coding of videotaped lessons to provide insights into classroom activities in terms of the time spent on teaching and the frequency of various teaching-learning activities, their sequencing, and the quality of delivery. (See box I.2 for a description of the method used in this trial.)

Political Economy Analysis

The second important methodological aspect of this book is the analysis of the PE that shaped the reform. Early in the development of this book, it became clear that the full story of the origin, evolution, implementation, and impact of the teacher reform process in Indonesia could only be told against the

Box I.2 Design and Standards of the TIMSS Eighth-Grade Mathematics Video Study in Indonesia

The video study took place in two phases (2007 and 2011) and involved 205 eighth-grade mathematics teachers and over 6,000 students. The two-phase approach allowed for the identification of general patterns and changes in teaching practices since the beginning of the teacher reform. The teachers and students in the study also participated in Trends in International Mathematics and Science Study (TIMSS), providing unique benefits in terms of nationally representative sampling; extensive student, teacher, and school background surveys; and student assessment results.

The use of video provided many advantages. Because the videos are permanent records of classroom activities, multiple analyses could be performed in an iterative manner and revisited whenever necessary. Different observers were also able to focus on the same video as the basis of a shared analysis. The videotaping sessions involved two cameras, with one on the teacher and one on the students, allowing different aspects of the classroom to be captured simultaneously.

A mixed-methods (quantitative and qualitative) analytical approach was used. The quantitative analysis used advanced forms of multilevel and value-added modeling. The coding of teaching practices followed a model developed for the international 1999 TIMSS Video Study (Hiebert 2003). The codes have their foundation in prominent theories on effective teaching and cover the themes of Structure of Lessons, Content of Lessons, Actions of Participants, Instructional Practices, and Classroom Climate and Resources. The practices were linked to student, teacher, and school survey data and student learning outcomes as measured through pre- and posttesting in the eighth grade.

The qualitative analysis used case studies of 10 relatively high-impact teachers to provide an in-depth examination of the "how" and "why" aspects of practices. Over intensive one-week visits, the teachers participated in multiple interviews, additional videotaping of lessons, stimulated recall sessions (where teachers watched their own videotaped lessons and discussed specific events), and a mathematical scenarios game. Specific topics included teachers' use of questioning, the selection and use of problems, the handling of student misconceptions, and the decision-making process for teaching approaches. It also explored two apparent drivers of teaching practices: teachers' mathematical beliefs and mathematical knowledge in teaching.

Its scope, magnitude, and distinctive approach make the study unique and allow it to contribute significantly to the understanding of how key background and contextual factors play a role in determining what takes place in the classroom as well as the relationship between teaching practices and student learning outcomes.

background of the political and economic context that influenced this process. This insight resulted in the development of a detailed questionnaire exploring various aspects of a PE analysis and a series of interviews with individuals both involved in and affected by the teacher reform. (See box I.3 for a more detailed description of this process.)

Box I.3 Design and Methods of the Political Economy Analysis

"Political economy (PE) is the study of both politics and economics and specifically the interactions between them. It focuses on power and resources, how they are distributed and contested in different country and sector contexts, and the resulting implications for development outcomes. Political economy analysis involves more than a review of institutional and governance arrangement: it also considers the underlying interests, incentives, rents/rent distribution, historical legacies, prior experience with reforms, social trends, and how all of these factors effect or impede change" (World Bank 2011). It is these PE drivers or triggers that explain why things are the way they are and therefore also help to explain the content of the reform and the process by which it came about.

Based on these principles outlined in "Political Economy Assessments at Sector and Project Level" (World Bank 2011), a detailed questionnaire was developed regarding the following issues:

- *Rationale for, and origin of, the Teacher Law*—for example, the problems that the law was meant to solve, the political and economic context of and reasons for the law, and the most controversial components of the law
- *Implementation of the Teacher Law at both national and local levels*—for example, what institutional, structural, and financial changes had to be made to implement the law; the key actors, challenges, and internal and external obstacles to its implementation; the monitoring and evaluation of the law's implementation; the capacity building required to improve the implementation of the law; and the "rent" processes (corruption, favoritism, political interference), if any, that might have had an impact on its implementation
- *Impact of the reform*—for example, its perceived success, most powerful impacts, and greatest failures; its effect on the balance of power among key political actors; and the gaps between the reform's vision, design, and implementation

A stakeholder analysis, central to this process, required information concerning which levels and actors in the system benefited (or lost) because of the reform, what kind of resistance or opposition to the reform existed and how it was overcome, and the major champions of the reform. The stakeholders examined were teachers and teacher associations, politicians and parliamentarians, individual units of the Ministry of Education and Culture (including the minister), local governments, the private sector, external development partners, the media, civil society organizations, the general public, and parents.

The authors interviewed important original designers of the Teacher Law, both in the Ministry and in Parliament; the leadership of the largest teacher association of the country; the president of a well-known private university in Jakarta; and the educational leaders of two districts, including the head of the district education office in West Java, a member of the district legislature's education commission, the chair of the local district-level Education Council, and the secretary of the local branch of the teacher association. Interviews at the district level focused especially on the impact of decentralization on the implementation of the reform.

Policy Trade-Off Analysis

The third important focus in this book is its in-depth analysis of the trade-offs that policy makers face when a decision is made to significantly increase investment in education. The Indonesian government has invested heavily in education. Between 2001 and 2012, spending doubled in real terms, partly from the fulfillment in 2009 of a constitutional commitment to spend 20 percent of the government budget on education. By far, most of this additional spending has gone to teachers through increased recruitment as well as significant improvements in pay (Cerdan-Infantes and Makarova 2013). Despite these massive investments in education, Indonesia's scores on international assessments of educational achievement have not improved significantly. The book looks closely at the trade-offs associated with the higher investment in teacher salaries and explores the extent to which it has crowded out investments in other areas to improve educational quality and expand pre- and postbasic educational opportunities

Virtually every country in the world—in every region of the world—faces similar trade-offs related to teacher quality improvement, management, and development. This is especially true for countries such as Indonesia that have had relatively high and stable rates of growth and therefore can (or could, if they wished) significantly increase their investments in education. Equitably distributing teachers across all schools regardless of their location is a challenge faced by all countries. And demand for schools and teachers in rural and remote areas is also moving to towns and cities even as the need to keep good teachers in less-developed parts of the country, where they are often needed the most, remains large.

Lessons from Indonesia

The Indonesian experience is particularly relevant because it not only presents a comprehensive approach to reform but also highlights the interplay among the complex political and economic contexts of the nation, policy-making processes, and the challenges in both implementing a comprehensive reform and creating an evidence base for future actions. Although few countries have to deal with Indonesia's size (or, for that matter, its problems of a teacher surplus and unreasonably low student-teacher ratios), most have serious concerns about the whole range of challenges related to teacher management and development.

Indonesia's experience, as described in this book, can provide useful lessons in regard to these concerns—lessons that involve examining questions such as these:

- What can be done to raise the status of the teaching profession, especially in countries where teaching is seen as a second-class, last-choice profession?
- What is the impact of the level of remuneration as a result of certification on the number and quality of candidates to the teaching profession?
- How can teacher education institutions be reformed to better ensure that their graduates (both new students and in-service trainees) have the subject and

pedagogical competencies required of the education system? What is the impact of a more systematic certification process on the number, nature, and programs of teacher education institutions?

- How and when are teachers best "qualified" and "certified"? How can one guarantee that formal qualification and certification result in better teaching and enhanced learning?
- What are the likely short-term and long-term impacts of a more systematic certification process and higher remuneration on teacher behavior and attitudes, teaching-learning methods, and student outcomes?
- What is the cost of serious imbalances in the distribution of teachers—especially to remote, isolated, and difficult areas—and the effectiveness of various mechanisms to solve this problem?
- How can in-service training be made both more accessible and of better quality—for example, through distance learning, formal training in teacher education institutions, within schools, or through school clusters?
- What role should processes such as induction and probation play in the certification process?
- What can be said about the ultimate cost, and cost-effectiveness, to an education system of a more systematic teacher certification process and a considerably higher remuneration for certified teachers?
- What is the potential impact, negative or positive, of decentralization on an improved teacher development and management process? What tensions around this process might arise between central and decentralized authorities?

Organization of the Book

Answers to these questions are sought in the chapters that follow, briefly described here:

- *Chapter 1*: The PE and situation of teachers in Indonesia prior to the reform
- *Chapter 2*: The book's conceptual framework of quality education
- *Chapter 3*: The pre- and postreform structure and processes of the entire teacher management and development system
- *Chapter 4*: The impact of these efforts on teacher status, motivation, and skills and on student outcomes generally
- *Chapter 5*: The impact of reform efforts in relation to eighth-grade mathematics teaching
- *Chapter 6*: An in-depth analysis of the pre- and postreform efficiency of Indonesia's education system—both financially and in terms of teacher distribution and student-teacher ratios—and of what is still needed to ensure that the current reforms are, in fact, sustainable
- *Chapter 7*: A summary of the major impacts and key messages arising from the entire reform process and of the influence of Indonesia's PE on the reform's outcomes

Teacher Reform in Indonesia • http://dx.doi.org/10.1596/978-0-8213-9829-6

It is hoped that the data and analyses discussed in this book will be able to unravel some of the complexities of the teacher reform process in Indonesia and, therefore, make available insights and recommendations useful to other countries faced with similar challenges.

Notes

1. Though exact numbers vary according to source and, of course, over time, for the purpose of this book, data from the school census of 2010 are used. These indicate approximately 2.7 million teachers managed by the Ministry of Education and Culture (from kindergarten to senior secondary school), with around 2 million at the primary and junior secondary level; these 2 million are the priority target of the teacher certification process. The Ministry of Religious Affairs manages close to an additional 1 million teachers. These figures have certainly increased since 2010 (NUPTK 2010).

2. At the time of the Teacher Law of 2005, the Ministry was named the Ministry of National Education. In 2011, its name changed to the Ministry of Education and Culture.

References

Bruns, B., D. Filmer, and H. A. Patrinos. 2011. *Making Schools Work: New Evidence on Accountability Reforms*. Human Development Perspectives Series. Washington DC: World Bank.

Cerdan-Infantes, P., and Y. Makarova. 2013. Spending More or Spending Better: Improving Education Financing in Indonesia. Jakarta: World Bank.

De Ree, J., K. Muralidharan, M. Pradhan, and H. Rogers. 2012. "Double for What? The Impact of Unconditional Teacher Salary Increases on Performance." Unpublished manuscript, World Bank, Washington, DC.

Hiebert, J. 2003. "Teaching Mathematics in Seven Countries: Results from the TIMSS 1999 Video Study." National Center for Education Statistics, U.S. Department of Education Institute of Education Sciences, Washington, DC.

NUPTK (Unique Identifier for Educators and Education Personnel, *Nomor Unik Pendidik dan Tenaga Kependidikan*) (database). 2010. Teacher database maintained by NUPTK, Jakarta.

World Bank. 2011. "Political Economy Assessments at Sector and Project Levels." How-To Notes, Government and Anticorruption (GAC) in Projects Initiative, World Bank, Washington, DC.

CHAPTER 1

Indonesia as a Case Study for Comprehensive Teacher Reform

Introduction

> Indonesia has constructed a definition of 'teacher' that fits the unique contours of the nation's social, historical, and political landscape. The structure and goals of the government have exerted a particularly powerful influence on the behavior of school employees.... State authority in Indonesia is, and has always been, so pervasive that few individuals question their lack of power in the schools. As civil servants they have learned to follow the directives of upper level officials, not dispute them.... The Indonesian government has ensured... that educators treat the civil servant identity as 'superordinate'.... One effect of that emphasis is that teachers have not established an identity for themselves separate from that applied to all civil servants, or a distinct set of professional standards.
>
> —Christopher Bjork, *Indonesian Education: Teachers, Schools, and Central Bureaucracy* (2005)

The story of teacher reform in Indonesia must begin with a description of the historical status and significance of its teaching profession. As in many other countries of the world, teaching was once a highly respected and desirable occupation in Indonesia. Given the limited number of schools during both Dutch colonial rule and the Japanese occupation and the important role given to education by the early leaders of independent Indonesia—a feeling shared by the leaders of virtually all of the nations that became independent as the world of colonialism crumbled—teaching was originally a vocation of choice. Only the best of students were admitted, with scholarships, into teacher education programs. As a result, teachers, especially those in rural areas, were not only often the best educated and most influential members of the community; they were also, in a larger perspective, the actors who were meant to transform Indonesia into a democratic, prosperous nation and bring it into the modern world. The image of the wise, incorruptible, and hard-working teacher—often struggling alone under difficult circumstances, in remote villages and urban slums, with little pay but much dedication—is one that an older generation of Indonesians still fondly remembers.

But eventually several issues came into play. First, the education system expanded rapidly in the 1970s and 1980s with a massive national program promoted by then-President Suharto. This program built tens of thousands of new primary schools between 1975 and 1987 and rapidly hired and trained hundreds of thousands of new teachers who were often thrust into classrooms with only a minimum amount of initial teacher education, few opportunities for further training, and therefore limited subject knowledge and inadequate pedagogical skills. This infusion of new, but not very rich, blood diluted the strength of the teacher cadre; blurred the mythic image of the teacher as community leader and nation builder; and ultimately, combined with a large expansion of the rest of the civil service, reduced the salaries of teachers and other civil servants relative to other professions. "The principal attractions of a career in the civil service became job security, undemanding work, short work hours, and lifetime employment. Low expectations led to decreased productivity" (Bjork 2005, 96). The result was an increase in second jobs (often quite menial in nature), an increase in teacher absenteeism, an ultimate decline in many teachers' work ethic, and consequently a further decrease in the status of the profession.

This loss of a sense of "vocation" and the "deprofessionalization" of teaching in the decades before the turn of the century were significant. Teachers were clearly seen—and were meant to see themselves—as civil servants first, answering "up" the system rather than "out" to students, parents, and local school boards. At a time of considerable political uncertainty and even instability in the transition from the rule of President Sukarno to the "New Order" of President Suharto, teachers were meant to demonstrate loyalty and obedience to the government and to transmit the national curriculum, promote the national creed of *Pancasila*,[1] and thereby strengthen national unity. "This designation of teacher as civil servant carried profound implications for the definition of the educator and for the way that Indonesian instructors approached their work. Educators, like post office workers and tax collectors, conceived of themselves as public servants first and foremost" (Bjork 2005, 94). Teachers, in other words, "came to define their professional responsibilities quite narrowly: to faithfully disseminate a set of ideas formulated in the capital" (Bjork 2005, 110)—in other words, to "educate" their pupils in terms of moral and ethical development rather than to "teach" them in terms of intellectual growth (Bjork 2005, 107).

As the new century approached, however, Indonesian political life became more stable and predictable, and its economy began to grow. Along with these developments came an increase in the number of community members— village leaders, government extension workers, private entrepreneurs—with educational levels and salaries equal to or exceeding those of teachers, thus further weakening teachers' earlier privileged position within the community.

And then the education system as a whole became larger, more complex, and more challenging to teachers in many ways:

- Partly as a result of efforts following the Jomtien and Dakar Education for All (EFA) commitments[2] and the Millennium Development Goals (MDGs) for education (the latter two made in 2000),[3] the system rapidly expanded with much higher enrollment and an increasing number of teachers (which led finally to an oversupply of teachers and one of the lowest student-teacher ratios in Southeast Asia).

- Educational programs and options at all levels of the system (from preschool to tertiary education) became more diversified, each demanding better and more specialized facilities, teachers, and materials.

- The curriculum also frequently changed and often was made more complicated, all within less than 10 years—from a competency-based curriculum introduced in 2004 to a school-based curriculum in 2006 and now to a very different curriculum for 2013. Overall, the curriculum became both more accelerated (teach faster) and congested (teach more)—moving from the essentials of reading, writing, and arithmetic (and the national creed of *Pancasila*) to a wider range of content areas (such as sustainable development and life skills) and new ways of teaching (for example, child-centered and interactive). Sometimes the new content areas have been treated as separate subjects, and sometimes they have been integrated into a basic subject such as language. These frequent changes have often been difficult for most of the teachers, many of whom are quite senior but with weak subject knowledge, limited professional support, and few opportunities for further training.

- Schools and individual teachers faced more learners of ever more diverse backgrounds and identities, who have (a) varying values, ways of thinking, behaviors, and motivations; (b) greater independence, creativity, and open-mindedness and more enterprising minds; and (c) skills often better than their teachers' skills in using new information and communication technologies.

- The governance of the education system was quite radically and rapidly decentralized, leading to new and sometimes difficult accountabilities and expectations of teachers—changes often made more difficult by newly empowered school committees (SCs) and more educated parents who demanded more from their schools.

- Finally, despite the frenzy surrounding the annual national examinations at the end of primary, junior secondary, and higher secondary school and the exceedingly high rates at which they are passed, increasing evidence from both international and national studies of achievement showed that despite the best intentions, higher enrollments, greater investments, and steady progress toward quantitative global targets, the Indonesian education system and its teachers were failing to achieve the results expected of them.

Indonesia's answer to these challenges was the pioneering Teacher Law of 2005. The most salient feature of this law was its attempt to "reprofessionalize" teaching—to once again make it a "profession"—both through formal certification and through the doubling or even tripling of teacher incomes by granting a professional allowance upon certification. The law also called for a comprehensive package of reforms that established an ambitious agenda for improving the national education system by laying out the roles and responsibilities of teachers, principals, supervisors, and local education authorities as well as the strategies needed to improve their quality and welfare in support of the earlier Education Law of 2003.[4]

The Status of Indonesian Education before Teacher Reform

The Indonesian experience in reforming the nation's teacher management and development structures and processes has been unique both in its comprehensiveness and in the attention paid to analyzing and assessing its implementation and impact. Before we assess the reform's impact on teachers, teaching, students, and the system as a whole, we must understand the status of teachers before the reform, why reform was considered essential, what the reform's major components were, and the political-economic context in which the reform was developed and has been implemented.

For a decade and more from 1990, Indonesian education policy was generally directed at increasing the number of children with access to formal education. Given the focus of the MDGs on universal primary enrollment and gender equity and the prioritization of EFA targets toward enrollment (MDG Goal 2) rather than quality, the country's education system was most concerned with increasing access to school. The result was a significant increase in the primary school net enrollment rate to 94.76 percent by 2010.

But with its stronger focus on a more comprehensive definition of quality, the Dakar World Conference on EFA in 2000 shifted government thinking around the world to greater concern about the nature and relevance of the education being provided. This shift led to more careful analyses of a range of indicators seen as useful proxies for quality. One important set of indicators focused on teachers—particularly their educational level, subject matter competency, and pedagogical skills. (This analysis was later followed by systematic studies of student outcomes such as the Trends in International Mathematics and Science Study [TIMSS], the Program for International Student Assessment [PISA], and the Early Grade Reading Assessment [EGRA].)

Before enactment of the 2005 Teacher Law, the Ministry of National Education in Indonesia had identified a number of shortcomings in the education system related to teachers. First, *teaching standards were ill-defined.*

Although standards were specified, they were neither sufficiently detailed nor clearly defined, and therefore, were difficult both to translate into the curricula of the wide range of teacher education institutions in Indonesia and to enforce through supervision at the school level.

Second, *the teacher management system in Indonesia was characterized by both inefficiency and inequality*. The certification of teachers was nonexistent (beyond successfully passing probation), and the appointment, deployment, and further professional development of new teachers, haphazard. Standards regulating these processes were inconsistent over time and across regions and often subject to personal relationships rather than professional training or competence, especially for temporary and contract teachers. This confusion worsened during the decentralization that began in 2000, which the Education Law of 2003 later defined.

In theory, the Education Law mandated that the employment and remuneration of teachers (except in Islamic schools), the setting of standards, the monitoring of performance, and the implementation of sanctions and remediation should be transferred from the Ministry of National Education to district offices. But issues around the granting of incentives, the dismissal and deployment of teachers (both within and across districts), the appointment and training of school principals and supervisors, the continuing professional development of teachers, and the request for the establishment of new civil service posts for teachers remained ambiguous. In fact, the overhiring of teachers was rampant and was partly the consequence of decentralization, which gave local governments strong incentives to hire more teachers whether needed or not. As a result, national student-teacher ratios were low, but inefficient distribution meant that many schools had insufficient teachers. Schools in rural and remote areas also tended to have teachers with lower academic qualifications.

The Low Status of Teachers

A third shortcoming was that teacher status was low compared with other occupations in Indonesia and with teachers in some neighboring countries. Such status derives from a combination of many factors, including the following:

- Educational qualifications
- Salary or income level
- Competence in both subject matter and pedagogy
- Perceived motivation to teach (the extent to which teachers are considered committed to their work)
- Official certification (in the Indonesian case, official recognition that a teacher is a "professional")

Educational Qualifications

Before 2005, Indonesian teachers, in general, had relatively low educational qualifications, and a significant proportion of serving teachers were

Teacher Reform in Indonesia • http://dx.doi.org/10.1596/978-0-8213-9829-6

Table 1.1 In-Service Teacher Training Requirements in Indonesia, 2006

Teacher category	Postsecondary education required before 2005 Teacher Law (years)	Teachers below required level before 2005 Teacher Law (%)	Postsecondary education required by 2005 Teacher Law (years)	Teachers below required level set by 2005 Teacher Law (%)
Primary	2	34	4	83
Junior secondary	3	23	4	38
Senior secondary	4	18	4	18

Source: Calculations based on the 2006 NUPTK/SIMPTK teacher's census.
Note: NUPTK = Unique Identifiers for Educators and Education Personnel (*Nomor Unik Pendidik dan Tenaga Kependidikan*). SIMPTK = Management Information System for Educators and Education Personnel (*Sistem Informasi Manajemen Pendidik dan Tenaga Kependidikan*). SIMPTK is the teacher database maintained by NUPTK.

underqualified. Counting all teachers—kindergarten through senior secondary school and vocational secondary schools (excluding Islamic schools)—more than 60 percent did not hold the four-year degree required by the Teacher Law. In fact, around 25 percent of the teachers had failed to go beyond high school.

Table 1.1 illustrates how the new higher-qualification mandate in the Teacher Law compounded the training requirement for in-service teachers.

Salaries

As discussed above, the salaries of teachers were also low and contributed to their low status. Although traditionally high relative to other occupations, especially in rural areas, teacher salaries had been declining in real terms as the number of teachers increased. By 2005, incomes from teaching were low relative to those of other occupations requiring a similar educational level.

Also, teacher salaries in Indonesia compared unfavorably with those in other middle-income countries in the region. For example, in 2008, the starting salary of a primary or junior secondary school teacher in Indonesia was approximately 40 percent of average per capita income. However, in the Philippines, starting teaching salaries were around 145 percent of average income (UNESCO Institute of Statistics 2010).

Absolute differences were also large. Compared with other nations in the East Asia and Pacific region, salaries of starting primary school teachers in Indonesia, in U.S. dollars, were less than one-third the salaries of teachers in Malaysia and the Philippines and less than half of those in Thailand. Their top salaries showed even greater disparities with those in Malaysia and Thailand. In Indonesia, a primary school teacher earned \$1,002–\$3,022 per year or a mere 50 percent of gross domestic product (GDP) per capita, according to United Nations Educational, Scientific, and Cultural Organization (UNESCO) estimates. Primary school teachers in the Philippines and Thailand earned over twice as much in terms of GDP per capita—in relative terms, a fourfold greater salary than their Indonesian counterparts.

Figure 1.1 Primary School Teacher Wages in Indonesia Relative to Nonteacher Wages, by Educational Level, 2004

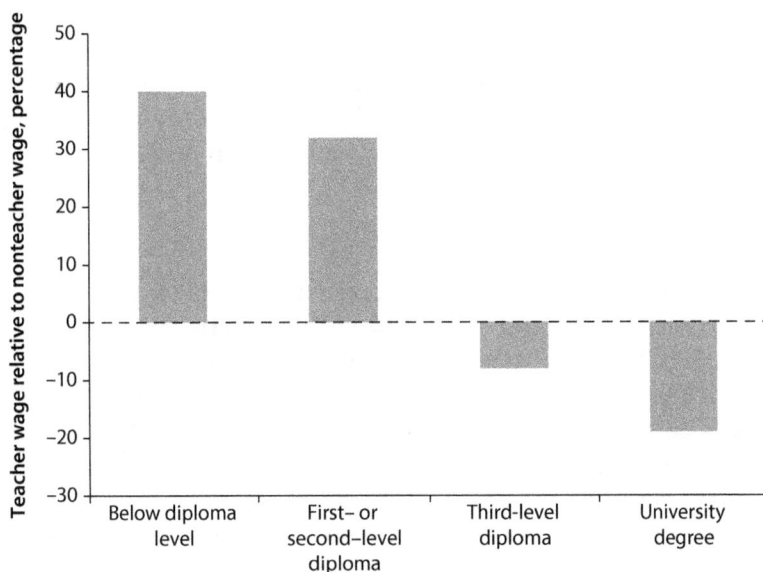

Source: Ragatz 2010.
Note: The bars show the percentage difference between a teacher's salary and the salary of other workers of the same educational level. For example, primary school teachers with a first- or second-level diploma earn 32 percent more than individuals of the same educational level who are engaged in a nonteaching occupation.

Thus, the teaching profession was unattractive for individuals who were better educated and had more opportunities for more challenging, better-paid jobs, as shown in figure 1.1. On the other hand, wages for the three-quarters of primary school teachers with second-level diplomas or below were high in comparison with the wages they could expect to receive outside of the teaching profession—indicating strong incentives for individuals with these qualifications to enter the teaching profession. However, the wages of better-qualified teachers were significantly below the wages of individuals with similar qualifications who worked outside of education. The wage structure, therefore, created incentives for less well-qualified candidates to enter the profession, while better-qualified and more-able candidates were likely to opt for nonteaching careers.

Pedagogical and Subject Matter Competency

Also related to status, Indonesian teachers in general demonstrated low competency on subject matter tests. Such results were due not only to the relatively low levels of initial education for many teachers—especially those hired at the time of the great expansion of primary education in the 1970s and 1980s—but also to relatively few opportunities for systematic in-service training. Thus, for example, in a study completed by the Ministry of National Education in 2004, a large percentage of one million teacher applicants competing for 64,000 positions as civil service teachers (many of whom were already likely teaching on local, temporary contracts) demonstrated poor content mastery, even in the subjects that they would be required to teach. On a general test for primary school teachers, the average score was 34 correct answers for 90 questions (with a range from 6 to 67); on tests in 14 special subjects (for example, civics, art, language, biology, and art), in only 4 subjects was the average score more than 50 percent (Ragatz 2010).

Motivation

In terms of commitment and motivation to teach, many factors before enactment of the Teacher Law of 2005 reinforced doubts about the status and professionalism of teachers. The low wages of teachers were perceived to have a significant effect on teacher behavior; many teachers, especially those in primary schools, were concerned quite correctly about the welfare of their families. This led in many cases to second jobs and high teacher absenteeism. A teacher absenteeism study covering the academic year 2002/03 showed that 19 percent of teachers were absent when enumerators made surprise visits to a random sample of primary and junior secondary schools (Usman, Akhmadi, and Suryadarma 2004). These relatively high rates of absenteeism were likely to have been driven by the fact that many teachers held second jobs to supplement their incomes from teaching. Such absenteeism affects the quality of teaching, of course, because it disrupts the learning process by reducing teacher-student contact time and interfering with the relationship between teachers and students.

The commitment of teachers to their profession was also put in doubt because of what was seen as a relatively light workload. Many had few teaching hours per week in classes with low student-teacher ratios. A World Bank study in 2005 found considerable variety in teacher work, but the "total percentage of teachers whose teaching workload [was] below the set minimum of 18 hours per week [was] 23 percent for primary schools and 44 percent for junior secondary schools" (Jalal *et al.* 2009). The average number of hours taught by teachers in remote schools was considerably higher than in urban and rural schools, likely indicating an undersupply of teachers in these remote areas. Indonesia also had (and still has) some of the lowest primary and junior secondary student-teacher ratios in the world, as shown in figure 1.2. At the primary level in 2003, Indonesia had a teacher for every 20 students, a ratio similar to Japan's and much lower than the Republic of Korea's. The student-teacher ratio for junior secondary schools in Indonesia was 12 to 1. These low ratios have arisen because of the practice of providing staff to schools based on the number of classes rather than the total number of students.

Official Certification

Prior to the reform, the government fully relied on and trusted the preservice teacher training universities to certify teachers. The universities issued two types of certificates for the universities' graduates: academic certificates (for example,

Figure 1.2 Student-Teacher Ratios Preceding Indonesian Teacher Reform, Selected Countries and Country Income Groups, 2003

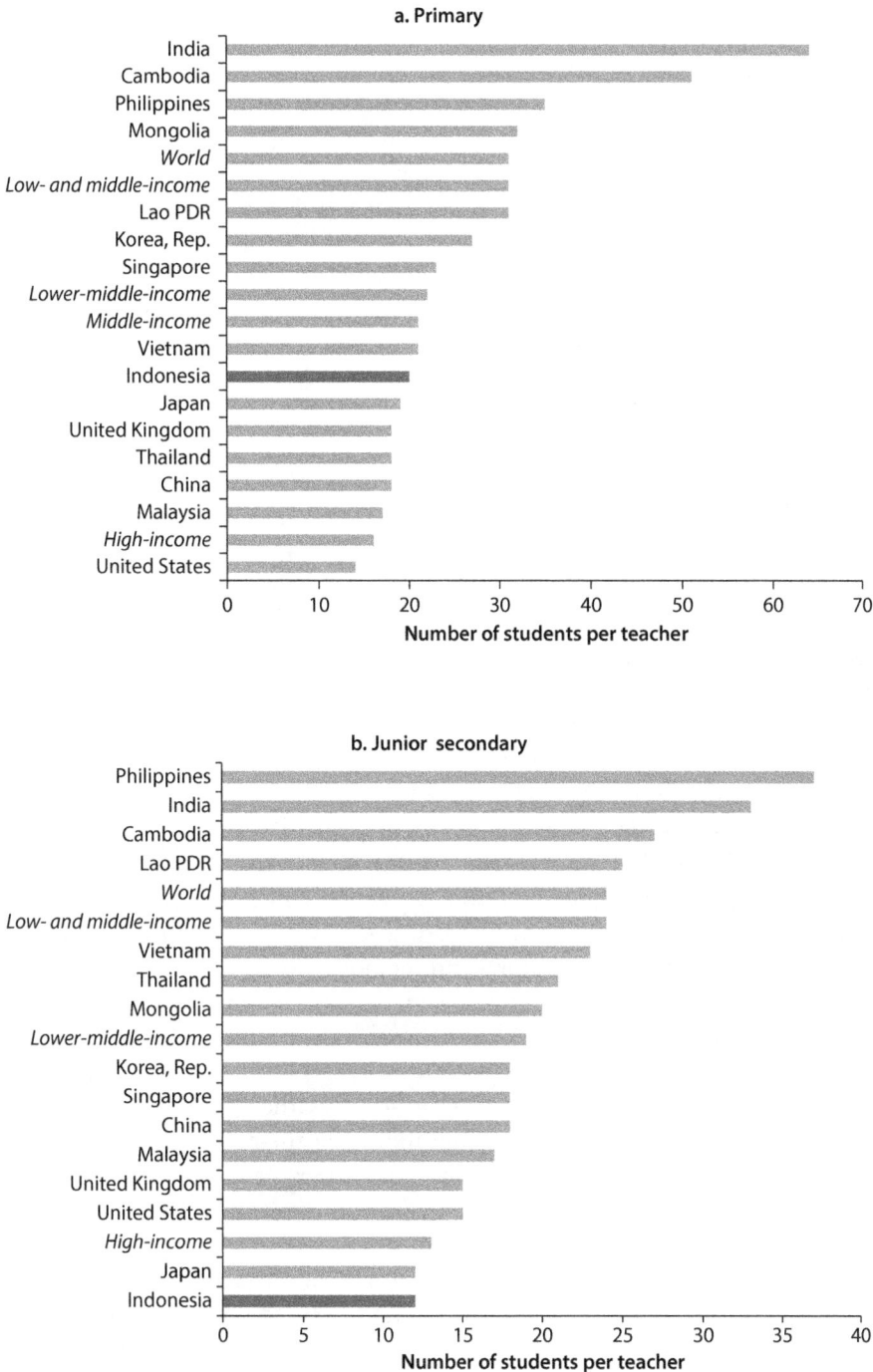

a. Primary

b. Junior secondary

Source: World Bank Education Statistics (EdStats database, http://go.worldbank.org/ITABCOGIV1) data for 2003, cited in World Bank 2008.

for three-year and four-year education programs) and teaching licenses at different levels to accompany the academic certificates. No further certification by the Ministry was required.

Teacher Supply and Distribution Issues

Another shortcoming identified as a serious problem in relation to teachers in Indonesia concerned supply and distribution. Before the education reforms in the mid-2000s, there was no attempt to match teacher education institutions' intake with the demand for teachers. Most countries rely on the demand for teachers to signal prospective teacher trainees about the benefits of becoming a teacher. However, in Indonesia, a far greater number of individuals enter teacher education institutions than required relative to overall needs. A recent study showed that only 53 percent of students graduating from teacher education courses could actually be employed as teachers (Ragatz 2010).

In 2005, a survey using the existing entitlement formula showed that 55 percent of primary schools in Indonesia were overstaffed and 34 percent understaffed. Despite incentives to overhire and the low aggregate student-teacher ratios that result, the distribution of teachers before the reforms was uneven. In 2004, the primary student-teacher ratio ranged from less than 10 to 1 in some districts to more than 30 to 1 in others (World Bank 2008). In junior secondary schools, approximately 20 percent of all districts had a student-teacher ratio of less than 20 to 1. Small schools tended to have low student-teacher ratios because of low enrollment and generous staffing standards. Remote schools tended to have higher than average student-teacher ratios because of the difficulty in deploying teachers to these schools.

Although nationally there was an oversupply of teachers in 2004, poor distribution meant that a significant number of schools did not have enough teachers (World Bank 2008). In 2005, it was estimated that approximately a third of all primary schools were short of teachers according to the prevailing staffing standards at the time. Rural and remote areas tended to have a greater proportion of schools with shortages compared with urban schools. Conversely, 55 percent of primary schools had more teachers than the minimum standards set at the time.

Another aspect of inequitable distribution was that teachers in rural and remote schools tended to have less education than their counterparts in urban areas. A 2005 survey showed that less than 10 percent of primary school teachers in remote areas had a four-year degree compared with 27 percent of urban school teachers (World Bank 2008). The differences in teacher qualification levels, as shown in figure 1.3, tend to reinforce patterns of inequality across Indonesia. Remote areas tend to be the poorest, and children in these areas, the most disadvantaged. To the extent that teacher characteristics are causal factors in student learning, it is likely that the prereform teacher distribution pattern widened disparities in learning achievement for children in rural and remote areas.

Figure 1.3 Educational Levels of Primary School Teachers in Indonesia, by Location, 2005

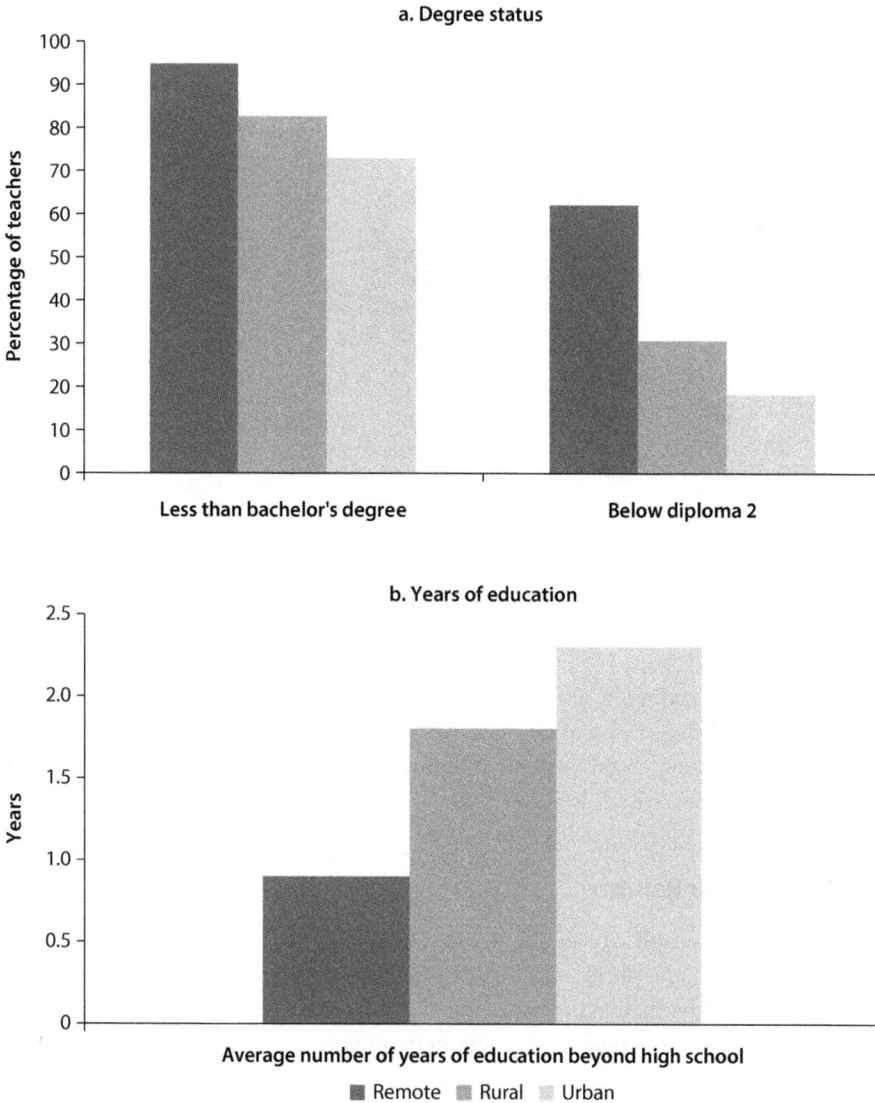

a. Degree status

b. Years of education

■ Remote ■ Rural ■ Urban

Source: World Bank 2008.

Low Level of Student Outcomes

A final—and critical—shortcoming related to teachers in Indonesia was the low level of student outcomes, especially as measured by international comparative tests. Indonesian students simply performed poorly relative to students in other countries. International benchmark tests showed (and continue to show) that student outcomes in Indonesia are lower than those in neighboring countries. For example, in 2007, Indonesia ranked 36th out of 49 countries in the TIMSS test. In science, it ranked 35th. In the 2006 PISA, which focuses on how well 15-year-olds are prepared for real-world situations, Indonesia ranked 48th out of

Figure 1.4 Indonesian PISA Scores, 2000–09

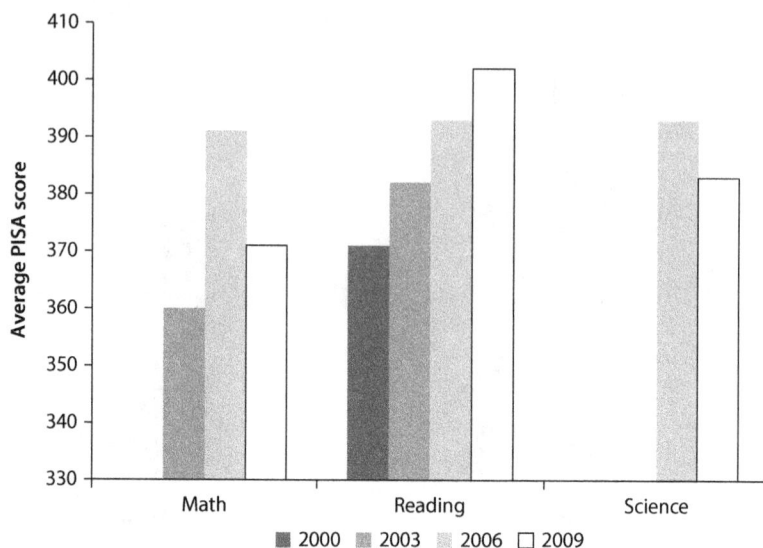

Source: OECD 2010.
Note: PISA = Program for International Student Assessment.

56 countries in reading. It also ranked 52nd in science and 51st in mathematics. As figure 1.4 shows, most of the country's PISA scores remain well below the average score among Organisation for Economic Co-operation and Development (OECD) countries, which is about 500.

Key Triggers for Reform

The increasing complexity of the education system in Indonesia, as outlined in the Introduction, and an increasingly sophisticated and insightful analysis of the challenges faced by its teachers convinced policy makers of the need for a major reform of the country's teacher management and development system. Originally, the key trigger for the reform was the relatively low pay and low status of the teaching profession, leading both to (a) the prevalence of second jobs and high absenteeism rates, and (b) the generally small number and poor quality of candidates applying from secondary education to teacher education institutes. This situation created a general consensus around the need to improve teacher "welfare" (greater income) but to do this not through a routine increase in the base salary (which would have led to demands for similar increases from other civil servants) but rather through a "professional allowance." Such an allowance would also reinforce the sentiment, strongly endorsed by Indonesia's teacher associations, that teaching had to be seen again as a "profession"—closed to those who are not adequately qualified and not officially certified.

As described above, this focus on income and status was linked to the realization that a large percentage of the teachers in 2005 had been hired during the large expansion of the system in the 1970s–80s with a relatively low level of initial education; little preservice education; few opportunities for later systematic in-service upgrading; and exposure to a school culture that rewarded passivity and loyalty rather than proactive, innovative approaches to the improvement of student outcomes. Many of these teachers still had another decade or more to work but had little incentive and few opportunities for further professional development (in 2005, some 77 percent of Indonesia's teachers were 41 years of age or older, with a retirement age of 60), all at a time when they were faced with many changes in the education system: a more diversified and accelerated competency-based curriculum, a more child-centered pedagogy, a more varied student body, and more empowered SCs.

The realization by the Ministry of National Education that the teacher cohort of the time was not only failing to respond adequately to these changes but also producing disappointing student outcomes led it to insist that any increase in the status, welfare, and income of teachers as professionals would need to be accompanied by an increase in quality. It therefore saw both (a) the need to condition the granting of the professional allowance to active teachers on some system of certification, and (b) the opportunity presented by the retirement of such a large cohort of teachers in a relatively short period of time to recruit and educate new generations of higher-quality teachers. This marriage of the "status trigger" with the "quality trigger" produced a rare consensus among the major actors on the need for a comprehensive new law on teachers.

Over time, another set of triggers added incentives to the implementation of the Teacher Law and led to a variety of complementary guidelines and regulations to help ensure the law would achieve what it was expected to achieve. These triggers included

- The need to enhance the capacity of teachers and their role in school self-assessment and improvement given the increasing decentralization of the system, which has given more authority (and accountability) for improving the quality of education to the school (that is, the school principal and his or her teachers);

- The increasing amount of funds being transferred directly to schools on a per-student basis for quality improvement through an operational cost program, which puts more demands on teachers to take part in school self-assessment and improvement programs and to produce better student outcomes; and

- The eventual flood of new funding into the system, from both internal and external sources (resulting from the constitutional amendment to earmark 20 percent of the national budget for education), which gave the Ministry of National Education an opportunity to undertake a range of programs under the reform.

Major Components of the Teacher Law of 2005

These various triggers sparked enactment of the pioneering Teacher Law of 2005, which laid out the roles and responsibilities of teachers as well as the strategies needed to improve their quality and welfare in support of the earlier Education Law of 2003. The Teacher Law defined the competencies required of teachers in four areas (pedagogic, personal, social, and professional); the incorporation of those competencies into national teacher standards; the role of various ministry units and agencies in supporting teachers to reach these competencies; the teacher certification process and the qualifications required for such certification; and the conditions under which teachers could receive special and professional allowances. The law also raised important issues concerning teacher management and development that required further consideration: continuing professional development and its link to promotion and salary increments, teacher performance appraisal, and the role of principals in instructional leadership. In other words, the Teacher Law provided a comprehensive, clearly defined package of reforms that established an ambitious agenda for improving the national education system.

Specifically, the 2005 law and the many presidential and ministerial regulations that govern its implementation have major components covering virtually all aspects of teacher management and development. These include the following:

- The core principle that teaching is a "profession." Teachers who fulfill certain established academic qualifications and demonstrate essential pedagogic, personal, social, and professional competencies must be considered "professional" and therefore worthy of a professional allowance equal to their base salary.
- The development by the National Education Standards Board of a standards framework for courses, tests, role definitions, and other education elements to underpin change. The board centered its core standards and indicators on the four core competencies mandated in the Teacher Law.
- The requirement that all teachers meet a minimum standard of a four-year degree before being certified.
- A course of additional professional training after the four-year degree—mostly classroom-based—of six months for primary school teachers and one year for secondary school teachers.
- The requirement that all teachers be formally certified after the four-year degree has been gained, through either a portfolio of the teacher's education and teaching achievements or a 90-hour remedial in-service course.
- The reform of preservice teacher education institutions so that their subject and pedagogical courses were closely linked to the school curriculum competency standards to ensure that all graduates meet the new performance standards for the teaching profession and are eligible for certification.
- Reformed practicum experience through improved links with districts and schools, the key feature of which is the requirement that education students

undertake the largest part of their pedagogical training and practice under supervision in the classroom.

- A mandatory 24 period-hour (18-hour) per week workload required to gain and maintain certification.
- A "special" area allowance to be paid to teachers in defined areas (such as in remote or border regions).
- Improved processes of in-school induction, mentoring, and probation to ensure that a beginning teacher receives close supervision and guidance in the workplace to successfully make the transition from university education to the school.
- A system of teacher appraisal and public service salary increases that links the teaching objectives of schools to individual teacher performance appraisal, career progression, and salary increments.
- A more systematic program of continuing professional development that links backward to the teacher appraisal process and forward to salary increments and career progression in a new career development framework for teachers.
- The strengthening of teacher working groups to bring teachers together in a forum to discuss teaching problems and to work cooperatively to undertake common tasks such as curriculum development, the creation of teaching aids, and the design of test items.
- The more systematic, merit-based appointment of principals and supervisors based on mastery of the four core competencies for educators, meant to be achieved through early identification of promising candidates, careful selection, and further training before promotion to more senior positions.

The Political-Economic Context of the Teacher Law

As can be seen, the Teacher Law of 2005 and the plethora of regulations that flowed from it produced an unusually substantial and comprehensive reform of not only teacher management and development but also many other aspects of the education system. Such a reform—both its content and its implementation—did not happen in a vacuum but rather must be understood in terms of the political and economic environment of the day. This environment has always been particularly complex in Indonesia given its history; its geographic spread; its large and growing population; and its cultural, religious, and linguistic diversity. In general, therefore, a range of political economy factors were important in the context of the development of the Teacher Law.

Part of the environment of decision making in Indonesia relates to the complexity of the nation itself. This complexity derives from many sources. In the most ordinary sense, Indonesia is one of the most ethnically and linguistically diverse, and geographically challenged, countries of the world. A combination of 722 language groups spread out over a 3,000-mile archipelago of more than 17,000 islands—with a matrix of Islamic, Buddhist, Hindu, Protestant, and Catholic faiths (and dozens of animistic beliefs) underlain by English, Dutch, and Chinese heritages—makes any standardized or centralized approach to change difficult. The primacy of the national language, Bahasa Indonesia, which has penetrated at least administratively to all regions of the country, has facilitated standardization to some extent, but cultural, religious, and historic differences have still prevented full achievement of the national aspiration of "*bhinneka tunggal ika*": unity in diversity. Related to this diversity is another challenge to the implementation of reform: the sheer isolation and remoteness of many of the country's communities, be they found on small, distant, rarely visited islands or equally hard-to-reach mountain peaks and valleys.

History of Reform

At the beginning of the century, Indonesia aspired to play a larger role both within the Association of Southeast Asian Nations (ASEAN) and internationally. This role required a government both more visibly stable and democratic and—at least in the eyes of the major international development agencies (both bilateral and multilateral) active in the country—having long-term, systematic national and sectoral development plans. In the context of increasing globalization and the economic changes this process demands, Indonesia also began to more clearly understand the importance of a better-trained workforce, educated within a more diversified, responsive education system and ultimately more adaptable to the ever-changing demands of a growing and changing economy.

Development of Consensus

This understanding led to the unusual mandate, contained in a 2002 amendment to the 1945 Constitution, requiring that 20 percent of the national and local budgets be devoted to education—a percentage often promoted internationally but rarely made legally binding at the national level. But the size of Indonesia's population and of its teaching cadre presented a difficult financial challenge: how to make a significant impact in terms of qualifying and certifying so many teachers and then radically increasing their remuneration in a country as large as Indonesia, even when 20 percent of the national budget is reserved for education.

At the same time, evidence began to accumulate that despite the best intentions and increased resources, the education system was not producing the kind of graduates needed to face the political and economic challenges of the new century. This was the challenge to be addressed. The aging, relatively poorly paid, poorly educated, and often demotivated (and "deprofessionalized") teaching force (at least relative to Indonesia's comparable ASEAN partners) began to be considered as a major factor in the perceived poor quality of the education system and its graduates. But teachers were also considered to be important opinion leaders in the communities where they taught (though considerably less so than in the decades following independence) and therefore were an important political constituency to support.

As a result of a combination of these various factors—national aspirations regarding Indonesia's role in an expanding global community, the need for more education resources, and the realization that the system was not producing the results it should—the various stakeholders concerned with teachers began to reach consensus on what to do next: an unusual "win-win" situation in the process of educational reform.

Discussions about some kind of government regulation concerning the welfare and protection of teachers started before the turn of the century and took several years (and a number of presidents and ministers of education) to come to fruition. The various teacher associations in Indonesia argued strongly that the income and status of teachers—and therefore, the quality of their teaching— were in such desperate straits that serious action was required. This conviction caused what was first proposed as a government regulation to be upgraded to a law to be approved by the Indonesian Parliament. It also led to the agreement that teacher salaries had to be doubled (an increase of 100 percent). But because such an increase, in effect, would have led to two streams of civil servant pay scales and, therefore, demands for equal increases for all civil servants, and because the associations argued that teaching needed to be considered a profession (like law and medicine), the proposal was made to identify the increase as a "professional allowance." With the professional allowance, teacher income indeed became commensurate with that of doctors and lawyers (and even exceeded them, especially given teachers' low teaching load).[5]

At about the same time, within the Ministry of National Education, a new Directorate General for the Quality Improvement of Teachers and Education Personnel was created and given responsibility for virtually all aspects of the management of teachers, both in formal schools and in nonformal education programs, and at both primary and secondary levels of education. One of the Directorate General's first acts was to develop a profile of the teacher population of Indonesia. This profile reinforced the view that teachers, in general, were badly paid, poorly motivated, inequitably deployed, increasingly disrespected by the communities they served, and with few opportunities for further training. The profile helped convince the ministry that any additional professional allowance had to focus not only on teacher welfare, but also on teacher quality, and therefore on some process of certifying that teachers who were provided this allowance were, in fact, professional.

Finally, the newly elected Parliament contained a number of representatives who themselves had been teachers and therefore had experienced directly the results of low status and inadequate pay. Supported by their political parties and leaders who recognized the importance of teachers as a voting constituency and as local opinion leaders, they therefore enthusiastically supported the move for a comprehensive Teacher Law that would directly address the twin issues of welfare and quality. (Rather late in the process, this officially became the Teacher and Lecturer Law to allow some coverage of university-level staff.) This enthusiasm persisted even after the ministry showed what the likely budget would require for putting in place the structures and processes needed for the certification process and paying the allowance.

Thus, in the early 2000s, there was considerable consensus among the major education stakeholders of the country—the government (the Ministry of National

Education, the Ministry of Finance, and the National Planning Board), the political parties and the Parliament, and teachers as represented by their various associations—that what became known as the Teacher Law of 2005 was necessary to clarify the roles, responsibilities, and desired competencies of teachers and to identify the strategies needed to improve their quality and welfare.

Debate on the Law's Provisions

Once the general framework of the Teacher Law was set, however, the consensus on its implementation began to fall apart among the stakeholders. A major issue in this regard was the means proposed to prove "competency" (after the gaining of a minimum four-year degree) for the purposes of certification and receipt of the professional allowance. The ministry, supported by a new National Education Standards Board, wished to assess the four core competencies (professional, pedagogical, personal, and social) through both written tests and classroom observation.

The teacher associations, however, harking back to the original focus on welfare, contended that the proposed competency tests were an assault on the fact that most candidates for certification had already earned a four-year degree and, in many cases, also had many years of experience accompanied by a range of in-service training activities. A majority in Parliament agreed with this opinion and therefore refused to provide funds to implement the competency tests. Instead, they agreed that proof of competency would be based only on the submission of "portfolios" of achievement (such as personal references, publications, certificates of attendance at in-service courses, and model lesson plans). Insistence by the ministry that some kind of competency assessment was essential in this process led to a compromise whereby those teachers whose portfolios were evaluated and approved by local teacher education institutions (selected and oriented by the ministry) would pass immediately to certification, while those who did not gain such approval would be required to undertake a 90-hour training program and then be tested on its content—a test that was ultimately passed by most who took it. In other words, the process of certifying teachers (and thus of providing them a professional allowance equal to their base salary) was not strongly linked to demonstrated competencies in either subject content or pedagogical skill.

Implementation Issues

Early in the process of implementing the Teacher Law, and from a political economy perspective, a range of bureaucratic, political, and financial problems began to appear at both the national and local levels:

- The new directorate general responsible for the process was understaffed, and many of its officers were new to the process of implementing a major, comprehensive, and largely untested reform. The management of such a programmatically and bureaucratically complex process in a system known for administrative inefficiency was not easy—a task made even more difficult by the sense of independence, nourished by the process of decentralization, felt by many district officials and principals who were reluctant to listen to the mandates of the central ministry in the absence of clear incentives.

- Detailed guidelines were therefore needed to try to ensure that district offices would follow the directions of the ministry.
- District education offices had no units comparable to the new directorate general and, therefore, continued to handle teacher management and development in a piecemeal and often uncoordinated fashion.
- The regulations determining which teachers in a given school or district would first enter the queue for certification (in theory, senior teachers with a four-year degree) were not always followed, leading to charges of favoritism and corruption both in schools and in district education offices.
- Reports emerged of fictitious and falsified portfolio documentation—for example, with sample lesson plans, upgrading certificates, and other documents shared among applicants.
- Too few teacher education institutions involved in assessing the large number of portfolios, and in some cases, they were pressured into passing a much larger percentage of portfolios than the 20 percent the ministry had anticipated; not enough teachers, therefore, were seriously assessed in terms of their existing competencies.
- Because funding to be provided to the teacher education institutions for the portfolio assessment and the 90-hour training course was seriously delayed, what was meant to be a leisurely seven-month planning and implementation process had to be completed in two months. This truncated process led to the development of standard training modules (rather than modules tailored to fit profiles of teachers' needs at different levels of competence); inefficient training processes (for example, up to 25 parallel classes in one institution and a large percentage of time devoted to breaks and administrative tasks); and an almost 100 percent pass rate at the end of the training.

When the Teacher Law was passed in 2005, only about 15 percent of the government's budget was devoted to education. The government recognized that the introduction of the professional allowance and a commitment to certify all teachers by 2015 would put significant pressure on the education budget. Despite evidence showing this impact, the pressure to improve the welfare of teachers meant that the provisions for the professional allowance remained. These budgetary pressures were partially relieved after 2008 when the constitutional court ruled that the government was failing to meet its constitutional obligation to spend 20 percent of its budget on education. Government education spending increased significantly, and its share has remained above 20 percent since 2009.

Early Challenges

In addition to these implementation problems, other, more subtle issues arose to complicate the process. Three years after the passing of the Teacher Law, the Directorate General for Quality Improvement of Teachers and Education Personnel was dismantled, and different aspects of teacher management and development were again placed not only in different directorates but also in a new Board for Educational and Cultural Human Resources Development and Quality Assurance for Education. Partly as a result, the original intention of the reform to adapt its strategies to the particular needs of different regions of Indonesia, different districts, and even different teachers—adaptations such as greater variety, more local content, and more options in the 90-hour course—was never carried out.

In addition, these practical setbacks arose:

- The expectation that certified teachers would use a portion of their new allowance for continuing professional development has rarely been fulfilled.
- Detailed regulations around a new mandate that every certified teacher teach a minimum of 24 period-hours per week (a rule hotly contested by teacher associations, which preferred 18 period-hours) were also only belatedly developed.
- Plans to implement other aspects of the reform focused more on quality assurance of both the process and the products (such as more effective and merit-based procedures for the appointment of school principals and supervisors and new and more rigorous mechanisms for induction, probation, and teacher appraisal) were either delayed or remained only central government regulations not actively implemented down to the district level. Funds available at the district level for continuing professional development of certified teachers were therefore often unspent.

Worries about the impact of the Teacher Law on private schools and systems also arose. Although the law itself does not distinguish between "public" and "private," priority for entry into the certification queue was usually given first to (a) public school teachers, who were much more likely to have both a civil service post and financial support to obtain the four-year degree necessary for certification, and then (b) to temporary teachers with government contracts. It is therefore said that many of the best private school teachers moved to public schools, even as contract teachers, with the intention of eventually gaining a post and then certification.

Ultimately, however, doubts began to accumulate both about the integrity of the content and the fairness of the portfolio assessment procedure across teacher education institutions and about the efficacy of the 90-hour training program. This evidence was compelling and convinced the ministry, despite opposition from some teacher associations, that a test of actual competency before certification was required. The ministry therefore eliminated the portfolio as a means to gain certification and developed both a Pre-Test of Teacher Competency (which determines whether a teacher remains in the certification queue) and a post-training Teacher Competency Test (to determine whether the teacher has achieved the desired competencies and thus is eligible for certification and the professional allowance). Even in this process, however, political pressures (from teacher associations to find most teachers competent) and financial exigencies (from the Ministry of Finance for the Ministry of Education and Culture[6] to spend its budget for professional allowances) caused the ministry to set the passing score at 30 percent for the competency pretest given in early 2012.

Impact of Decentralization

Another aspect of Indonesia's political and economic environment that became important in the implementation of the Teacher Law was the strong policy of decentralization of authority and resources from the center to regional (district and municipal) governments and agencies. This decentralization policy, starting in 2000, was expected to weaken the hierarchical, almost feudal attitudes that made Indonesia's bureaucracy so unwieldy and often so unimaginative by increasing the efficiency of the system and making it more innovative and responsive to the needs of its constituencies and ultimate "clients." However, by stopping much of the decentralization process at the district office level—where one office can be in charge of 1,000 schools or more—little reform or change, in fact, may happen at the level where it matters the most: the community and the school.

This decentralization process both (a) transferred substantial policy making and planning authority (and resources) from the central level down to the district level, and (b) moved implementation processes (and resources) from the subdistrict level up to the district level—changes that resulted in much larger and much more powerful district-level offices. But the unclear and incomplete division of labor among the different levels of the system and the lack of management and technical skills in planning, budgeting, procurement, and accounting needed at lower levels of the system to take on more authority (and the willingness of the upper level to give up its authority) made decentralization a problematic process. Also, because decentralization took away most of the central government's carrots and sticks—which can be used to ensure that decentralized entities still work within some kind of central framework—the pressure for district offices to do much more than merely send the reform messages downward is limited.

Decentralization and the introduction of school grants led to increases in the size of the teaching force, increasing further the future costs of certification. The intergovernmental transfer system introduced to allocate resources across levels of governments included incentives to hire civil service teachers (Cerdan-Infantes and Makarova 2013). Part of the overall fund transfer was determined by the size of the civil service establishment and local governments, with large civil services receiving more central funds. This led to an increase in teacher hiring, which has meant that student-teacher ratios have declined substantially since decentralization began. Incentives to hire more teachers were also exacerbated by the large increase in school-hired teachers following the introduction of the school grants program in 2005. This program, School Operational Assistance (*Bantuan Operasional Sekolah*, or BOS), was launched nationally, and schools used these resources partly to hire more teachers. Between 2006 and 2010, an additional

260,000 teachers were recruited in this way in primary and junior secondary schools across Indonesia.

What decentralization did mandate was the popular election of district-level legislatures and district "regents" (chiefs) and the subsequent appointment by these regents of the heads of local government sectoral offices such as education—appointments open to favoritism and manipulation rather than reliance on experience and merit. Decentralization gave these heads of district education offices a mandate over processes such as the appointment of subdistrict office heads and school principals (in one reported case, 120 principals were replaced at one time by new district education authorities); the request for and deployment of new teaching posts; and the prioritization of candidates for obtaining the four-year degree and, subsequently, entry into the certification process. And although the Teacher Law gives to district offices the right to withhold the professional allowance from teachers who fail to meet given criteria of quality, this right is seldom exercised because of various local personal and political pressures.

Another objective of decentralization is a stronger voice in education decision making and budget oversight on the part of parents and the community through elected SCs, an essential component of a major program on school-based management (SBM; further described in box I.1). Despite some progress in this regard in districts and schools that consciously attempt to promote this process, local voices are generally not an important factor in issues around teacher reform. As a recent review of the SBM program concluded, "Parents generally had a small voice in school matters. Parents' deferential attitudes toward school staff, perceptions of the effective division of labor between school and home, and schools' lack of outreach appear to prevent parents from effectively exercising their voice in school affairs. Parents are rarely part of final decisions on school matters" (Chen 2011).

Thus, both the economic impact of more resources available to local governments and the political impact of more power exercised by these governments have caused considerable concern about the fairness and propriety of a range of activities in the teacher management and development cycle, especially at the district and school level. As a result, the Teacher Law's focus on longer-term, continuing quality improvement achieved through flexible, more adaptable, and individualized implementation has in some ways been lost because of (a) political pressures for rapid certification and standardized treatment for all, and (b) economic pressures to quickly and completely spend the new funds moving into the education system.

More generally, perhaps, the focus on a "structural" rather than a "cultural" solution to the low status and competency levels of teachers—including a formal degree, portfolios and multiple-choice tests, standardized certification processes, and standardized content for quality improvement, all leading to formal professional labeling and greater income—resulted, in some people's view, in the downgrading of what in the past had actually been the basis for status: a strong commitment to and passion for teaching.

Box 1.1 School-Based Management in Indonesia

As part of a broad decentralization of governance responsibilities to districts, the Indonesian government adopted school-based management (SBM) principles through regulations in the National Education Law of 2003. SBM is a form of education governance that grants responsibilities and authority for individual school academic operations to principals, teachers, and other local community-based stakeholders. The expectations are that local, and often shared, decision making will lead to more efficient and effective policies and programs aligned with local priorities, which in turn will lead to improved school performance and student achievement. Because of the limited scope of past research on the implementation and effects of SBM in Indonesia during its eight years of implementation, the Ministry of Education and Culture and the development partners expressed the need to undertake a study that aimed to (a) provide a nationwide quantitative and qualitative status report on the implementation of SBM, (b) identify factors associated with successful practices of SBM, and (c) assess the effects of SBM on student achievement.

The study was carried out in 2010 and 2011 and was based on face-to-face surveys of principals, teachers, school committee (SC) members, and parents in 400 elementary schools; surveys of district staff in 54 districts; and case studies in a subsample of 40 schools (Chen 2011). Although the study determined that in general the structures (such as SCs, district-level supervision, and teacher councils) and processes (such as SC elections and principal-teacher consultations) supportive of SBM were nominally in place, successful implementation of the SBM program—still, in the history of things, relatively young—would require greater clarity of the roles and responsibilities of the various administrative levels of the system, more capacity building of all the system's actors, and a stronger commitment to its goals and objectives.

Based on the findings of the study and given the importance of SBM in the further development of Indonesian education, recommendations for improving the implementation and the outcomes of SBM focused on three actions: (a) expanding principal, teacher, and SC member capacity to implement SBM; (b) increasing school staff ability to make managerial and instructional changes; and (c) developing district capacity to support schools and SBM.

Conclusions

The Indonesian Teacher Law of 2005 is unusual in the comprehensiveness of its various components and of the institutions, mechanisms, strategies, and processes put in place to implement it. It is also unusual in the principal incentive designed to inspire it: the granting of status as a "professional" and, probably more important, the large and unconditional increase in income provided upon gaining this status.

But the evolution of the Teacher Law of 2005 from its original conceptualization to its current state of implementation is not unusual for major reforms. From larger macro-level political and economic considerations to more personal and institutional rivalries, a number of complications have arisen to delay or derail the implementation of various parts of the reform. These are well understood by the Ministry of Education and Culture, and steps are being undertaken to resolve many of them. Whether these steps are successful will go a long way toward determining whether the lofty goals and aspirations of the Teacher Law are finally met.

With the context of this comprehensive reform now in place, the next chapter turns to the conceptual framework for quality education through reformed teacher management and development, which forms the basis for the remaining chapters of this book.

Notes

1. *Pancasila* is the official philosophical foundation of the Indonesian state. The term consists of two Old Javanese words (originally from Sanskrit): "*pañca*" meaning five, and "*sīla*" meaning principles. It comprises five principles held to be inseparable and interrelated: (a) belief in the one and only God; (b) just and civilized humanity; (c) the unity of Indonesia; (d) democracy guided by the inner wisdom in the unanimity arising out of deliberations among representatives; and (e) social justice for all of the people of Indonesia.

2. The World Conference on Education for All was held in Jomtien, Thailand, in 1990. From this conference, the World Declaration on Education for All (EFA) was adopted, and six goals were set for 2000. In 2000, the international community met again at the World Education Forum in Dakar, Senegal, and set further goals for achievement by 2015. The United Nations Educational, Scientific, and Cultural Organization (UNESCO) has the overall coordination and leadership role in the EFA effort, whose goals also contribute toward the global pursuit of the United Nations' MDGs.

3. For more information about the UNESCO-led EFA movement, see http://www .unesco.org/new/en/education/themes/leading-the-international-agenda/education-for-all/. For more about the UN's MDGs regarding achievement of universal primary education, see http://www.un.org/millenniumgoals/education.shtml.

4. The previous law governing the National Education System needed to be adjusted to implement the principles of the democratization of education. The Law on National Education System (2003) covers all aspects in the Indonesian education system, including its functions and aims; the rights and obligations of learners, parents, citizens, the community, and the government; the streams, levels, and types of education; the medium of instruction; compulsory education; national education standards; the curriculum; the educators and education personnel; educational facilities and equipment; financing of education; educational management; community participation in education; evaluation, accreditation, and certification; criteria for the establishment of educational institutions; and supervision.

5. According to one source, although beginning medical doctors and teachers receive almost the same base pay of over Rp 1,900,000 per month, the professional allowance for certified teachers (for teaching 24 period-hours or 18 hours per week) is equivalent to this base pay, while for a doctor (working 40 hours per week), the professional allowance is Rp 325,000 (Sri 2011). The maximum allowance for senior doctors is Rp 1,400,000 and for senior teachers, Rp 4,100,000.

6. At the time of the Teacher Law of 2005, the Ministry was named the Ministry of National Education. In 2011, its name changed to the Ministry of Education and Culture.

References

Bjork, C. 2005. *Indonesian Education: Teachers, Schools, and Central Bureaucracy*. London: Routledge.

Cerdan-Infantes, P., and Y. Makarova. 2013. *Spending More or Spending Better: Improving Education Financing in Indonesia*. Jakarta: World Bank.

Chen, D. 2011. "School-Based Management, School Decision-Making, and Education Outcomes in Indonesian Primary Schools." Policy Research Working Paper 5809, World Bank, Washington, DC.

Jalal, F., M. Samani, M. Chu Chang, R. Stevenson, A. B. Ragatz, and S. D. Negara. 2009. *Teacher Certification in Indonesia: A Strategy for Teacher Quality Improvement*. Report of the Development Education Program, World Bank, Washington, DC.

OECD (Organisation for Economic Co-operation and Development). 2010. *PISA 2009 Results: Learning Trends. Changes in Student Performance Since 2000*. Vol. V. Paris: OECD Publishing. http://dx.doi.org/10.1787/9789264091580-en.

Ragatz, A. 2010. *Transforming Indonesia's Teaching Force*. Vol. II of *From Pre-service Training to Retirement: Producing and Maintaining a High-quality, Efficient, and Motivated Workforce*. Human Development Series. Jakarta: World Bank.

Sri, Y. 2011. "Gaji Guru Vs. Gaji Dokter." Kompasiana.com., August 16. http://kesehatan .kompasiana.com/medis/2011/08/16/gaji-guru-vs-gaji-dokter-387357.html.

UNESCO Institute of Statistics. 2010. *Global Education Digest 2010: Comparing Education Statistics across the World*. Montreal, Canada: UNESCO Institute of Statistics.

Usman, S., Akhmadi, and D. Suryadarma. 2004. *When Teachers Are Absent: Where Do They Go and What Is the Impact on Students?* Field report, SMERU Research Institute, Jakarta.

World Bank. 2008. *Teacher Employment and Deployment in Indonesia: Opportunities for Equity, Efficiency and Quality Improvement*. Study report 45622, World Bank, Jakarta.

CHAPTER 2

Teachers as the Cornerstone of Educational Quality

A Definition of Educational Quality

> Available studies suggest that the main driver of the variation in student learning in school is the quality of the teachers .... Studies that take into account all of the available evidence on teacher effectiveness suggest that students placed with high-performing teachers will progress three times as fast as those placed with low-performing teachers.
>
> —Sir Michael Barber and Mona Morshed, "How the World's Best-Performing Schools Come Out on Top"

The evolution of the definition of *quality in education* has been a complex and nonlinear one. But in simplified terms, early definitions of quality focused on inputs and outputs. More schools and classrooms, more books and teachers, would inevitably lead not only to higher enrollments but also to higher completion rates and greater achievement. When such logic did not always lead to the expected results, attention eventually turned to the "black box" in the middle—the quality of the teachers, the teaching-learning process, and the curriculum it was meant to deliver—where the inputs were meant to be used in creative ways to produce the outcomes desired. Efforts were also focused on the "quality" of the children who entered school: were they healthy, well-nourished, motivated to learn, and ready for school? Still later, the school climate or environment (what surrounded the "black box") also became of interest. Was the school a physically healthy and psychosocially friendly and protective place to be—a sanctuary for children rather than a place with poor hygiene and unhealthy facilities, corporal punishment, peer bullying, and teacher indifference and even cruelty?

Even later, the larger environment of parents, families, and communities was included in the definition. Are families willing and able to be involved in making the school better and helping their children learn more? And is the school willing and able to accept their involvement? Is the larger community supportive of—rather than dismissive of—the school? Is the school sensitive to and supportive of the local community and its culture(s)?

Most recently, the nature and quality of school governance have become important. Do individual schools—through a collaborative partnership of school staff, parents, and the community—develop efficient school-based management mechanisms and procedures, including sensitive self-assessments of school conditions (inputs, processes, outcomes) and forward-looking, innovative, and (ideally) adequately financed school improvement plans?

Such a comprehensive definition of *quality* was at the core of the Dakar Framework for Action for Education for All (EFA) of 2000 (UNESCO 2000).[1] It contained both a target and a strategy on quality:

- *Target 6*: Improving all aspects of the quality of EFA
- *Strategy 8*: Create safe, healthy, inclusive, and equitably resourced educational environments with clearly defined levels of achievement for all

The Dakar Framework also focused on 10 characteristics of educational quality:

- Healthy, well-nourished, and motivated students
- Well-motivated and professionally competent teachers
- Active learning techniques
- A relevant curriculum
- Adequate, environmentally friendly, and easily accessible facilities
- Healthy, safe, and protective learning environments
- Adequate evaluation of school environments, processes, and outcomes
- Participatory, school-based management
- Respect for and engagement with local communities and cultures
- Adequate and equitable financing

With this list, the definition of quality became truly comprehensive and multidimensional. The definition included characteristics of the major actors (students, teachers, parents, the community); inputs (books, learning materials, facilities); processes (teaching and learning, school governance, monitoring and evaluation, financing); environments (of the classroom, the school, and the surrounding community); and, ultimately, outcomes (enrollment, retention, completion, achievement).

Whatever the definition of "good" education has been—and particularly in any more comprehensive definition used today—the role of the teacher in providing an education of good quality is seen as ever more critical: "The quality of education, in other words, cannot exceed the quality of its teachers" (Barber and Mourshed 2007, 16). It is the teacher who must use more student-centered, active teaching-learning techniques to deliver a relevant curriculum; who, often in the context of increasingly powerful school-based management, must promote community support for the school and demonstrate respect for and engagement with local communities; who must demonstrate both good practice and strong ethical principles; and who must ultimately motivate students, ensure their health and safety, and help them learn what they want—and need—to learn. A strong, rigorous, merit-based teacher management and development system is therefore essential in creating the teachers who can fulfill this increasingly important role.

A Conceptual Framework for Teacher Quality

Defining a Good Teacher

The comprehensive and multidimensional definition of quality provided above requires an equally comprehensive and multidimensional framework for teacher quality. But describing the nature and quality of a teaching force in any nation is a complex task; this is even truer in an education system as large and diverse as Indonesia's. The logical place to start, of course, is with an assessment of its quality: just how good are the teachers, how well do they teach, and what kinds of outcomes do they achieve for their students?

What constitutes effective teaching is a matter that psychologists, sociologists, and educators have long deliberated with a general focus on which teaching strategies, techniques, and devices contribute most effectively to student learning. Although there is often an attempt to simplify it, learning is a complex and contextual process. It requires specifics of which teaching methods, under which conditions, with which students, in which subject areas, and at which grade levels are essential to achieve effective learning (O'Neill 1988).

The quality of teachers and teaching can be conceptualized and measured in many ways.[2] One approach focuses principally on teacher productivity, perhaps best assessed by general classroom performance and specific teacher practices. In recent decades, greater attention has been given to such practices, in part because of landmark studies that found classroom effects to be greater than school effects (see, for example, Sanders and Rivers 1996 and Scheerens 1992). One result has been that research related to effective teaching has been expanding rapidly.

Process-Product Function

Teaching behavior and its relation to student achievement had traditionally been studied through what became known as "process-product" studies, in which teaching practices and behavior are statistically linked to student outcomes to determine which practices or behaviors positively or negatively affect outcomes (Muijs and Reynolds 2002). But this process-product model is limited—seen as often too subjective, undertaken by principals or supervisors rather than neutral assessors, sporadic, and unsystematic—and new models are emerging to replace it (Seidel and Shavelson 2007). Such models of teaching and learning have changed to emphasize cognitive and affective components. A critical reason for this shift is that, in the past decade,

Teacher Reform in Indonesia • http://dx.doi.org/10.1596/978-0-8213-9829-6

teaching effectiveness research has concentrated on more global aspects of teaching and on analyzing teaching patterns or regimes instead of single teaching acts (Borko 2004).

In this shift, two distinct approaches have emerged. One approach has focused on large-scale surveys with sophisticated multilevel statistical models of students nested within classes nested within schools with extraneous variables controlled. This has increased statistical power in detecting effects (Raudenbush 2004; Rowan, Correnti, and Miller 2002). The second approach focuses on processes of learning in specific knowledge domains (Bereiter and Scardamalia 2003, 55–68; Greeno, Collins, and Resnick 1996). This approach typically involves experimental or quasi-experimental studies of specific instructional approaches and how these approaches affect student learning.

In both of these approaches, student performance is often used as a more easily measurable proxy of teacher effectiveness. An important feature of such measurement is that student learning is characterized as multidimensional, making it quite distinct from the older process-product studies. Student outcomes are often examined not only on cognitive outcomes but also on affective and metacognitive outcomes (Snow and Lohman 1984). This view holds teaching to be the creation of a learning environment for students to undertake cognitive activities through which they can build knowledge and reasoning capacity. This approach, of course, has its own challenges, especially at the primary school level where, over a number of years, students may experience a variety of different teachers. Furthermore, student performance in, say, arithmetic is conditioned not only by a wide range of external factors (such as the student's health and nutritional status, family background, prior experience in an early childhood development program, and the extent of exposure to the language of instruction used in school) but also by many internal school factors beyond teacher quality, including the availability of texts and other materials, the language of instruction, and the physical and psychosocial environment of the school as a whole.

Assuming that such factors can be taken into account in any systematic assessment, resulting student outcomes can be correlated with a number of policy indicators related to teacher management and development. For example, Rice (2003) identifies a number of these as follows:

- *Teacher preparation programs and degrees*. What is the structure of teacher education in terms of the balance between practice and theory, what percentage of teachers has how many years of formal preservice education, and what percentage has attained the desired or required degree mandated by the Ministry of Education and Culture?
- *Teacher experience*. Experience includes both induction and mentoring in the early years of a teacher's career and in-service training in later years.
- *Subject matter credentials*. These include, in both preservice and in-service education, the extent to which teachers have taken coursework relevant to the subject area(s) they teach and the pedagogical skills needed to teach it.

- *Test scores*. Knowledge may be not only measured by the teachers' own test scores, especially the teacher's literacy level or verbal abilities but also subject knowledge.
- *Teacher certification*. Ultimately, based on a mixture of some or all of the above, some kind of formal teacher certification is desirable (especially when certification is in the subject that the teacher is assigned to teach).

Unfortunately, the literature on the impact of these policy indicators is not altogether clear. This is especially the case in regard to issues of qualification and certification—often used as a measure of teacher quality—and a great deal of research has been done examining educational levels (for example, a four-year degree), degree types (for example, mathematics versus mathematics education), and qualifications (for example, certification and training received). A study employing multiple years of the reading and mathematics assessments of the National Assessment of Educational Progress (NAEP) examined the relative contributions of teacher qualifications, other school inputs, and student characteristics to student achievement (Darling-Hammond 2000). After controlling for student poverty and student language background, this study found that "measures of teacher preparation and certification were the strongest correlates of average student achievement in reading and mathematics. The most strongly significant predictor of achievement was the proportion of well-qualified teachers, defined as the proportion holding both full certification and a major in the field being taught." Darling-Hammond and Berry (2006) also note that the less-advantaged students benefit most, stating, "Studies show that well-prepared and well-supported teachers are important for all students, but especially for students who come to school with greater needs."

On the other hand, many other studies have found certification programs and other qualifications to be poor measures of teacher quality. Leigh (2007) argues that formal qualifications of teachers and other information frequently recorded on a database of teachers (for example, gender, age, degrees held, and certification) seldom predict effectiveness in raising student achievement. Others (Wayne and Youngs 2003) agree, finding "little different in the average academic achievement impacts of certified, uncertified, and alternatively certified teachers" (as quoted in Kane, Rockoff, and Staiger 2008). Many such instances relate to the inability to use effective pedagogy; there is often a significant discordance between knowledge of subject and ability to manage in the classroom. Clearly, aptitude and calling have a place in the teaching profession.

Teacher Knowledge and Classroom Behavior

A second way to conceptualize and measure teacher quality looks not at outcomes but rather at what teachers should know and be able to do—essential knowledge and skills rather than outcomes. Research in this vein suggests that high-quality, effective teachers who can increase the academic achievement of their students tend to share many of the characteristics listed in table 2.1.

Table 2.1 Characteristics of Good Teachers from International Research

• Demonstrate commitment • Have subject-specific knowledge and know their craft • Love children • Set an example of moral conduct • Manage groups effectively • Incorporate new technology • Master multiple models of teaching and learning • Adjust and improvise their practice • Know their students as individuals • Exchange ideas with other teachers • Reflect on their practice • Collaborate with other teachers • Advance the profession of teaching • Contribute to society at large	• Know their subject matter • Use pedagogy appropriate for the content • Use an appropriate language of instruction and have mastery of that language • Create and sustain an effective learning environment • Find out about and respond to the needs and interests of their students and communities • Reflect on their teaching and children's responses and change the learning environment as necessary • Have a strong sense of ethics • Are committed to teaching • Care about their students
Source: OECD 2009.	*Source:* Craig, Kraft, and Du Plessis 1998.

This approach also recognizes that the role of a teacher involves a broad range of knowledge and skills. The teacher needs to have an in-depth understanding of the subject matter being taught and the requirements of the curriculum. The teacher also needs to understand child development (physical, cognitive and linguistic, social, and moral); appreciate factors that facilitate or inhibit learning; and have a good understanding of the context for learning, including both factors in the classroom (such as its climate) and factors in the home and community (such as their general support for the school). Also necessary is a good knowledge of instructional psychology, including theories of teaching and learning and methods of teaching that foster active learning and problem solving, facilitate group learning and constructive student interaction, and develop in children a love of reading and learning.

Beyond this knowledge base, the teacher needs a range of skills in the following areas:

- *Classroom management*: planning lessons, organizing structured but personalized learning experiences, delivering the required content in the language of instruction (and helping children weak in that language to gain this content), providing appropriate reinforcement, assessing what students learn, and being alert to children who show evidence of being at risk of failure
- *School relationships and improvement*: collaborating with colleagues in assessing the school's status, developing school improvement plans, and building a positive school climate
- *School-community relationships*: providing appropriate reports to parents and motivating their support of and involvement in school affairs
- *Self-reflection and improvement*: being able to reflect on their own teaching (including with their peers) and improve their performance accordingly

Such teaching skills—perhaps less easily measured but essential indicators of quality—have been among the major focuses of the reforms in Indonesia and are addressed in different ways in most chapters of this book. For example, many of the key skills have been built into the teaching-learning packages used by the Ministry of Education and Culture through the local teacher working groups, as discussed in chapter 3. The video study discussed in chapter 5 also focuses clearly on the nature of the teaching-learning process and presents a pioneering in-depth analysis of secondary school mathematics teaching that directly links student outcomes with teacher knowledge and behaviors.

Also examined in this book are more general values and behaviors related to teacher quality, including professional commitment, ethical behavior, and—more concrete and measurable—absenteeism, the holding of second jobs, and workload. The assumption that higher status and remuneration will somehow automatically lead to better outcomes in regard to such behaviors is subject to detailed analysis.

Such a plethora of desired knowledge, skills, and values makes imperative some set of professional competency standards. The standards also include measures and methods to assess their achievement. These standards usually underpin training courses, assessment instruments, and accreditation requirements as well as professional development courses. They should be (but seldom are) developed collaboratively by ministry staff, academics and teacher trainers, and representatives of professional teacher associations. Such standards have also been a major focus of the Teacher Law reforms and associated regulations.

Conceptual Framework for Quality Education: Managing and Developing Good Teachers

> Countries that have succeeded in making teaching an attractive profession have often done so not just through pay, but by raising the status of teaching, offering real career prospects, and giving teachers responsibility as professionals and leaders of reform. This requires teacher education that helps teachers to become innovators and researchers in education, not just deliverers of the curriculum.
>
> —Andreas Schleicher, *Building a High-Quality Teaching Profession: Lessons from Around the World*

Managing teachers—individually (both in a classroom and throughout a career) and collectively (as an entire cadre)—is a difficult enough task. Ensuring that they progressively develop in their profession, from first recruitment to final retirement, only adds to the complexity of the challenge facing ministries of education around the world. Meeting this challenge successfully requires a comprehensive framework of teacher reform encompassing essential standards and competencies as well as the institutions, mechanisms, strategies, and processes required to ensure that these competencies are achieved, assessed, continuously improved, and ultimately rewarded. Figure 2.1 reflects such a framework.

Teacher Reform in Indonesia • http://dx.doi.org/10.1596/978-0-8213-9829-6

Figure 2.1 Conceptual Framework for Quality Education

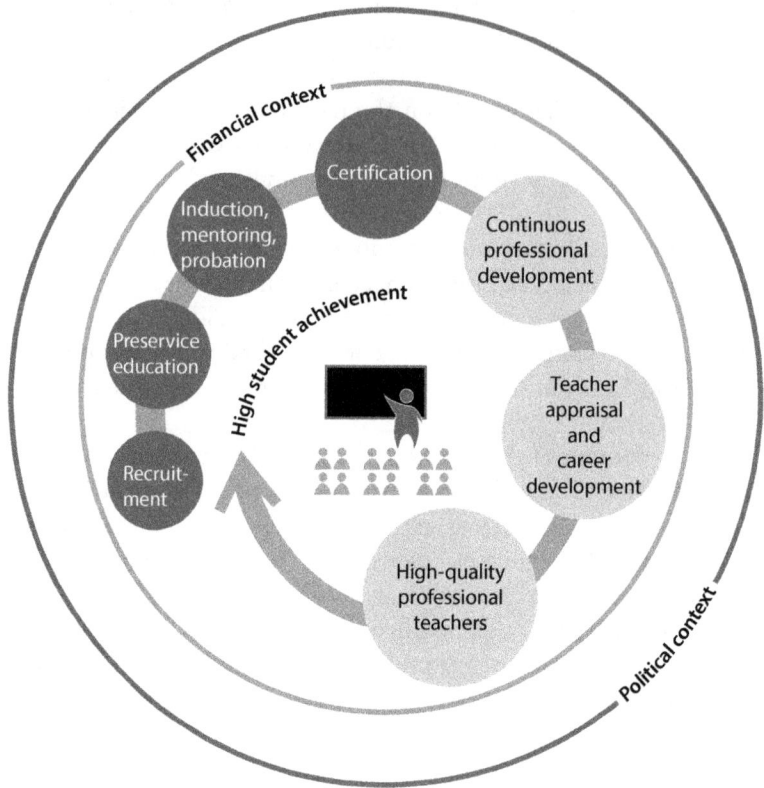

The Political and Financial Context

Policy design and implementation is a complex, multi-directional, fragmented, and unpredictable process. A political economy lens broadens operational considerations beyond technical solutions to include an emphasis on stakeholders, institutions, and processes by which policy reform is negotiated and played out in the policy arena .... A vital component of understanding context is the political dynamics of policy change—how reforms get tabled and why; how they are perceived; and who will support, oppose, or attempt to change the proposals which have been made.

—World Bank, "The Political Economy of Policy Reform: Issues and Implications for Policy Dialogue and Development Operations"

No education policy is perhaps more complex, multidirectional, fragmented, and unpredictable than that regarding teacher management and development. Teachers often represent a large percentage of the total civil service, and in many societies they play an important and influential role in the community as well as in the school. Thus, all of the various stages of teacher reform described below, both in general and in relation to Indonesia, must be analyzed in terms of the larger political context surrounding them—both the historical context relevant to education (which has played an important role in the development of Indonesian education) and the current structure and nature of the government and the Ministry of Education and Culture that propose the reform, those who support and oppose it (and why), and those who win or lose from it.

Equally important is the financial context—on the national, local, and school levels as well as community support to education and the start-up and recurring costs of the reform itself—which helps determine what can be done, how quickly, and how rigorously. More and more middle-income countries, such as Indonesia, are finding additional resources to put into education, and the financial decisions they make about these resources, whether teachers or infrastructure, preschools or universities, will have important long-term effects on the development of their education systems.

Recruitment

A comprehensive framework for high-quality education requires attention to many different steps in the teacher management and development framework. Recruitment into teacher education institutions is the first step in the career of a new teacher, and countries are using an ever wider range of strategies to recruit higher-level candidates for the teaching profession. Higher pay, of course (competitive with other "professions") helps, but many other strategies are also being applied, including the following (Barber and Mourshed 2007; World Bank 2008):

- *Active recruitment campaigns*, especially (a) among secondary school graduates with the highest achievement levels and, in some countries, "nontraditional" candidates (for example, mid-career professionals seeking a career change); and (b) among teachers of subjects (usually science and mathematics) and in regions (rural and remote) where shortages of good teachers are often the greatest
- *Rigorous selection processes*, based not only on graduation records and entrance examinations but also on the testing of subject knowledge, literacy, numeracy, and communication skills and interviews to assess motivation, personality, and sensitivity to student needs—processes that can help prove to candidates and the larger public that teaching is, in fact, a high-status profession
- *Financial incentives* such as fee waivers, loans, and scholarships, perhaps biased toward underrepresented fields and teachers destined for difficult locations
- *More flexible approaches to teacher education*, such as part-time study and distance education, especially for nontraditional candidates and those from usually underrepresented groups such as ethnic minorities, people with disabilities, and males in preschool and primary education
- *A clearly defined career path* that holds out the possibility of both merit-based promotion and diverse opportunities within the system
- *The prospect of ultimately being a "professional,"* able to exercise responsibility, autonomy, and innovativeness in one's daily work

Teacher Reform in Indonesia • http://dx.doi.org/10.1596/978-0-8213-9829-6

Preservice Teacher Education

Once the candidate is selected, the nature and quality of preservice teacher education become paramount. There are many options for such education, including the following (Stevenson 2009c):

- A multiyear course (for example, four years leading to a bachelor's degree in education) that integrates pedagogy, subject content, and practical teaching experience
- An "end-on" option that adds one or two years of professional training (pedagogy and practical experience) to a subject-matter university degree
- A double degree (a major and a minor) with additional training in education
- For mid-career professionals, a short course on pedagogy and practical experience with continual supervision in school by the training institution

In all such programs, there are a number of essential, basic principles (Barber and Mourshed 2007; Schleicher 2011):

- *Clear and concise profiles or standards outlining desired teacher competencies*— what teachers are expected to know and be able to do in specific subject areas—which can guide not only teacher education but also certification, evaluation, professional development, and career advancement
- *More innovative content in teacher education* with emphases on such skills as personalized instruction based on the individual learner's needs; reflective practice; and in-school, on-the-job research
- *Training for special circumstances*—for example, multigrade and double-subject teaching for small, remote schools; teaching in the students' mother tongue; and teaching learners with disabilities and in (post-) emergency or conflict contexts
- *Preparation of professionals in school settings*, separate from the largely academic preparation in the training institution, thus finding a proper balance between theory and practice

Regarding the last point, it has become increasingly important to place candidate teachers into classrooms as early as possible. This initial placement should not happen in the second semester of the last year, as is often the case, but as early as possible so that future teachers can both practice and improve the whole range of skills they need and clearly see the challenges (and rewards) of being a teacher (thereby perhaps weeding out those not committed enough to face the challenges).

The success of this professional component of preservice education depends on both (a) an effective partnership among the lecturers of the teacher education institution, the school coordinator of the professional experience, the supervising classroom teacher(s), and, of course, the candidate teacher; and (b) the use of a range of "real" schools for this professional experience, demonstrating good practice in a number of often-challenging contexts rather than only in elite, often university-based laboratory schools (Stevenson 2009c).

The role of assessment, both of teacher education institutions and of the newly educated teacher, has become especially critical. In many countries, such as Indonesia, which are moving aggressively toward a more systematic process of teacher certification, there have been increasingly greater demands on their teacher education institutions and a greater need for their formal accreditation. What standards should be used for such accreditation, and should there be different levels of accreditation? Who should accredit? For what level(s) of teaching and what subject content? Is there a maximum number of institutions that should receive accreditation, and what should be done to control what is often a mushrooming of such institutions, especially in remote areas of a country such as Indonesia? And how, using what criteria and mechanisms, will these institutions determine when a candidate teacher is adequately prepared for assignment to a school? When, how, and by whom is such an assessment made? And, ultimately, how serious is the system of assessment if it is not willing to "push out" candidates who are not qualified—or qualifiable?

Induction, Mentoring, and Probation

Getting new teachers into a school is only the first step in a career-long program of professional development. In the best of worlds, an education system attracts better candidates to become teachers—most likely through a combination of higher pay, higher status, and appeals to commit oneself to an honorable profession—and, one way or another, provides them during their preservice education with the basic knowledge, skills, and values needed to be good teachers. But even if this initial education is soundly based in classroom experience, it is not easy to make the transition to being a full-time teacher responsible for the education of one or more classes of learners; being expected to fit in and work well with a team of strangers; and being accountable both *up* the system to the principal and supervisor or inspector and (more and more often) *out* of the system to parents and the community. Facilitating this transition, helping teachers succeed at the beginning of their careers (and easing out those who cannot succeed), continuously enhancing teacher motivation and improving teaching practice, and systematically assessing teacher performance for the sake of both their students' learning and their own career progression—these are all essential components of continuing professional development.

The processes of induction, mentoring, and probation should be linked seamlessly to the teacher's future professional development. These are especially important because "the learning curve during the first years of teaching is particularly steep. Having support to confront this learning curve in a gradual but steady manner is important to build new teachers' self-confidence, help them cope with the demands of the profession, and reduce drop-outs" (Stevenson 2009b). Induction, well-implemented, is important for new teachers for several reasons: "familiarization with the responsibilities of teaching and the culture of the school in which they teach … increased competency through improvement of their professional skills in the classroom by learning from experienced teachers in an authentic environment ... assessment of their classroom performance to ensure they are effective in their duties as a teacher ... [and] improved retention of teachers in the profession" (Stevenson 2009b).

A range of activities can be considered as induction, varying from the informal (a welcome by the principal) to the formal (mentoring, workshops, observation of model classes, and so on). However, a well-planned induction should at least include orientation to the school community; the provision of a systematic program of formal instruction in areas such as curriculum content, teaching methods, classroom management and assessment, advice to students, and school policies; and mentoring by an experienced teacher.

Of course, the latter—mentoring—links into the other important part of early professional development: probation. Probation is in theory a trial period (often one year with the possibility of extension) when new teachers can be evaluated as to whether they are genuinely suited to teaching. In a sense, the evaluation concerns the extent to which the teacher has become successful in the practice of teaching. In other words, can the teacher be confirmed as a permanent civil servant? The tools of probation are several—all designed to assess whether the new teacher has met the required teaching standards—and can include written tests, classroom observation of content knowledge and teaching practice, the teacher's classroom documentation, feedback from parents and students, interviews, the assessment of the teacher's relationships with other teachers and his or her general contributions to school activities and decision-making processes, and so forth.

Certification

For permanent employment as a teacher, most school systems require teachers to hold certification. This is official recognition that the teacher has reached the standard endorsed by the education authorities and is a mark of the teacher's competence in subject-matter knowledge and teaching methodology. It also indicates that the teacher possesses the attitudes and personal characteristics necessary for the special relationships of trust and guidance he or she must have to effectively impart knowledge and skills to the young. Certification is usually based upon the academic achievement of teachers in their teaching subjects as well as their knowledge of child development and education. However, skill and expertise in the classroom delivery of effective learning experiences for students is also part of certification.

In making certification decisions, some authorities consider the academic qualifications provided by the university or college to the teacher on graduation but will accept the practical professional capability of the teacher only following a formal assessment by a school principal, usually during the probationary period. In this situation, the certification award is based on a balance between academic excellence as judged by the lecturers and teaching expertise as judged by the employer. This seems to be a worthwhile method of ensuring that only well-rounded teachers with the best knowledge, skills, and attitudes are certified to educate children.

Continuing Professional Development

Accompanying these early-career experiences and continuing beyond them, throughout a teacher's career, is more focused continuing professional development or in-service education. New and updated content knowledge, curricula, and textbooks have to be mastered; existing skills have to be refined and new ones acquired in new teaching contexts and derived from new research learned; and new challenges facing teachers need to be met. These challenges, among others, include

- New roles for teachers in the context of decentralization and newly empowered school committees;
- More diversified programs requiring more specialized skills;
- New kinds of learners with more diverse backgrounds and identities, different values and different ways of thinking and acting, and greater independence and open-mindedness; and
- New information and communication technologies (which students often master more quickly than their teachers) (Shaeffer, forthcoming).

The professional development needed to help teachers both improve what they currently do and meet the new demands thrust upon them can be carried out in several ways. Unfortunately, the most typical development programs are one-off seminars and in-service short courses that are often conducted, as in Indonesia, in cascade fashion (whereby each trainee in turn trains others) and the message received at the bottom of the cascade bears little resemblance to that delivered at the top. What is needed instead, and what teachers reportedly want, is both (a) training linked to some kind of longer-term qualification process; and (b) more ongoing, school-based, research-focused training, practice, and feedback with adequate time, follow-up support, and involvement in learning activities that are similar to those they will use with their students (Schleicher 2011, 21).

Much of this development, of course, is best done through effective teacher collaboration. "Teachers report relatively infrequent collaboration with colleagues within the school, beyond a mere exchange of information and ideas; direct professional collaboration to enhance student learning is rarer" (Schleicher 2011, 23). Much of this collaboration can be promoted in schools through group- and inquiry-based collaboration, but in many systems with relatively small schools (as in Indonesia), school clusters—groups of schools in close geographical proximity—can serve a useful function by promoting collaboration in what can become genuine learning communities. Teachers of the same grade or subject can meet regularly to share lesson plans and teaching practices, explore the use of new materials and media, and work through issues such as teaching children with special needs or in the mother tongue.

A further mechanism of professional development is distance learning. This is especially useful for teachers in distant or difficult contexts in which they cannot get to institution-based in-service programs and perhaps not even to cluster meetings. Such distance learning ranges from radio- and television-based programming directed at the individual school and teacher to immense open universities providing a range of distance-learning services to teachers throughout the nation.

Teacher Appraisal and Career Development

A final component of continuing professional development relates to the appraisal of teachers' performance, ideally linked to progression, promotion, and diversification in their careers. Such appraisal usually considers three aspects of professional competence (Stevenson 2009a):

- *Professional knowledge and understanding*—of their students, school, and community; of the curriculum they are meant to deliver; and of the education system (and its policies and practices) of which they are a part.
- *Professional skills and abilities*—to plan and deliver coherent programs, in well-managed classrooms, appropriate to their pupils' needs and abilities; to use relevant media, teaching strategies, and resources; to work cooperatively with their colleagues, parents, and the community; to implement appropriate and fair assessment and reporting of student progress; and to systematically reflect on and improve one's performance.
- *Professional values and personal commitment*—to promoting social justice and inclusion, to continuing professional learning and development, and to valuing and respecting the partners with whom they work.

Just as important as the competencies to be gained is the nature of the appraisal process itself. Whoever is involved in the appraisal (for example, the principal or supervisor) must work with the teacher at the beginning of the process to identify individual goals and performance indicators; to review progress midyear and later at an annual performance review; and to make decisions regarding actions such as confirmation (or not) of probationary teachers and the need for further development and training in areas of weakness or areas for future growth.

Formal appraisal can also support a system's merit-based progression (and promotion) process. Goal setting, appropriate professional in-service training, and advanced mentoring can improve teacher quality and motivation and also prepare teachers for accelerated professional progression, promotion, and future educational leadership.

One final point concerning teacher management and student achievement: a rapidly expanding body of research evaluates the effects of bonus payment schemes on teachers' work. Bonus payment schemes, or pay-for-performance schemes, add to salaries in ways that are conditional on performance. Performance can be measured based on inputs (such as absenteeism levels) or outputs (such as student learning gains). It has been shown that pay-for-performance schemes can work in developing-country settings. (See Bruns, Filmer, and Patrinos 2011 for a summary, or Muralidharan and Sundararaman 2011 for one of the most comprehensive studies on this topic to date.)

For example, individual teacher incentives work—and work better than group incentives—which, in turn, work better than unconditional block grants to schools (Muralidharan and Sundararaman 2011). However, even though some literature shows that bonus payment schemes can work, there are perhaps insurmountable difficulties associated with implementing such schemes in real-world, whole-system contexts. Pfeffer and Sutton (2006, 22–23) sum up the debate as follows: "It turns out that merit pay for teachers is an idea that is almost 100 years old and has been the subject of much research … that evidence shows that merit pay plans seldom last longer than five years and that merit pay consistently fails to improve students' performance."

Another view is as follows: "In an influential article, Murnane and Cohen (1986) suggest that merit pay and education do not mix because the complex work that teachers do is difficult to evaluate. Without clear measures and criteria for judging success, decisions about rewarding performance are, at best, subjective and, at worst, unworkable. They also suggest that merit pay is problematic because it raises the potential for dysfunctional (or, as they call it, opportunistic) behavior: that is, teachers may end up focusing only on tasks that are rewarded by a merit pay plan at the expense of additional goals or tasks valued by the public (e.g., promoting citizenship, or reducing drug use or violence). Furthermore, at its worst, merit pay may have a demoralizing and counterproductive effect on the work place, corroding teacher collegiality by introducing competition. In sum, this is the view that there is something about the nature of teaching and schooling that makes the effective use of merit pay in public education unlikely" (Goldhaber *et al.* 2008).

Teacher Reform around the World

The literature on comprehensive teacher reform around the world, covering all aspects and stages of teacher management and development, is limited. The literature that does exist, like the reforms themselves, is largely piecemeal in nature—some on incentives, some on preservice education, some on principal and supervisor training—which is why the reform in Indonesia and the analysis of it offered by this book are so potentially useful. The following are some of the issues addressed and lessons learned from this literature:

- *Teacher status:* "Successful countries have shown how a teaching profession that assumes a high level of responsibility and is well rewarded can attract some of the best graduates into a teaching career. Dramatically increasing the quality and prestige of a nation's teaching corps is far from easy and cannot be done overnight. However, solutions include measures at recruitment stage, but more importantly involve transforming the teaching profession from within …. Above all, professional development needs to be integrated into both an individual teacher's career and school and system changes. At the career level, in-service education, appraisal and reward need to be closely aligned. At the same time, learning that improves individual competencies and collaboration among teachers to produce better instruction in the classroom must go hand-in-hand" (Schleicher 2011).

- *Recruitment:* "The issue of teacher demand and supply is both complex and multi-dimensional, as it reflects several challenges: how to expand the pool of qualified teachers, how to address shortages in specific subjects, how to recruit teachers to the places where they are most needed, how to distribute teachers in equitable and efficient ways, and how to retain qualified teachers over time. Policy responses are needed at two levels. The first concerns the nature of the teaching profession itself and teachers' work environment. Such policies seek to improve the profession's general status and competitive position in the job market and are the focus of this paper. The second involves more targeted responses and incentives for particular types of teacher shortage, which recognizes that that there is not a single labor market for teachers, but a set of them, distinguished by school type and characteristics, such as subject specialization. Competitive compensation and other incentives, career prospects and diversity, and giving teachers responsibility as professionals are important parts of strategies to attract the most talented teachers to the most challenging classrooms" (Schleicher 2011).

- *Teacher education:* "What teacher preparation programs are needed to prepare graduates who are ready to teach well in a 21st-century classroom? One of the key challenges for the teaching profession is to strengthen the 'technical core' of its professional practices, which requires the development of educational ecosystems that support the creation, accumulation and diffusion of this professional knowledge. Such ecosystems need to draw on four sources: innovation and knowledge inspired by science (research and evaluation); innovation inspired by firms (entrepreneurial development of new products and services); innovation and knowledge inspired by practitioners (teachers, school heads); and innovation inspired by users (students, parents, communities)" (Schleicher 2011).

- *School autonomy:* "School leaders can make a difference in school and student performance if they are granted the autonomy to make important decisions. To do this effectively, they need to be able to adapt teaching programs to local needs, promote teamwork among teachers, and engage in teacher monitoring, evaluation and professional development. They need discretion in setting strategic direction and must be able to develop school plans and goals and monitor progress, using data to improve practice. They also need to be able to influence teacher recruitment to improve the match between candidates and their school's needs. Last but not least, leadership preparation and training are central, and building networks of schools to stimulate and spread innovation and to develop diverse curricula, extended services and professional support can bring substantial benefits" (Schleicher 2011).

- *School leadership:* "School leadership and particular school personnel practices may be a driving force in effective schooling. Not only are school leaders responsible for personnel practices, but recent prior work has highlighted the importance of personnel practices and other organizational management practices for distinguishing (if not causing) effective schools (Grissom and Loeb 2009; Horng, Klasik, and Loeb 2010). The results are also not surprising. Teachers strongly affect students' educational opportunities. Higher performing schools seem better able to build a staff of strong teachers through differential retention of good teachers, through recruitment and hiring, and through providing supports for teacher improvement … [and] more effective schools are doing all three. In addition, these schools appear to use their teaching resources more efficiently, not assigning new teachers to lower performing students" (Loeb, Kalogrides, and Beteille 2011).

- *Teacher appraisal:* "Teacher appraisal and feedback has a positive impact on teachers … both to teachers personally and to the development of their teaching. Positive impacts on job satisfaction and, to a lesser extent, job security are important, given that the introduction of systems of teacher appraisal can be met with criticism and potential negative reactions, especially where it is linked to accountability. Moreover … such systems contribute to school improvement. Numerous initiatives developed by policy makers aiming to lift school improvement have had teacher development at the core …. The school evaluative framework is often policy malleable so that not only can the strength of the evaluative framework be altered but also its focus. The criteria by which schools are evaluated and teachers are appraised and receive feedback should be aligned with the objectives of the system of school education. These objectives may relate to aspects of student performance, teacher development, specific teaching practices, the maintenance of specific standards and procedures, and a variety of aspects of the work of teachers and school principals. Aligning criteria for school evaluation with those for teacher appraisal and feedback would emphasize the importance of policy objectives at the school level and could give teachers and school principals an incentive to meet such objectives" (OECD 2009).

- *Focus on learning:* In its groundbreaking study of learning in the best school systems in East Asia (Hong Kong SAR, China; Republic of Korea; Shanghai; and Singapore), the Grattan Institute shows that success in high-performing systems is not always the result of spending more money. These four systems all focus on "things that are known to matter in the classroom, including a relentless, practical focus on learning, and the creation of a strong culture of teacher education, research, collaboration, mentoring, feedback and sustained professional development. These are precisely the reforms that Australia and other Western countries are trying to embed" (Jensen 2012).

Finally, some of the most sensitive analysis of comprehensive (as opposed to piecemeal) educational reform derives from the work of Michael Fullan. In essence, he argues that "*all* really does mean *all*. You can't solve the problem of whole-system reform through piecemeal efforts that try to get parts of the system improving in order to show the way. System reform does not, cannot work that way" (Fullan 2010, 5). On the one hand, this refers to *whole-school reform*—not one teacher being trained (or certified) at a time, which means pupils move from good to bad teachers and back again, but all teachers, with the school leadership, the parent-teacher association, and the community as a whole involved in the process. This focus on both the individual teacher and the collective school community makes possible change that is essential in the school culture. "The obvious point is that the culture of the school, itself a collective capacity by definition, is more important, in fact essential for full success .... Thus, individual capacity thrives if it is integrated with strategies and experiences that foster collective capacity. There is no other way. The top-performing countries have quality teachers, but they have them in numbers—that is, the entire profession or virtually all teachers, not just a percentage of selectively rewarded ones" (Fullan 2010, 87).

But, significantly, Fullan is also talking about *whole-system reform*, which "involves *all* schools in the system getting better, including reducing the gap between high and low performers. Whole-system reform produces higher levels of education performance on important cognitive and social learning goals, and it does so while reducing the gap toward a more equal public education system" (Fullan 2010, 18).

Ultimately, therefore, change is systemic. In most contexts, "political pressures combine with the segmented, uncoordinated nature of educational organizations to produce ... a steady stream of episodic innovations—cooperative learning, effective schools research, classroom management, assessment schemes, career ladders, peer coaching, etc., etc.—come and go. Not only do they fail to leave much of a trace, but they also leave teachers and the public with a growing cynicism that innovation is marginal and politically motivated ... [Rather] 1) reform must focus on the development and interrelationships of all the main components of the system simultaneously—curriculum, teaching and teacher development, community, student support systems, and so on, and 2) reform must focus not just on structure, policy, and regulations but on deeper issues of the *culture* of the system" (Fullan and Miles 1992, 745–52).

Notes

1. The World Declaration on Education for All (EFA) was adopted in 1990 at a world conference in Jomtien, Thailand. In 2000, the international community met again at the World Education Forum in Dakar, Senegal, and set further goals for achievement by 2015. The United Nations Educational, Scientific, and Cultural Organization (UNESCO) has the overall coordination and leadership role in the EFA effort.

2. Much of this analysis derives from Helen Craig (personal communication, April 18, 2012).

References

Barber, M., and M. Mourshed. 2007. *How the World's Best Performing School Systems Come Out on Top*. Study report, McKinsey & Company, New York.

Bereiter, C., and M. Scardamalia. 2003. "Learning to Work Creatively with Knowledge." In *Powerful Learning Environments: Unravelling Basic Components and Dimensions*, edited by E. D. Corte, L. Verschaffel, N. Entwhistle, and J. V. Merrienboer, 55–68. Oxford, U.K.: Elsevier Science.

Borko, H. 2004. "Professional Development and Teacher Learning: Mapping the Terrain." *Educational Researcher* 33 (8): 3–15.

Bruns, B., D. Filmer, and H. A. Patrinos. 2011. *Making Schools Work: New Evidence on Accountability Reforms*. Human Development Perspectives Series. Washington, DC: World Bank.

Craig, H. J., R. J. Kraft, and J. Du Plessis. 1998. *Teacher Development: Making an Impact*. Washington, DC: U.S. Agency for International Development and World Bank.

Darling-Hammond, L. 2000. "Teacher Quality and Student Achievement: A Review of State Policy Evidence." *Education Policy Analysis Archives* 8 (1).

Darling-Hammond, L., and B. Berry. 2006. "Highly Qualified Teachers for All." *Educational Leadership* 64 (3): 14–20.

Fullan, M. 2010. *All Systems Go: The Change Imperative for Whole System Reform*. Thousand Oaks, CA: Corwin.

Fullan, M., and M. Miles. 1992. "Getting Reform Right: What Works and What Doesn't." *Phi Delta Kappan* 73 (10): 745–52.

Goldhaber, D., M. DeArmond, D. Player, and H. Choi. 2008. "Why Do So Few Public School Districts Use Merit Pay?" *Journal of Educational Finance* 33 (3): 262–89.

Greeno, J. G., A. M. Collins, and L. B. Resnick. 1996. "Cognition and Learning." In *Handbook of Educational Psychology*, edited by D. Berliner and R. Calfee, 15–41. New York: Macmillan.

Grissom, Jason A., and Susanna Loeb. 2009. "Triangulating Principal Effectiveness: How Perspectives of Parents, Teachers, and Assistant Principals Identify the Central Importance of Managerial Skills." CALDER Working Paper 35. The Urban Institute, Washington, DC.

Horng, Eileen Lai, Daniel Klasik, and Susanna Loeb. 2009. "Principal Time Use and School Effectiveness." CALDER Working Paper 34. The Urban Institute, Washington, DC.

Jensen, B. 2012. *Catching Up: Learning from the Best School Systems in East Asia*. Study report, Grattan Institute, Melbourne, Australia.

Kane, T., J. Rockoff, and D. Staiger. 2008. "What Does Certification Tell Us about Teacher Effectiveness? Evidence from New York City." *Economics of Education Review* 27 (6): 615–31.

Leigh, A. 2007. "Estimating Teacher Effectiveness from Two-Year Changes in Students' Test Scores." Unpublished paper, Australian National University, Canberra.

Loeb, S., D. Kalogrides, and T. Beteille. 2011. "Effective Schools: Teacher Hiring, Assignment, Development, and Retention." Working Paper 17177, National Bureau of Economic Research, Cambridge, MA. http://ssrn.com/abstract=1879039.

Muijs, D., and D. Reynolds. 2002. "Teacher-Level Effects in School Effectiveness Research: First Findings of a Longitudinal Study." Paper presented at the International Congress for School Effectiveness and Improvement (ICSEI) 2002, Toronto.

Muralidharan, K., and V. Sundararaman. 2011. "Teacher Performance Pay: Experimental Evidence from India." *The Journal of Political Economy* 119 (1): 39–77.

Murnane, R. J., and D. K. Cohen. 1986. "Merit Pay and the Evaluation Problem: Why Most Merit Pay Plans Fail and Few Survive." *Harvard Educational Review* 56 (1): 1–17.

OECD (Organisation for Economic Co-operation and Development). 2005. *Teachers Matter: Attracting, Developing and Retaining Effective Teachers.* Paris: OECD.

———. 2009. *Creating Effective Teaching and Learning Environments: First Results from TALIS [Teaching and Learning International Survey].* Paris: OECD.

O'Neill, G. P. 1988. "Teaching Effectiveness: A Review of the Research." *Canadian Journal of Education* 13 (1): 162–85.

Pfeffer, J., and R. Sutton. 2006. *Hard Facts, Dangerous Half-Truths, and Total Nonsense.* Boston, MA: Harvard Business School Press.

Raudenbush, S. W. 2004. "Schooling, Statistics, and Poverty: Can We Measure School Improvement?" Paper presented at the William H. Angoff Memorial Lecture Series, Educational Testing Service, Policy Evaluation and Research Center, Princeton, NJ, April 1.

Rice, J. K. 2003. *Teacher Quality: Understanding the Effectiveness of Teacher Attributes.* Washington, DC: Economic Policy Institute.

Rowan, B., R. Correnti, and R. J. Miller. 2002. "What Large-Scale Survey Research Tells Us about Teacher Effects on Student Achievement: Insights from the Prospects Study of Elementary Schools." *Teachers College Record* 104 (8): 1525–67.

Sanders, W. L., and J. C. Rivers. 1996. *Cumulative and Residual Effects of Teachers on Future Student Academic Achievement.* Research project report, University of Tennessee Value-Added Research and Assessment Center, Knoxville, TN.

Scheerens, J. 1992. *Effective Schooling: Research, Theory and Practice.* London: Cassell.

Schleicher, A. 2011. *Building a High-Quality Teaching Profession: Lessons from Around the World.* Paris: Organisation for Economic Co-operation and Development.

Seidel, T., and R. J. Shavelson. 2007. "Teaching Effectiveness Research in the Past Decade: The Role of Theory and Research Design in Disentangling Meta-Analysis Research." *Review of Educational Research* 77 (4): 454–99.

Shaeffer, S. Forthcoming. *The Quality of Basic Education: Issues and Challenges for Asia.* Manila: Asian Development Bank; National University of Singapore.

Snow, R. E., and D. F. Lohman. 1984. "Toward a Theory of Cognitive Aptitude for Learning from Instruction." *Journal of Educational Psychology* 76 (3): 347–76.

Stevenson, R. 2009a. "Approaches to the Management of Underperforming Teachers in Indonesia." Unpublished manuscript, Human Development Unit, World Bank, Jakarta.

———. 2009b. "Induction of Beginning Teachers." Unpublished manuscript, Human Development Unit, World Bank, Jakarta.

———. 2009c. "Some International Perspectives and Ideas on Pre-service Teacher Education." Background paper, World Bank, Washington, DC.

UNESCO (United Nations Educational, Scientific, and Cultural Organization). 2000. "The Dakar Framework for Action, Education for All: Meeting Our Collective Commitments." Framework document adopted by the World Education Forum, UNESCO, Paris, April 26–28.

Wayne, A. M., and P. Youngs. 2003. "Teacher Characteristics and Student Achievement Gains: A Review." *Review of Educational Research* 73 (1): 89–122.

World Bank. 2008. *The Political Economy of Policy Reform: Issues and Implications for Policy Dialogue and Development Operations.* World Bank and Oxford Policy Management study, Report 44288-GLB, Social Development Department, Washington, DC.

CHAPTER 3

The Comprehensive Reform of Institutions, Mechanisms, Strategies, and Processes

Countries that have succeeded in making teaching an attractive profession have often done so not just through pay, but by raising the status of teaching, offering real career prospects, and giving teachers responsibility as professionals and leaders of reform. This requires teacher education that helps teachers to become innovators and researchers in education, not just deliverers of the curriculum.

—OECD (2011), *Building a High-Quality Teaching Profession: Lessons from Around the World* (2011)

The Laws and Regulations Supporting Teacher Reform

Past attempts in Indonesia to deal with issues of teacher quality have had limited impact partly because they have been conceived and implemented in a piecemeal fashion. Salary increases, higher training requirements, professional development courses, promotion opportunities, and other strategies, in themselves, have had only limited impact. Only the Teacher Law of 2005, with its emphasis on the certification of all teachers, has attempted to comprehensively address the issue of teacher quality improvement by linking a range of strategies to the powerful incentive of a significant increase in income. This reform has resulted in a period of fundamental change, with the whole teaching service being subject to new rules and regulations governing the conditions of teachers, including the following:

- Performance appraisal being linked to career progression
- Major educational institutions being subject to new standards and required to deliver new services such as four-year degrees and professional training courses
- Teachers being required to do continuing professional development
- Districts and schools being required to enforce new workload rules

The period since the enactment of the Teacher Law has therefore been one of constant pressure to change the education system to meet the changing requirements of a modern and dynamic Indonesian state. The law has been the springboard for this extensive change.

Most impressive (given the massive size and complexity of the Indonesian education system) has been the financial capacity and sustained energy required to transform a poorly paid and ineffectively managed teaching service. This transformation has required an almost fearless determination to develop and implement procedures to deal with the system's large numbers of districts, schools, and teachers. Over it all, certification has been adopted as a requirement for both in-service and preservice teachers and designed to act as a benchmark for all teachers, both government and nongovernment. It is intended to provide the community with a guarantee of the quality and professionalism of all teachers, everywhere—their standard of training, their skills and capacity, and their ability to shape the next generation in a way that is agreeable and satisfying to the wider community.

The remarkable comprehensiveness of the reform in Indonesia regarding its systematic attempt to cover all institutions, mechanisms, strategies, and processes related to teachers from recruitment to retirement is evident in not only the 2005 Teacher Law but also in a series of national and ministerial regulations (sometimes as annual updates) that outline, often in considerable detail, the definitions and procedures to be followed in the implementation of the law. These are summarized in table 3.1 and further described in the pages that follow.

Setting Standards

An early essential step in the complex process of teacher reform was the establishment of the National Education Standards Board in May 2004 to provide a sound basis for the reform process. The board's work consists of establishing, monitoring, and evaluating standards in eight areas: graduate competencies, subject content, education processes, teaching personnel and training, infrastructure and facilities, management, education funding, and educational assessment. Its standards and indicators for graduate teachers are based on the four core competencies (professional, pedagogical, personal, and social) mandated in the Teacher Law. They have been the basis for developing the competencies that now underpin the instruments used in the certification of teachers; the redesigned university training courses; university accreditation requirements; competency tests; statements of duties for supervisors, principals, and teachers; performance appraisal instruments; and other key elements of the reform.

The standards, as defined by Regulation 19/2009, create a unifying point for the reforms and ensure that the new training programs are designed to better meet international best practice. These standards were developed through the collection of data on national and international best practice,

Table 3.1 Teacher Reform Laws and Regulations in Indonesia, 2003–14

Key aspects of reform	Government regulation	Regulations for implementing the law	Status of implementation
Law on the National Education System (2003)			
Principles of implementation of education, national education standards, education legal entities, boards of education and school committees, teachers and educators as professionals, school accreditation, education funding at 20 percent of national and regional budgets, and education conducted in Indonesia by overseas institutions.	Government Regulation on the National Education Standards (2005) Establishment of the National Education Standards Board. The eight national standards of education are graduate competencies, subject content, education processes, teaching personnel and training, infrastructure and facilities, management, education funding, and educational assessment. Government Regulation on the Management and Implementation of Education (2010) Educational management by government at all levels, the management of community-based schools, types of education, international cooperation, the roles and responsibilities of teachers and education staff, the establishment of education institutions, and community involvement in education.	Ministerial Regulation on Standards for School Supervisors (2005) Ministerial Regulation on Standards for School Principals (2007) Ministerial Regulation on Standards for Academic Qualifications and Competencies of Teachers (2007) Ministerial Regulation on Standards for School Administration Staff (2008) Ministerial Regulation on Standards for School Librarians (2008) Ministerial Regulation on Standards for Academic Qualifications and Competencies of Counsellors (2008) Ministerial Regulation on Minimum Service Standards for Basic Education in Districts/Cities (2010)	The ministerial regulations on the national education standards are used for educational planning and implementation. Because many schools have not reached the national standards, minimum service standards have been set as intermediate targets toward the national standards. The minimum service standards are now being used to raise the quality of schools. District education budgets are to be used to reach the minimum service standards.

table continues next page

61

Table 3.1 Teacher Reform Laws and Regulations in Indonesia, 2003–14 *(continued)*

Key aspects of reform	Government regulation	Regulations for implementing the law	Status of implementation
		School Operational Assistance program (Bantuan Operasional Sekolah, or BOS)	
	Amendment to Government Regulation Number 17/2010 on the Management and Implementation of Education (2010) Changes and additions to existing chapters and paragraphs of the Government Regulation.	Decree of the Minister of Home Affairs on Guidelines for the Management of the School Operational Assistance (2011) Ministerial Regulation on Technical Guidelines for the School Operational Assistance and its Financial Report for 2012 Fiscal Year (2011) Ministerial Decree on the Quality Assurance System for Education (2009)	Guidelines for the financing, implementation, and administration of the School Operational Assistance are issued annually. The technical guidelines are also annually issued. The quality assurance system is a subsystem of the national education system and is used to improve the quality of all aspects in education.
		Teacher competencies and certification	
Law on Teachers and Lecturers (2005)[a] Principles of professionalism; protection of teachers through the regulation of all components of teacher reform, such as teacher qualification, competencies, and certification; rights and responsibilities; appointment, placement, transfer, and release; development; rewards; leave; and professional organizations.	Government Regulation on Teachers (2008) Regulations on teacher competencies and certification, professional allowances, functional allowances, special allowances, allowances for non-civil-service teachers, rewards, promotion, the chance to participate in the development of education policy, teacher workload, appointment, placement, transfer, and sanctions.	Ministerial Decree on the Establishment of a Consortium for Teacher Certification (2007) Ministerial Regulation on the Certification of In-Service Teachers through Education Upgrading (2007) Joint Circular on the Certification of Religious Education Teachers and Madrasah Teachers (Ministry of Religious Affairs [MORA] and Ministry of National Education) (2007) Ministerial Regulation on the Certification of In-Service Teachers (2007) Ministerial Regulation on the Teachers' Competency Test (2012)	This was first issued in 2007 and reissued in 2009 and 2011. Universities were appointed to conduct this educational program. Teachers can attend a two-semester program. Religious education teachers in schools are to be certified through MORA. This was first issued in 2007 and updated annually. The regulation issued in 2012 mentioned that teachers had to pass an initial competency test before participating in the certification process. Certified teachers have to be tested on their competencies for mapping and upgrading purposes.

table continues next page

Table 3.1 Teacher Reform Laws and Regulations in Indonesia, 2003–14 (continued)

Key aspects of reform	Government regulation	Regulations for implementing the law	Status of implementation
		Teachers' functional positions	
		Ministerial Regulation of the State Minister of Administrative and Bureaucratic Reform on Teacher Functional Positions and Credit Points (2009)	Career progression will be managed in regard to teachers' functional positions, continuing professional development, criteria and components to be evaluated, credit points, appointment, and release.
		Joint Regulation of the Minister of National Education and the Head of the Government Employment Agency on Implementation Guidelines for Teacher Functional Positions and Credit Points (2010)	Guidelines for teacher progression came into force on January 1, 2013.
		Ministerial Regulation on Technical Guidelines for the Implementation of Functional Positions and Credit Points (2010)	Assessment of teacher performance according to the technical guidelines in this Ministerial Regulation became effective on January 1, 2013.
		Ministerial Regulation of the Minister of Administrative and Bureaucratic Reform on School Supervisor Functional Positions and Credit Points (2010)	A career progression for school supervisors and related criteria are to be used for the recruitment of new school supervisors and the upgrading of existing ones.
		Joint Regulation of the Minister of National Education and the Head of the Government Employment Agency on the Implementation Guidelines for School Supervisor Functional Positions and Credit Points (2011)	Requirements to become school supervisors became effective on January 1, 2013. Requirements to become a member of the evaluation team will be effective on January 1, 2014.
		Ministerial Regulation on the Adjustment of Teacher Functional Positions (2010)	The adjustment and adaptation of previous teacher positions to new teacher functional positions was to be finished by December 2012.

table continues next page

Table 3.1 Teacher Reform Laws and Regulations in Indonesia, 2003–14 *(continued)*

Key aspects of reform	Government regulation	Regulations for implementing the law	Status of implementation
		Induction of new teachers	
		Ministerial Regulation on an Induction Program for New Teachers (2010)	Guidelines have been developed for school principals, school supervisors, and senior teachers to conduct an induction program for new teachers. When new teachers pass the induction program, they can become permanent, fully paid government officials and are eligible for certification.
		Teachers' professional development	
		Ministerial Regulation on the Implementation of the Requirement of a Four-Year Degree in Education for In-Service Teachers (2008)	Recognition of prior learning (RPL) can be applied for existing teachers to upgrade themselves to a four-year degree in education up to a maximum of 65 percent of the total credit semesters that are needed for the degree. Several universities and study programs have been appointed to implement the RPL for in-service teachers.
		Ministerial Regulation on the Teacher's Competency Test (2012)	This test was conducted online and manually in August 2012. The results will be used as a basis for the teacher's individual professional development.
		Ministerial Regulation on the Assignment of Teachers as School/Madrasah Principals (2010)	Criteria for teachers to become school or madrasah principals are to be used for the selection process. The selected teachers have to undergo training, and when they pass the evaluation, they will get a certificate that will be listed in a database.

table continues next page

Table 3.1 Teacher Reform Laws and Regulations in Indonesia, 2003–14 *(continued)*

Key aspects of reform	Government regulation	Regulations for implementing the law	Status of implementation
		Teacher training and upgrading	
		Ministerial Decree on the Appointment of Universities to Deliver a Four-Year Degree for In-Service Teacher Qualification Upgrading (2007)	This decree selected universities eligible to conduct four-year programs to qualify existing teachers for certification.
		Ministerial Decree on the Appointment of Universities to Deliver a Pre-Service Four-Year Degree in Teaching for Elementary School Teachers (2009)	This regulation selected universities to conduct a four-year degree program for elementary school teachers. Universities will be evaluated each year.
		Ministerial Regulation on the Pre-Service Teacher Professional Education Program (2009)	This regulated the Teacher Professional Education program for those who want to become teachers.
		Ministerial Decree on Appointment of Alpha Universities to Deliver In-Service Education for Teachers in 2010	This regulation selects universities to conduct in-service education for teachers in 2010 and determines a quota for each educational program. Universities will be evaluated every three years.
		Efficiency of teachers	
		Joint Decree of the Minister of Education and Culture, the Minister of Administrative and Bureaucratic Reform, the Minister of Home Affairs, the Minister of Finance, and the Minister of Religious Affairs on the Structuring and Distribution of Civil Service Teachers (2011)	Effective January 2, 2012, districts and cities have the responsibility to map teacher distribution to know whether there is a surplus or shortage of teachers in each school and then take steps to redistribute teachers as needed.

Note: RPL = Recognition of prior learning.
a. Also commonly referred to as the Teacher Law of 2005.

the inductive gathering of academic and practitioner opinion, and the testing of draft material in wider public forums to ensure that the standards finally adopted reflected the highest levels of practice. Once finalized, the developed standards were mandated in a series of regulations and decrees (such as those listed in table 3.1) and provide a blueprint for quality. Reference to the incorporation of these standards in various instruments and processes used in the reform attests to the work of this board and the desire to align all educational activity with the values and standards that represent the nation's expectations of the education sector. However, as described in chapter 1, although the intention was to ensure consistent and high standards as implied in the Teacher Law, the use of suitable instruments for measuring teacher competencies, and therefore ensuring quality, was met with opposition from teacher associations; therefore, their use was significantly compromised during implementation.

Recruitment

Indonesia has not yet formally adopted all of the strategies available to attract more and better candidates to the teaching profession, including active recruitment campaigns and rigorous selection processes (from, say, the top 20 percent of a graduating secondary school class). But the country has adopted, or is experimenting with, several other strategies:

- Financial incentives such as fee waivers, loans, and scholarships
- More flexible approaches to teacher education such as part-time study and distance education
- A clearly defined career path
- The prospect (with the Teacher Law) of being considered a "professional"

As has been seen, the latter has been achieved by the doubling of teachers' income through the provision of a professional allowance equal to a teacher's base salary for all teachers meeting the four-year degree qualification followed by official certification. This allowance has definitely made teaching an attractive profession in Indonesia. Details of the impact of this allowance on recruitment are presented in chapter 4.

Training Pathways Available to Indonesian Teachers

Once the standards are set and new candidates attracted to the profession, Indonesia has a plethora of agencies involved in both preservice education and in-service teacher education or continuing professional development— ranging from both traditional and open teacher education institutions to a variety of in-service actors and to what is meant to be ongoing support through district education offices (further described in box 3.1). Before exploring in detail how these agencies have changed as a result of the Teacher Law, an overview of their scope and function is presented in table 3.2.

Table 3.2 Agencies Involved in the Preservice Education and Continuing Professional Development of Teachers in Indonesia

Teacher education universities and institutions	Regular universities with a faculty for training teachers	The Open University
a. Preservice training facilities		
There are 12 public teacher education institutions and approximately 120 private ones. They provide study programs in the various teaching areas: primary teaching, secondary subject areas, early childhood, special education, and other areas.	There are approximately 270 faculties for the training of teachers within regular universities, of which 19 are public and the balance private. These faculties provide subject knowledge in the relevant teaching areas as well as practical classroom training for teachers.	The Open University, established in 1984, is the traditional supplier of distance learning courses in Indonesia. It has a number of faculties, but the largest number of students enrolled are in-service teachers seeking to upgrade their qualifications.
These universities train the great bulk of preservice teachers. They have their origin in the early teachers colleges, which have subsequently been upgraded to university status on the condition they incorporate faculties for additional subjects and careers. In general, however, their main focus remains on teacher education. Since the Teacher Law, 23 universities have cooperated to introduce distance education programs, using a jointly prepared set of modules—representing the first competition with the Open University's offerings.	These operate similarly to the teacher education universities, except their focus is more clearly academic and draws on the full academic status of the university. These universities offer greater academic choice and the opportunity to more easily transfer between faculties in response to a change in career destination.	In 2009, over 485,000 of its 600,000 students were in-service teachers upgrading to four-year degree status. In-service teachers can receive RPL of up to 28 credits toward a complete degree of 145 credit points. The Open University sends learning materials to many teachers in printed form. However, it also provides learning materials through its website. The program has local workshops coordinated through its 36 regional centers throughout Indonesia.

Institute for Educational Quality and Assurance	Centers for the development and empowerment of teachers and education personnel	Teacher working groups
b. Continuing professional development facilities		
There are 33 quality assurance agencies—one in each province. They are closely linked with the Ministry of Education and Culture rather than the provincial authorities. Although in the past, these agencies have been heavily involved in teacher education at the local district level, in recent years their function has become largely related to the evaluation of programs and the quality assurance of schools.	There are 12 national subject training centers responsible for providing in-service training to teachers in specialized subjects, particularly at the secondary level. However, management courses and school leadership courses are also provided. Some adopt an entrepreneurial approach and run some fee-based courses for outside groups.	Teacher working groups are organized by a cluster of schools in close proximity. They operate at the local level to provide a program of training activities for teachers and have been fostered in Indonesia for over 20 years. They are operated by a committee that identifies agreed-upon priorities for funding and a program of activities in teaching and learning. The groups may receive grant funds from the district or provincial level.

table continues next page

Table 3.2 Agencies Involved in the Preservice Education and Continuing Professional Development of Teachers in Indonesia *(continued)*

Institute for Educational Quality and Assurance	Centres for the development and empowerment of teachers and education personnel	Teacher working groups
In spite of their heavy programs of school visits to undertake quality assurance, these institutions have a residual role in teacher training—particularly in management and consultancy roles—and are also facilitators for train-the-trainer programs.	One subject training center in Jogjakarta, for example, specializes in mathematics and offers training courses in subject content and pedagogy. This includes developing teaching resources and supplying materials to teacher working groups throughout Indonesia.	Separate working groups exist for teachers, principals, and school supervisors. Not all schools and teachers have access to such a working group. However, the number of active working groups has increased in recent years to around 35,000. They represent a relatively effective mechanism for channeling training to local schools.

Note: Although the agencies in this table have been categorized as mainly "preservice training" or "continuing professional development" facilities, some agencies offer elements of both. Ideally, the preservice institutes will also develop increasingly greater capacity for in-service training. RPL = Recognition of prior learning.

Box 3.1 District Education Authorities

The district office is responsible for the schools and teachers under its management, ranging from 14 primary schools (in Anambas Island) to 1,986 in Garut and from 10 junior secondary schools in Asmat to 809 in Malang. Districts have an initiating and coordinating role in the training of teachers. In this regard, for example, they facilitate the establishment of local teacher working groups, identify key teachers from schools to receive training to act as consultants and trainers in the rollout of national training programs, and conduct their own training programs using these trainers.

District officers are responsible for the administration and implementation of the certification program within the district, and technical teams have been organized at the local level to plan, monitor, and report the progress of implementation to Ministry of Education and Culture agencies. The districts are also involved with socialization of the certification process to principals and teachers. In addition, district authorities collaborate with local universities regarding teacher education matters, provide scholarships for teacher upgrading, and identify areas of teacher shortage. The effectiveness of training programs usually depends heavily on the enthusiasm with which district authorities identify school and teacher needs and then support and follow up on training activities. The response of districts to training initiatives varies widely.

Preservice Teacher Education

The significant increase in the number and quality of entrants to teacher education institutions as a result of the enactment of the Teacher Law has given these institutions both new obligations and new challenges. In other words, new ways to strengthen the efficiency and effectiveness of preservice teacher education institutions in the context of implementing the Teacher Law have become essential. These approaches include effective delivery of a new four-year degree educational program for all elementary teachers (replacing the previous two-year diploma) as well as revision and upgrading of existing primary and secondary training courses to incorporate the newly mandated competencies and the adoption of new teaching methodologies.

As a consequence, universities have had to change many of their practices. New competency-based curricula and methodologies are being introduced to improve the knowledge and skills of new teachers. Changed management structures and new resources have been identified to cater to the larger numbers of candidates staying longer in training. In short, a number of new challenges facing preservice teacher education institutions have arisen:

- The need for the better selection and retention of high-caliber candidates for teacher education
- The need for more coordinated planning to ensure that the number of teacher education graduates more closely meets the demand from schools and district authorities
- The need to improve the preparation of candidates to become more effective teachers
- The need to strengthen preservice institutions to become "after-sales" service centers to support improved classroom effectiveness of recently graduated students

These challenges have created an extensive agenda for the reform of preservice teacher education. In essence, university-level preservice programs now need to prepare teachers for the latest curriculum at the national, provincial, or district levels and see this preparation as part of a lifetime of continuing professional development. Subject and pedagogy courses need to be closely linked to school curriculum competency standards and ensure that all graduates meet new performance standards for the teaching profession and are eligible for certification. This agenda for reform includes the following aspects:

- Increased course time for practical classroom teaching, with coaching and mentoring by lecturers and, periodically, by experienced classroom teachers
- More extensive school-based experience, observation, tutoring, small-group assistance, school-based action research, and collaboration during the induction year
- Greater school-university collaboration by using more on-campus microteaching to exhibit best practices

- Closer cooperation between the universities and teacher working groups to ensure higher-quality experiences for both pre- and in-service teachers
- Employment of expert classroom teachers to supervise future teachers, assist in or teach courses in the preservice university programs, and collaborate on action research with university faculty
- Appropriate university infrastructure in terms of science and language laboratories, curriculum development centers and libraries, and instructional technology including Internet connection

These new challenges require the universities to make significant changes, and grants have been made available to support preservice teacher education institutions. The government's BERMUTU (Better Education through Reformed Management and Universal Teacher Upgrading) program, supported by the World Bank, provided $25 million for reforming university-based teacher education courses in light of the Teacher Law's requirements and for strengthening the national accreditation agency for higher education, especially to accredit the newly established four-year preservice education programs for primary school teachers. By 2011, for example, 56 study programs (26 for the four-year primary teacher degree and 30 for junior secondary teachers) had participated in the accreditation incentive grants program to revise their programs and purchase resources to implement these innovations. In addition, the funding provided distance learning grants for a consortium of universities to develop and promote a distance learning initiative (Hybrid Learning for Indonesian Teachers [HYLITE])[1]; grants to support technological improvements at the Open University to enhance distance learning capacity; and scholarships for lecturers to update their knowledge and skills in delivery of the new courses to upgrade in-service teachers. The government has reinforced this support by widening the number of universities involved to 90 and mandating that courses be competency-based.

The national accreditation agency for higher education also received funding to improve its capacity to assess the quality of the new courses and the ability of the universities to meet the new standards. The new standards, procedures, and instruments are covered in a series of eight manuals that relate data collection and analysis to the set of seven national standards shown in table 3.3. These documents can be found on the website of the accreditation agency.[2] For each of these national standards, there are a number of items in the accreditation instrument that require the assessors to explore the evidence the university can provide regarding implementation and outcomes for the program being accredited.

Universities are under some pressure to incorporate these new approaches if they wish to gain accreditation for their redesigned courses. For the new courses to be accredited, for example, universities should be able to provide evidence of new student-centered and interactive teaching methodologies; international best practice in teacher internship and practicum; actual school teaching experience by their lecturers; willingness and ability to recognize the prior learning of teachers upgrading their qualifications; and highly skilled lecturing staff to work with teachers, schools, and district staff in the assessment of teachers and the conduct

Table 3.3 National Standards for Indonesian University Program Accreditation

Standards	Items for evaluation (no.)	Proportion of marks given (%)[a]
1. Vision, mission, goals, objectives, and strategy achievement	3	3.12
2. Governance, leadership, management, and quality assurance system	6	6.24
3. Students and graduates	17	15.60
4. Human resources	23	21.90
5. Curriculum, learning, and academic atmosphere	27	18.81
6. Finance, facilities and infrastructure, and information systems	16	15.64
7. Research, service or community service, and cooperation	8	18.78

Source: BAN-PT 2008.
a. "Proportion of marks given" represents the relative weight assigned to each standard. The percentages add up to more than 100 due to rounding.

of training activities within schools. Whether the new courses have improved the quality of graduates or have resulted in higher student scores will be a project for the future.

An added complication in the reform of teacher education institutions is that their curriculum structures and content often work against the efficient and effective deployment of school staff. Within teacher education institutions, courses are organized into study programs for each teaching subject. Each study program consists of two main elements: (a) the knowledge content of the particular subject adapted for the needs of teaching; and (b) the pedagogy appropriate to the teaching of that subject (the latter is a relatively small component of only two to four months over four years). In this fairly self-contained structure, each study program is separate from the others with little interprogram exchange of either students or activities.

Such an arrangement has some inherent difficulties:

• The level of content is specific to teaching rather than to a corpus of academic knowledge so that there is little equivalence between, say, a mathematics course taken by an engineer and one taken by a teacher. A later career change for a teacher then becomes difficult, and, on a broader scale, limits the flexibility of the Indonesian labor force with a consequent cost to the whole economy.

• Although all teachers gain a "major" teaching subject from the study program in which they enroll, it is rare for teachers to have a "minor" or second teaching subject because they usually do not have the opportunity to study outside their particular study programs. This means that many secondary teachers who cannot gain sufficient teaching periods in the "major" subject they have been certified to teach are officially unable to teach a second "minor" subject to achieve the teaching load necessary to gain their professional allowance (24 period-hours per week). This limitation also unnecessarily increases the number of teachers a secondary school requires—yet another reason for the apparent overstaffing in some secondary schools.

Box 3.2 Adopting New Training Approaches

The city of Surabaya district government implemented a pilot (World Bank 2009a) to solve the subject mismatch problem by enrolling teachers at the University of Surabaya or the Open University to improve their competencies in the other subjects they have been asked to teach but for which they have no training. The plan is that by 2015 there will be no further mismatch problems. Currently, the university faculty has established a cooperative relationship with the local government and is obtaining the necessary equipment to improve the practical part of the subject instruction. Additional workshops will be held to raise the quality of instruction.

Likewise, many small primary schools in Indonesia have a surplus of teachers because they receive teaching staff based on the number of classes they have rather than on the number of students. Other schools, however, do not meet this criterion, having perhaps only four teachers or fewer—a situation that will become more common as teacher distribution inequities are reduced. When schools are staffed more equitably on the basis of student enrollments, smaller schools will receive fewer teachers, which will require teachers to instruct students in multigrade classes. Currently, however, most primary teachers are not trained for multigrade teaching. Universities will therefore need to ensure that their graduates have the skills to promote this form of class organization through their subject and pedagogical instruction.

Some teacher education institutions are attempting to resolve these problems of mismatch and provide other flexibilities in teacher education. Because teachers at the secondary level are trained and certified in only one subject, principals sometimes have difficulty obtaining a specialist teacher for some subject areas and must ask capable (but subject-untrained) teachers to teach classes outside their areas of expertise. This mismatch means students in that class are denied the expertise of a correctly trained teacher. Although regulations concerning multigrade teaching and multisubject teaching have not been issued, some universities have found creative ways of solving the problem of teacher over supply as well as the mismatch between the teacher's subject area and the subject they actually teach. The University of Surabaya, for example, trains such teachers at courses conducted during school vacations (see box 3.2).

Some universities offer innovative solutions to meet local needs, including a wide range of practical experiences to prepare teacher candidates for their teaching careers. The University of Manado provides a model for active involvement in the training of local teachers (see box 3.3).

Although a renewed emphasis on practical classroom training is necessary to produce good teachers, it has been difficult to identify high-quality teachers in these schools to work alongside the trainees in improving their practical knowledge and skills for classroom teaching. Furthermore, universities have not budgeted for their lecturers to spend more time in the schools and classrooms supervising and guiding their trainees and supporting the mentors. Maintaining

---

Box 3.3 The University of Manado's "In-Service, On-Service" Program Model

The University of Manado has been helping many teachers to upgrade their training. To support this government policy, it has developed an "in-service, on-service program" that started in 2009. This is an integrated program that caters to both preservice and in-service teachers. The university trains preservice teachers Mondays through Thursdays and trains in-service teachers on Fridays and Saturdays. The preservice teachers (third-semester students) will take the school positions of those teachers who go to campus on Fridays and Saturdays. This, in turn, will create an opportunity for them to gain teaching experience.

This program is particularly worthwhile for several reasons:

- In-service teachers have a chance to upgrade their knowledge (supporting the certification process).
- Schools welcome the practicing students.
- Many students from remote areas are willing to be assigned to teach in their own areas.
- Students are exposed to real situations (from the early period of their study) and know what schools need.
- Students and lecturers develop the learning model together, encouraging action research.

The university does not provide financial assistance for the practicing students because of financial constraints. However, it lets the students pick schools in their hometown areas. In addition, to support the monitoring of practical training, the university has budgeted funds to cover the transport costs of staff lecturers who supervise these practicum students in more-distant locations. This is an imaginative response to the need to find regular and longer-term placements in schools to implement the policies of the new training program.

---

productive and ongoing relationships with schools is also proving to be difficult to sustain because of the number of trainees to be placed and the longer time period they are expected to remain in the schools.

District scholarships for high-achieving graduates are seen to be an essential part of the larger strategy of teacher education reform. Schools in remote and disadvantaged areas are forced to hire temporary, often poorly trained, teachers to fill their vacancies. Some universities recognize that almost all districts face some challenges in terms of appointing the appropriately trained teacher to the appropriate vacancy. One university has reported that it will focus its postgraduate professional training course on teachers prepared to serve in remote areas. A number of other universities have signed memoranda of understanding with their local district offices to ensure they provide local government scholarships for selected students. These teachers are then guaranteed a position in those districts on graduation. This approach is most used for secondary subject areas, particularly in shortfall areas such as science and mathematics. These scholarships can reduce the mismatch caused when teachers are employed for a subject vacancy for which they are not qualified. The benefits of coordination at the district level are highlighted in box 3.4.

Teacher Reform in Indonesia • http://dx.doi.org/10.1596/978-0-8213-9829-6

Box 3.4 Coordination between Districts, Universities, and Schools

Close coordination between district offices, teacher education institutions, and schools has important benefits. District offices first need to work more closely with their schools and local universities to identify the district's teacher profile to match the schools' demand for teachers (particularly subject specialist teachers) with the supply available from the universities. Such a profile, constantly updated, can map teachers according to academic qualifications and schools' need for teachers at each educational level. This is especially true in preparing teachers to teach dual subjects in secondary schools in remote areas.

As teachers retire or resign, further vacancies arise, transfers occur, and new hiring takes place. One district conducts an annual district workshop to plan teacher appointments for each level of school and each subject area, incorporating known retiring teachers as well. This process addresses the problem of overstaffing in some schools and the shortage of teachers in other schools to ensure more efficient personnel deployment and resource use.

The Postgraduate Professional Teacher Training Course

International experience has shown that a postgraduate focus on pedagogy will enable greater flexibility in student entry to teaching. By providing a one-year professional teacher education course as an "add-on" diploma to a regular three-year or four-year degree in a teaching subject, universities can increase the options available for candidates who may seek a future career change. This model is often offered as an alternative to a four-year "integrated" degree.

The great benefit of the "3+1 year" model is that it enables greater flexibility for students than would a straight four-year teacher education degree at an Indonesian university. For example, it enables subject graduates to make a last-minute decision to opt for a teaching career if they can apply for and be accepted into the postgraduate training course. In addition, it may also facilitate the entry of mature graduates making a mid-life career change from another profession into teaching if they already have a relevant subject degree. Provided the enrollment opportunity into the postgraduate course remains open in this manner, a great deal more flexibility will exist to enable movement into and out of teaching as a career. This movement will enrich the experience of the teaching workforce and enhance the exposure of students to a wider range of teacher backgrounds.

In Indonesia, the Teacher Law requires that a postgraduate course of professional study and classroom practice be undertaken by all teachers seeking certification. This course is of one year's duration for secondary teachers and six months for primary teachers and is in addition to the four-year teacher education degree course taken by all. The course is designed to focus on interactive, student-centered teaching methodologies, with 60 percent of the course time being spent in classrooms involved in practical classroom work (watching and analyzing the lessons of master teachers, preparing and conducting lessons prepared by the trainee, and so on). However, in addition to providing effective training, the postgraduate course is also meant to be used as a filter to restrict the number of candidates being employed in teaching to ensure that only the most highly skilled teachers enter the profession in the future. By reducing the number of teacher graduates currently entering the profession, the course will also help to ensure that the supply of graduates more closely matches the demand for new teachers.

Selection for enrollment will involve a more rigorous testing regime—clearly a move in the right direction. However, by coming at the end of the four-year teacher education degree, the test does not effectively manage the number entering the education profession in the first place, and thus does little to improve efficiency of resource use by teacher education institutions.

Teacher candidates for the new postgraduate professional year must have already completed their four-year degrees. In 2012 the quota for this professional training was 3,000 degree graduates. Most openings will be filled by newly graduated teachers. Because of the incentive of the professional allowance, competition for these limited places has been vigorous. Priority entry to the postgraduate course advances a teacher in the queue for employment and the opportunity to gain the professional allowance.

Regulation 8/2009 governs the introduction of this postgraduate professional course. A team from the Directorate General of Higher Education ensures that the teacher education institutions meet the following conditions before receiving approval to give this course:

- In curriculum, a course of subject-specific pedagogy and a field experience program for each study program
- In human resources, a permanent faculty of two with PhDs and four with master's degrees for each program
- In infrastructure, the necessary specialist equipment and materials
- An improvement program for all instructional activities
- An organized partnership program with schools
- A professional postgraduate course for every study program, although an organizing university may arrange shared programs
- A regular Directorate General of Higher Education evaluation of programs with reapproval necessary after three years

Of particular importance in the conduct of the postgraduate professional training program is the need for universities to build closer links with schools, which reinforces the more general mandate for all teacher education institutions to do so. The key feature of this regulation is the requirement that students undertake the largest part of their pedagogical training and practice under supervision in the classroom.

The program has four core areas:

- Content in at least two teaching subject areas
- Teaching methodologies that are both generalist and subject-oriented

- Foundations of education, including child psychology and stages of child growth
- Professional practice in the classroom

Regulation 8/2009 particularly emphasizes practice teaching or a professional experience component that should be carried out in a number of schools, including a variety of observations and practice opportunities with an experienced teacher or lecturer mentor. The trainee should also have one or two blocks of teaching, each for a number of weeks, to teach a defined topic from the curriculum, using a range of methods, and to gain experience in testing students and analyzing their scores to judge their progress and their reaction to different methodologies. Reflection time should be included so that student teachers can consider the responses to their teaching and can also have a debriefing session with their mentors.

The final advantage of the professional postgraduate program has been to ensure the more equitable distribution of teachers. In spite of its teacher surplus, Indonesia has a continual shortage of teachers in rural and isolated areas. Inadequate teacher provision in remote, border, and disadvantaged areas was recognized by the Teacher Law, which provided a generous locality allowance (equal to the professional allowance) to attract teachers to these areas. Other incentives such as subsidized housing, payment of travel expenses, and longer vacations have also been tried but without much success. Figure 3.1 indicates

Figure 3.1 Teacher Shortfall in Remote Areas of Indonesia, 2011–12

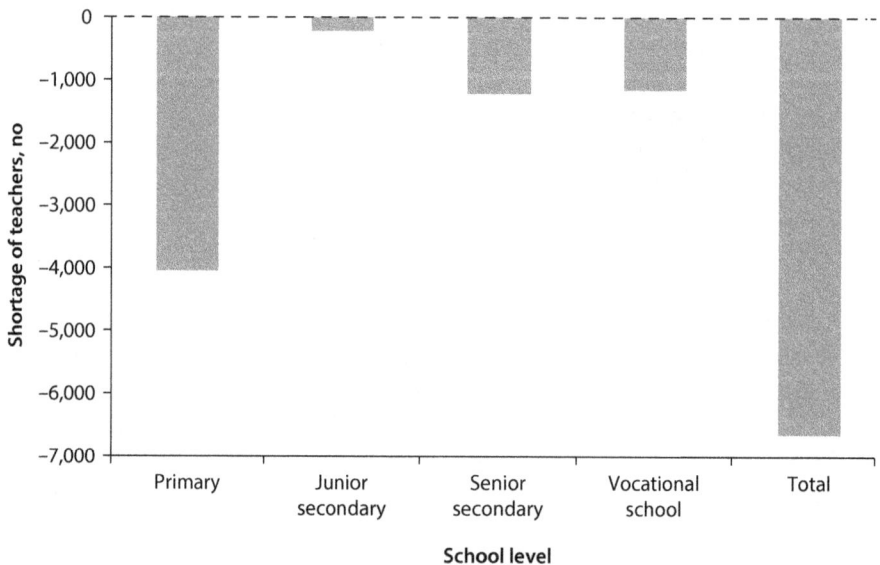

Source: Rustad 2012.
Note: The Ministry of Education and Culture defines "remote areas" as frontier, outer islands, and disadvantaged areas (Terdepan, Terluar, Tertinggal, or 3T). The ministry maintains a list of districts that fit these criteria. "Remote" is the inclusive term most often used to describe these areas.

Box 3.5 The SM-3T Program for Frontier, Outermost, and Disadvantaged Areas

In January 2012 the Ministry of Education and Culture reported that it had recently dispatched nearly 3,000 fresh graduate teachers on a one-year teaching assignment in frontier, outer islands, and disadvantaged areas (*Terdepan, Terluar, Tertinggal*, or 3T) under the "Education Bachelor's" program (*Sarjana Mendidik*, or SM) in 3T areas. This program is in line with the government's concentrated effort this year to expand education access in 3T locations in East Nusa Tenggara, Aceh, Papua, Maluku, and Kalimantan.

Demand for teachers in the 3T areas reaches 6,000 people annually, which the government attempts to meet by redistributing 3,000 in-service teachers and supplying 3,000 preservice teachers through the SM-3T program. The SM-3T is not a teacher recruitment program, but it offers fresh graduates of teacher education institutions the opportunity to gain firsthand experience in teaching before continuing with their professional postgraduate teacher education. There was a strong demand to enter the SM-3T program: a total of 7,000 graduates applied for the assignment.

---

the number of vacancies in the defined remote and border areas that were to be addressed in 2011–12. Twelve universities have been approved to commence a series of strategies, using access to the postgraduate professional training year as an incentive.

Priority to undertake the postgraduate professional course has therefore been given to teachers prepared to accept appointment to a school in a remote locality, a border zone, or a rural area. On their return, they are awarded a scholarship to complete postgraduate professional training and can then immediately undertake certification. This process not only helps remote schools to fill their vacancies with up-to-date and specially selected graduates but also ensures that teachers have a unique opportunity to practice in a special type of school. Clearly, the Ministry of Education and Culture is using this kind of teacher placement strategy to address the issue of staff shortages in remote areas (see box 3.5).

Induction, Mentoring, and Probation

One of the most important reforms emerging from the Teacher Law is the development of a school-based (or local working group-based) induction program for beginning teachers. This policy is meant to link the beginning teacher induction program and the school's classroom assessment report with the certification process and completion of the probationary period.

Currently, a teacher, like any other member of the civil service, has a one-year probationary period (with a possibility of having an extension to two years) after joining a school staff and commencing his or her teaching career. Traditionally, any civil servant, including teachers, must complete induction training in civics and administrative routines through the district government. However, it is also important to prove to the authorities that the teacher meets the chosen profession's required standards (both in subject knowledge and classroom pedagogy).

Teacher Reform in Indonesia • http://dx.doi.org/10.1596/978-0-8213-9829-6

The government intends to defer certification until the end of the teacher's probationary year, when the principal's report can also be incorporated into the process and be sent to the university for inclusion in the certification and probationary process. This gives a better balance between the university's view and the employer's view of the overall ability of the prospective teacher. It also retains some of the links from the previous year between the practice teaching and the university lecturer's teaching.

The teacher induction process became mandated through Regulation 27/2010. This marks an important point for the quality of Indonesia's teaching profession because it acknowledges that a beginning teacher requires closer supervision, mentoring, and guidance in the workplace than other teachers to successfully make the transition from university training to the school workplace.

It has been recognized that such an induction and probation program is best delivered by principals able to take a true leadership role within the school. After mentoring and monitoring the new teacher during the probationary year, the principal can undertake a classroom performance assessment of the beginning teacher before writing a report on the teacher's work. To help complete this task, the government's BERMUTU program made funding available for a professional development program to strengthen the capacity of principals and supervisors. Twelve modules were developed for school principals and supervisors to mentor beginning teachers and to assess them at the end of their first year. The material emphasizes the adoption of an important new duty for the principal—that of school instructional leader—which requires all principals with beginning teachers to take an active role in the professional development of those teachers. The materials also include classroom video lessons to be shown and discussed in workshops with the principal that also constitute an instrument for the assessment of beginning teachers at the end of their probation.

This teaching resource is critical for building the capacity of school instructional leaders and underlines part of the professional duty of principals as set out in Regulation 28/2010 on the role of the principal. The knowledge and skills gained by a principal through the use of this course material with his or her beginning teachers will have application right across the school into other classrooms and will assert the right and duty of the principal to enter classrooms and take an active part in the improved performance of all teachers, including those who are underperforming. By June 2011, the modules had been prepared and trialed to support the induction procedure, and training materials had been developed to socialize the process. Core teams have also been trained at the national and district levels to support this reform. Training will be largely through the supervisors' and principals' working groups.

This reform has closed a gap in Indonesian in-service training. Preservice university teacher education has a strong focus on subject matter and education theory with only a small component of face-to-face teaching practice in schools and classrooms. The new requirement that principals and supervisors adopt a more active role in mentoring new teachers in the classroom during the probationary year is an important new reform. By inducting beginning teachers into their new school role, the principal is providing the first comprehensive training of the teacher within the intensive, everyday environment of the school and classroom. This is a critical step in the training of teachers because they are, for the first time, under pressure to prepare and present lessons while controlling students in the class. It would be unfortunate if teachers finished their probationary year and were confirmed as civil servants before the employer's representatives (the principals) could confirm their efficiency and effectiveness.

Continuing Professional Development

The Teacher Law had a dramatic impact on the quantity of teachers undertaking in-service training. With 65 percent of the country's 2.7 million teachers not meeting the new minimum of a four-year degree academic requirement, the process of in-service upgrading has been the starting point for reform. In fact, it represents the area with the greatest potential for improving the quality of in-service teachers. This is an area where a range of training options and other useful initiatives is now becoming available, including the following:

- An expanded role for the Open University, whose enrollment of external students doubled by about 300,000 in-service students almost overnight
- Adoption of distance learning modes by a limited number of education faculties of the teacher education institutions
- Learning modules for use at the local level through the school cluster teacher working groups
- Recognition of prior learning (RPL)
- University accreditation of local cluster-based training

Distance Education Reforms

The Open University is the traditional supplier of distance learning in Indonesia, as further described in box 3.6. The ability of the Open University to rapidly expand its capacity to supply upgrade training for in-service teachers has made a significant contribution to the certification process. As figure 3.2 indicates, in 2009 over 485,000 in-service teachers were enrolled. Enrollment in the four-year degree in primary teaching and the degree in early childhood education constituted 86 percent of all students of the university.

The Open University has provided learning materials to teachers in printed form throughout Indonesia, and it conducts over 14,000 local workshops for in-service teachers, which are coordinated by its 36 regional centers. Additional support materials and e-resources have recently become available through its website, Guru Pintar (Clever Teacher) Online.[3]

Another open and distance learning approach—the first time distance learning strategies were used in Indonesia outside of the Open University—is the innovative HYLITE training mode, which has also been used to increase the capacity of regular universities to provide distance learning. With the increased demand from teachers seeking to upgrade their qualifications, the government

Teacher Reform in Indonesia • http://dx.doi.org/10.1596/978-0-8213-9829-6

Box 3.6 Using the Open University's Experience with Distance Learning Materials

Materials developed for distance learning are quite different from those meant for the traditional learning process. Open and distance learning (ODL) materials need to be more engaging and encourage learners to use them. To achieve that goal, developers of ODL materials need to have specific knowledge, skills, and experience. In this regard, the Open University's learning materials for the four-year degree for in-service teachers are well designed according to ODL instructional design principles.

Indonesia's Open University has significantly more experience in developing ODL materials than the regular teacher education institutions that have more recently entered the field under the HYLITE program. From interviews with the Open University's rector and staff, it is clear that it receives feedback from its users and continues to develop its staff's capacity in instructional design. This experience could usefully be shared with other universities in supporting the development of ODL materials in Indonesia and making them more instructionally effective.

Figure 3.2 Indonesia Open University Student Enrollments, by Faculty, June 2009
Percent

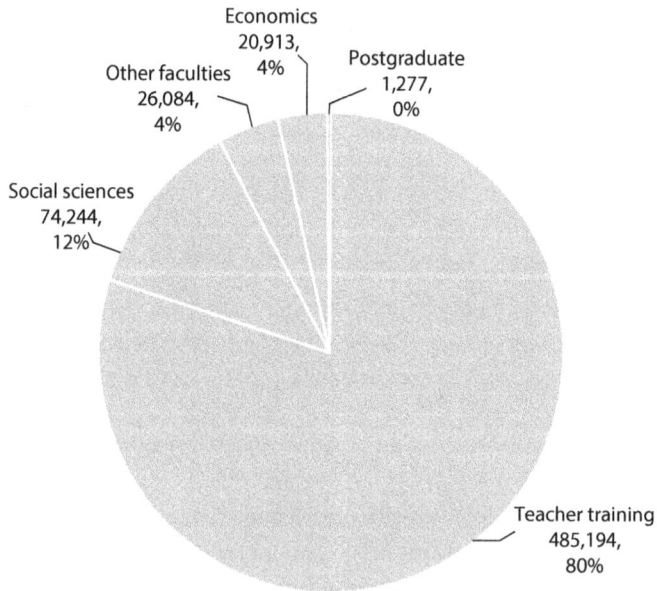

Source: Indonesia Open University website: www.ut.ac.id/. Accessed in 2011.

established a trial program using regular universities in 2007. A consortium of 13 universities was commissioned to create a program to support primary teachers seeking to upgrade their qualifications to a four-year degree for certification. Grant funding supplied by the BERMUTU program was used to develop these materials, and 23 universities agreed to adopt the program. This new four-year degree expanded existing teachers' access to upgrading opportunities through provision of instructional materials and packages for 32 courses. These comprised audiovisual materials, printed booklets, a web-based format, additional test items, sets of assignments and other online initiations, and tutorial plans and materials.

This change in government policy created a new mode of study for teachers seeking to upgrade and has established the principle that regular universities can deliver distance instruction. By the end of 2010, over 7,000 incumbent teachers had used this avenue to upgrade (Directorate General of Higher Education 2011).

Recognition of Prior Learning

As part of the reform process, the principle of RPL has been introduced for in-service teachers who enroll for upgrading (see box 3.7). Many teachers needing academic upgrading to a four-year degree may already be effective

---

Box 3.7 International Experience with Recognition of Prior Learning

The theoretical benefits of recognition of prior learning (RPL) make it an attractive policy option in a number of countries. However, practical implementation has often proved difficult, and take-up has frequently been lower than anticipated. According to the City and Guilds Centre for Skills Development in London, countries have encountered the following challenges in implementing RPL (Sims 2010):

- Lack of demand from learners who, even when eligible for RPL, prefer the conventional learning process and the social interactions that accompany it
- Lack of awareness of the process
- Perception that RPL is an "easy option" not valued by stakeholders
- Complexity of the process, which requires a sophisticated understanding of subject unit structures and may end up being mired in heavy bureaucracy
- Difficulty that many students have in gathering evidence acceptable to the institution

The core requirement for successful RPL is an established framework of credit, qualifications, and occupational standards. The support of stakeholders and efforts to raise awareness among universities and candidates are necessary, as is a fairly rigorous assessment process to ensure quality. Clear, jargon-free information is also essential. There should be minimal difficulty in accessing the process and substantial support from the university to help practitioners and candidates through the process.

If RPL is seen as a tool for skill identification and capacity building, it is argued, the emphasis should lie even more on using it as a way to bring individuals into further education and training. Such an outcome may, however, require a change in culture and mind-set. In a number of RPL initiatives in developing countries, outcomes were linked to occupational standards rather than curricular structures, leading to a lack of connectivity with further education and a mind-set that receipt of a certificate of recognition is an end rather than a means to further development.

---

teachers with a depth of workplace experience. It was recognized that, as in other education systems, such knowledge and skills could be assessed to count toward their degrees. RPL was therefore included under the banner of in-service teacher upgrading, and universities received the authority to determine how much advanced standing to give for in-service teachers enrolling for training. Accordingly, a policy and instruments for RPL were developed and trialed in 2008. All 81 universities appointed to offer upgrade courses for underqualified teachers were also approved to offer RPL. In 2009, implementation commenced. The Open University was excluded from this regulation because the process is not a new one for that institution.

The Open University has adopted a straightforward approach to RPL based on a simple formula taking into account a teacher's educational level at point of entry, additional in-service training received, and the number of years' experience as a teacher. It is difficult to judge how successful this formula is in determining the quality of the candidate upon entry. However, up to 28 credit points toward a degree of 145 credit points can be awarded for this work.

Although the number of teachers awarded RPL has increased significantly, the relatively slow uptake by the universities has been a cause for concern. They may remain resistant to the idea of gaining the four-year degree through in-service training at regular universities; thus, the overwhelming majority of upgrading in-service teachers are enrolled at the Open University. In addition, the slow uptake may be due to the following factors:

- Refusal of some district education offices to permit their teachers to leave their classes for an extended period
- Lack of partnerships between many of the appointed universities and local districts, rendering their programs inaccessible for many teachers
- Teachers' failure to receive the allocated subsidy from the provincial office because of the limited quota and the provincial policy to prioritize enrollment at the Open University
- Failure of many districts in general to allocate subsidies for in-service teachers to upgrade their qualifications

Thus, despite progress in the socialization and implementation of the RPL and its procedures, only about 35,000 teachers have gained access to such recognition through regular universities (Ministry of Education and Culture 2011a).

Establishment of a quality assurance system for RPL will increase confidence in this reform. To date, university practices to calculate the levels of RPL to be awarded have varied considerably. The Ministry of Education and Culture is aware of a growing lack of rigor in the procedures being used in some universities and is taking steps to carefully audit how procedures are being applied to ensure that standards are maintained. Although it is understandable for universities to resist the adoption of practices they believe will lower standards, the justification for offering RPL is quite sound and is a common international practice.

It saves time and money and also avoids the needless repetition of material that late entrants to academic courses often experience.

Cluster-Based Working Groups

Teacher working groups (KKGs and MGMPs)[4] have been recognized as "the most viable and accessible avenue for most teachers to receive continuing professional development" (Ministry of Education and Culture 2011a). They have played an integral role in supporting teachers in training and professional development activities for over 20 years and provide a forum for teachers to discuss teaching problems and work cooperatively to undertake common tasks such as curriculum development, the creation of teaching aids, and the design of test items as well as more advanced activities such as lesson study and classroom action research. However, support for these groups has varied over the years, and although many are still active and productive, a large number have become inactive or fail to provide effective support for career development. They often wax and wane in importance in the local education community, depending upon the support of the district and subdistrict education offices or the interest of teachers.

With the surge of training generated by the Teacher Law reforms, however, the teacher working group has been seen as providing a model method of delivering in-service training at the local level. This model required attempts to reactivate and strengthen these groups. Although the Ministry of Education and Culture began a revitalization process through a block grant program in 2005, funding for this process has been supplemented from other sources in selected districts (such as the government's BERMUTU program, which is supported by the World Bank) with the intention of using the groups to support teachers for upgrading, certification, and professional development activities. In 2005, the status of working groups was also not well understood, and thus the World Bank undertook a comprehensive study (World Bank 2009b). The 2007 report[5] described the groups' activities, confirmed their potential benefits, and identified the characteristics of a model working group.

The study produced a number of important findings regarding the profile of an effective working group—for example, confirming the following central features of the best working groups:

- Sizes of approximately 6–10 schools for a KKG (cluster of primary schools) and 10–12 schools for an MGMP (cluster of subject-based secondary teachers from a group of high schools)
- Biweekly working meetings (approximately 16 meetings per year)
- Financial and technical support and frequent visits from the district education staff, supervisors, and principals
- Focused meetings that last approximately four hours
- Small-group work
- Nearly full attendance by all teachers in the school cluster working group
- Office-bearers consisting of at least a chair, a secretary, and a treasurer

- A focus on providing core activities such as the development of syllabi and lesson planning, discussions of subject matter, the development and practice of active and innovative teaching methods, the design of teaching aids, and student testing and achievement

A second study conducted in 2010 was undertaken by the Ministry of National Education using a sample of 30 of the 75 BERMUTU project districts (Ministry of Education and Culture 2011b). It estimated that 267,000 teachers were participating in a total of 6,155 working groups under BERMUTU. On this basis, it can be estimated that there are well over 60,000 working groups in Indonesia. This is a massive structure through which to deliver teacher in-service training and is probably the most significant avenue through which teachers receive their continuing professional development—particularly in rural and remote areas where teachers' access to professional training is limited. Figure 3.3 looks at the key activities conducted by working groups in 2007 and again

Figure 3.3 Changing Activities in Local Teacher Working Groups in Indonesia, 2007–10

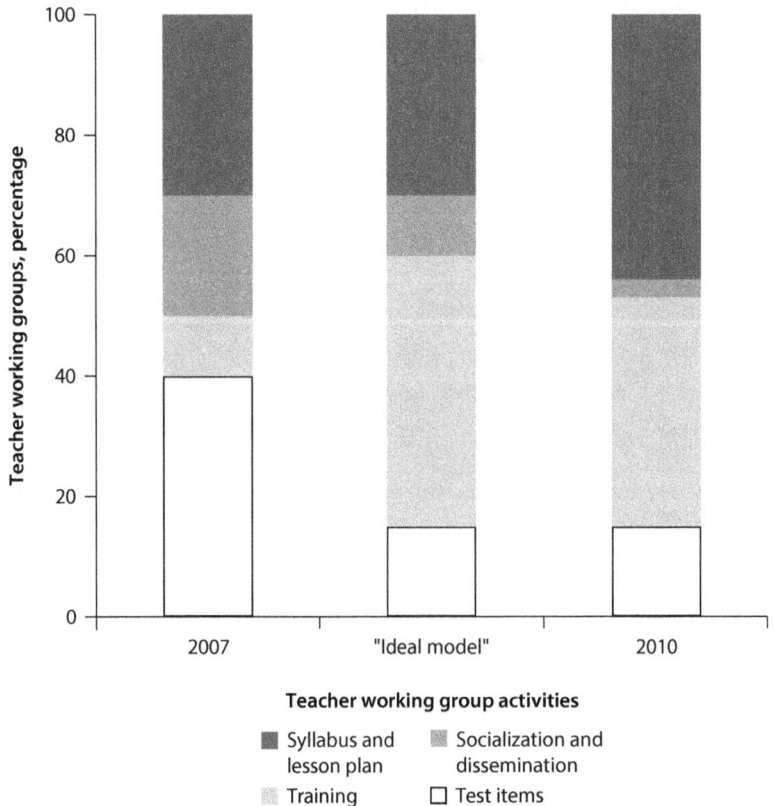

Teacher working group activities

- ■ Syllabus and lesson plan
- ▨ Socialization and dissemination
- ▨ Training
- □ Test items

Sources: 2007 results and "ideal model" from World Bank 2009b; 2010 results from baseline data collected for Ministry of Education and Culture 2011b.
Note: The "ideal model" represents a consensus of how a teacher working group should operate based on the 2007 World Bank study of 45 school districts in Indonesia (World Bank 2009b).

in 2010; an "ideal model" of an effective working group appears in the center as a comparison.

The first column shows the range of teacher professional development activities and their relative importance as identified in the 2007 World Bank study of 45 districts (World Bank 2009b). From this study, it was possible to postulate a theoretical or "ideal" model of how a teacher working group should operate—in particular, what sort of teacher education a group should deliver to local teachers. In terms of teacher effectiveness and improvement, the "training" element was considered the most critical one to examine. The consensus was that the chief function of working groups should be one of training—not just in terms of the amount of training but also in terms of the quality of subject content and methodology. The graph shows a training component in working group activities of 10 percent in 2007 when the preferred level was postulated to be 45 percent (that is, a difference of 35 percentage points at the cost of "socialization and dissemination" and writing "test items").

By the time of the 2010 ministry study, the actual figure for training had grown from 10 percent in 2007 to 38 percent in 2010 (Ministry of Education and Culture 2011b). In addition, the types of training activities were more diverse and classroom-focused. The data mentioned "learning models, teaching aids, and classroom action research," so the quality of what was undertaken during this larger slice of working group time was more classroom- and teaching-focused. This additional time came from reductions in the proportion of time spent developing "test items" (reduced from 40 percent to 15 percent) and in "socialization and dissemination" of administrative and routine circulars (reduced from 20 percent to 3 percent).

Although there was only a small district overlap in these two studies, the working group activities indeed appear to have been reoriented. This change is in two directions: (a) a significant growth in the time spent in training activities, and (b) an improvement in the nature and quality of activities on which that time was spent. This is good news for those involved in educational reform because the local school working groups represent a critical strategy for bringing in-service training to the grassroots and into schools where the greatest improvement in teacher quality is desired (see box 3.8).

Teacher working groups depend heavily on the availability of resource people. These are usually provided by universities, provincial institutes for quality assurance, Centres for the Development and Empowerment of Teachers and Education Personnel in subject areas, expert teachers from district schools, and sometimes private consultants. In general, however, the number of such facilitators is small, and funding for payment to them is scarce.

Teacher Appraisal and Career Development
Teacher Appraisal
As part of the teacher reforms, the ministry has also begun to implement some changes to the teacher accountability system. The focus is on a revision to the teacher performance appraisal scheme and a stronger link to the professional

Box 3.8 Impact of Teacher Working Groups

There is some evidence that teacher working groups are effective in increasing knowledge levels of teachers. Teachers in working groups receiving a direct grant under the BERMUTU program show a significant improvement in cognitive and pedagogical ability. A ministry study of a sample of 1,015 teachers, drawn from working groups in the 75 BERMUTU districts, showed that some improvement in teachers' abilities had occurred (Ministry of Education and Culture 2011b).

Generally, the same teachers were tested twice: at baseline (2010) and at midline (2011) of a three-stage study. The tests used contained linked (anchor) items, which means that a small percentage of questions were the same in both baseline and midline tests. This methodology can be used to construct test scores that are comparable over time. From figure B3.8.1, it is possible to conclude that the sample teachers improved in 2011 over 2010, in both cognitive and pedagogical ability.

All regular primary-school working groups in the BERMUTU program received a direct grant through the provincial quality assurance agency of $5,200 (or $5,500 for junior secondary groups) over the three years of the program that had elapsed at that time. This funding was conditional on adhering to the program guidelines, which meant expenditures were to be directed toward the purchase of learning materials and activities associated with modules of work provided by the program. These modules predominantly focused on class action research, lesson study, active learning, group work, and other effective classroom methodologies. A further requirement was that each working group would meet 16 times each year (fortnightly) to conduct activities—a more intensive pattern than in the past. As figure B3.8.1 shows, while there was some gain in cognitive (subject) ability, the larger gain was in pedagogical (teaching method) ability. This finding is in line with the reorientation of working group activities toward syllabus development, lesson study, and training.

Figure B3.8.1 Standardized Gains in Abilities of Primary School Teachers Attending Working Groups in Indonesia, 2010–11

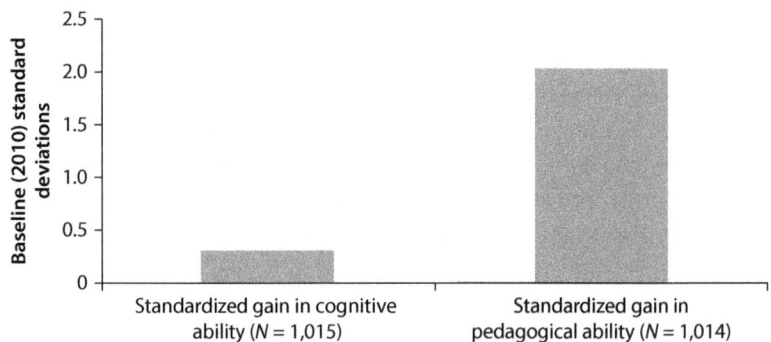

Source: Based on Rahmawati 2011.
Note: Teachers tested were drawn from teacher working groups in districts participating in the Ministry of Education and Culture's BERMUTU grant program. BERMUTU = Better Education through Reformed Management and Universal Teacher Upgrading.

box continues next page

Box 3.8 Impact of Teacher Working Groups (*continued*)

The findings concerning the effectiveness of teacher working groups are significant for policy makers. Although the working-group structure has been in place for many years as a meeting point for teachers to exchange ideas, it is not sufficient to simply leave them on their own without guidance if real teacher improvement is to take place. The groups do need some regular funding, and they do need a structured program of improvement to implement. Such a program should be clearly focused on subject content framed within a comprehensive program of classroom lesson improvement. Furthermore, through the working group, the roles of teachers, principals, and supervisors also need to be aligned. Regular scheduling of meetings should be a requirement for funding (perhaps 16 sessions per year), and auditing should be rigorous. However, this audit must be of two kinds: first, it must record details of the teachers' classroom products, including lesson implementation and improvement; and second (and only second), it should require financial records and receipts of funds expended. If done systematically, the training available at the local level can be shown to have a significant impact on teacher ability.

---

development system. The implementation of an annual performance appraisal scheme will ensure that school principals and supervisors take an active part in the work and performance of each teacher. Through an annual review of a teacher's work in relation to the knowledge and skills he or she is required to demonstrate and the standards mandated by the Teacher Law, a principal can identify the weaknesses of a teacher's performance and require that the necessary professional development take place.

With scores from the performance appraisal instrument linked to a teacher's salary increment and future progression, teachers will have a strong incentive to undertake the necessary development coursework recommended for improvement. Furthermore, if this performance is a component of future promotion opportunities, the cycle is complete and an integrated framework is established. Teachers who are identified as underperforming will receive support but also face sanctions for nonperformance. The teacher's clear link to accountability for work productivity is thus established.

It is therefore critical to develop an integrated framework to sustain and continually enhance the quality and accountability of teachers after they have been certified. This is being achieved by

- Reforming existing policies, procedures, and instruments for performance appraisal and for progression and promotion
- Linking incentives created under the Teacher Law to career advancement
- Clarifying lines of accountability between principals and supervisors and their teachers

In this context, a recent ministerial memorandum has promoted the principle of integrated training, which involves providing courses through the cooperation of a number of education and training agencies acting together. In this case, the ministry has brokered an agreement among universities, the provincial Institutes for Educational Quality Assurance, and the subject-focused Centres for the Development and Empowerment of Teachers and Education Personnel, and a memorandum of understanding has been signed and funding provided for the development of additional accredited teacher education modules to be delivered jointly by these agencies. It has been agreed that these will form part of the continuing professional development requirement for all teachers set out in the Teacher Law and will be linked to teacher performance appraisal for the calculation of credit points for progression and salary increments. This integrated framework now links the key elements shown in figure 3.4. This diagram shows the elements that will govern the performance cycle for all teachers. It consists of three basic processes:

- *Competency tests* completed as part of certification and at subsequent times to determine the competency levels being achieved by teachers and being applied in the classroom
- *Performance appraisal* for all education professionals that is annual, evidence-based, and criterion-referenced
- *Continuing professional development* based on identified teacher and school needs

For example, a teacher failing the competency test must undertake a course of basic training available in the continuing professional development circle before he or she can undertake performance appraisal. Should the appraisal

Figure 3.4 An Integrated Framework to Sustain Teacher Quality and Accountability after Certification in Indonesia

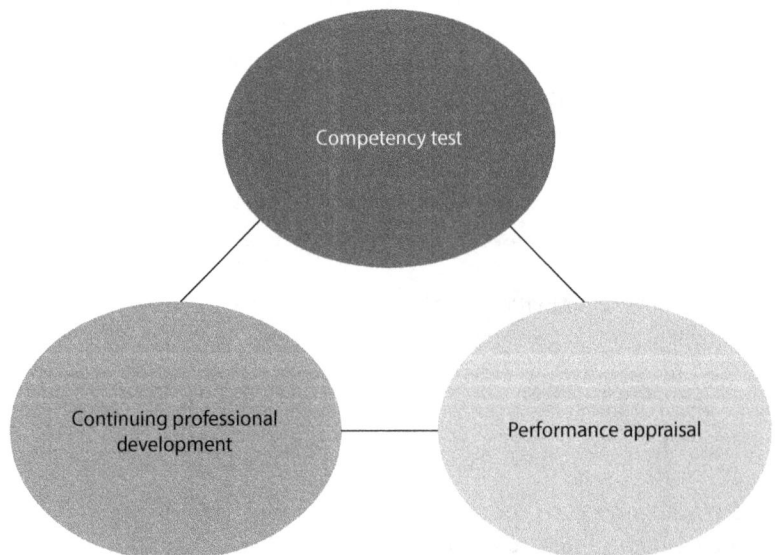

Teacher Reform in Indonesia • http://dx.doi.org/10.1596/978-0-8213-9829-6

reveal further weaknesses in the teacher's work, a specific remedial course must be undertaken as part of continuing professional development. However, a teacher shown to be performing at the minimum standard or better will progress to an improved salary and the opportunity for promotion.

The management of performance and career progression of all education personnel is, therefore, now governed by structures and procedures based on a comprehensive legislative framework. The reforms have resulted in a revised operational and functional framework supported by legislation specifying the competency requirements of teachers and counselors.[6] This framework includes specific core competencies required for increased levels of responsibility as well as additional competencies related to career stages. Teachers will thus have ongoing, career-long incentives that provide the motivation for improvement upon which modern education systems function.

The Ministry of Education and Culture is currently preparing an online teacher assessment recording system to measure the subject content knowledge and classroom performance of teachers.[7] This e-system will record the data from each teacher's performance appraisal and competency test results into a specially designed computer database. The information will be used to develop individual teacher profiles in the legislated competencies and will enable management to measure progress toward their achievement. These data will enable the targeted planning of continuing professional development programs for teachers from the individual to the national level of demand. Teachers, principals, and district authorities will have access to this information. It is intended that this database be an invaluable tool to help teachers make professional decisions about their annual professional development plans.

Career Development

The ultimate goal of this cycle, of course, is a new career development and salary framework based on the achievement of required competencies and successful continuing professional development. As a result of negotiations between the Ministry of National Education and the Ministry of Administrative Reform, a new career framework was agreed on and formalized in Regulation 16/2009. This regulation clusters the many salary increments defined for the Indonesian civil service into four major career levels (five levels with the inclusion of teacher induction). This is a particularly significant reform because the teacher-specific framework it adopts differs from the overall civil service pay scale.

Policy makers have agreed that at each annual teacher performance appraisal, a total credit-point score will be calculated for each teacher. The score achieved will vary according to how well a teacher performs on each dimension of the instrument. Every two years, a teacher will have these scores matched against the salary scale and a decision made about progression to the next increment. In the final step of implementation of this project, principals will be able to enter the scores by computer and transfer the data to the district level.

The performance appraisal instrument will refer to the professional development activities undertaken by the teacher. Many professional development modules have already been developed. Others will be prepared. A framework is being developed to incorporate all these modules and to ensure they are graded according to the types of professional development required at different levels of a teacher's career. The various themes for training are as follows:

- *Induction*: Beginning teachers who need support from developed modules
- *Novice Teacher (Guru Pertama)*: Teachers just starting out who need material to focus on competency development
- *Junior Teacher (Guru Muda)*: More experienced teachers seeking material to focus on improvements in student performance and school management
- *Senior Teacher (Guru Madya)*: Associate teachers needing material to focus on the development of the school
- *Master Teacher (Guru Utama)*: Senior teachers needing material on school leadership and teacher development

With appropriate legislation, this process could lead to a full performance-related pay scheme. For example, teacher certification could be linked in future reforms to specific professional levels rather than the current practice of one-off certification qualifying a teacher for a lifelong entitlement to a professional allowance. If such a route is taken, it would move the whole teacher performance management process closer to the goal of linking incentives to career advancement.

In implementing this system, particular attention is being given to building the capacity of the personnel needed to complete key tasks, including the following:

- Management of teacher performance appraisal and continuing professional development by the district education office
- Management and use of databases by relevant users
- Training to implement the control and support system including school supervisors, provincial staff, and the outside monitoring agencies to be involved
- Training of personnel at national Centres for the Development and Empowerment of Teachers and Education Personnel to produce, deliver, and train in the use of distance learning materials to be provided to local teacher working groups and schools
- Further development of the professional working groups for supervisors, principals, and teachers to deliver the needs-based modular continuing professional development program
- Inclusion of preparatory training to deliver programs for induction, teacher performance appraisal, and continuing professional development in the professional development programs of supervisors and principals

These are complex and ambitious reforms requiring negotiation with a number of agencies, professional bodies, and teacher associations. Principals and supervisors, for example, have only recently been involved in making professional judgments and preparing reports on the competency of their teachers. The performance appraisal process will require them to regularly enter this sensitive field, which some consider to be "culturally inappropriate." Although some training has been given, there is need for ongoing work in this area to build confidence and enhance their role as instructional leaders in schools. The associations will also need assurance that principals and supervisors are acting in a supportive role and on developmental activities to improve the quality of teaching. The methods of dealing with underperforming teachers will be particularly important.

This point is important: when certification of teachers is complete, the continued motivation of teachers to improve quality will depend heavily on the teacher management structures in place and the quality of leadership at the local level—of the district education offices, of principals, and of supervisors. In the past, particularly since decentralization, the quality of leadership at this level has been poor and often tainted by patronage or reflective more of administrative function than genuine educational leadership. This state of affairs must change if teacher quality is to improve. Two recent regulations[8] define the future competencies demanded by these positions and establish a list of requirements for them, including civil service level, maximum age limit, a competency test based on the standards of specialized training, and a selection test. However, there is no mention of selection on merit. Since the promulgation of these decrees, a major training course for principals has been developed and a specialist unit established to visit districts to train principals and supervisors who, if successful, will be "licensed" to practice. These actions will create a pool of eligible candidates from which district education authorities can draw when they wish to fill a vacancy.

Selection for these key positions should be based on ability to undertake educational leadership at the local level. The need to improve teacher quality means that principals and supervisors must be skilled in direct classroom assessment of teachers and the identification and support of poorly performing teachers. They must undertake an instructional leadership role in teaching methodologies and pedagogy, including student-centered teaching, classroom management, and student achievement measurement. Although both of these positions will require some administrative responsibility, great time must be devoted toward their leadership roles in curriculum development and management. School supervisors, in particular, should take a significant role in the training of principals in educational management, including mentoring and coaching their decision making and supporting their school leadership on a day-to-day basis. Part of their commitment must be to facilitate the work of teacher working groups management committees in providing continuing professional development programs for schools. Only the direct involvement of principals and supervisors in the observation and improvement of teaching in the classroom will sustain continued development of teacher competency.

Principals. Although many principals in Indonesia are well educated and capable, their training and knowledge of school management is often inadequate for modern requirements. Most principals simply implement education policy and administrative requirements as a matter of routine without the knowledge and skills of an instructional leader. Often their professional development as school leaders consists of little more than a briefing on policy documents issued by the district office. They are poorly paid and have little authority over the teachers they supervise. Consequently, few adopt a proactive supervisory and developmental role toward their teaching staffs. They are often selected following an examination or are simply nominated by a district education officer. They are rarely selected by a formal merit process and receive little training for the task.

Ministerial Regulation 44/2002 mandated school-based management in Indonesia, which placed educational management firmly in the school with the principal as the key decision maker. The commencement of the School Operational Assistance funding program in 2005 placed resources at the school level to facilitate this decision making. Principals now have an effective role in a range of areas including school planning, curriculum development, school finance and budgeting, staff management, and community involvement. The principal thus has a key responsibility at the center of a devolved system where school-based management is the expectation. Principals in Indonesia now need greater skill in more effectively managing these processes.

In time, it is anticipated that school principals will take a more active role in the management of their schools in terms of the effectiveness of their personnel, efficient use of financial resources, and their accountability for student results and achievements to parents and the wider community. Principals will also become instructional leaders taking a positive role in the improvement of the quality of instruction at their school, and this improvement will be reflected in improved student scores.

School Supervisors. The school supervisor (*pengawas*) employed by the district office to visit schools provides an accountability link between the school principal and the district officers. When visiting schools, supervisors may have a range of tasks, such as collecting and analyzing reports and providing information about curriculum implementation and school effectiveness to the district office. Unfortunately, following the decentralization of education administration, the nature of the role now varies widely from district to district and usually focuses more on administrative issues than on the improvement of the classroom performance of teachers. A recent review of the capacity of the school supervisor concluded as follows: "School principals, teachers and school committee members regard the position of school supervisor as a low status position rather than an attractive career pathway. School supervisors reported that they have limited access to training and development opportunities" (Australia-Indonesia Basic Education Project 2007).

However, there is considerable potential in this position: a well-trained school supervisor can be a significant change agent operating across a cluster of, say, 10–15 schools. Freed of many administrative tasks and equipped with the knowledge and skills of a modern instructional leader, a school supervisor can effectively mentor and coach principals and arrange workshops and seminars for teachers in the new methodologies during visits to each school. This role is a significant one and needs continual strengthening through training and the selection of capable officers with good qualifications and extensive experience.

Ministerial Decree 12 of March 28, 2007, recognizes the potential in this position for reorienting the face of Indonesian education. It defines the competencies required of school supervisors in six dimensions: personal competence, managerial supervision competence, academic supervision competence, education evaluation competence, research and development competence, and social competence. But the review mentioned above identified a large number of deficiencies in the knowledge and skill of school supervisors to undertake the newly defined tasks, as shown in figure 3.5.

This summary of qualitative data shows the extent to which principals and teachers agreed or disagreed with the proposition that school supervisors possess competency in each of the six dimensions. The small percentage of those in agreement indicates the generally low perception of school supervisor competencies reported in interviews and focus group discussion. Clearly, this creates a considerable agenda for the professional development of school supervisors.

Data from the Directorate of Basic Education Educational Personnel Development indicate an increasingly aging school supervisor workforce, with 35 percent of the 21,627 school supervisors in the government system reaching retirement age within the next five years. Within the Ministry of Religious Affairs (MORA), 67 percent of the 7,060 school supervisors will retire in the next five years. The extent of imminent retirement presents an important

Figure 3.5 Perception of School Supervisor Competencies in Indonesia, 2007

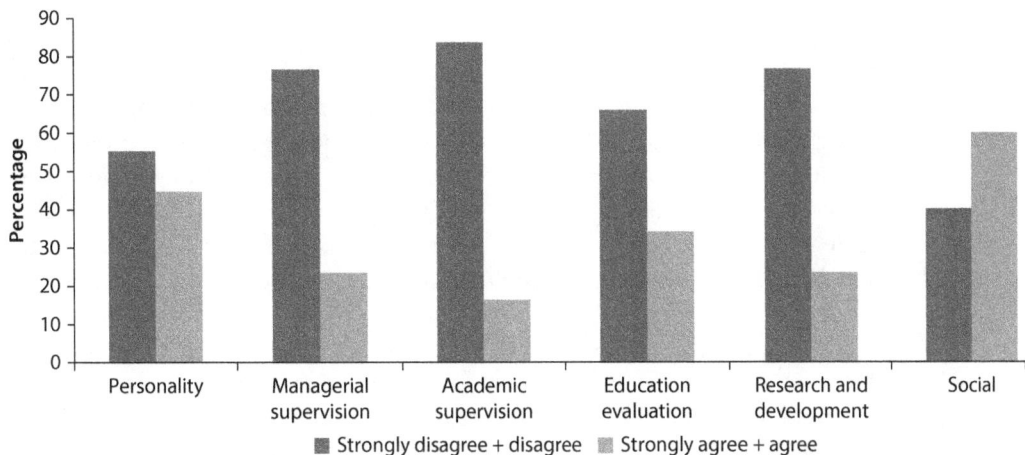

Legend: ■ Strongly disagree + disagree   ■ Strongly agree + agree

Source: Australia-Indonesia Basic Education Project 2007.
Note: Ministerial Decree 12 of March 28, 2007, defined the six dimensions of competencies required of school supervisors, shown on the x-axis. A sample of principals and teachers from all provinces were asked whether they agreed or disagreed that their own school supervisors possessed each dimension of competency.

Box 3.9 Selecting Supervisors in Karawang District

The new district head of education at Karawang intends to improve the quality of his school supervisors (who each manage 10 schools) to establish them as "quality advisers" to lead the district's teacher quality improvement program. School supervisors are to form a cadre of experienced educational leaders to help teachers and principals to improve the standard of teaching in schools and hence lift student achievement scores. His plan is to select from a pool of school principals who have had eight years (two four-year terms) of successful experience in managing a school and have returned to the classroom for two years. This selection strategy is based on the need to have school leadership experience as well as a classroom-teaching "refresher experience."

   The district head's intent is clear: he recognizes the need to focus closely on improvement in classroom teaching as the essential core of teacher quality and improvement. However, in discussion he spoke of his uncertainty about how to select the type of school supervisor who could successfully undertake such a task. Although these personnel can face special training and competency tests, at the final point of selection they rarely face an interview or go through a serious merit process in which a panel deliberates over matching the best person from a number of applicants for the position.

---

opportunity to replace over 40 percent of all school supervisors over the next five years and create a new elite workforce of these key personnel to drive educational improvement in schools and districts. Box 3.9 discusses one such effort that reflects the intention of district authorities to drive improvement in teacher quality.

Conclusions

In the long run, the reforms being promoted in the teacher career cycle—from attracting better recruits to ensuring that they know their subjects well and can teach them effectively through better and more school-based training—are most important in developing a cadre of teachers who deserve both professional certification and the rewards that come with it. To the extent these reforms are implemented successfully, of course, less time and fewer resources will need to be devoted to "catch-up" in-service training, and more time and more resources can be used for more systematic, career-long continuing professional development.

   Although many ministerial reforms have been introduced to improve the system of teacher management, a major factor in their implementation and final success is the proper recruitment and selection process for the posts that can help ensure adequate attention to quality—namely, principals and supervisors. Mechanisms are now being piloted to guarantee that this process is based on merit and competence instead of political or personal favoritism.

The preservice education and continuing professional development needed to make these reforms succeed has also involved significant policy changes for the institutions providing this training, particularly the following:

- The closer linking of teacher education institutions with schools and district offices
- The introduction of limited distance-mode training by regular universities
- The authority for universities to facilitate training through new rules for RPL

These policy changes are essential for the ongoing professional development of the new generation of teachers and will also have a wider impact on university operations of the future.

But there are two critical caveats: First, this comprehensive and systematic teacher management and development process is based on the assumption that teachers begin with some minimum level of competence and a certain degree of motivation: to teach and to help their students learn. Earlier chapters have described the sometimes indifferent attitude of teachers (many of whom, given their seniority, are now certified), whose priorities, according to the exigencies of the time, were obedience and loyalty *up* the system rather than proactive service *to* their students and *out* to the larger community. Ensuring that the postcertification quality assurance process works for them as well as for the new generation of teachers mentioned above is a major challenge.

Second—and equally challenging—is the need, as Fullan (2010) maintains, to focus not only on individual capacity building (as the current preservice, induction, probation, certification, professional development, and teacher appraisal process does) but also on whole-school, collective capacity building. This is where the new roles for the principal, supported by the supervisor, become so essential in the process of reprofessionalizing teaching.

Notes

1. HYLITE is a distance learning program prepared by a consortium of 13 universities for use by 23 universities to train underqualified primary school teachers.
2. Further details can be found on the accreditation agency's website: http://ban-pt .kemdiknas.go/id.
3. http://gurupintar.ut.ac.id.
4. These working groups include *Kelompok Kerja Guru* (KKGs), which are clusters of primary schools, and *Musyawarah Guru Mata Pelajaran* (MGMPs), which are clusters of subject-based secondary teachers from a group of high schools.
5. An initial exploratory report was undertaken by the World Bank in 2007 and unpublished. A second report (World Bank 2009b)—which was more extensive and undertaken by the Centre for Assessment in the Ministry of Education and Culture— enabled comparisons in some dimensions with the data from the 2007 study.
6. Ministry of Administrative Reform, PermenMenpan 16/2009, Chapter 3.

7. For more information, see the Ministry of Education and Culture website: http://ekinerjaguru.org/.

8. Ministerial Regulation on Standards for School Supervisors (2005) and Ministerial Regulation on Standards for School Principals (2007).

References

Australia-Indonesia Basic Education Project. 2007. "Review of the Capacity of School Supervisors." AusAID, Jakarta.

BAN-PT (National Board of Accreditation for Higher Education, Badan Akreditasi Nasional—Perguruan Tinggi). 2008. *Accreditation of Degree Study Programs, Book 5.* Operational manual. Jakarta: BAN-PT.

Directorate General of Higher Education. 2011. "Distance Education for Primary Teachers." Paper presented at Directorate General of Higher Education, Ministry of Education and Culture, Jakarta.

Fullan, Michael. 2010. *All Systems Go: The Change Imperative for Whole System Reform.* Thousand Oaks, CA: Corwin.

Ministry of Education and Culture. 2011a. "Aide-Mémoire: Better Education through Reformed Management and Universal Teacher Upgrading (BERMUTU)." Mid-Term Review, World Bank, Jakarta, October 19.

———. 2011b. *Report on 2010 BERMUTU Study: Impact of Block Grants to KKG/MGMP (Teacher Working Group/Forum of Subject Teachers.* Centre of Education Assessment, Jakarta.

OECD (Organisation for Economic Co-operation and Development). 2011. *Building a High-Quality Teaching Profession: Lessons from Around the World.* Paris: OECD.

Rahmawati. 2011. "BERMUTU KKG/MGMP Study report". Background paper, Education Assessment Center, Jakarta.

Rustad, Supriadi. 2012. "National Policy for Teacher Education." Paper presented at Directorate General of Higher Education, Ministry of Education and Culture, Jakarta.

Sims, Chris. 2010. "Recognition of Prior Learning." Briefing note 27, City and Guilds Centre for Skills Development, London.

World Bank. 2009a. "Rapid Assessment Study in Pre-service Training of Teachers." Background paper, World Bank, Jakarta.

———. 2009b. "Teacher Working Groups in Indonesia: A Study of the Current Situation and Opportunities for Increased Effectiveness." Background paper, World Bank, Jakarta.

CHAPTER 4

The Impact of the Reform on Teacher Quality and Student Outcomes

The Certification Tool: A Quality Assurance Mechanism and a Potential Way to Improve Learning

> Over the last decade, many developing countries have embarked on large educational reforms aimed at rapidly expanding the supply of education, achieving equity in the provision of education, and significantly improving the quality of education. Some of these reforms have been far-reaching, transforming the budget priorities of many countries .... A number of developments have served as catalysts for reform.
>
> —Erwin R. Tiongson,
> "Education Policy Reforms," in *Analyzing the Distributional Impact of Reforms* (2005)

The Teacher Law of 2005 shaped a major proportion of the Indonesian teacher reforms of the past decade. The law aimed to address a wide range of teacher quality issues simultaneously. Most of the evidence provided in this chapter is used to discuss the impact of a key component of the law: the teacher certification program. The label of "professional" gained by certification and the associated professional allowance were meant, in part, to improve teachers' welfare and increase their status and recognition.

Teachers with a four-year university degree or with a high rank in the civil service (rank IV) or very senior teachers qualify for certification. Since the start of the program, the government has admitted 200,000–300,000 (qualified) teachers into the certification process each year. The eligibility conditions for certification were meant eventually to ensure that all teachers in the system had minimum levels of defined competencies. Since the program started, teachers have passed through the certification process either through an assessment of a portfolio of past experiences and training or through 90 hours of additional training. Overall passing rates of this process have been high, at around 95 percent.

The financial implications of the program are, of course, enormous. The teacher wage bill, already the largest expense of the Ministry of Education and Culture, will approximately double over the years to come (Cerdan-Infantes and Makarova, 2013). The question is whether this is money well spent. This chapter, therefore, discusses some of the impacts of certification on the quality of learning in Indonesia.

The analysis can provide important information to policy makers in countries with conditions similar to those in Indonesia. A number of developing countries combine high economic growth rates with relatively poor performance of the education system as a whole. Such conditions mean that, in the years ahead, governments will be able to budget increasing amounts for quality improvements to the education system.

The current teacher certification process in Indonesia can improve the quality of teaching in the country through three different channels:

- *The attraction channel.* The professional allowance makes the teaching profession considerably more attractive (and competitive). This results in better-qualified high school graduates entering teacher education institutions across the country. The attraction channel applies to high school graduates who are confronted with the choice to become a teacher or to choose another career. The higher salaries and status now given to teachers should increase the relative attractiveness of the teaching profession. High school graduates who might have opted for careers in engineering or business in the absence of certification might now be persuaded to choose teaching careers.

- *The upgrading channel.* Teachers who do not qualify for certification normally need to acquire a four-year degree. In this process of upgrading, teachers acquire skills that improve their capacities as teachers. The upgrading channel applies to in-service teachers who do not yet qualify for certification. Such teachers must normally enroll in courses to upgrade their academic qualifications to the four-year postsecondary degree level. Certification and the related professional allowance provide a strong financial incentive to upgrade these qualifications. At the start of the certification program, 84 percent of the primary school teachers and 40 percent of the junior secondary school teachers did not qualify for certification (Ragatz 2010). This large group of teachers is expected to upgrade to the four-year degree level. Because this mechanism applies to most in-service teachers, the aggregate effect of the certification program, channeled through academic upgrading, is potentially large.

- *The behavioral channel.* Certification implies increased recognition and a doubling of income, which motivate teachers to become more productive in their profession. The behavioral channel applies to all teachers who become professionally certified and receive the professional allowance. The allowance is permanent and not conditional on subsequent performance in the classroom except for the requirement to teach 24 period-hours per week. Teachers who are certified, therefore, have few explicit financial incentives to change their teaching practices. But teachers might feel a moral obligation to invest more effort in their work and be absent less often. At the same time, their need to take second jobs decreases, which means that teachers have more time in a day for professional work such as classroom preparation and participation in teacher working groups.

Whether certification in its current form has positive effects on teacher quality and student learning outcomes depends on the potency of these three channels. Separating the different channels for analysis will aid in the discussion of the effects of certification.

The Attraction Channel: Certification, Recruitment, and the Attractiveness of the Teaching Profession

This section discusses the effects of certification on prospective teachers—that is, on high school graduates who might or might not choose a career in teaching. Depending on the nature and rigor of the selection mechanisms used in accepting these graduates, higher demand could translate into better quality if higher-ability graduates are selected over those with lower ability.

Figure 4.1, panel a, shows that the number of students enrolled in education programs in universities in the country increased fivefold in the years following the Teacher Law—from 200,000 in 2005 to over 1 million in 2010. The regained

Figure 4.1 Enrollments of Higher Education Students in Indonesia, 2005–10

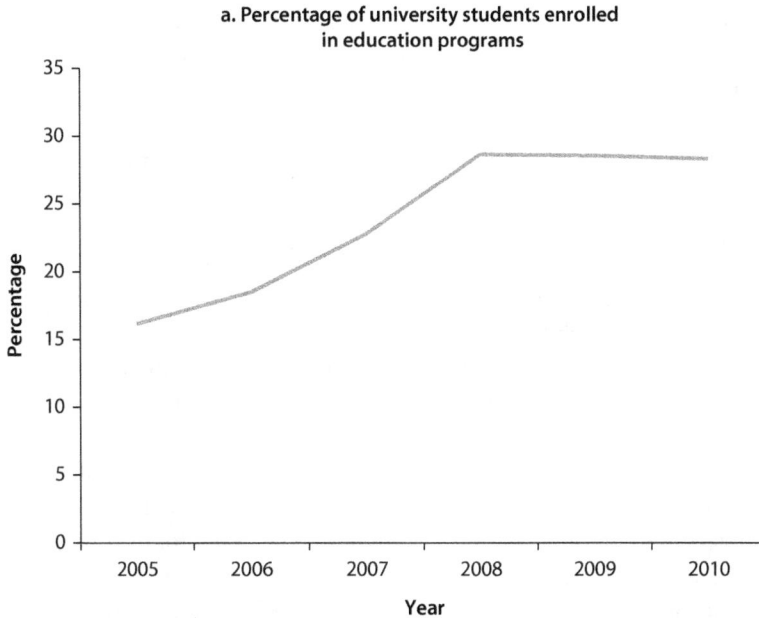

a. Percentage of university students enrolled in education programs

figure continues next page

Figure 4.1 Enrollments of Higher Education Students in Indonesia, 2005–10 *(continued)*

b. University Students Enrolled in Education Programs

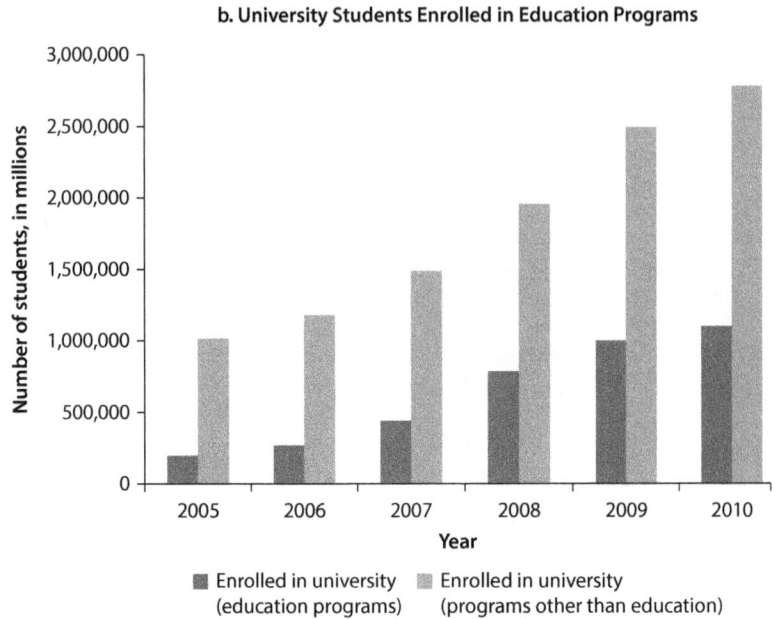

Source: Dashboard PDPT (Pangkalan Data Pendidikan Tinggi), Indonesia Ministry of Education and Culture, Directorate General of Higher Education: http://www.PDPT.dikti.go.id/dashboard/v002.

Note: The 1 million enrolled in education programs in 2010 are recent high school graduates and exclude the approximately 500,000 in-service teachers enrolled in Indonesia Open University.

attractiveness of the profession is more clearly visualized by the increase in the percentage of students enrolled in education programs, as shown in figure 4.1, panel b. The percentage increased from 15 percent before the Teacher Law to almost 30 percent in 2008. The 1 million enrolled in education programs in 2010 are recent high school graduates and exclude the approximately 500,000 in-service teachers enrolled in the Open University. Certification seems to have significantly increased the attractiveness of the profession.

One of the intended results of the certification program was that a more attractive teaching profession would increase the quality of teacher intake because higher-caliber high school graduates would want to become teachers. There are indications that, at least for some specific teacher education institutions, the demand for vacancies has increased and that in some cases the quality of the intake has gone up over time.

Figure 4.2 compares the attractiveness of education study programs with programs that are similar but are not for training to become a teacher across 15 universities in Indonesia. English language education, for example, received many more applicants than just English language and literature, and the number of applicants has been increasing at a faster rate. The same is true for mathematics and mathematics education. From 2005 to 2009, the number of applicants for mathematics education programs increased by 100 percent. The figure indicates

Figure 4.2 Number of Applicants to Selected Education and Other Study Programs at 15 Universities in Indonesia, 2005 and 2009

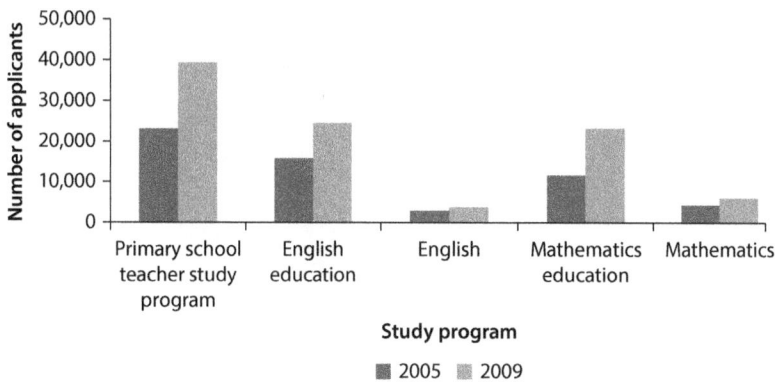

Source: Ministry of National Education 2009.

that these universities could have been more selective in enrolling the best candidates out of the increased pool of applications. Whether this has happened and whether it has increased the average quality of the accepted applicants, however, depends largely on whether the group of graduates applying to the college includes enough high-caliber candidates.

More competition for places is expected to have led to higher quality of those accepted. Figure 4.3 traces the average scores for the senior high school national exit examination for three different graduation cohorts (2006, 2008, and 2009). It compares the average scores of a sample of primary teacher candidates from 15 universities (the same 15 as used for the construction of figure 4.2) with the average scores of the total exiting population of senior high school students in the country. The first observation is that the average score of primary-school teacher candidates is higher than the national average. The second observation is that the scores of the new cohorts of teacher candidates tend to increase at a faster rate than the national average. If this trend continues, it could eventually lead to improvements in the quality of the future teaching service.

Teacher education institutions became more attractive in the five-year period leading up to 2010–11. The supply, however, has kept pace with the increase in demand, which has limited the beneficial effects of competition. As indicated in figure 4.1, the number of applicants who gained a position in a teacher education program saw a manifold increase.

The supply of and demand for vacancies in education study programs have increased to the point that an oversupply of newly graduated, highly motivated, and aspiring teachers is a relevant concern. Such an oversupply would present a new problem: even if the quality of new intake is higher on average, it does not necessarily mean that the best students eventually get the jobs. Indeed, finding jobs as (certified) teachers might be difficult in a situation where the number of

Figure 4.3 National Exam Scores of New Teacher Candidates Compared with All Senior Secondary Graduation Cohorts, 2006–09

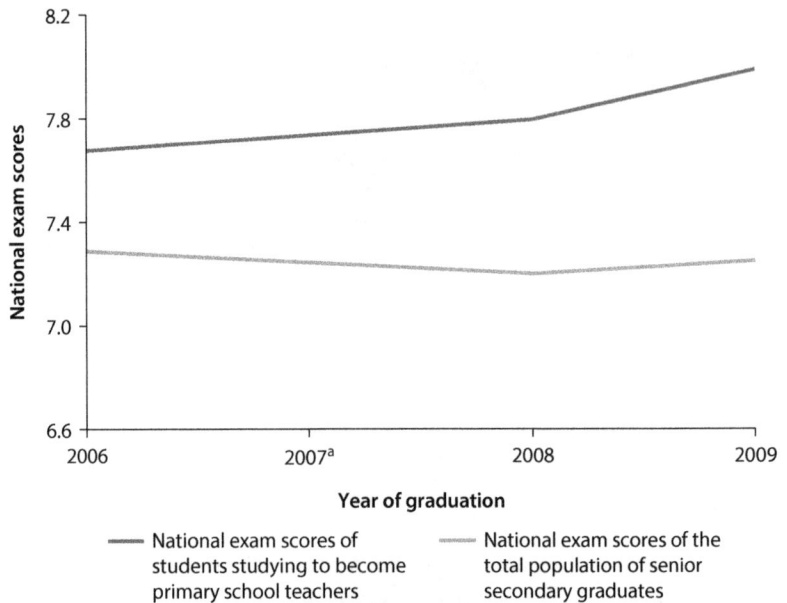

Year of graduation

— National exam scores of students studying to become primary school teachers

⸺ National exam scores of the total population of senior secondary graduates

Source: Scores of students studying to become primary school teachers from Ministry of National Education 2009. Scores of the total population of senior secondary graduates based on population-level data (school-level) published yearly by the Center for Educational Assessment, Research and Development Board, Indonesian Ministry of Education and Culture.
a. Comparative data for the 2007 cohorts are not available.

new teachers entering the market greatly exceeds the demand for teachers from schools. With around 3 million teachers currently active in the system, roughly 100,000 will retire each year.[1] With around 1 million students enrolled in preservice education programs today, it is expected that, for the years to come, about 250,000 new teachers will enter the labor market each year. Not all of these will be able to find jobs as teachers.

The disconnect between demand and supply in the labor market for teachers creates another concern about the quality of the teachers who finally end up being hired. Hiring procedures in Indonesia are not always efficient or based on merit, and it is not evident that systems are in place to guarantee that the best candidate will get the job. A second-order effect of the impending oversupply may be that current high-caliber candidates internalize this situation in their decision making and opt out of teaching careers—not because they do not want to become teachers but because they are uncertain about whether they will find jobs.

The system needs amendments to curb these unintended consequences of the certification program. Competition can be increased by requiring universities to produce the right number of graduates to meet labor market demands and by calling a halt to the proliferation of private universities of dubious quality. Policy makers are aware of this changing scenario, and commencing in 2013 the government has set an annual quota of 40,000 teacher candidates to enroll at private and state universities. This decision is intended to ensure that the number of student teachers admitted each year will match the number of teachers expected to retire four years later (when the cohort is graduating). In the past and in the near future, however, the inflow of new teachers to the system has exceeded and will exceed the outflow due to retirement.

Individual teachers deal with this situation by often approaching schools directly and applying informally with their curricula vitae. The school then employs these extra teachers using school funding (salaries paid for such teachers are often quite low), after which the teachers often attempt to gain greater permanency (for example, by seeking civil service status). This loose management of extra teachers by schools and district authorities is a major reason for the constant oversupply of teachers in the Indonesian school system.

The net results of these inefficiencies are clearly visible in table 4.1. The number of primary school teachers has increased by over 30 percent in five years. The increase in the number of teachers has outpaced the increase in the number of students over that same period (Cerdan-Infantes and Makarova 2013). Only much stricter regulation of teacher graduates and hiring will help balance the oversupply of teachers found in Indonesia—an issue to be examined further in chapter 6.

The Upgrading Channel: Certification as a Financial Incentive for Academic Upgrading

Teachers with a university four-year degree and with high rank in the civil service as well as very senior teachers qualify for certification. Because rank and seniority are not easily manipulated by individual teachers, those without these qualifications should normally obtain their four-year degrees. The prospect of receiving the professional allowance is a strong financial incentive to acquire this degree. The Open University—the traditional supplier of distance learning courses for upgrading teachers' knowledge and skills—reports on its website to have close to 500,000 teachers actively enrolled to upgrade their academic qualifications to the required level. In the process of upgrading to the four-year degree level, teachers' knowledge and pedagogical skills should increase. The extent to which this happens is ultimately an empirical question.

Figure 4.4 reports increases in the percentage of teachers with a four-year degree based on the teacher census of the Unique Identifier for Educators and Education Personnel (*Nomor Unik Pendidik dan Tenaga Kependidikan*, or NUPTK). The rising percentages suggest that the professional allowance had important effects by encouraging unqualified teachers to upgrade academic qualifications. From other data sources, such as the recent 2011 Village Potential Statistics (PODES) school facility census, even higher percentages emerge. Based on calculations from PODES, close to 44 percent of primary school teachers currently have a four-year degree.[2] These are important changes to the situation preceding the Teacher Law and are quite likely directly attributable to

Table 4.1 Number and Education of Primary School Teachers in Indonesia, 2006 and 2011

	Untrained	1-year postsecondary diploma	2-year postsecondary diploma	3-year postsecondary diploma	4-year academic diploma or 4-year degree	Master's degree	Doctorate	Total
2006	414,310	11,673	586,709	24,431	209,798	1,198	4	1,248,123
2011	388,454	11,647	449,720	211,406	578,111	5,579	8	1,644,925
Change (no.)	−25,856	−26	−136,989	186,975	368,313	4,381	4	396,802
Change (%)	−6	0	−23	765	176	366	100	32

Sources: Based on 2006 SIMPTK/NUPTK and 2011 NUPTK teacher census.

Note: Teachers of Islamic schools are not included in these figures. SIMPTK = Management Information System for Educators and Education Personnel. NUPTK = Unique Identifiers for Educators and Education Personnel.

Figure 4.4 Proportion of Teachers with a Four-Year Postsecondary Degree in Indonesia, 2006–11

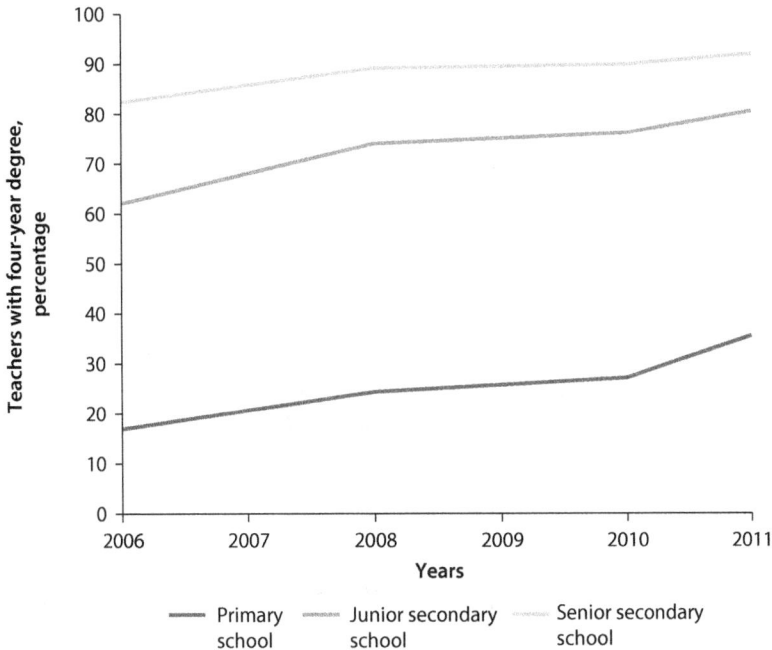

Source: Calculations based on NUPTK/SIMPTK teacher censuses of 2006, 2008, 2010, and 2011.
Note: Teachers of Islamic schools are not included in these figures. NUPTK = Unique Identifier for Educators and Education Personnel. SIMPTK = Management Information System for Educators and Education Personnel.

the financial incentives internal to the certification program. In some cases the upgrading was made possible through central, provincial, and district government scholarships.

This wave of academic upgrading has only recently started, and many teachers are, in one form or another, still in the middle of the process. Thus, the full scale of the effects of this academic upgrading should only appear over the years to come. The ultimate test, perhaps, will be to continuously monitor the changes in Program for International Student Assessment (PISA) and Trends in International Mathematics and Science Study (TIMSS) scores: does a massive increase in the number of teachers with an academic diploma lead to simultaneous increases in the students' PISA and TIMSS scores?

To date, there do not appear to be any improvements that are systematic across all subjects, at least not in Indonesia's PISA scores (see figure 4.5). Given uncertainty about whether Indonesia will continue to participate in cross-country comparison studies such as PISA and TIMSS, it would be useful for Indonesia to set up its own system for monitoring student achievement gains over time and across geographical areas. The current national examinations given at the end of grades 6, 9, and 12 are inadequate for this purpose.

Figure 4.5 Indonesian PISA Scores, by Subject, 2000–09

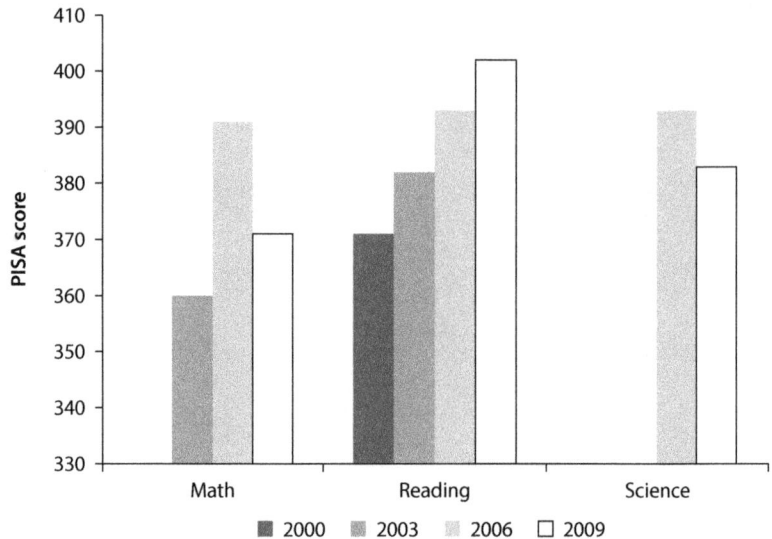

Source: OECD 2010.

Note: PISA = Program for International Student Assessment. Only the scores for reading can be straightforwardly compared across all four periods. Trend comparisons for math and science are possible only for a shorter period (OECD 2010).

The upgrading mechanism is likely to have the largest impact in primary schools because at the time of the Teacher Law in 2005, only about 40 percent of primary school teachers qualified for certification (mostly because of rank or age). Seventy percent of the junior secondary school teachers qualified in 2005/06, mainly because a four-year degree was already required before the introduction of the law. Figure 4.6 shows the percentage of teachers who qualified for certification at the start of the program and the criteria on which this qualification was based.

Further evidence on the effects on schools of teacher upgrading can be provided through a database collected by the government in partnership with the World Bank. The study sample comprised 240 public primary schools and 120 public junior secondary schools—representative of approximately 40 percent of the public primary and junior secondary schools in Indonesia. All core-subject teachers[3] and all students in these schools were administered a multiple-choice subject matter test. Furthermore, all core-subject teachers were interviewed. The data collection was repeated three times: a baseline was held in November 2009, a midline in April 2011, and an endline in April 2012 (the latter not yet available for analysis). The study has an experimental component that is used to evaluate the certification process and the effects of unconditional teacher salary increases on teacher performance. These results are presented in the next section about the behavioral channel (See the Introduction and De Ree *et al.* 2012 for a more detailed description of this study).

Figure 4.6 Percentage of Teachers Qualifying for Certification at Start of Indonesian Certification Program, 2005/06

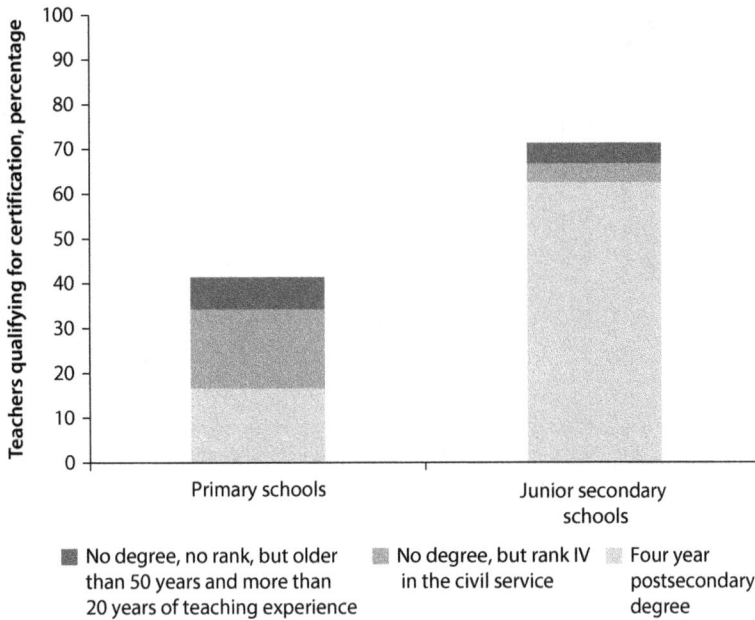

Source: Calculations based on NUPTK/SIMPTK teacher census of 2006.
Note: NUPTK = Unique Identifier for Educators and Education Personnel. SIMPTK = Management Information System for Educators and Education Personnel.

The survey data confirm that academic upgrading is continuing on a massive scale. Only a small fraction of teachers with a four-year degree report to be further upgrading their academic qualifications, as shown in figure 4.7. Around 30 percent of the few teachers who qualify for certification based on the civil service rank or seniority still try to upgrade academic qualifications, although they do not strictly need to in order to be qualified for certification. The vast majority of the unqualified teachers (70 percent), however, are actively engaged in the upgrading process. These data show clearly that teachers take the incentives provided by the certification program seriously. The financial incentives for academic upgrading seem to work.

The potential for quality improvements through academic upgrading are enormous, but they are not automatic. Most teachers who upgrade to the four-year degree level already have a two-year postsecondary diploma. These teachers therefore really "upgrade" rather than start a full-fledged four-year academic program. Upgrading typically happens remotely through the Open University but also, more and more, through other higher-education institutions accredited to offer the four-year degree program in education.

The quality of the Indonesian universities is highly variable. Figure 4.8 shows that primary school teachers both with and without four-year degrees do rather

Figure 4.7 Proportion of Indonesian Teachers Upgrading Academic Qualifications, by Certification Status, 2011

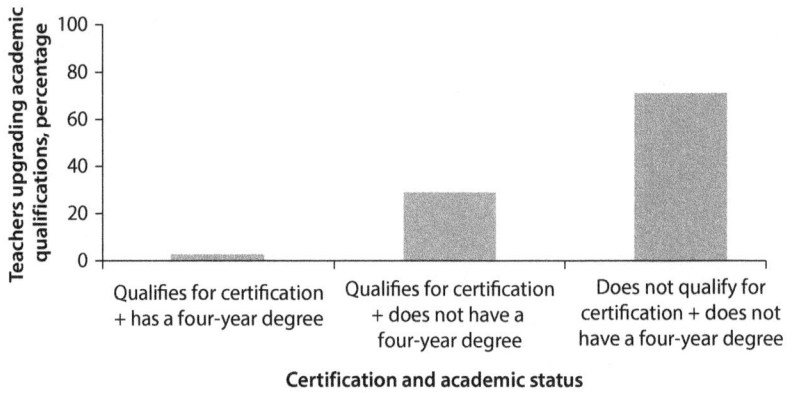

Source: Calculations based on survey information from the teacher certification impact assessment study.
Note: The teacher certification impact assessment study included 1,746 primary school teachers from a sample of 240 public primary schools in Indonesia.

Figure 4.8 Subject Matter Test Scores of Primary School Teachers in Indonesia, by Four-Year Academic Degree Status, 2011

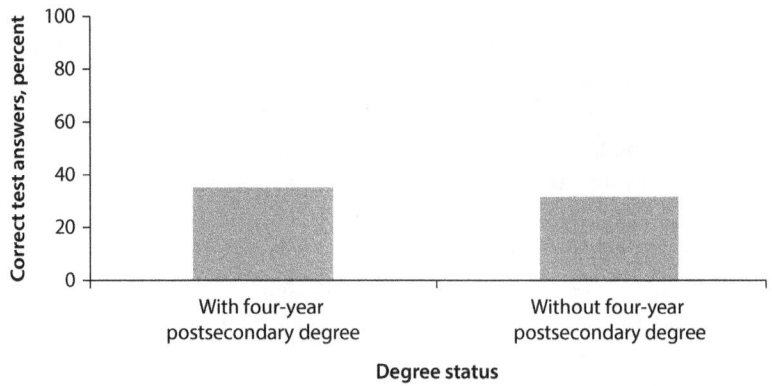

Source: Calculations based on subject matter test information from the teacher certification impact assessment study.
Note: The teacher certification impact study included 1,714 primary school teachers from a sample of 240 public primary schools in Indonesia.

poorly on the subject matter test that was part of the data collection for the impact assessment study discussed briefly above. The tests were designed by the government's Centre of Educational Assessment and were explicitly designed to measure competencies deemed necessary for effective teaching. Teachers with degrees perform somewhat better than teachers without degrees.[4] (Whether these data differ according to the grade being taught is discussed in box 4.1.) These differences are smaller than expected and suggest that teachers, on average, do not gain enough extra knowledge from obtaining a degree. A minimum

Box 4.1 Teacher Education and Competency by Grade

An interesting aside from the data on teacher background (with or without a four-year degree and subject matter competency) relates to how these data differ according to the grade being taught. One could argue that, given the importance of ensuring a strong foundation for learning in the early grades of primary school (especially for children who have not had a preschool experience), it would be essential for principals to assign highly qualified teachers to those grades. Figure B4.1.1 shows the data from the impact assessment study broken down by grade.

Figure B4.1.1 Primary School Teacher Qualifications and Test Scores in Indonesia, by Grade Level Taught

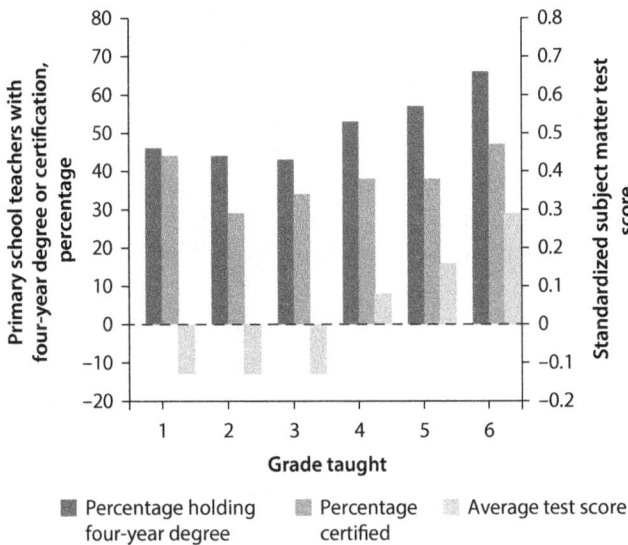

Source: Calculations based on subject matter test information from the teacher certification impact assessment study.

Note: The green bars indicate the average standardized subject matter test score (right y-axis) of all teachers in a given grade level regardless of degree or certification status. The teacher certification impact study included 1,714 primary school teachers from a sample of 240 public primary schools in Indonesia.

box continues next page

Box 4.1 Teacher Education and Competency by Grade *(continued)*

The percentage of teachers in grades 1–3 holding a four-year degree is considerably lower than that of the teachers in grades 4–6. More important, the standardized scores for the subject matter test show dramatic differences—much lower for the teachers of the early grades than for those of the upper grades. In a system where a relatively small percentage of grade 1 entering teachers have had preschool experience and where later student achievement (for example, in the PISA and TIMSS studies) is of great concern, the fact that the teachers with least subject matter mastery are assigned to the youngest pupils should encourage both the Ministry of Education and Culture (in terms of national policy) and individual principals (in terms of teacher assignments) to reconsider how they can guarantee a high quality of teachers in the grades that need them most.

---

amount of subject matter knowledge is a prerequisite for being an effective teacher. This knowledge deficit may, therefore, appear to present a challenge for the future.

One question regarding teacher knowledge is whether teachers who received their four-year degrees in a more full-time, preservice, perhaps residential setting (say, before the Teacher Law was passed) have more knowledge and skill than teachers who have earned their degrees over a longer period of time, at a distance, or more recently (through the greater number of institutions now accredited to provide the degree). On the one hand, perhaps the online distance learning methods prevalent today; the considerable amount of the required curriculum gaining recognition as prior learning; and the mushrooming of new, smaller, and private (even if accredited) institutions offering the four-year degree add up to a less rigorous approach to obtaining the four-year degree and therefore to less impact on teacher content knowledge, pedagogical skills, and student outcomes. On the other hand, it could be argued that teachers with more recent, presumably up-to-date content and more explicitly child-centered methods would perform better than those trained a decade or more ago in a more traditional style. The survey information is not sufficiently informative to support either one of these theories.

The authors did, however, investigate whether teachers who actively participated in the upgrading process between the baseline and midline data collections gained more knowledge than those who did not. The group of teachers who acquired a four-year degree between baseline and midline and those who report to be actively in the process of upgrading were compared to the rest. At baseline in November 2009, the *upgraders* scored lower than the others. But after two years of actively engaging in the upgrading process, they scored higher than the others. The relative increase, however, is relatively small and not statistically significant, which confirms the pattern previously observed in figure 4.8.

On the whole, therefore, having a four-year degree is an imperfect marker for subject matter knowledge of teachers. Many teachers without a four-year degree do very well on these subject matter tests. At the same time, a fair number of teachers with a four-year degree do extremely poorly. This fact can be used as an argument against using objective indicators such as formal degrees as the primary basis for admission to the certification process. Whether academic degrees are useful indicators of trainable competencies such as subject matter knowledge depends in part on the quality of the universities. Distinguishing high-quality teachers from low-quality teachers on all levels of competency is even more challenging; the huge variability in quality among teachers is typically not easily explained by observable indicators such as academic qualifications or experience (Rivkin, Hanushek, and Kain 2005).

Primary school teachers with a four-year degree have more subject knowledge than those who do not, and some of that seems to be due to their education. The differences, however, are not large, perhaps suggesting that the process of academic upgrading is not leading to the large increases in teacher quality that Indonesia needs to catch up with economically more developed nations.

The evidence provided in figure 4.8 is only part of the story, however. As the literature suggests, there is much variation in teacher quality related to student learning outcomes that is not easily explained. Figure 4.8 focuses only on the subject matter knowledge of teachers. Teachers, however, might acquire a variety of pedagogical skills when undertaking the upgrading process.

It is not straightforward to evaluate whether academic upgrading leads to improvements in student learning outcomes and by how much. Experimental or quasi-experimental evidence on the effects of teachers' academic upgrading on student learning outcomes are not available for Indonesia. However, some evidence does shed light on the issue.

Teacher academic qualifications and student learning gains are positively related, even after controlling for teachers' subject matter knowledge. Figure 4.9 estimates the additional learning gains of having a teacher with a four-year degree. It attempts to answer the question: do students of teachers with four-year degrees progress faster? The answer is affirmative.

Learning gains here are an estimated 0.15 standard deviations higher for students with a teacher with a four-year degree. This "four-year degree" effect can be broken down into a subject matter component (0.05 standard deviations) and an additional effect (0.10). The analysis suggests that teachers with academic degrees are better teachers, not only because they score (slightly) higher on subject matter tests but also because they have additional skills such as pedagogical skills.

It should be realized that the evidence presented in figure 4.9 shows correlations that are not necessarily causal. Teachers with a four-year academic degree have students that do better for a variety of reasons, only one of which may be that these teachers are truly better teachers. A similar correlation can be found if students from better socioeconomic backgrounds are sent to schools with a higher proportion of teachers with four-year degrees. Also, higher ability and greater motivation make some teachers more likely to obtain a four-year degree.

Figure 4.9　Value Added by Primary School Teachers with a Four-Year Degree in Indonesia

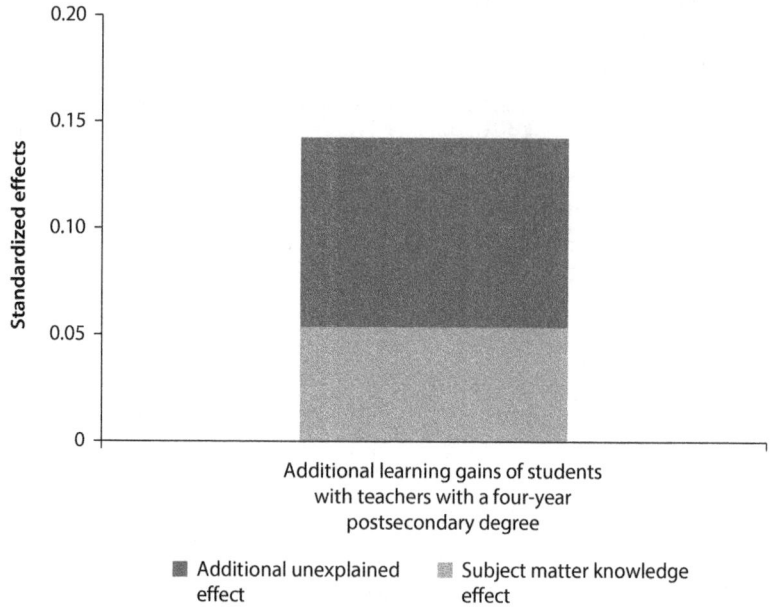

Source: Analysis based on data from the teacher certification impact assessment study.
Note: The figure is constructed based on a regression of midline student test scores, baseline student test scores, the (subject matter) test score of the teacher, and a dummy variable that indicates whether the teacher has a four-year degree. Both teacher subject matter knowledge and the indicator for having a teacher with a four-year degree appear statistically significant in this regression. This indicates that subject matter knowledge matters, and that the academic degree of teachers matters over and above a difference in subject matter knowledge.

As a consequence, teachers with a degree perhaps are not better because they have a degree, but rather because they are more motivated and capable to begin with. More in-depth research is needed to make any final claims about whether academic upgrading works and, consequently, how well it works. We cannot be certain, therefore, whether this finding can be used to project the effects of academic upgrading into the future. But if all teachers who upgrade to the four-year degree level would improve learning outcomes by 0.15 standard deviations, the total effects of upgrading will indeed be substantial.

Another notable fact of figure 4.9 is that the 4 percentage point difference in teacher test scores between teachers with and without four-year degrees (see figure 4.8) is associated with a 0.05 standard deviation increase in learning gains. That such (apparently) small differences in teachers' subject knowledge are associated with fairly substantial student learning gains indicates that teachers' subject matter knowledge is important. The subject matter component shown in the figure is smaller than the additional, unexplained effect because differences in subject knowledge for teachers with and without degrees are really quite small. From a policy point of view, the findings suggest that large learning gains can be achieved by attempting to increase subject knowledge among teachers.

The Behavioral Channel: Impact of the Certification Process and the Professional Allowance as Shown from a Randomized Field Experiment

One of the well-established results of the recent empirical literature on teacher effectiveness is that there are very good and very bad teachers in a population: teachers matter! There is much less certainty, however, about what makes for a good or a bad teacher. Rivken, Hanushek, and Kain (2005) find, for example, that formal certificates, degrees, experience, and so forth explain little of the variation in teacher quality. This finding suggests that whereas some teachers are better in delivering a message than others, this skill is not easily acquired from either teacher education institutions or experience. Whether money matters depends in large part on whether there is some dormant "unused" potential that can be realized if additional incentives appear. In other words, one argument is that teachers could do better, but they hold back because they are not paid enough.

This chapter presents experimental evidence on the effects of certification (and the associated professional allowance) through the behavioral channel—that is, the effects of certification through changes in motivation or behavior of qualified in-service teachers. The analysis basically evaluates the effects of doubling a teacher's income, although certified teachers would have also successfully passed a portfolio assessment or graduated from a 90-hour training course.

This is the first empirical study that attempts to evaluate the relationship between permanent, unconditional pay increases and teacher productivity using experimental methods. The experimental nature of the study means that there can be high levels of confidence in the findings presented here. (See De Ree *et al.* [2012] for more details on the methodology and findings.) Furthermore, the study is unique in that it evaluates the effects of a real-world program that is a very expensive one in the context of Indonesia.

At the moment teachers become certified, neither the continuation of the certified status nor the payment of the professional allowance is conditional on subsequent performance. This evaluation, therefore, complements a rapidly expanding body of research that evaluates the effects of bonus payment or pay-for-performance schemes. These schemes link pay levels explicitly to the performance of teachers. Teacher performance can be measured based on inputs (such as low teacher absenteeism levels) or outputs (such as high student learning gains). As discussed earlier, it has been shown in some developing-country settings that pay-for-performance schemes can work but also that there are perhaps insurmountable difficulties associated with implementing such schemes in real-world contexts.[5]

The Indonesian teacher salary system leaves little room for explicitly rewarding top performers individually. Indonesia is, in that respect, not very different from many other countries in the world. Salary levels are determined based on academic degrees and seniority. Moreover, the current design of Indonesia's certification program does not allow for merit-based rewards. It is largely true that the most experienced and best-educated teachers entered the certification process first, but eventually all teachers must be certified by 2015.

Figure 4.10 Pathways to Certification of Teachers in Indonesia, 2006–11

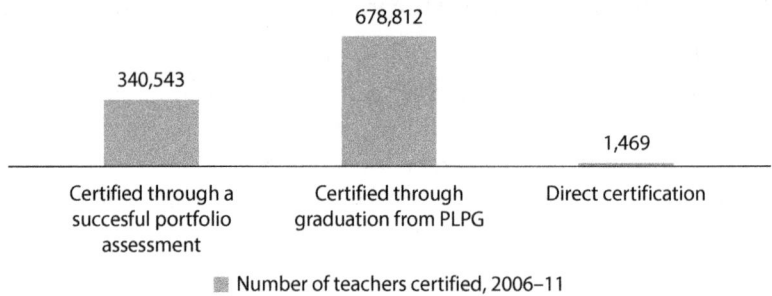

Number of teachers certified, 2006–11

Source: Data provided by an Indonesian Ministry of Education and Culture official in 2012.
Note: PLPG = Education and Training for the Teaching Profession (*Pendidikan dan Latihan Profesi Guru*), which is the 90-hour training program for in-service teachers to gain certification.

This experimental evaluation is relevant for at least two reasons: First, unconditional salary increases are much easier to implement than pay-for-performance schemes. This is especially true in developing countries where monitoring systems to operate functional pay-for-performance schemes are generally not well established. Indeed, Indonesia's certification program is currently being rolled out across the country and, by 2011, had certified about 1 million teachers. Second, there is no experimental evidence on the effects of large, permanent, and unconditional salary increases on teacher performance (as measured by student learning outcomes).

As mentioned earlier, there has been an evolution in the procedure for gaining certification—from an original option of portfolio assessment (for those who failed to enroll in a 90-hour training program) to the current situation where almost all candidates go through (and rarely fail) the 90-hour course. Figure 4.10 illustrates the pathways to certification and the number of teachers using these pathways.

The income for certified teachers practically doubled as a result of certification. Based on findings from the teacher certification impact study, close to 100 percent of teachers who entered the certification process in a given year had been certified in the next. Around 30 percent of teachers reported having received payment of the professional allowance one year after entering the certification procedure. Two years after entering the certification quota, all teachers had received the allowance. Baseline data were collected before certifying the teachers who were targeted by the intervention but after they enrolled in the quota. At midline, all teachers who entered the 2009 quota (which includes the teachers who were targeted by the intervention) were certified and were paid.

Money Affects Teacher Behavior

The survey also found that because of certification, teachers rely less on second jobs and have fewer difficulties financially supporting their households. Figure 4.11 presents the effects of certification on teacher characteristics.[6] Overall, the livelihoods of teachers have improved. Certification can lead to a 27

Figure 4.11 Effects of Certification on Selected Teacher Characteristics in Indonesia, 2009–11

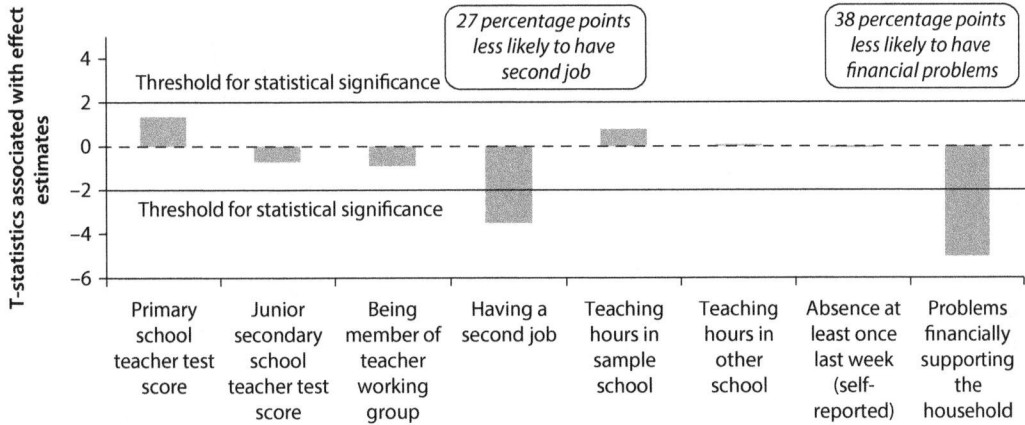

Source: De Ree *et al.* 2012.

percentage point decrease in the likelihood of teachers holding a second job because the professional allowance decreases the need to rely on such jobs to supplement income. This income effect is also reflected in a decrease in the number of teachers who report problems financially supporting their households. However, there is no evidence that certification makes teachers more likely to participate in teacher working groups, teach more hours, or self-report to be absent[7] less often.

The first two bars present the effects of certification on teacher subject knowledge. As part of the study, teachers were tested on their subject matter knowledge with a multiple-choice test. Subject matter tests are, admittedly, an incomplete measure of teachers' overall competencies, although they do measure subject matter knowledge that is a prerequisite but not sufficient for overall teacher quality. Certification has not caused any measurable changes to these scores. The certification process and the payment of the professional allowance do not make teachers more knowledgeable. This finding is hardly a surprise; however, it does indicate that the 90-hour training, which was part of the certification procedure for many teachers, is perhaps not quite sufficient to bring the competence of teachers to the next level.

Changes in Time on Task

To be eligible to receive the professional allowance, teachers must teach a minimum of 24 period-hours. This regulation should force teachers who teach less to find employment in other (nearby) schools. But given the current oversupply of teachers in the system, it might not be easy to find these additional hours. It was assumed that the 24-hour workload rule would help to push surplus teachers out of the system. Because the pressure on teachers to adhere to the 24-hour rule is much higher in treatment schools than in the control schools, it would be expected that the former teachers would teach more hours. This appears not to be the case.

Figure 4.12 Student-Teacher Ratios in Indonesia, by School Level, 1995–2010

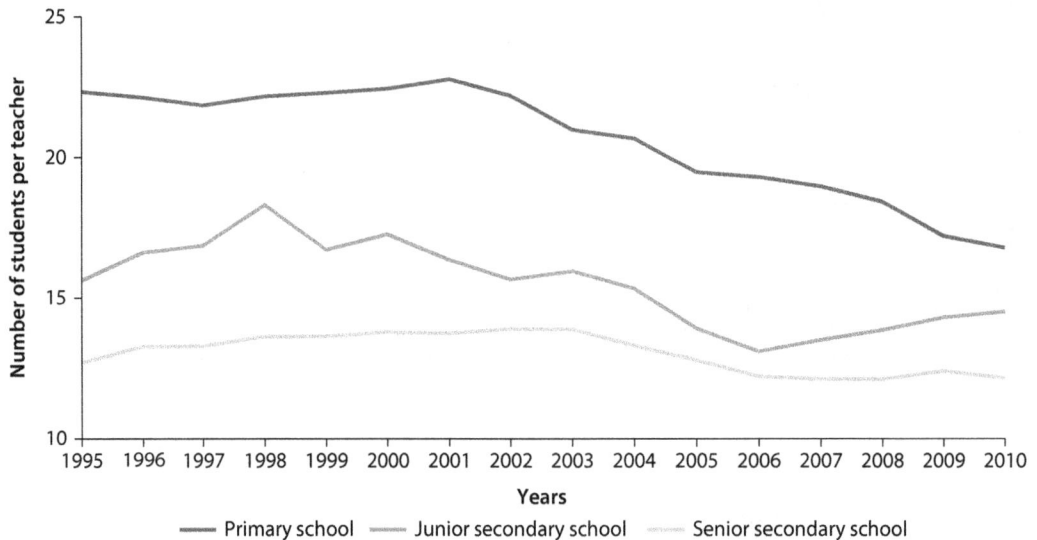

Source: Ministry of National Education *Statistical Yearbook.*

The idea that the 24-hour rule has not worked as planned can also be inferred following trends in student-teacher ratios. Although there have been weak increases in student-teacher ratios in junior secondary schools since 2006, there is still a steady decrease in primary schools. Thus, the implementation of the 24-hour workload rule has not led to the desired improvement in efficiency in the use of teachers, although figure 4.12 suggests that the rule has worked better with junior secondary schools.

Recent changes in regulations are expected to have additional beneficial effects. For example, the recently introduced restrictions on team teaching will now prevent schools from simply appointing two teachers to single classes and double-counting teaching hours just to build teacher workloads up to the 24-hour minimum workload to ensure that teachers receive the professional allowance. It seems unlikely, however, that the 24-hour rule alone can solve the problem with teacher oversupply in the country. (See chapter 6 for further discussion of this issue.)

No Apparent Changes in Learning Outcomes

Professional certification increases the well-being of teachers, but does it also benefit students? Figure 4.13 presents the estimates of the effects of certifying teachers on the learning outcomes of their students. There is no evidence that certification makes teachers teach better, at least not in ways that are measurable through student test scores. The effects shown are well within the boundaries for statistical significance. The first column relates to the effects of certifying a primary school class teacher on student learning outcomes in primary school. The second to fifth columns present the effects of certifying a subject teacher in junior secondary school on student learning gains in the specified subject.[8] Overall, the experimental evidence presented in figure 4.13 shows that the certification process and the payment of the professional allowance do not benefit student learning. (Box 4.2 describes the results of another empirical investigation that draws similar conclusions.)

In summary, fewer certified teachers have second jobs, and fewer worry about providing adequate financial support to their families, but these changes in behavior have not led to significant improvements in teacher productivity. With regard to the broader picture, the conclusion is that the greatest impact of certification is expected from the academic upgrading of teachers who did not yet qualify before the law was passed and from the higher quality of new inflow. Variability in the quality of the upgrading courses and the apparently large increases in supply of seats in university programs in education, however, also limit the potential effectiveness of these channels.

Figure 4.13 Effects of Teacher Certification on Student Learning Gains in Indonesia, 2009–11

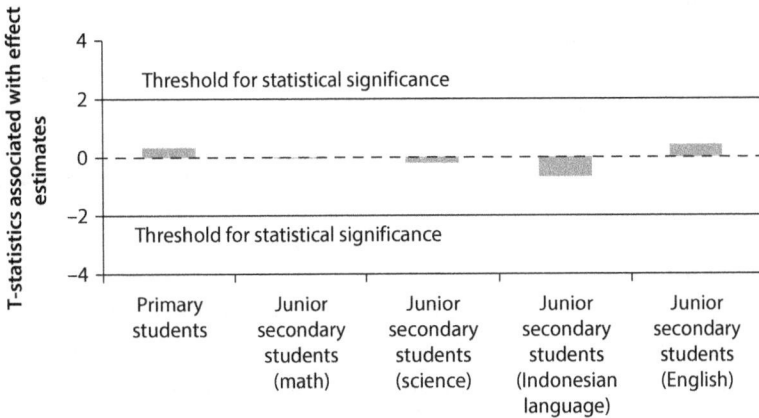

Source: De Ree *et al.* 2012.

Box 4.2 The Effectiveness of the Certification Process

The results of the randomized field experiment discussed above indicate that the actual process of certification (either through a portfolio assessment or after passing the 90-hour training course) and the doubling of income do not lead to learning improvements in the classroom.

A 90-hour training course is possibly not sufficiently intensive to lead to significant changes. A study by the ministry assessed the capacities of teachers graduating from this 90-hour training course (Ministry of National Education 2010). The analysis does not provide a definitive before-and-after comparison to assess quality improvements. It does make

box continues next page

Box 4.2 The Effectiveness of the Certification Process *(continued)*

some judgments about whether teachers who graduate from the course really meet the minimum standards along the lines of the four competencies spelled out in the Teacher Law: professional, pedagogical, personal, and social.

This face-to-face course—supposedly with 30 hours of theory and 60 hours of practice (but with many hours taken over by rest breaks and administrative matters)—provides a peer-teaching experience as well as observation and feedback on teaching skills demonstrated by participants. The curriculum follows the competency requirements of the Teacher Law and is based on a child-centered, active learning model. Instructors are university-trained with minimum qualifications of a master's degree and at least 10 years of teaching experience. There is a separate curriculum for each category of teacher. The course is structured around the four competencies mandated by the Teacher Law.

The basic curriculum of the 90-hour program requires participants to complete 90 hours (in 50-minute lessons) as specified in the guidelines. This includes general content, subject content, and a written test consisting of a pretest and a posttest. In the learning process, instructors use multimedia and follow the principles of active, creative, joyful, and effective learning. In practice, participants are trained using case analysis, group discussion, and peer teaching (three days continuously with the instructor acting as a supervisor). The learning approach adopted is intended to stimulate participants into discovering their potential as teachers and to become sensitive to new problems. This interaction results in a two-way learning process (geared both for the more active participants who might raise an issue and to the less active who may find a solution to a problem by themselves).

The 90-hour course is therefore focused on both professional (subject) and pedagogical (methodology) competencies. Personal and social competencies are integrated into the other activities, which are assessed continuously throughout the duration of the course. The assessment at the end of the course is based on four components: (a) 35 percent from written examination; (b) 40 percent from practicum (teaching); (c) 10 percent from participation; and (d) 15 percent from peer teaching. Scores from the four areas form 75 percent of the final determination toward certification. The remaining 25 percent is the score originally obtained in the portfolio assessment, if applicable. The final test verifies that the participating teacher has met the standards in the four competency areas as referred to in the Teacher Law and subsequent regulations.

In 2010 a qualitative study was undertaken to explore the impact of the 90-hour course on teacher knowledge and skills (Ministry of National Education 2010). The course was already being taken by approximately 50 percent of the applicants, and it became important to identify whether the course: (a) increased the competency and performance of teachers, (b) established a pattern of regular developmental activities to be taken by teachers, and (c) identified potential strategies that could be used to enhance the professional skills of teachers.

Instruments to gather data were based on the standards established in the four competency domains. In the study, two major areas were assessed: (a) subject knowledge

box continues next page

Box 4.2 The Effectiveness of the Certification Process *(continued)*

Figure B4.2.1 Ratings of Professional and Pedagogical Competence of Teachers after Training in Indonesia, 2010

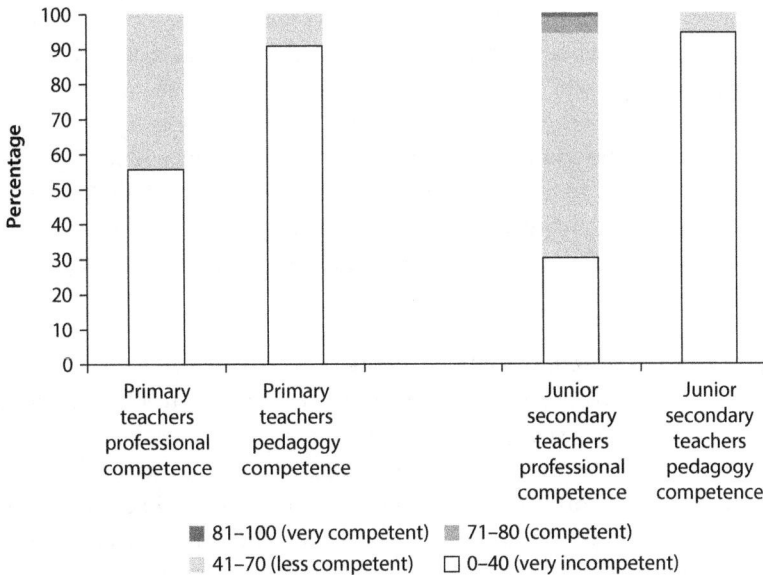

■ 81–100 (very competent) ▨ 71–80 (competent)
▨ 41–70 (less competent) □ 0–40 (very incompetent)

Source: Ministry of National Education 2010.
Note: The teachers assessed had completed a 90-hour training course required for certification. "Professional" competence refers to subject knowledge. "Pedagogical" competence refers to teaching methods.

with a competency test, and (b) classroom performance through completion of a questionnaire on the teacher's work by the principal. A score of 1–4 (very incompetent [1], incompetent [2], competent [3], and very competent [4]) was given for each item. Figure B4.2.1 was prepared from the data collected to illustrate the levels of proficiency of the professional and pedagogical competencies of the sample of teachers measured.

In general, the scores suggest that most primary school teachers had less than optimal training results in terms of both professional and pedagogical competence. More than 90 percent of the teachers who passed the 90-hour training course were classified as "very incompetent" in the pedagogical domain. Scores were also inadequate for professional capacities (that is, subject knowledge), but they were considered better than the pedagogy scores. Competency scores for personal and social competencies were higher and generally not below standard.

In regard to junior secondary school teachers, the test results showed that most had less than optimal training in terms of both professional and pedagogical competence. This is an important finding and an indication that the desired level of support needs to be much higher than the current structure provides.

Conclusions

Certification sets minimum quality standards and provides recognition and higher levels of pay for teachers who adhere to these standards. In the case of Indonesia, because of the instruments used for the certification, the certification program has had a number of different consequences: The attractiveness of the teaching profession has increased. More high school graduates apply for places in the country's teacher education institutions, and there is some indication that the increased competitiveness has also led to increased quality of the candidates enrolled. At the same time, however, universities providing teacher education have responded to market forces, leading to an increased intake of new students. This process might further contribute to the general oversupply of teachers in the country and dampen the beneficial effects on the average quality of the intake.

Impact of Certification: The Evidence

Certification has provided the financial incentive for teachers to upgrade to the four-year degree level, which applies to most of the teachers currently active in the system. Although academic upgrading of the majority of the teaching forces should, at least intuitively, lead to important increases in student learning gains, the evidence provided in this chapter shows that such a result is not automatic. For example, teachers with degrees do not display much higher levels of subject matter knowledge than teachers without degrees. But, at the same time, there are correlations between student learning gains and academic degrees of teachers that cannot be explained solely by subject matter knowledge differences between teachers with and without degrees: teachers with degrees seem to be better teachers for reasons other than their subject matter knowledge.

The general conclusion drawn from the evidence, perhaps somewhat prematurely, is that the process of academic upgrading itself (currently happening at a massive scale) does not automatically translate into substantial steps forward in terms of the quality of teaching. This conclusion implies that the universities supplying these degrees should be rigorously controlled in terms of the quality of the training they provide and properly accredited when they do.

The law mandates that all Indonesian teachers must be certified by 2015.[9] All of them therefore go through the certification process and receive the professional allowance at some point in their careers. This chapter has discussed experimental evidence on the effects of certifying teachers and doubling their income. The certification tool used at the beginning of the reform fell short of measuring competence; as a result, a number of teachers who lacked minimum subject knowledge and pedagogical skills received double income but did not improve the outcomes of their students. However, teachers did respond to their new status by refusing second jobs and by being much less likely to have financial difficulties. Teachers' welfare and well-being have improved.

There is no evidence that the certification procedure and the increased levels of pay have led to better performance in the classroom. It seems that there is no dormant, unused potential that can be activated by paying teachers more money. This finding is not surprising, given that there are no clear theoretical reasons for why salary increases that are not conditional on classroom performance or further professional development would lead to better performance. It is also not surprising given the earlier analysis of the civil service mentality of many (mostly older) teachers who have focused for many years more on "educating" their students than on "teaching" them.

All evidence combined suggests that efforts must be made to closely monitor the upgrading process and make sure that academic upgrading, which currently happens at a massive scale, is of high quality. At the same time, the increased popularity of the teaching profession among young high school graduates should be used to select the best among the pool of applicants rather than to increase the levels of intake.

Improving the Rules of the Game

The Indonesian government realizes the huge benefits the certification program could have in improving the quality of the system. Despite the pressure of various interest groups such as the teacher associations, the Ministry of Education and Culture has made changes to the system that are likely to improve it. Whereas the first batches of teachers passed the certification process only through an assessment of a portfolio of past training and professional experience, later batches had to pass a 90-hour training program to become certified. The latest batch, which entered the certification quota in 2012, also needed to pass an entrance examination for this 90-hour training. (Even though close to 90 percent of the enrollees passed this test, it implied an additional selection on quality.)

Notes

1. The 100,000 is a rough estimate, and it may differ from year to year. With 3 million teachers in the system, and with an average length of service of 30 years, the number of retirees is estimated at 100,000 per year. Because of the skewed distribution of age in the population of teachers, however, retirement figures over the next 10 years are likely to be higher than 100,000 per year.

2. The difference between the NUPTK and the PODES school census is perhaps due to imperfect updating of the NUPTK census, which was established in 2006 as SIMPTK (Management Information System for Educators and Education Personnel, *Sistem Informasi Manajemen Pendidik dan Tenaga Kependidikan*). The figures of 2006 are therefore perhaps more likely to be accurate than the later ones. The increase from 2010 to 2011 may also be partly attributed to administrative data updates.

3. Core-subject teachers are class teachers in primary schools and Indonesian language, English language, mathematics, and science (biology and physics) teachers in junior secondary schools.

4. Note, however, that the difference in test scores is statistically significant at the 1 percent level, and, even though the 4 percentage point difference seems small, it still amounts to about 0.3 standard deviations in the population.

5. There are theoretical reasons to believe that pay explicitly tied to performance would work better than pay that is not (in which case the financial incentive to perform is lacking). The practical implementation of pay-for-performance schemes in the real world, however, is not straightforward at all. The main concern is whether measures of "value added"—that is, average learning gains of students of a particular teacher—are sufficiently accurate measures of teacher performance (see, for example, Guarino, Reckdase, and Wooldridge [2011]). Also, difficulties with practical implementation are one likely reason why pay-for-performance schemes are not adopted on a large scale.

6. The empirical specification used to obtain the results of figure 4.12 is one in which the outcome variable of interest (for example, a dummy variable of having a second job) is regressed on the baseline value, a full set of district dummy variables, and a dummy variable that indicates whether a teacher is certified or not. To account for nonrandom selection, the certification dummy is instrumented with the random treatment indicator that measures whether a school is in the treatment or the control group. The procedure obtains so-called local average treatment effects. This measures the average effect of certification on the group of teachers that was granted preferential access to the certification process in 2009. It can be seen as the effect of certification on those teachers who would normally enter the certification quota in 2010 or later. A final note is that, for observations that did not have baseline values (new teachers or teachers who were absent at baseline), the baseline scores are set to zero. Included is an additional dummy variable that is marked as "one" if baseline scores are missing. Similar effects are found, however, if the model is run on a balanced panel—that is, only on those observations for which there are baseline and midline observations. See De Ree *et al.* (2012) for more details.

7. A more generally accepted way of measuring absenteeism is by doing surprise visits. This was not done in this study.

8. The teacher survey and the information on the answer sheets of students were used to match teachers to students. The results presented in figure B4.2.1 were obtained using an empirical model similar to that used for the results of figure 4.12. The midline score of students was regressed on the baseline score, a full set of district dummies, and a dummy variable that indicates whether the student had a certified teacher over the past year. This indicator was instrumented with a dummy variable indicating whether the student's school was treatment or control. Here, also, baseline values were set to zero if they were not available (for example, for first-grade students at midline, there are no baseline scores). This procedure was accounted for by including a dummy variable that is "one" if baseline scores are not available.

9. In fact, in the current regulation, all civil servants and all government-hired contract teachers should be certified by 2015. School-hired contract teachers who are not explicitly recognized by the district government are not eligible for certification even if they have a four-year postsecondary degree.

References

Cerdan-Infantes, P., and Y. Makarova. 2013. *Spending More or Spending Better: Improving Education Financing in Indonesia.* Jakarta: World Bank.

De Ree, J., K. Muralidharan, M. Pradhan, and H. Rogers. 2012. "Double for What? The Impact of Unconditional Teacher Salary Increases on Performance." Unpublished manuscript, World Bank, Washington, DC.

Guarino, C. M., M. D. Reckdase, and J. M. Wooldridge. 2011. "Can Value-Added Measures of Teacher Performance Be Trusted?" Discussion paper 6602, Institute for the Study of Labor (IZA), Bonn, Germany.

Ministry of Education and Culture. Various years. *Statistical Yearbook (Seri Ikhtisar Data Pendidikan Nasional)*. Jakarta: Centre for Educational Statistics Data, Ministry of National Education.

Ministry of National Education. 2009. "Dampak Peningkatan Kesejahteraan Guru terhadap Mutu Input (Quality Enrollment) dan Pemberian Bantuan Dana Kompetitif terhadap Kemampuan Lulusan LPTK." Data prepared by the Research and Development Board, Ministry of National Education, Jakarta.

———. 2010. *Studi Kualitatif: Pelaksanaan Sertifikasi Guru (Kinerja Pendidikan dan Latihan Profesi Guru/PLPG dan Pola Pembinaan Guru)*. Study report, Research and Development Board, Jakarta.

OECD (Organisation for Economic Co-operation and Development). 2010. *PISA 2009 Results: Learning Trends. Changes in Student Performance Since 2000* Vol. 5. Paris: OECD Publishing. http://dx.doi.org/10.1787/9789264091580-en.

Ragatz, A. 2010. *Transforming Indonesia's Teaching Force. Volume II: From Pre-service Training to Retirement: Producing and Maintaining a High-Quality, Efficient, and Motivated Workforce*. Human Development Series, Jakarta: World Bank.

Rivkin, S. G., E. A. Hanushek, and J. F. Kain. 2005. "Teachers, Schools, and Academic Achievement." *Econometrica* 73 (2): 417–58.

Tiongson, E. R. 2005. "Education Policy Reforms." In *Analyzing the Distributional Impact of Reforms*, edited by S. Paternostro and A. Coudouel, 261–94. Washington, DC: World Bank. http://siteresources.worldbank.org/INTPSIA/Resources/490023 -1120845825946/Education.pdf.

CHAPTER 5

Looking Inside the Classroom Black Box

Teacher Classroom Practice

The teacher reform effort has a strong focus on increasing teacher qualifications by requiring the attainment of both a four-year degree and certification. These qualifications are, of course, not the end goal but are instead part of a chain. Qualifications are expected to subsequently improve what takes place in the classroom, which should in turn lead to improved student learning outcomes. The certification study, elaborated in chapter 4, explored the "bookends" to determine how qualifications are related to learning outcomes. It found no difference between the learning outcomes of students taught by certified teachers and those taught by uncertified teachers. However, students taught by teachers with four-year degrees did have better learning outcomes than those with teachers having lower degrees—and the effect is quite large. The study further identified a "teacher knowledge" component as measured through teacher competency tests, which helps to partially explain the contribution made by four-year-degree teachers.

This chapter extends the certification study analysis by exploring the "in between"—the black box—of what takes place in the classroom through a video study of 8th-grade mathematics classrooms that participated in the Trends in International Mathematics and Science Study (TIMSS). When looking at the same "bookends" dimensions used in the certification study, the findings are strikingly similar: The students of certified teachers did not have better learning outcomes than students of uncertified teachers. There was also no difference between certified and uncertified teachers in their subject matter and pedagogy assessment scores. Educational level, on the other hand, did have a positive relationship with student outcomes. Teacher knowledge—in both subject matter and pedagogy—stood out as having a particularly strong relationship with, and a large effect on, student learning outcomes. Teacher degree type was also explored, and a striking difference emerged between the outcomes of students taught by teachers holding a mathematics education degree and students of teachers with a pure mathematics degree. Although the pure-mathematics-degree teachers tended to have slightly higher subject matter scores on the teacher assessment, when it came to student outcomes, students with teachers having a mathematics education degree actually performed better than those with teachers having a pure mathematics degree.

Although the video study can provide insights on qualifications, its true power comes through its comprehensive information on classroom process. Videos of 200 teachers working in classrooms were coded in great detail with multiple layers of teaching practices. These practices were then analyzed and linked with the critical dimensions identified in the certification study. When looking at the certification study dimensions through the lens of teaching practices, some telling results emerged in the areas of certified versus uncertified teachers, teachers with a four-year degree, and teachers with higher knowledge as measured through assessments.

By analyzing the use and frequency of teaching practices and relating them to student learning outcomes, further insights were gained on which practices tend to be related to better learning. Some results confirm what would be expected, but there were also some surprising results that tend to contradict some well-known teaching-learning theories.

With a two-phase design involving nationally representative samples for each year, the video study was designed to examine not only what teaching practices were used but also how the use of those practices changed between 2007 and 2011. Although some changes in teaching practices appear to be related to the teacher reforms, it seems that other factors beyond the teacher reforms are having greater influence on teaching practices—in particular, an increased emphasis on the national examination and changes in school resources.

Methodology and Analytical Approach

The Indonesia TIMSS Video Study uses detailed coding of videotaped lessons of 200 teachers to provide insights on classroom activities in terms of time spent, frequency, sequencing, and quality of delivery. The fact that the study examined TIMSS participants provided unique benefits in terms of nationally representative sampling; extensive student, teacher, and school background surveys; and student assessment results. The coding of the videos followed the coding structure developed for the 1999 TIMSS Video Study (Hiebert *et al.* 2003). This was beneficial not only in providing a high-quality, proven coding scheme but also in providing a context for a comparison of Indonesia's results with those of other countries.

A mixed-methods approach involving both quantitative and qualitative analysis was used. The quantitative analysis used advanced forms of multilevel and value-added modeling. The qualitative analysis used case studies of relatively high-impact teachers to provide in-depth insights on specific practices and also to explore two factors seen as driving teaching practices: *teacher mathematical beliefs* and *mathematical knowledge in teaching.*

The data collection took place in two phases (2007 and 2011),[1] allowing for exploration of changes that had taken place since the beginning of the teacher reform. The TIMSS rigorous sampling approach provided nationally representative samples for each year. That the video study is based on these samples allowed for general snapshots of teaching practices to be created for each year.[2]

Multilevel and value-added concepts were used in the analysis of the relationships between teaching practices and student learning outcomes. The multilevel model used advanced techniques developed by the Centre for Multilevel Modeling and included students nested within classes nested within provinces. The value-added approach relied on measurement of student learning over the 8th-grade year by using a pretest at the beginning of the 8th-grade year and a posttest at the end.[3] The pretest provides a baseline of the level of knowledge for students as they enter the year, and the posttest provides an exit level of knowledge.

Findings: Use of Practices and Relation to Student Learning

Teaching practices were examined from various angles to understand their frequency of use, how the practices relate to student learning outcomes, and how the teacher reforms and other factors may be influencing trends in practices.

The first step in the analysis below examines categorizations of teaching practices in relation to the following questions:

- In looking at the teaching practices for the full, nationally representative samples of teachers in 2007 and 2011, are there any changes where teachers are using certain practices more or less frequently?
- Is there a statistically significant positive or negative relationship between practices and student learning outcomes?

If there were, in fact, changes in the use of specific teaching practices between 2007 and 2011, an additional two questions were asked:

- Would the changes be considered positive or negative from the perspective of student learning outcomes?
- What might have caused these changes from the perspective of policies, training, demographics, or some other factor?

The relationship between teaching practices and student learning outcomes is presented through two models (as summarized in table 5.1): The first is a regression that includes 30 background variables on student, student home, classroom, school, and community characteristics. The second is the same regression as the first but also includes multiple teacher background characteristics (such as experience, gender, whether the teacher is a civil servant, degree type, and so on) as well as variables that could be seen as indicators of quality, including teacher competency scores, educational level, and certification.

Table 5.1 Two Models to Examine the Relationships between Teaching Practices and Student Outcomes

Model	Variables	Logic behind model
Base regression	Key home, student, school, and classroom variables but *not* including teacher background and quality variables	Shows a picture of the relationship of teaching techniques with student learning, without accounting for teacher dimensions
Regression with teacher variables	Same variables as in the base regression but also including a small set of teacher background and quality variables	Shows how the results of the base regression change when teacher background and quality aspects are controlled for, therefore giving a picture of the relation of practices across teachers

When looking at teaching practices, the first model can generally be interpreted as how the practices relate to student learning when not taking teacher-related factors into account. The second can be interpreted as how practices relate to student learning with teacher background and quality aspects taken into account.

As an example for comparing the two models, teachers holding a mathematics education degree tend to use the expositional teaching approach less than teachers holding pure mathematics degrees. In the first regression, this information would not be captured and would give the relationship of exposition to student learning outcomes *without considering which teachers use it*. The second model, on the other hand, takes the teacher degree (and other teacher variables) into consideration so it captures the relationship between exposition and student learning outcomes while controlling for teacher degree and other teacher variables. By controlling for these variables, the teaching practice can be thought of as applying *across teachers of various backgrounds*. Both provide interesting perspectives, and although the second model would generally be considered more relevant because it provides the relationship across all teachers, the first gives an important contrast when thinking about teaching practices and what role teachers' background and quality play in the use of the teaching practice.

The relationship of teaching practices to student outcomes, however, must be interpreted with caution. The analysis identifies statistically significant relationships based on the frequency and extent of use for given practices. Any statistically significant relationship that emerges is an important signal of how practices relate to student outcomes but should not be oversimplified or misinterpreted to provide a right way of teaching. Below are some important points to keep in mind regarding what is measured and the pitfalls to avoid in interpretation:

• *It is important to measure not only the amount of time spent for a given practice but also the quality of how the teacher conducts the practice.* A practice may emerge as having a positive relationship with student learning based on overall frequency and extent of use, but individual teachers may use the practice effectively or ineffectively.
• *Each lesson requires a unique set of practices.* There is no optimal formula to apply to all lessons; in fact, particularly effective teachers are able to vary their

practices according to the material and the needs of the students within a given lesson.

- *Context is important.* The regressions take into account many contextual factors in an attempt to determine effects across various contexts, but the results certainly should not be interpreted to indicate a standardized approach to mathematics teaching.[4]
- *The teaching practices are typically measured as proportions within a given category.* A negative relationship should not necessarily be interpreted as being a bad practice. It could possibly indicate that relatively too much of the proportional time tends to be allocated to the practice.
- *For any category, teachers typically use multiple practices rather than just one.* In looking for the relationship of a practice to student learning outcomes, the interpretation is not whether teachers do or do not use a practice but rather *to what extent* the practice is used.

Keeping these important points in mind, the results still create an overall picture of practices and trends and thus provide critical insights into what takes place in Indonesia's mathematics classrooms and how practices relate to student learning outcomes. In relating these practices to student learning, many statistically significant results are obtained, giving insights into the teaching-learning process and how it might be improved.

Lesson Structure: Time Spent on Mathematics

In what could be considered the foundational layer of classroom time allocation, all lesson time was first categorized as being either *mathematical, mathematical organization,* or *nonmathematical* in nature. The theoretical heart of this layer is based on research related to time on task that has its roots in Carroll's "A Model of School Learning" (Carroll 1963) and has been one of the most widely discussed concepts in the education community since the 1970s. Mathematical time also represents what has been called Academic Learning Time (ALT),[5] which represents when learning takes place. Mathematical organization time may be effective and necessary for setting up a learning situation but could be detrimental if not conducted efficiently or if it breaks the rhythm of learning. Although some nonmathematical time may not be avoidable, it clearly takes away from learning time and may also be an indicator of classroom management and behavior issues (for example, Doyle 1990; Kounin 1970; Wragg 1993).

The teaching practices in the *Lesson Structure* category have the following definitions:

- *Mathematical:* Time spent on mathematical content presented either through a mathematical problem or outside the context of a problem
- *Mathematical organization:* Time devoted to preparing materials or discussing information related to mathematics but not qualifying as mathematical work
- *Nonmathematical:* Time devoted to nonmathematical content such as taking roll call, prayer time, disciplining a student while other students wait, or listening to school announcements on a public-address system

Figure 5.1 Proportions of Lesson Structure Practices in Indonesia TIMSS Video Study of Mathematics Classes, 2007 and 2011

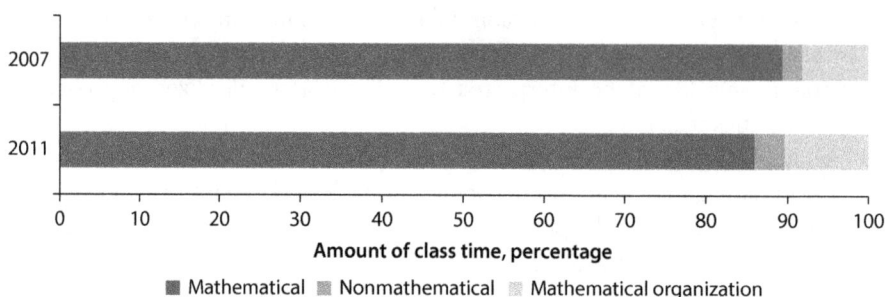

Note: Changes in mathematical time and mathematical organization time were statistically significant. TIMSS = Trends in International Mathematics and Science Study. "Mathematical" time refers to time spent on mathematical content. "Nonmathematical" time refers to time spent on materials preparation or discussing information related to mathematics but not qualifying as mathematical work. "Mathematical organization" refers to time spent on nonmathematical contents such as roll call, school announcements, or other administration.

Comparison between 2007 and 2011

Teachers spent less time on mathematics and more time on mathematical organization. The data from 2007 to 2011 indicate (as shown in figure 5.1) that the proportion of classroom time spent on mathematics fell from 89 percent to 86 percent while mathematical organization time increased from 8 percent to 10 percent and that these changes were statistically significant. Nonmathematical time increased slightly, but the change was not significant.

Although not specifically intended for mathematics classrooms, the Stallings benchmarks for effective time use indicate that instruction time should make up at least 85 percent of class time while classroom management should be 15 percent or less, and off-task time should be 0 percent (Stallings and Knight 2003). Indonesia's instructional time (mathematics time) is just above the benchmark, but off-task time (nonmathematics time), while low, is considered something to be eliminated in the benchmark.

Relationship to Student Learning Outcomes

The relationship of these time categories to student learning outcomes was examined starting with a base regression controlling for student, classroom, school, and community characteristics and then with a second regression that also included teacher background and quality characteristics. As shown in figure 5.2, mathematical time had a positive relationship with student outcomes while nonmathematical time had a negative relationship. As would be predicted in time-on-task theory, students in classrooms with a higher proportion of time spent on mathematics tended to have higher learning outcomes, while classes with higher share of time spent on nonmathematical tasks tended to have lower outcomes. Mathematical organization did not have a statistically significant relationship to learning outcomes.

The coefficients indicate that a percentile increase in the proportion of time spent on mathematics is related to an increase in student test scores by

Figure 5.2 Relationship of Lesson Structure Teaching Practices to Student Learning Outcomes in Indonesia TIMSS Video Study of Mathematics Classes, 2007–11

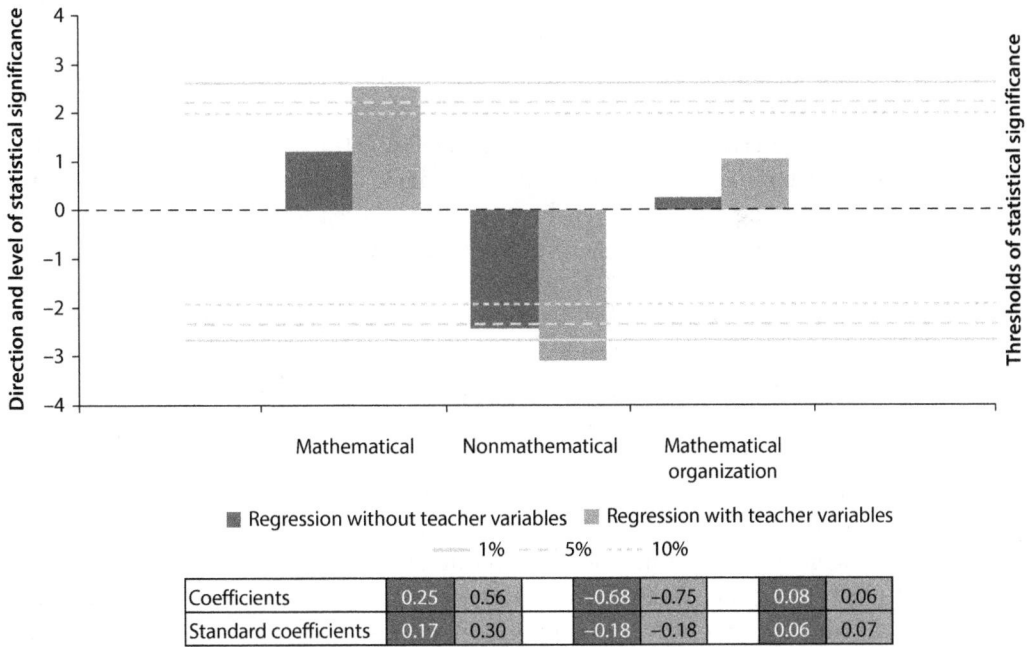

| Coefficients | 0.25 | 0.56 | | −0.68 | −0.75 | | 0.08 | 0.06 |
| Standard coefficients | 0.17 | 0.30 | | −0.18 | −0.18 | | 0.06 | 0.07 |

Note: Full regression results can be found in appendix A at the end of this book. TIMSS = Trends in International Mathematics and Science Study. "Mathematical" time refers to time spent on mathematical content. "Nonmathematical" time refers to time spent on materials preparation or discussing information related to mathematics but not qualifying as mathematical work. "Mathematical organization" refers to time spent on nonmathematical contents such as roll call, school announcements, or other administration.

0.56 percentage points while an increase of a percentile point in the proportion of nonmathematical time is related to a decrease of 0.83 percentage points. An alternative way to look at the relationship is by using standardized coefficients, which allow for easier comparison with other variables examined in this chapter. The standardized coefficients indicate that a 1.0 standard deviation increase in mathematical time is related to a 0.30 standard deviation increase in student test scores, while a 1.0 standard deviation increase in nonmathematical time is related to a 0.18 standard deviation decrease. Both of these changes are large in comparison with other teaching practices.

The trend of decreased time spent on mathematics is of concern because, in line with expectations based on theory, mathematical time should have a positive relationship with student outcomes. Nonmathematical time tends to have the strong negative relationship with student outcomes, but the change between 2007 and 2011 of this variable (from 3 percent to 4 percent) is not statistically significant and represents a small proportion of lesson time; the highest proportion in the sample was 11 percent.

Although the result of time on task having a positive relationship and time off task having a negative relationship is not surprising, it drives home an important fundamental point: that teaching requires management of time, and the trend toward less mathematical time, while not dramatic, should raise a flag. The other seven countries in the 1999 TIMSS study all had at least 95 percent of classroom time allocated to mathematics, and no country had more than 1 percent of time on nonmathematics (Hiebert *et al.* 2003, 39).

Time on task extends to the breakdown of mathematical time into problem and nonproblem time. Indonesia's results showed a decrease in problem time from 76 percent in 2007 to 67 percent in 2011, but lessons with a higher proportion of problem time tended to have a positive relationship with student learning outcomes. Teachers also have increased the proportion of mathematical time used for the introduction of new material from 46 percent in 2007 to 58 percent in 2011 while reducing practice time from 39 percent to 26 percent. The reason for the decrease may be related to the increased availability of textbooks and to greater ease in giving practice work as homework rather than using class time. Teachers now seem to be using that time instead to introduce new material, possibly allowing for the coverage of more topics and material. Interviewed teachers also spoke of the curriculum being spread thin, meaning it is difficult to get through all the topics expected to be covered over the course of the year. This may be a contributing factor to teachers' rebalancing to use time for the introduction of new material.[6] These examples of changing time indicate that classroom resources and influences, such as the curriculum, can alter the composition of time on task and teaching practices.

Teaching Approaches

The teaching approaches used in classroom activities can also play an important role in how students learn. Various models of teaching approaches have been developed, with a progressive (socioconstructive) versus traditional (behaviorist) model often used to distinguish between ways of teaching (for example, Dewey 1938; Handal 2003). The teacher's conception of role is also an important factor, with Kuhs and Ball (1986) defining categories of (a) instructor (for skill mastery), (b) explainer (for conceptual understanding), and (c) facilitator (for confident problem solving).

In the coded approaches used in the video study, *exposition* (or lecturing) encompasses an approach that is highly prevalent in many countries and is often associated with traditional or teacher-centered learning where student participation is limited.[7] *Discussion* becomes more student-centered with dialogue between the teacher and students, while *problem solving, practical work,* and *investigation* are approaches that revolve more around mathematical problems and tend to encourage more student-centered learning.

The practices in the *Teaching Approaches* category have the following definitions:

- *Exposition:* Time when the teacher lectures while students listen and answer closed questions (with no discussion)
- *Discussion:* Time when the teacher and student(s) discuss their own ideas about mathematics

Figure 5.3 Time Spent on Different Teaching Approaches in Indonesia TIMSS Video Study of Mathematics Classes, 2007 and 2011

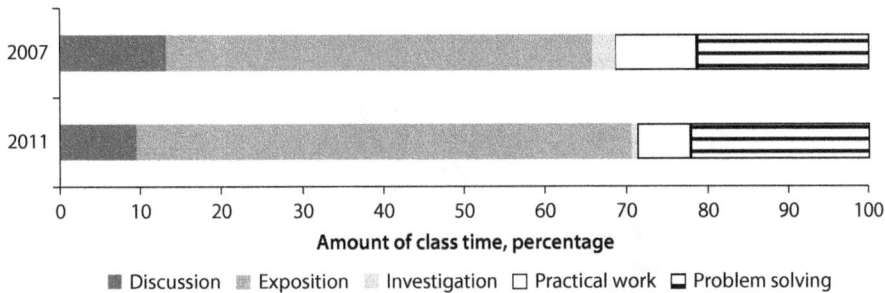

Note: The changes between 2007 and 2011 are statistically significant for discussion, exposition, and investigation.
TIMSS = Trends in International Mathematics and Science Study.

- *Problem solving:* Time when the teacher provides a problem or situation as a basis to discuss ideas in mathematics
- *Practical work:* Time when equipment or situations in the real world are used to explore ideas in mathematics
- *Investigation:* Time when students explore the issues (problems) in various mathematical situations

Comparison between 2007 and 2011

Compared with 2007, Indonesian teachers in 2011 tended to use much more exposition while discussion, practical work, and investigation all decreased, as shown in figure 5.3. This result is somewhat surprising in that the practices taught in many recent government programs (for example, through the national mathematics training organization and in teacher working groups) generally encourage teachers to use *less* exposition and *more* student-centered learning.

The mathematics experts involved in the study have proposed various theories as to why this trend occurred, including the possibility that certification is influencing teachers to be more teacher-centered, either through the pride they may feel by being certified (that is, as "professionals") or through a greater sense of obligation. This theory did not bear out in further analysis where certified teachers were not found to be any more likely to use exposition. Another possibility is that teachers consider exposition to be an easier or more direct method to prepare students for the national examination. This and other possible reasons for this trend are continuing to be explored.

Relationship to Student Learning Outcomes

In examining the relationship between teaching approaches used and student learning outcomes, some striking differences emerged, as shown in figure 5.4. Exposition had a negative relationship to learning outcomes and surpassed the statistical threshold. Investigation, practical work, and problem solving all had positive tendencies, with investigation and problem solving both reaching thresholds of statistical significance.[8] These three approaches tended to involve a

Figure 5.4 Relationship of Teaching Approach Practices to Student Learning Outcomes in Indonesia TIMSS Video Study of Mathematics Classes, 2007–11

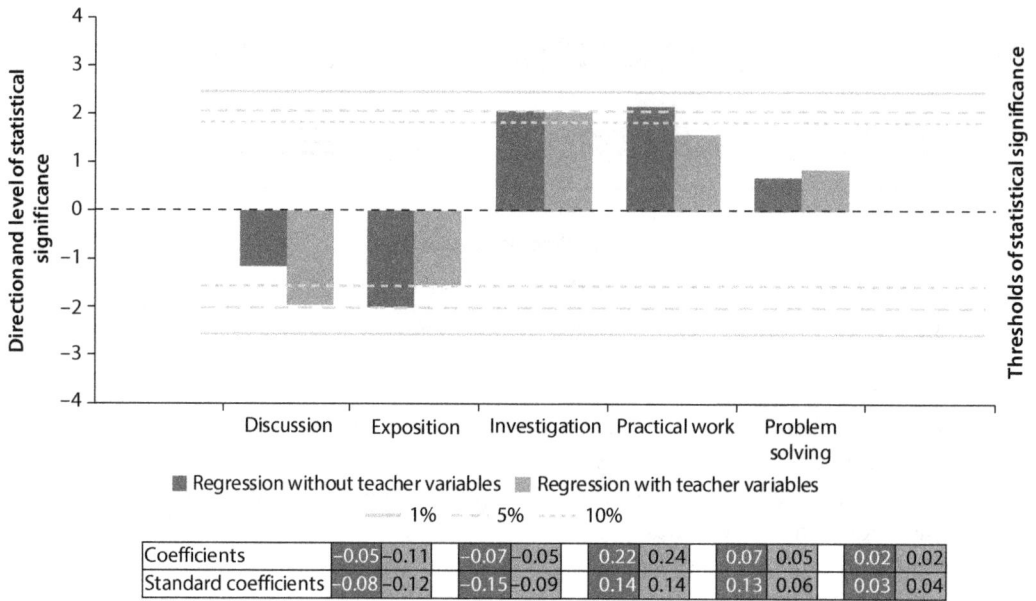

Coefficients	-0.05	-0.11		-0.07	-0.05		0.22	0.24		0.07	0.05		0.02	0.02
Standard coefficients	-0.08	-0.12		-0.15	-0.09		0.14	0.14		0.13	0.06		0.03	0.04

Note: Full regression results can be found in appendix B at the end of this book. TIMSS = Trends in International Mathematics and Science Study.

mathematical problem focus and tended to encourage active student engagement and participation.

The trend in teaching practices, in combination with the evidence of their relationship to student learning outcomes, raises some flags. Exposition had a large negative relationship, yet it increased significantly in use from 2007 to 2011. On the other hand, the techniques of investigation and practical work, which had positive relationships, were decreasing in use (although practical work never reaches the 5 percent threshold of statistical significance). Exposition and problem solving, the two approaches with increases, could often be used as a way of "teaching to the test," whereas investigation and practical work could lead to greater understanding but require a more indirect approach to getting students to be able to answer typical national examination questions.

Public (Whole Class) Interaction Time by Participants

Mathematical time was divided into public time (when the whole class participates in a task) and private time (when students are broken up into groups or do individual seatwork). In 2011, the allocation was 64 percent whole-class time and 36 percent group or seatwork time. There was no statistically significant relationship between the proportions of these categories and student learning outcomes, but a further breakdown of the interaction uncovered interesting results in terms of changes from 2007 to 2011 and in how those changes relate to student learning outcomes.

Whole-class time was further broken down into the types of interaction by the participants. The division of whole-class time into teacher-only, teacher-student, and student-only interaction is closely linked with traditional versus progressive teaching approaches. Teacher-only interaction is considered traditional whereas teacher-student and student-only interactions are often associated with progressive and student-centered learning. These divisions also relate to the teacher's conception of his or her role as instructor (for skill mastery), explainer (for conceptual understanding), or facilitator (for confident problem solving) (Kuhs and Ball 1986).

The practices in the *Public Interaction Participants* category have these definitions:

- *Teacher interaction:* Time when the teacher leads the class and presents to all students
- *Teacher and student interaction:* Time when a presentation is made by both the teacher and students (in intervals), intended for all students
- *Student interaction:* Time when a presentation is made by a student or students, intended for the teacher and all students

Comparison between 2007 and 2011
Within the public or whole-class interaction, there was much more teacher-only time in 2011 than in 2007. This time typically involved expositional or lecture activities. Student involvement in the form of teacher-student interaction fell dramatically, as shown in figure 5.5.

Relationship to Student Learning Outcomes
The standout feature of the different types of public whole-class interaction was the positive relationship of student learning outcomes with participation involving both teacher and students, as figure 5.6 shows. In contrast, activities that are teacher-only or student-only had negative, but not statistically significant, relationships to student outcomes.

Figure 5.5 Public (Whole Class) Interaction Time by Participants in Indonesia TIMSS Video Study of Mathematics Classes, 2007 and 2011

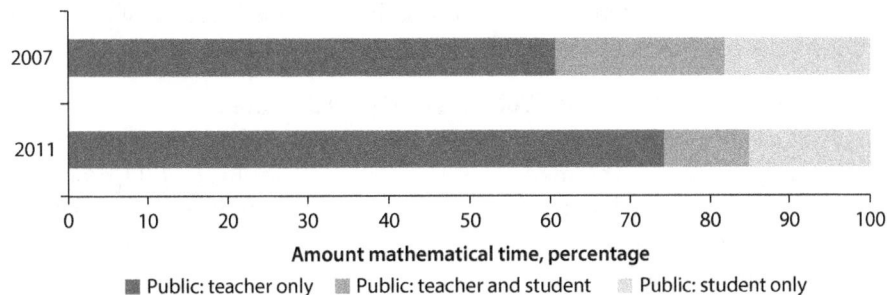

Amount mathematical time, percentage

■ Public: teacher only   ■ Public: teacher and student   ■ Public: student only

Note: The changes between 2007 and 2011 are statistically significant for "Public: teacher only" and "Public: teacher and student." "Public" time refers to time when the interaction, regardless of the participants, is intended for the whole class.

Teacher Reform in Indonesia · http://dx.doi.org/10.1596/978-0-8213-9829-6

Figure 5.6 Relationship of Public Interaction Categories to Student Learning Outcomes in Indonesia TIMSS Video Study of Mathematics Classes, 2007–11

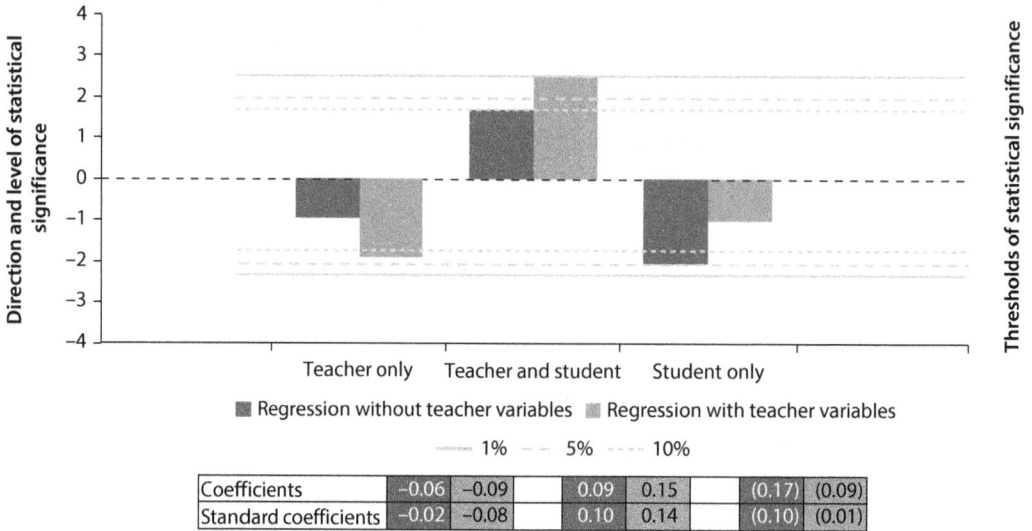

	Teacher only			Teacher and student			Student only	
Coefficients	−0.06	−0.09		0.09	0.15		(0.17)	(0.09)
Standard coefficients	−0.02	−0.08		0.10	0.14		(0.10)	(0.01)

Notes: Full regression results can be found in appendix C at the end of this book. TIMSS = Trends in International Mathematics and Science Study.

As will be shown later when looking at private interaction, a similar pattern emerged: activities that are student-only tend to have a negative relationship to student learning while teacher-student activities have a positive relationship. This pattern may indicate the importance of teachers being actively involved, even in student-led activities, to monitor, speak to, and encourage students. On the other hand, teacher-centered activities tended to be negative in relationship to learning.

The trend of decreasing teacher-student interaction goes against the practices reportedly encouraged by the Ministry of Education and Culture in its training and teacher working group activities.[9] Combining this trend with the fact that teacher-student interaction time has a positive relationship to student learning outcomes raises some concerns as well as questions as to why such interaction might be declining. As mentioned earlier, one possible explanation suggested by teachers and policy makers is that certification may indirectly encourage teachers to use more teacher-centered learning approaches because of a sense of pride and self-importance or even of obligation to earn their increased income.

The Context and Language of Problems and their Solutions

Problems can be presented in a variety of ways in terms of the context presented, the language used, and the method used to solve them. Real-world problems may provide a contextual understanding of how mathematical concepts relate to actual situations. Application of mathematical concepts to situations may also require more advanced cognitive thinking relative to problems presented in mathematical language. The use of mathematical language and symbols at times is associated with rote learning, but it can also be required for advanced and complex mathematical problems.

Similarly, problems may be considered routine or nonroutine, with the latter generally considered as requiring more advanced cognitive thinking. Routine problems can be solved directly through formulas, whereas nonroutine problems cannot be solved with a usual procedure but instead require a nonroutine strategy.

Generally, the application of mathematics to real-world problems and the use of nonroutine problem solutions tend to be seen as involving more higher-order thinking and requiring a deeper understanding of mathematics. This is not to say that problems in the context of mathematical language and symbols and problems that can be solved with a routine approach are inferior; indeed, they are necessary. Still, many advocates of progressive learning tend to promote real-world contexts and nonroutine problem solving.

The terms used in the *Problem Context* category have these definitions:

- *Real world:* Time spent on mathematical problems presented within a real-life context
- *Mathematical language:* Time spent on problems presented only with mathematical language and symbols

The terms used in the *Problem Solution* category have these definitions:

- *Routine:* Time spent on a problem that can be solved directly, using a formula, definition, or proposition
- *Nonroutine:* Time spent on problems that cannot be solved with a usual procedure (directly using a formula, definition, or proposition) but instead must be solved using a nonroutine strategy

The terms used in the *Problem Nature* category have these definitions:

- *Open:* Time spent on problems or questions where there is more than one correct answer
- *Closed:* Time spent on problems or questions where there is only one possible answer

Comparison between 2007 and 2011

In 2011, mathematical problems overwhelmingly involved mathematical language and symbols, and there was an increase in the amount of time during which mathematical language and symbols were used—from 89 percent in 2007 to 93 percent in 2011, as shown in figure 5.7. A likely explanation for the decrease in problems involving real-world contexts is that there had been a push for contextual teaching and learning (CTL) starting in the late 1990s, but it was promoted less in recent years. The change, therefore, possibly reflects a fading out of the CTL approach. Still, it is surprising to see how unbalanced the mix of problem contexts is, with the use of real-world contexts making up a very small proportion of the total.

Figure 5.7 Contextual Language Used during Problem Time in Indonesia TIMSS Video Study of Mathematics Classes, 2007 and 2011

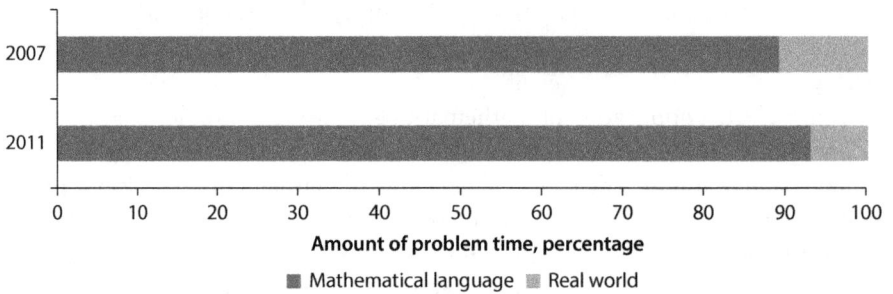

Notes: The changes between 2007 and 2011 are statistically significant for both the "mathematical language" and "real world" problem contexts. TIMSS = Trends in International Mathematics and Science Study.

Figure 5.8 Use of Routine vs. Nonroutine Approaches to Problems in Indonesia TIMSS Video Study of Mathematics Classes, 2007 and 2011

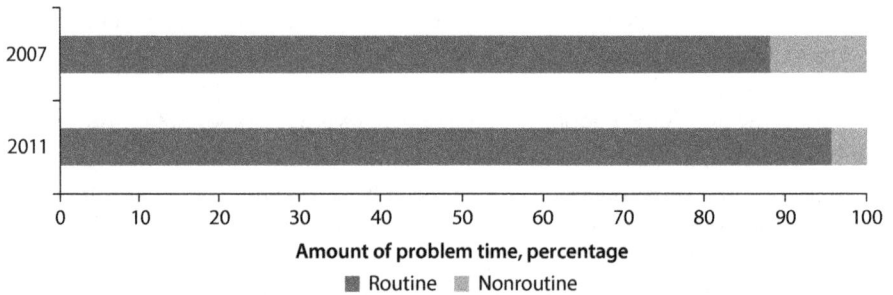

Note: The changes between 2007 and 2011 are statistically significant for routine and nonroutine. TIMSS = Trends in International Mathematics and Science Study. "Routine" refers to problems that can be solved directly using a formula, definition, or proposition. "Nonroutine" refers to problems that cannot be solved with a usual procedure (directly using a formula, definition, or proposition) but instead must be solved using a nonroutine strategy.

Teachers tended to present and spend time on problems that could be solved in a routine manner rather than through a nonroutine approach; this proportion increased between 2007 and 2011, as shown in figure 5.8. The fact that only 4 percent of problem time was spent on nonroutine approaches is of concern, particularly because nonroutine problem solving is typically considered to be related to higher-order thinking.

Teachers also overwhelmingly used problems and asked questions that were closed in nature. Only 3 percent of time spent involved open problems and questions, as shown in figure 5.9.

Relationship to Student Learning Outcomes

Surprisingly, problems within the context of mathematical language and problems solved through routine procedures had a positive relationship with student outcomes. The results shown in figure 5.10 combine the three separate categorizations of approaches to mathematical problems and questioning. On the left is the mathematical language versus real-world contexts; in the center is

Figure 5.9 Use of Open vs. Closed Problems in Indonesia TIMSS Video Study of Mathematics Classes, 2007 and 2011

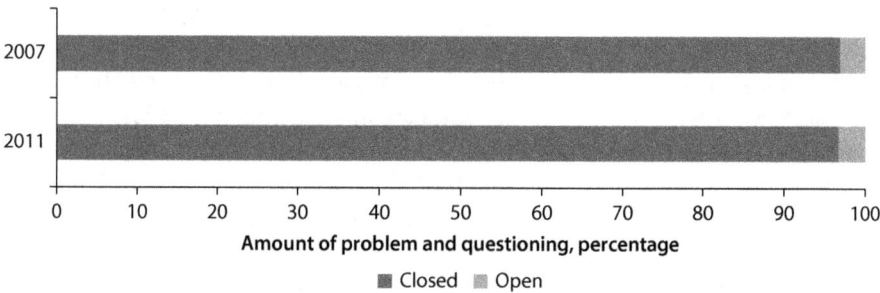

Amount of problem and questioning, percentage

■ Closed ■ Open

Notes: The changes between 2007 and 2011 are not statistically significant for open and closed. TIMSS = Trends in International Mathematics and Science Study. "Open" refers to problems for which there is more than one correct answer. "Closed" refers to problems for which there is only one possible correct answer.

Figure 5.10 Relationship of Problem-Solving Approach Categories to Student Learning Outcomes in Indonesia TIMSS Video Study of Mathematics Classes, 2007–11

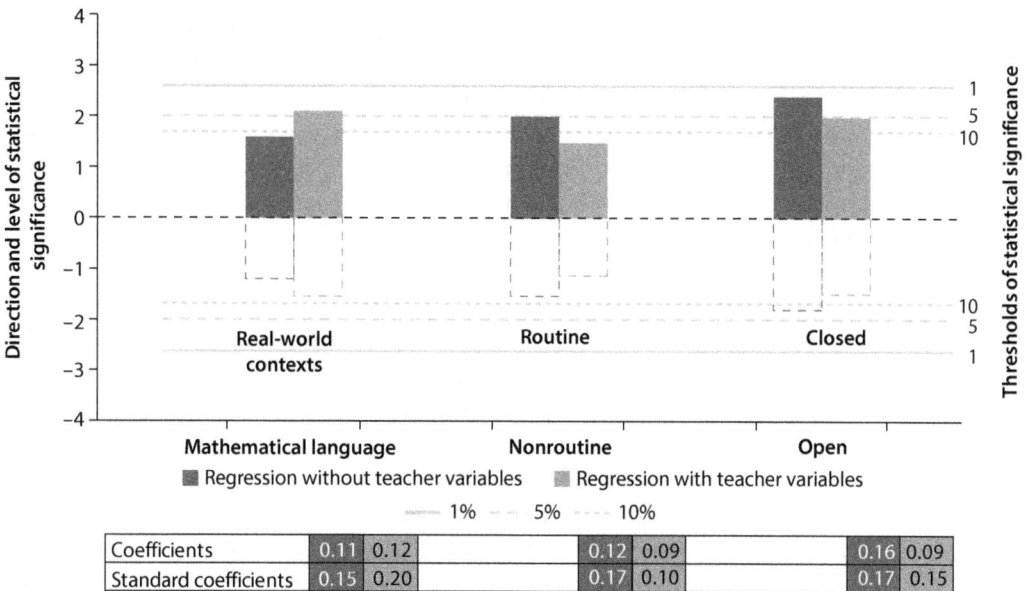

■ Regression without teacher variables ■ Regression with teacher variables

——— 1% ——— 5% ······ 10%

Coefficients	0.11	0.12		0.12	0.09		0.16	0.09
Standard coefficients	0.15	0.20		0.17	0.10		0.17	0.15

Note: The practices with the dotted lines are the same, mirrored values as the corresponding practices above but with negative values. Full regression results can be found in appendix D at the end of this book. TIMSS = Trends in International Mathematics and Science Study. "Routine" refers to problem solving using a formula, definition, or proposition. "Nonroutine" refers to problem solving instead using a nonroutine strategy. "Open" refers to problems for which there is more than one correct answer. "Closed" refers to problems for which there is only one possible correct answer.

routine versus nonroutine problem solving; and on the right is the open versus closed nature of problems and questioning. The results indicate that there was a strong positive relationship to learning outcomes for both mathematical language and nonroutine problem solving, while the real-world contexts and routine practices had a negative relationship. The use of open approaches also had a positive relationship with student learning outcomes.

Teacher Reform in Indonesia • http://dx.doi.org/10.1596/978-0-8213-9829-6

The results vary in terms of statistical significance depending on whether the regression includes the teacher variables. In the case of mathematical language and real-world contexts, the results become statistically significant only when the teacher background and quality variables are included. On the other hand, the routine versus nonroutine and the closed versus open distinctions are statistically significant when no teacher variables are included but are no longer significant when teacher variables are added. One interpretation is that the nonroutine and open practices are rarely used and typically only the "higher-quality" teachers use them, so once this is taken into account, the practices no longer become statistically significant. The mathematical language and real-world contexts, on the other hand, may be used by a mix of teachers, but once the background and qualities are taken into account, it appears that the use of mathematical language and symbols in problems has a positive relationship across teacher background and quality.

These problem context and approach categories bring up interesting aspects related to testing, what is truly being measured, and how teachers might change their teaching practices to better help their students succeed in high-stakes assessments such as Indonesia's national examination (in this case, held at the end of grade 9). Teachers seem to have moved toward more routine, formulaic, and possibly rote learning approaches, and these actions could be considered "teaching to the test." The increase in mathematical language and the use of routine approaches and closed problems and questions may have to do with an increased emphasis on performing well on the national examination, where questions typically require a routine approach in their solution.

There was a positive relationship between teachers' self-reported influence of the national examination and their use of routine problems and mathematical language contexts. Teachers were asked whether the national examination influenced their teaching. Those who said they were more influenced also tended to use routine problems, closed problems, and mathematical language contexts— evidence that these practices could be seen by teachers as being more effective or efficient in preparing students for the national examination. In addition, the percentage of teachers who said they were influenced by the national examination increased from 70 percent to 75 percent between 2007 and 2011, which indicates the national examination is increasingly influencing how teachers prepare and implement their lessons.

This finding raises an important contradiction: many educationalists argue that the teaching approach encapsulated in these routine, closed, and formulaic techniques does not promote true understanding of mathematics. Still, if teachers are "teaching to the test" and these approaches tend to help students score better (as at least the mathematical language relationship with student outcomes indicates), is it a wise strategy? Could it, in fact, lead to better learning, albeit more through a mechanistic, rote-learning approach? The results regarding nonroutine and open approaches are an indication that the less mechanistic approach could, in fact, lead to better learning, but it is used infrequently.

Impact of the Reforms

In light of the results presented in the previous section on the frequency and use of teaching practices as well as their relationship to student learning outcomes, the practices can now be seen in the context of teacher reform. This section explores key elements of teacher reform, including the cornerstone aspects of certification and the requirement that all teachers obtain a four-year degree. Regarding the latter, a special focus is also placed on teachers who did not have a four-year degree at the start of the reform (2005) but subsequently upgraded to a four-year degree.

Teacher Certification

As elaborated in chapter 4, the certification process itself did not have an impact on altering teaching performance as measured through student learning outcomes. The video study had similar results: there was no statistically significant difference between student learning outcomes for certified and uncertified teachers, and there was also no statistically significant difference in the certified and uncertified teachers' assessment scores. But differences may still emerge related to their teaching. In the 2011 sample, 53 percent of teachers were certified, providing a nice balance of certified and uncertified teachers for comparative purposes.

The teaching practices of certified and uncertified teachers may differ because of either teacher motivation or fundamental underlying differences between the two groups. Certified teachers may alter their teaching practices because of higher motivation from the increased salary, an increased sense of status, or an increased sense of obligation. They might also dedicate more time to teaching because of not having a second job, which could conceivably lead to changes in the way teachers plan and execute their lessons. In this section, the teaching practices of certified teachers are compared with those of uncertified teachers to determine whether any differences can be seen.

The queuing process of teachers for the certification process is important to take into account when analyzing certified and uncertified teachers. Teachers were selected first based primarily on age and years of experience. Civil servant teachers also received priority. These and other important background characteristics of teachers and the contextual characteristics of their working environment were controlled for in the analysis.

Teaching Practice Comparison

In looking at teaching practices, the striking feature is the *lack* of statistically significant differences between certified and uncertified teachers. Figure 5.11 shows results where the teaching practices of interest were placed (one at a time) into a regression model that controlled for multiple contextual variables. Only one difference emerged: certified teachers tended to use more public (whole-class) interaction and less private (group and seatwork) interaction. As demonstrated in the previous section, there is no statistically significant relationship between these practices and student learning outcomes.

Teacher Reform in Indonesia • http://dx.doi.org/10.1596/978-0-8213-9829-6

Figure 5.11 Differences in Teaching Practices of Certified Teachers vs. Uncertified Teachers in Indonesia TIMSS Video Study of Mathematics Classes, 2007–11

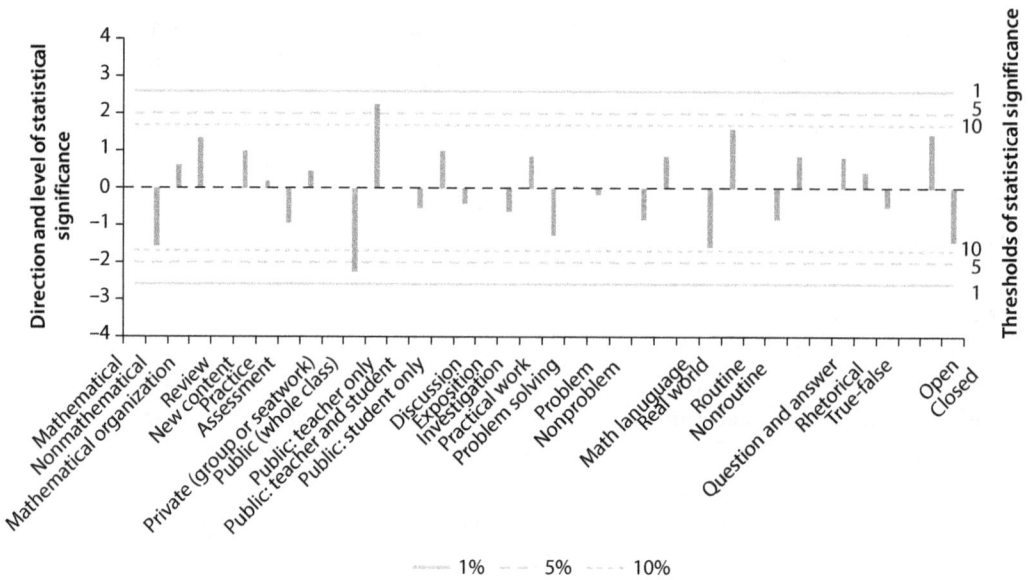

Note: Bars that pass the 5 percent threshold are considered to be statistically significant. Full regression results can be found in appendix E at the end of this book. TIMSS = Trends in International Mathematics and Science Study.

The results coincide with the certification study findings, giving further evidence that certification did not have an impact on teaching practices and behavior. This lack of difference is not particularly surprising. Almost every teacher who went through the certification process obtained it, so there was no separation of teachers during the process in terms of quality criteria.[10] Although approximately two-thirds of the teachers took an additional 90-hour course, such training would be highly unlikely to alter teaching practices in any measurable way. The certification study found that certified teachers were less likely to hold a second job, but it did not identify any other differences in teacher behavior such as teaching hours, absenteeism, or student outcomes. The video study accords with those results by further indicating no discernible differences in practices.

Teacher Education

The requirement that all teachers obtain a four-year degree by 2015 is based on the assumption that the teachers with a higher level of education will be more effective teachers. This section explores how a teacher's education relates to student learning outcomes. To meet the four-year-degree requirement, many existing teachers who had less than a four-year degree upgraded through additional in-service training. The section therefore explores how teachers who have upgraded to a four-year degree compare with teachers who obtained the degree directly through preservice training.

The video study sample in 2011 is made up almost completely of teachers who have already obtained a four-year degree, so it unfortunately doesn't lend itself well to analyzing differences between teachers who have met this critical threshold requirement for certification and those who have not. Still, the study obtained results similar to those of the certification study: students taught by teachers with a four-year degree tended to have higher learning outcomes. Such students tended to have posttest scores nearly 4 percentage points higher than those of students taught by teachers with less than a four-year degree after controlling for multiple background factors and the students' pretest scores. Because the average score on the posttest was only 34 percent, the 4-point difference is quite large and can be interpreted to represent a difference of nearly 12 percent relative to the average score.

Relationship of Degree Type to Student Learning Outcomes

One of the components of the teacher reform in Indonesia was the requirement that teachers hold a degree in the subject they teach. There was concern that many teachers were teaching subjects different from those of their training degrees and that the mismatch could potentially be harmful if teachers did not have sufficient subject competence. Teachers undergoing certification could obtain certification only in a single subject and were expected to teach only that subject.

One of the more striking results of the study is the difference in student learning outcomes of teachers holding a mathematics education degree compared with those holding a pure mathematics degree. Students of both teachers holding mathematics education and pure mathematics degrees had positive learning outcomes on average, but students taught by teachers having a mathematics education degree tended to perform relatively better. Students of teachers who held a mathematics education degree on average scored 1.3 percentage points lower on the pretest than those with teachers holding mathematics degrees but scored 1.3 percent higher on the posttest, showing bigger gains. Figure 5.12 highlights the contrast, with student learning outcomes of those taught by teachers with a degree in mathematics education having a positive and statistically significant relationship while teachers with degrees in pure mathematics having a strongly negative relationship to learning outcomes. It is important to emphasize that this negative relationship is relative to teachers who did not have a pure mathematics degree and does not indicate that students had negative learning outcomes. Their progress in learning was just relatively less.

Surprisingly, students with teachers lacking any formal mathematics training did not have lower student outcomes. Such nonmathematics teachers made up only 8 percent of the sample and held a diverse range of degrees in subjects including economics, Indonesian, chemistry, and even religion. Their results tended to be positive but did not reach statistical significance. It is not known what sort of training they received over their careers to possibly support their knowledge of mathematics, but the results at least do not indicate that their teaching is worse for lack of a mathematics focus in their degrees, as is feared in the case of mismatch.

Teacher Reform in Indonesia • http://dx.doi.org/10.1596/978-0-8213-9829-6

Figure 5.12   Relationship of Teacher Degree to Student Learning Outcomes in Indonesia TIMSS Video Study of Mathematics Classes, 2007–11

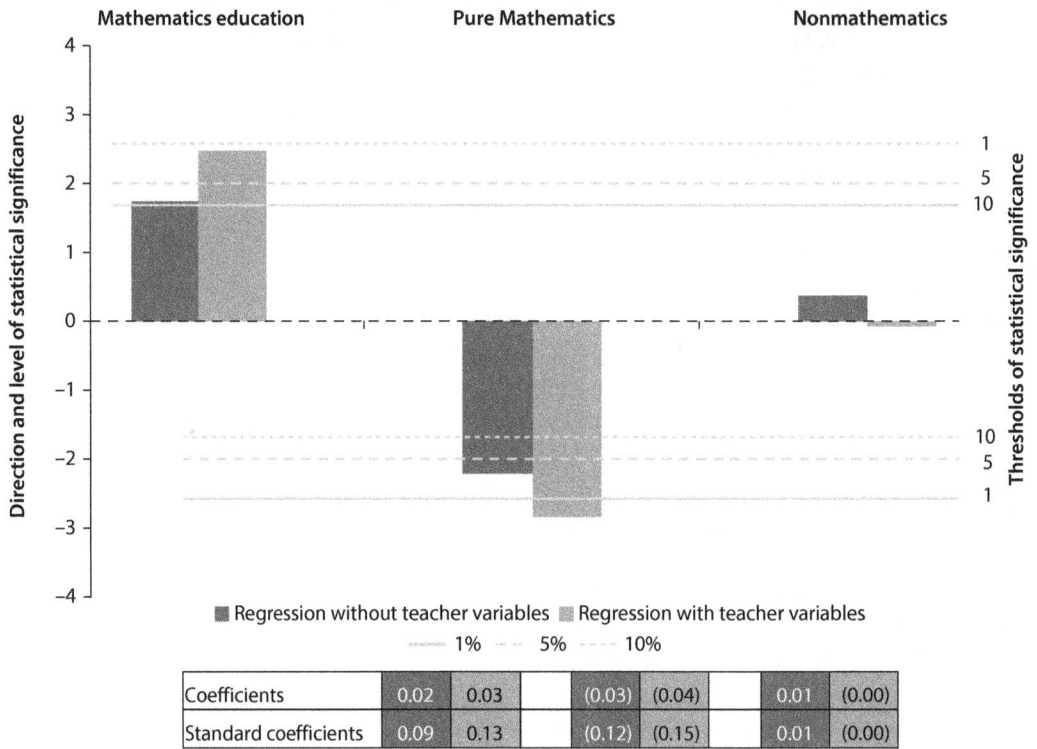

	Mathematics education			Pure Mathematics			Nonmathematics	
Coefficients	0.02	0.03		(0.03)	(0.04)		0.01	(0.00)
Standard coefficients	0.09	0.13		(0.12)	(0.15)		0.01	(0.00)

Note: Full regression results can be found in appendix F at the end of this book. TIMSS = Trends in International Mathematics and Science Study.

In interpreting the regression coefficient for the teacher degree type and its relation to student posttest scores, the students having a teacher with a mathematics education degree tended to have posttest scores that were 3 percentage points higher after controlling for multiple background factors and the students' pretest scores.[11]

It is important to note that this result *should not* be oversimplified to conclude that only teachers with mathematics education degrees should be hired. In fact, teachers with pure mathematics degrees do tend to have important foundational skills and can be very effective teachers. What is important about this result is that it may provide insights into how training can support teacher development. The result may be capturing important pedagogical skills that the teachers with mathematics education degrees obtain through their degree work. Ensuring that teachers with pure mathematics degrees receive similar additional pedagogical training could have a positive impact. It may also capture differences in the way the degree courses teach mathematics, with the mathematics degree teachers learning how to solve problems whereas mathematics education degree courses tend to approach problems within the context of teaching mathematical concepts and problem-solving approaches to students.

Figure 5.13 Practices of Teachers with Mathematics Education Degrees vs. Those with Pure Mathematics or Nonmathematics Degrees in Indonesia TIMSS Video Study of Mathematics Classes, 2007–11

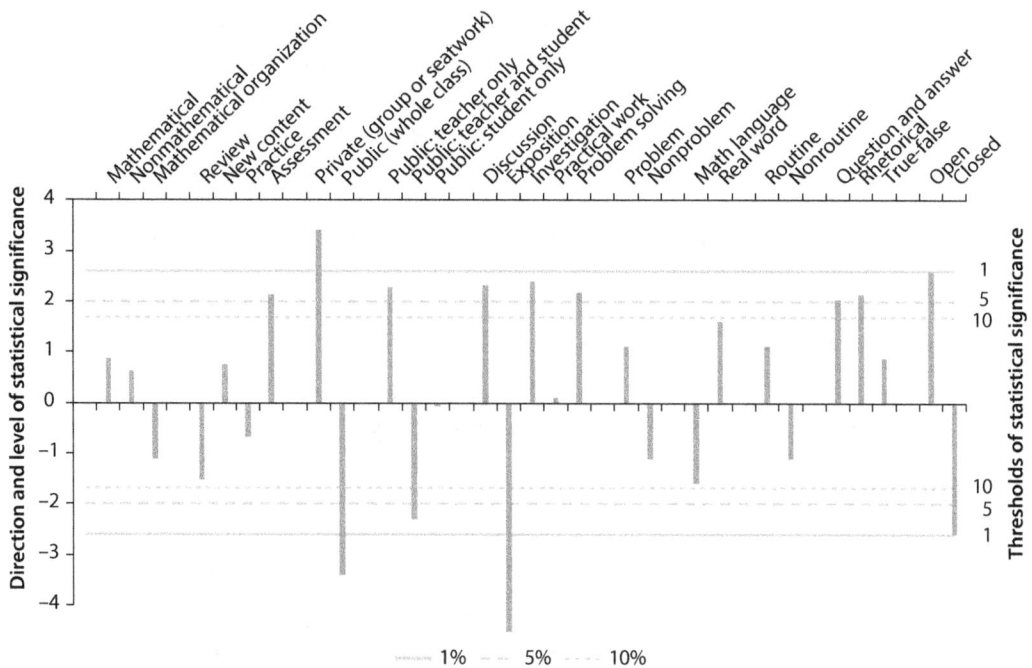

Note: Full regression results can be found in appendix G at the end of this book. TIMSS = Trends in International Mathematics and Science Study.

Teaching Practice Comparison

The difference between teachers holding mathematics education degrees and those holding pure mathematics degrees is one of the biggest distinguishing factors in terms of the types of teaching practices employed. As is shown in figure 5.13, teachers with mathematics education degrees tended to generally use the practices that are positively related with student learning outcomes. They tended to use a teaching approach of investigation, problem solving, and discussion more often than exposition, which has a strong negative relationship with student learning.

Questioning (as box 5.1 discusses further) was also an important distinguishing factor: Mathematics education teachers used questioning much more frequently and with various techniques including question-and-answer and rhetorical questioning. They also tended to do more private interaction teaching (group and individual seatwork) than public (whole-class) teaching and tended to do more monitoring of student activities.

It is not always the case that the techniques used more often by mathematics education teachers than mathematics-only degree teachers had a positive relationship with student outcomes. For example, they tended to do more teacher-only public interaction and less teacher-student public interaction. Real-world contexts in working on mathematical problems were also used more often by mathematics education teachers, and mathematical language and symbols (which have a positive relationship with learning), less often.

Box 5.1 The Use of Questioning from the Perspective of the Teacher's Goals

Questioning can be a powerful instrument in a mathematics teacher's repertoire of teaching practices and can serve various purposes in defining the dynamics of the classroom and developing student learning. Through interviews and the observation of case study teachers in the video study, an interesting picture emerged of how teachers conceive of and use questioning. Teachers said that they used questioning to check understanding (majority), keep the students' attention, direct the students' attention, and understand what students are thinking. They also explained that they called on individual students as a way of building their self-confidence, although some teachers at times used it as a punishment for not paying attention. Ainley (1988) developed a framework of questioning based on the teacher's goals by which questions were categorized in the following way:

• *Pseudo questions:* to establish an acceptable behavior or a social contract with students
• *Testing questions:* to find out whether students respond correctly
• *Genuine questions:* to seek information (thus, teachers do not know the answers to these types of questions)
• *Direct or provoking questions:* to provoke students' thinking by making new connections or clarifying existing ones and by exploring new areas of mathematical knowledge

   In Indonesia's classrooms, the use of pseudo and testing questions dominated, but the relatively effective teachers would more frequently use genuine questions and direct or provoking questions. The latter is considered to be particularly effective at encouraging higher-order thinking.

Teacher Knowledge

Teacher competency testing is an important recent inclusion in the certification process. In 2012, such testing was introduced into the process; teachers falling below the passing mark are not allowed to become certified and must reapply the following year. Whereas virtually all teachers were able to obtain certification in the previous process, the new process truly has the possibility of distinguishing between higher- and lower-quality teachers from a competency standpoint.

   But is competency testing a valid way of determining higher- and lower-quality teachers, and will it make a difference in terms of improving student learning outcomes? This section presents an analysis that indicates a strong relationship between teacher knowledge and student learning outcomes and also indicates that teachers with greater knowledge use different practices than teachers with less knowledge.

Relationship of Teacher Knowledge to Student Learning Outcomes

Of all factors explored, teacher knowledge had the strongest relationship to student learning outcomes. The results indicate that *both* subject matter knowledge and pedagogical knowledge, in almost all cases, were well above the generally accepted 5 percent statistical significance threshold and typically above

Figure 5.14 Relationship between Teacher Knowledge and Student Learning in Indonesia TIMSS Video Study of Mathematics Classes, 2007–11

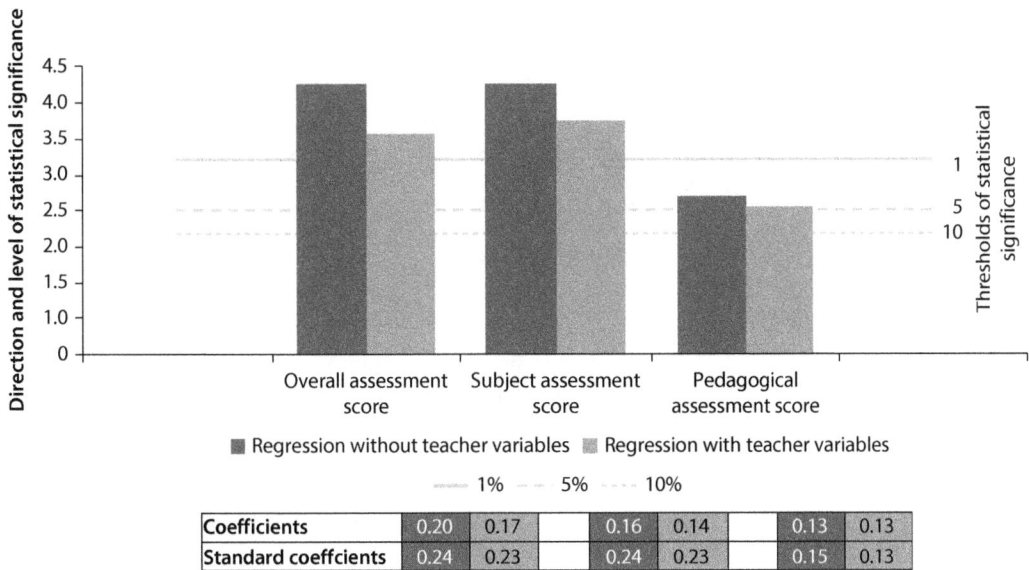

	Overall assessment score		Subject assessment score		Pedagogical assessment score	
Coefficients	0.20	0.17	0.16	0.14	0.13	0.13
Standard coeffcients	0.24	0.23	0.24	0.23	0.15	0.13

Note: Full regression results can be found in appendix H at the end of this book. TIMSS = Trends in International Mathematics and Science Study.

the 1 percent significance threshold (see figure 5.14). The significance levels tended to drop when including teacher background variables such as educational level and experience, likely indicating that other teacher characteristics also play an important role in student learning.

Teacher subject knowledge tended to have a stronger relationship with student learning than did pedagogical knowledge. This may, in part, be due to the measurements themselves, with subject matter knowledge lending itself well to a test whereas pedagogical knowledge is much more difficult to measure through a written test.[12] Still, the fact that pedagogical knowledge also tended to have strong results indicates its important role in learning outcomes.

In interpreting the regression coefficient for the degree and its relation to student posttest scores, a percentage point increase on a teacher's assessment score is related to a 0.17 percentage point increase in a student's posttest score after controlling for multiple background factors and the student's pretest score. Teacher assessment scores ranged from 7 percent to 75 percent, with an average score of 48 percent. For example, a 10-percentage-point higher teacher assessment score resulted in a student's posttest score being 1.7 percentage points higher. Again, because the average score on the posttest was only 34 percent, the 1.7 percentage point difference represents a difference of 5 percent relative to the average score. (Similar but lower coefficients were found when looking at the subject and pedagogy score in relation to students' posttest score, with a 0.14 and 0.10 percentage point increase, respectively.) The standardized coefficients indicate that a 1.0 standard deviation increase in teacher assessment scores is related to a 0.23 standard deviation increase in student test scores.

Figure 5.15 Relationship between Teaching Practices and Teacher Knowledge (Assessment Score Percentage) in Indonesia TIMSS Video Study of Mathematics Classes, 2007–11

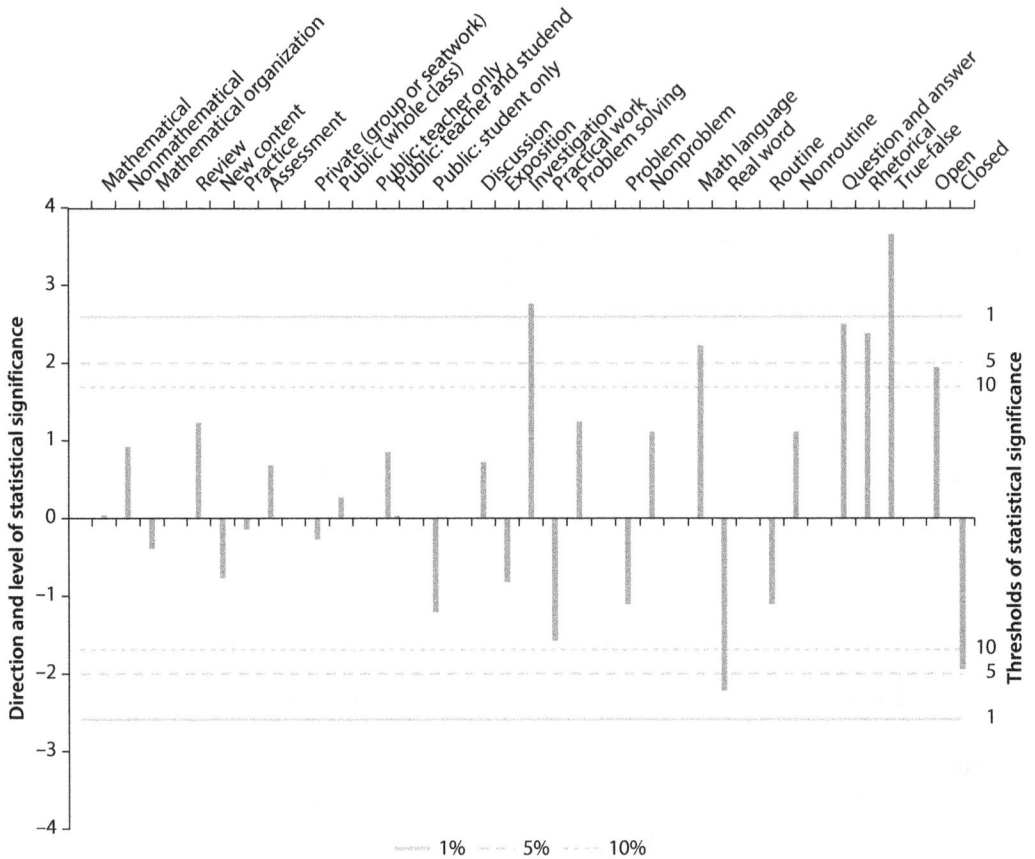

Note: Bars that pass the 5 percent threshold are considered to be statistically significant. Full regression results can be found in appendix I at the end of this book. TIMSS = Trends in International Mathematics and Science Study.

Teaching Practice Comparison

The strong relationship between teacher knowledge and student learning indicates that teachers with more knowledge tended to teach more effectively, but can this knowledge be communicated through the teaching practices employed in the classroom? When dividing teachers into high and low knowledge groups and then comparing the groups' frequency and approach in teaching practices, certain differences emerged as is shown in figure 5.15: Teachers with greater knowledge tended to use mathematical language rather than real-world contexts. They also tended to use questioning techniques, such as question-and-answer, rhetorical, and true-false questioning, more often. In terms of teaching strategy, they tended to use the investigative technique more.[13] All other teaching practices were not statistically significant.

The differences in teaching practices may reflect greater confidence with mathematics among teachers with greater knowledge. Teachers' use of problems with mathematical language may indicate a fluency in mathematics. The much greater use of questioning could possibly be related to greater confidence in dialogue with students, whereas teachers with less knowledge might shy away from questioning because it could lead to unexpected challenges. Finally, the teaching approaches of investigation (statistically significant) and discussion (positive but not quite statistically significant) may require a higher comfort level and fluency in mathematics depending on how they are used.

What is somewhat surprising is that students whose teachers have greater knowledge tended to do much better, but the teaching practices are *not* so drastically different. This likely indicates that the more knowledgeable teachers were more effective in using the same practices. For example, two teachers could conduct a review of previous material, but teachers with greater knowledge may tend to be more effective because they give clearer explanations and can spot and correct student errors and misconceptions and other factors because they have a better grasp of mathematics and pedagogical concepts.

Conclusions

In examining teaching practices in a sample of Indonesia's 8th-grade mathematics classrooms, important findings emerged that have implications for the teacher reform process and how the quality of teachers can be improved over time. Key aspects of certification and the four-year degree requirement were explored in the context of what takes place in the classroom and how they relate to student learning outcomes.

Qualifications Comparisons

The video study had results that were strikingly similar to the findings of the certification study when examining teacher qualifications and their relation to student learning outcomes.

The students of certified teachers did not have better student learning outcomes than students of uncertified teachers. This seems to indicate that teachers were not improved through the certification process itself. It also underscores the fact that the process did not separate higher-quality teachers from lower-quality ones; this is self-evident because virtually all teachers passed the certification process.

There was also no difference in the subject matter and pedagogy assessment scores of certified and uncertified teachers. Certification could have conceivably improved teacher competency in subject matter and pedagogy through the additional training received by teachers in the certification training course (for those who did not directly pass the portfolio process). Certified teachers also generally tended to participate in a greater number of training courses, possibly to strengthen their portfolios. But the fact that there is no statistically significant difference in the competency test scores of certified teachers is a further indication that the certification process itself has not boosted competency and has also not been separating out teachers in terms of quality. With the introduction of teacher competency testing as part of the certification process, however, this could change—especially if the testing and certification processes are carried out more rigorously than in the past.

Educational level, on the other hand, did have a positive relationship with student outcomes. The requirement that all teachers obtain a four-year degree may lead to a significant improvement in the quality of the teacher workforce over time.

A strong relationship exists between teacher knowledge—in both subject matter and pedagogy—and student learning outcomes. This result is particularly important. There are concerns about the quality of four-year degrees offered by many universities across Indonesia. That the competency test scores had such a strong relationship with student outcomes underscores the importance of including it as part of the certification process. Requiring teachers to meet a minimum threshold of skills and knowledge would likely have a significant impact on improving the teacher workforce over the long term, both by pushing teachers to improve their skills and by rewarding teachers who demonstrate higher quality.

Interesting differences also emerged by teacher degree type—comparing teachers holding mathematics education degrees with those holding pure mathematics degrees. The pure-mathematics-degree teachers tended to have higher subject matter scores on the teacher competency assessment, but when it came to student outcomes, students of teachers having a mathematics education degree performed better than those whose teachers had a pure mathematics degree. This result *should not* be interpreted to mean that teachers should be required to hold an education-oriented degree but rather that those coming into the system with a noneducation degree are likely to require pedagogical training. This could be given in the extra year of training now required for all wanting to become a teacher.

Teaching Practices Comparisons

When looking at the certification study dimensions through the lens of teaching practices, some telling results emerged. Of particular relevance was that the teaching practices of certified teachers *did not* differ from practices used by uncertified teachers.[14] This finding builds on the evidence that there is no difference in student learning outcomes of certified teachers and extends further to indicate that certification also appears to have no impact from the perspective of changing practices used in the classroom. It indicates that certification itself, even with increased income, doesn't appear to alter the way teachers teach. This can be seen in two ways: after certification, (a) teaching practices do not change, and (b) the *quality* of the practices used (which could have arisen through increased motivation and preparation) also does not change.

On the other hand, striking differences emerged in the teaching practices of teachers with greater subject and pedagogical knowledge (relative to those with less knowledge) and in the practices of teachers holding mathematical education degrees (relative to those with pure mathematics degrees). Both groups tended to more frequently use practices that correlated with higher learning outcomes.

Practices in Relation to Student Learning Outcomes

Some insights were gained on the extent to which specific practices were used, the trend in the use of these practices between 2007 and 2011, and how the practices related to student learning.

In the area of *teaching approaches*, teachers often used exposition (lecturing) in the classroom, and this tended to have a negative relationship with student outcomes, while other techniques such as investigation, practical work, and problem solving had a positive relationship. Student participation also emerged as an important differentiator. Teacher-centered activities tended to have a negative relationship with learning outcomes whereas active participation of students in learning activities tended to be positive. But interestingly, when those activities were student-only, they appeared to be less effective than those with teacher-student involvement. Time on task was also clearly important, and students with teachers who spent more time on mathematics and who used more problem time than nonproblem time tended to have better learning outcomes.

The change in practices between 2007 and 2011 also provided interesting insights. In terms of approach, teachers tended to use more exposition and less discussion and investigation in 2011. Teachers were also spending more time on new material and less time on practice. Teachers' time on task appears to have gone in the opposite direction from what would be hoped, with less time dedicated to mathematics and less of that mathematics time involving mathematical problems. Teachers also tended to use more mathematical language and routine approaches.

Although some teacher reform factors appear to be related to more teachers having a four-year degree, certification itself does not appear to be driving change in the classroom. It actually appears that other factors beyond the teacher reforms are having greater influence on teaching practices. Of particular importance is the increased emphasis on the national examination, which appears to lead teachers to use practices that better prepare students for the examination. This could be seen as positive or negative. With more "teaching to the test," students may be learning to answer questions rather than gaining true mathematical understanding. Still, techniques such as focusing on mathematical language and formulas as opposed to real-world contexts did have a positive relationship with student test scores.

The video study highlights the important relationship between what takes place in the classroom and student learning outcomes. It also highlights the fact that teaching practices evolve over time and that multiple system and cultural influences contribute to this evolution. The teacher reform is contributing to this evolution, although not always as intended and not working in isolation from other influential factors.

Notes

1. Different teachers and students participated in each phase, so the two-phase approach should not be seen as providing panel data.

2. By summarizing the practices of the full sample of teachers, a "lesson signature" of Indonesian 8th-grade mathematics teachers in general was obtained.

3. Although the study uses TIMSS student test results in some analyses, this measure provides only a snapshot of student achievement levels as they finish the 8th-grade year. For in-depth analysis of the relationship of teaching practices to student learning outcomes, an additional component of pre- and posttesting was added in the 2011 phase. Only the 2011 data were used for analyses involving student learning outcomes because pre- and posttesting are critical for properly measuring student learning progress within the 8th-grade year.

4. The effects of practices across contexts will be explored in great detail in the forthcoming full video study, but because of space constraints much of the detail cannot be presented in this chapter.

5. Academic Learning Time (ALT) is defined by Berliner (1990) as that part of allocated time in a subject matter area (physical education, science, or mathematics, for example) in which a student is engaged successfully in the activities or with the materials to which he or she is exposed and in which those activities and materials are related to educational outcomes that are valued (Berliner 1987; Fisher *et al.* 1980).

6. Full results for these layers are not shown because of space constraints.

7. At the same time, it is important to note that just because students are not actively participating through dialogue does not necessarily indicate a lack of engagement because students could still be actively thinking about and working on problems.

8. It is important to note that although investigation shows up as having a strong positive relationship, it was used by only three teachers in the sample, so the results should be interpreted with caution.

9. Examples of practices encouraged can be found in the ministry's teacher training branches and in documentation and learning modules distributed to teacher working groups for use in professional development. Student-centered learning and increased student participation are encouraged, while teacher-centered and rote learning tend to be discouraged.

10. The queuing criteria, such as experience and educational level, did mean that differences do exist between certified and uncertified teachers, but these factors were controlled for in the analysis.

11. As noted earlier, students of teachers with mathematics education degrees started out with lower pretest scores, so the 3 percentage point difference is based on their relative improvement.

12. A great deal of caution should be used in assessing a teacher through a pedagogy examination because a teacher's pedagogical effectiveness is not about knowing facts about teaching methods that can be reduced to a question in a multiple-choice examination. The video study is specifically intended to explore how teachers use their pedagogical knowledge "in the moment." Still, the fact that such a strong relationship exists between the pedagogy score and student learning indicates that the test is, in fact, capturing some aspect of the teachers' knowledge and appears to provide a proxy for what they do in the classroom.

13. There is an issue with using this variable in that only three teachers actually used the investigative technique, so any positive or negative relationship may be inaccurate because it was used so infrequently and by so few teachers.

14. One difference did emerge: certified teachers tended to have more whole-class interaction and less seatwork and group work interaction. These practices do not have a statistically significant relationship to student outcomes.

References

Ainley, J. 1988. "Perceptions of Teachers' Questioning Styles." Proceedings of the Twelfth Annual Conference of the International Group for the Psychology of Mathematics Education, 92–99. Veszprem, Hungary, July 20–25.

Berliner, D. C. 1987. "Simple Views of Effective Teaching and a Simple Theory of Classroom Instruction." In *Talks to Teachers*, edited by D. C. Berliner and B. Rosenshine, 93–110. New York: Random House.

———. 1990. "What's All the Fuss About Instructional Time?" In *The Nature of Time in Schools: Theoretical Concepts, Practitioner Perceptions*, edited by M. Ben-Peretz and R. Bromme, 3–35. New York: Teachers College Press.

Carroll, J. B. 1963. "A Model of School Learning." *Teachers College Record* 64 (8): 723–33.

Dewey, J. 1938. *Experience and Education*. New York: Macmillan.

Doyle, W. 1990. "Classroom Management Techniques." In *Student Discipline Strategies: Research and Practice*, edited by O. C. Moles, 113–27. New York: New York University Press.

Fisher, C. W., D. C. Berliner, N. N. Fully, R. S. Marliave, L. S. Cahen, and M. M. Dishaw. 1980. "Teaching Behaviors, Academic Learning Time, and Student Achievement: An Overview." In *Time to Learn*, edited by C. Denham and A. Lieberman, 7–32. Washington, DC: National Institute of Education.

Handal, B. 2003. "Teachers' Mathematical Beliefs: A Review." *The Mathematics Educator* 13 (2): 47–57.

Hiebert, J., R. Gallimore, H. Garnier, K. B. Givvin, H. Hollingsworth, J. Jacobs, A. Miu-Ying Chui, D. Wearne, M. Smith, N. Kersting, A. Manaster, E. Tseng, W. Etterbeek, C. Manaster, P. Gonzales, and J. Stigler. 2003. *Teaching Mathematics in Seven Countries: Results from the TIMSS 1999 Video Study*. Washington, DC: National Center for Education Statistics, Institute of Education Sciences, U.S. Department of Education.

Kounin, J. S. 1970. "Observing and Delineating Technique of Managing Behavior in Classrooms." *Journal of Research and Development in Education* 4 (1): 62–72.

Kuhs, T., and D. Ball. 1986. "Approaches to Teaching Mathematics: Mapping the Domains of Knowledge, Skills and Dispositions." Article, Center on Teacher Education, Michigan State University, East Lansing, MI.

Stallings, J., and S. Knight. 2003. "Using the Stallings Observation System to Investigate Time on Task in Four Countries." Unpublished paper for the International Time on Task (ITOT) Project, World Bank, Washington, DC.

Wragg, E. C. 1993. "Multimedia in Education: Bane or Boon?" *Journal of Educational Television* 19 (2): 73–79.

CHAPTER 6

The Impact of the Reforms on the Efficiency and Equity of Public Spending

Introduction

Progress in education in Indonesia over the past 15 years has been driven by significant increases in public spending. Since 2001, government education spending has doubled in real terms, and in 2009 approximately 4 percent of gross domestic product was devoted to the sector. These large increases in public spending have come about through the achievement of a constitutional obligation to devote a fifth of the government budget to education.

A significant proportion of the increased government investment in education has financed the teacher reforms outlined in previous chapters. Most notably, the 2005 Teacher Law introduced a professional allowance for certification and incentives for working in remote areas that have added significant commitments to government spending. As a way of balancing the increases in the education budget from rising teacher compensation, the government introduced measures to improve the efficiency of teacher use. For example, the Teacher Law requires teachers to teach for a minimum of 24 period-hours per week, and school staffing standards were revised to address the low national student-teacher ratios for basic education.

The purpose of this chapter is to assess the effect of these reforms on the efficiency and equity of teacher supply and distribution. The key message that arises from this assessment is that improvements in teacher pay have placed a significant additional burden on the government budget while reforms designed to improve efficiency and equity have had limited impact.

Many of the issues addressed in this chapter are relevant for other countries in the region and beyond. Countries, such as Indonesia, that have experienced relatively high and stable rates of growth have been able to—or have the potential to—rapidly increase their investments in education. Insights from Indonesia's experience of using these additional resources can provide valuable lessons for countries aiming to improve educational quality.

Getting the right number of competent teachers equitably distributed across all schools, regardless of their location, is a challenge faced by all countries. In Indonesia, these challenges are particularly acute given its geographical and socioeconomic diversity. Rapid rates of urbanization across the world are also shifting the demand for schools and teachers from rural and remote areas to towns and cities without neglecting the need to keep good teachers in less-developed parts of the country where they are often needed the most. Managing this shift in a cost-effective way is becoming an increasingly pressing problem in many countries in Europe and Asia. The analysis presented in this chapter highlights how these trends have affected school size and teacher demand in Indonesia.

To assess the effect of reforms on teacher pay and management, the next section outlines the specific aspects of the reform process that were designed to tackle some of the perceived inadequacies in teacher pay and the significant inefficiencies in teacher hiring and deployment systems. This is followed by a section that explores the effects of these reforms, and the final section offers some conclusions.

What Reforms Were Introduced?

Prior to the Teacher Law, the perceived low quality of the Indonesian education system was seen to be associated with low teacher motivation because of low relative rates of pay. As previous chapters have discussed, a professional allowance was introduced as the result of teachers being certified.

The Teacher Law also attempted to tackle the inefficiencies in teacher deployment by making certification conditional on a 24 period-hour teaching week. In many schools, particularly at the junior secondary level, teachers taught for a relatively limited amount of the working week. At the secondary level, teachers officially can teach only one subject; for many, teaching 24 hours in the same school is difficult because of the limited number of classes and the number of hours devoted to each subject in the curriculum. For example, the current curriculum suggests approximately four hours of teaching on mathematics, English, Bahasa Indonesia, the natural sciences, and social sciences per week for each grade. For a teacher certified to teach only one subject and teaching in a school with only one class in each grade—often the case for small, often isolated schools—it is only possible to teach a maximum of 12 hours. This has, in some cases, improved efficiency in teacher deployment because those unable to achieve 24 hours of teaching in their own school have fulfilled the criteria by teaching in more than one school.

Remote-area allowances were also introduced as part of the Teacher Law to address both the overall shortage of teachers and the poor educational background of existing teachers in these areas. These initial reforms have been supplemented with scholarships and upgrading programs for teachers already working in these areas. For example, as described in chapter 3, a program for graduate teachers to work in remote areas was introduced in 2011. The program promises scholarships for postgraduate professional training (a requirement for certification) if recipients are willing to move back to remote areas to teach for at least a year. Currently about 5,000 teachers are participating in this program.

Central and district hiring of non-civil-service (non-*Pegawai Negeri Sipil* [PNS]) teachers was also frozen in 2005, and a process of converting existing non-PNS teachers to civil servants began (Ragatz 2010). This was in part a response to low educational quality and the generally lower levels of education that non-PNS teachers had. At the same time, the School Operational Assistance (*Bantuan Operasional Sekolah* [BOS]) program was introduced that provided all primary and junior secondary schools with grants for operational spending. As much as 30 percent of these grants were used to finance non-PNS hiring (Ragatz 2010). Recognizing that this was contributing to the overstaffing of schools, the government introduced in 2011 a 20 percent ceiling on teacher payments from BOS funds.

At the same time, a number of other reforms also had an impact on the efficiency of the teaching force. Since 2007, staffing standards have been introduced not only to ensure that schools are adequately staffed but also to identify schools with surplus teachers who could potentially be moved to schools without enough teachers. The most recent set of regulations (issued as a joint decree by all central ministries with responsibility for teacher hiring and deployment in 2011) aimed to improve the distribution of teachers and tackle the incentives for overhiring.

The Impacts of Reform

Effects on Teacher Supply

Ensuring that the teaching profession attracts some of the brightest school graduates into preservice education is crucial for the quality of any education system. To do this, the teaching profession has to be attractive compared with other similar jobs in terms of remuneration, working conditions, and job satisfaction. In many of the best-performing countries, selection processes for teacher education ensure that only appropriate individuals are selected for teacher education and that intakes match with teacher needs. For example, in Singapore, only one in five applicants for teacher education programs is offered a place, but almost all of those graduating enter the teaching profession (Ragatz 2010).

In Indonesia, the increased salary of teachers brought about through certification has made teaching an attractive profession. Wages for noncertified teachers with a four-year degree are similar to nonteachers with the same qualifications, as shown in figure 6.1. However, certified teachers earn substantially more than other individuals with similar levels of education. In fact, certified teachers can earn approximately twice as much as individuals with similar qualifications. Although these wage increases have not led to significant improvements in

Figure 6.1 Average Lifetime Monthly Salary for Teachers and Nonteachers with a Four-Year Degree in Indonesia, 2010

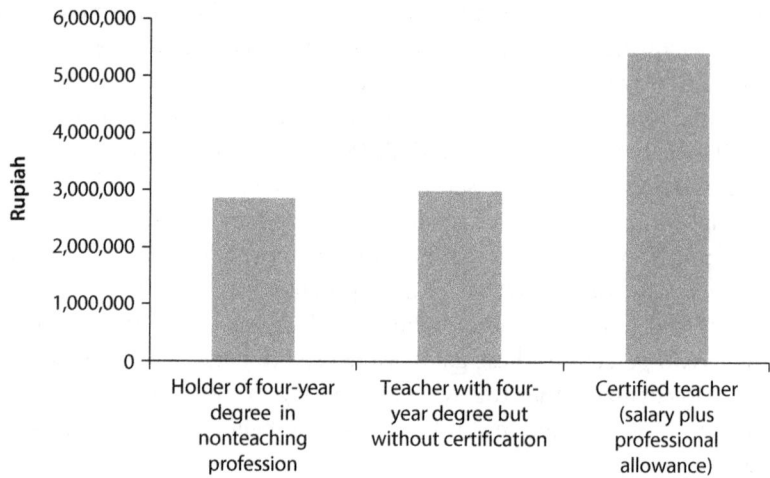

Sources: BPS 2010 and Ministry of Education and Culture teacher salary scales.
Note: Wages for teachers without certification and nonteachers include all categories of workers (for example, both public and private sector workers and both civil service and non-civil-service workers) and are calculated using the labor force survey (BPS 2010). Monthly wages are calculated as an unweighted average of four age groups (20–29, 30–39, 40–49, and 50–59). The wages for a certified civil service teacher are based on Ministry of Education and Culture salary scales and the size of the professional allowance. It is assumed a teacher is certified in the 30–39 age group.

teacher behavior and student learning outcomes, there is some evidence to suggest that high wages have begun to attract somewhat better candidates into teacher education programs (see chapter 3).

Although increases in teacher pay have raised the quality of student intakes in preservice education institutions, there is a significant mismatch between the numbers graduating from colleges and teacher need. Chapter 4 showed that in 2011 there were approximately 500,000 students currently training to be teachers. Given the limited need for new teachers over the next few years (see the next section, "Effects on the Efficiency of Teacher Use"), it is unclear how this magnitude of newly qualified teachers will enter the current teaching profession. They could possibly replace existing teachers who do not have the required qualifications to teach under the new law. However, almost all of these in-service teachers (approximately 500,000) are currently upgrading their qualifications to ensure that they comply with the new qualification requirements. Because many of these teachers are non-PNS teachers, the political consequences of replacing non-PNS teachers with newly qualified graduates would be significant.

Effects on Public Spending

Reforms to improve teacher quality, outlined in earlier chapters, have placed and will continue to place significant pressure on the education budget. In particular, the teacher professional allowance paid to teachers who become certified effectively doubles the basic pay of teachers' salaries. With over 2 million teachers currently teaching in primary and junior secondary schools across Indonesia, the resources necessary to implement the certification program fully are enormous.

The reforms have been largely financed by increases in government investment in education and the fulfillment in 2009 of the constitutional obligation to devote 20 percent of the public budget to education. Between 2001 and 2009, government spending on education increased by 120 percent in real terms (see figure 6.2). Increases in the education budget have been most rapid since the introduction of the certification program. Between 2006 and 2010, the overall education budget increased in real terms by 47 percent or Rp 66 trillion ($6 billion).

Implications of Increased Teacher Recruitment, Certification, and Salaries

A significant proportion of the increased public investment in education has been devoted to hiring more teachers and increasing their pay through the certification program. Between 2006 and 2010, an additional 450,000 teachers were recruited, and by 2010 approximately 30 percent of all teachers had been certified.[1] Approximately 60 percent of the increased resources going to education between 2006–08 and 2009 were absorbed by teacher salaries and allowances (Cerdan-Infantes and Makarova 2013). In 2011, the professional allowance associated with certification cost Rp 23 trillion or 9 percent of the overall education budget.

Until recently, the large proportion of non-PNS teachers has constrained the budgetary impact of the reform. Teacher salaries combined with the number of

Figure 6.2 Public Expenditure on Education in Indonesia, 2001–10

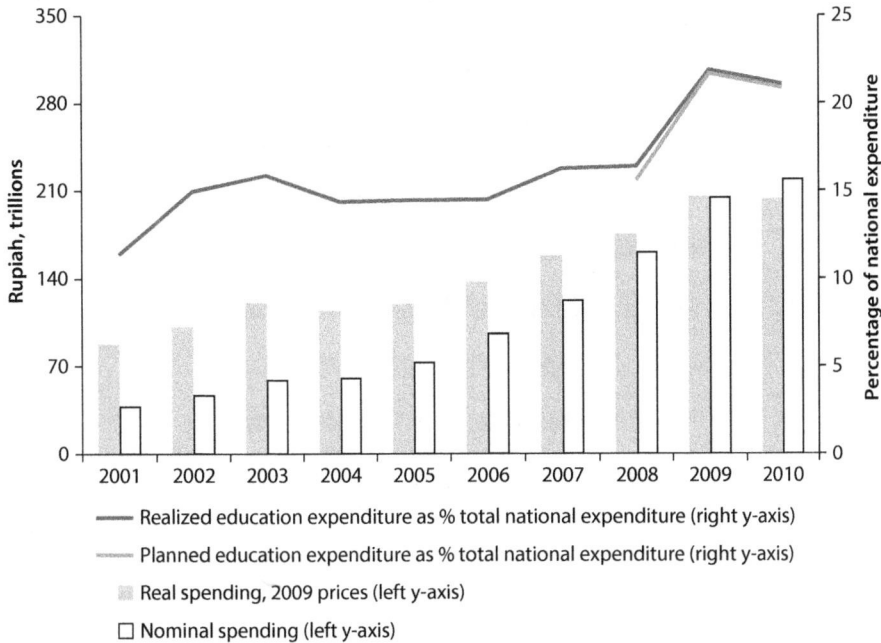

— Realized education expenditure as % total national expenditure (right y-axis)
— Planned education expenditure as % total national expenditure (right y-axis)
▨ Real spending, 2009 prices (left y-axis)
☐ Nominal spending (left y-axis)

Source: Cerdan-Infantes and Makarova 2013.

Teacher Reform in Indonesia • http://dx.doi.org/10.1596/978-0-8213-9829-6

students a typical teacher teaches are key drivers of the costs of education provision. Indonesia's low student-teacher ratios and higher salaries resulting from teacher certification imply that a large proportion of the education budget is devoted to paying teachers. However, 30 percent of the primary and secondary school teaching force is made up of non-PNS teachers who earn significantly less than their civil service counterparts. This limits overall salary expenditures and is a key factor in explaining Indonesia's relatively low share of teacher salaries in overall government education spending compared with other countries (see figure 6.3).

Certifying the remaining 1.7 million teachers (70 percent of the total) by 2015 will have enormous budgetary implications.[2] With the current pay scale and information on all teachers currently teaching in primary and junior secondary, it is possible to estimate the total cost of certification.[3] Using this approach, it is estimated that the provision of the existing professional allowance associated with only the certification of all primary and junior secondary school teachers

Figure 6.3   Share of Total Pretertiary Education Budget Spent on Salaries in Selected Countries, 2009

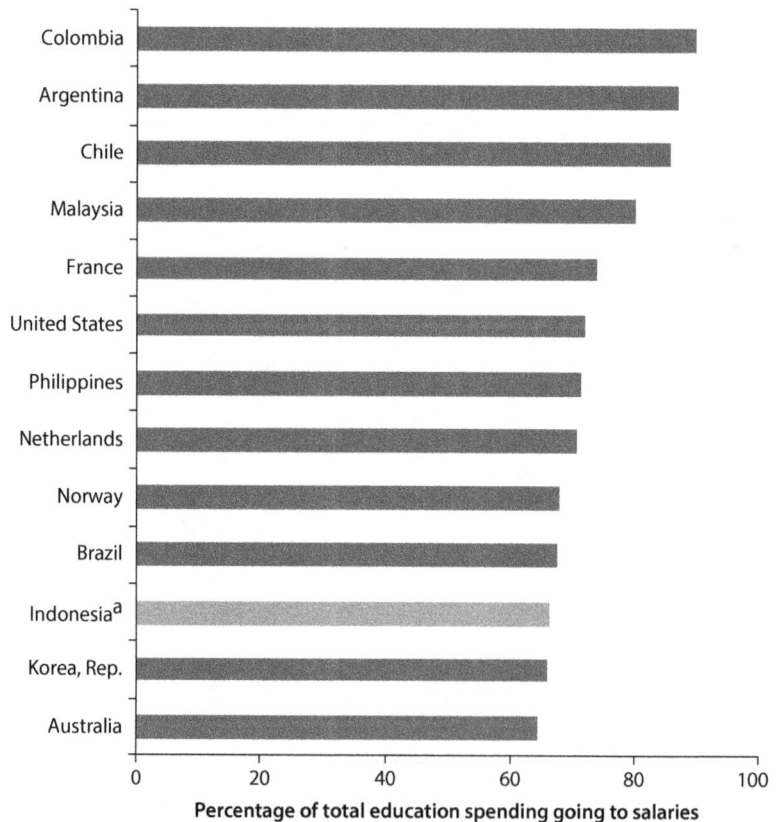

Percentage of total education spending going to salaries

Sources: UIS 2010; Indonesia data based on Cerdan-Infantes and Makarova 2013.
a. Indonesia's salary expenditure includes salary subsidies from certification and payment for contract teachers under School Operational Assistance (*Bantuan Operasional Sekolah*, or BOS) in addition to civil servant salaries.

would cost approximately Rp 68 trillion ($7 billion in constant 2012 prices).[4] Combining this with estimates of salaries and allowances suggests that the total salary bill for these teachers would rise in real terms to Rp 139 trillion ($16 billion), a 43 percent increase over the estimated 2012 salary bill.

In 2005, when the Teacher Law was introduced, the budgetary impact was even larger. At that time, the constitutional obligation to spend 20 percent of the budget on education had not been met, and the education budget had grown by only 37 percent in real terms between 2000 and 2005. Questions about the affordability of the program were raised at the time of its introduction. However, the strength of the demands of the teacher associations (supported by many parliamentarians) to raise teacher income appears to have trumped issues of the future affordability of the program.

Budgetary Trade-offs from Increased Certification Costs

There are substantial trade-offs associated with the increases in salary spending that result from certifying all teachers. Government medium-term budget projections show that overall government spending is estimated to grow by approximately 3 percent in real terms between 2012 and 2015 (World Bank 2012a). This projection also suggests that the education budget will increase only marginally over the next few years if it is assumed that the share of government spending going to education remains constant at 20 percent.

Certifying all eligible primary and junior secondary school teachers by 2015 will absorb approximately 41 percent of the total education budget in 2015 compared with 32 percent in 2012. If nonsalary spending in basic education is maintained at its 2012 level, this would imply that basic education would absorb 64 percent of the budget in 2015 compared with approximately 56 percent in 2012. This increased spending would require cutbacks in other levels of education. The remaining budget for other educational levels, after all civil service teachers were certified, would be Rp 113 trillion ($11.8 billion) in 2015, down from Rp 135 trillion ($14.1 billion) in 2012 (figure 6.4).[5]

The rising cost of the certification program will continue to limit investments in other areas crucial for improving educational quality. So far, the certification program has not had a significant impact on teacher quality and student learning outcomes. Improving other factors associated with teacher quality has the potential to deliver bigger impacts on student learning outcomes. For example, weaknesses in preservice and in-service teacher education, ongoing professional development, and incentive systems have all been highlighted as factors associated with low teacher quality. Improvements in these areas would likely have significant payoffs, but the costs of the ongoing certification program will limit the resources available to make these additional investments.

The future costs of certification will also threaten other government objectives in the education sector. For example, the government plans to expand early childhood education programs, including kindergartens, and to mandate that compulsory education should include the three years of senior secondary education. Conservative estimates suggest that the additional public costs of expanding

Figure 6.4 Projected Budgetary Impact of the Teacher Certification Program in Indonesia, 2012 vs. 2015

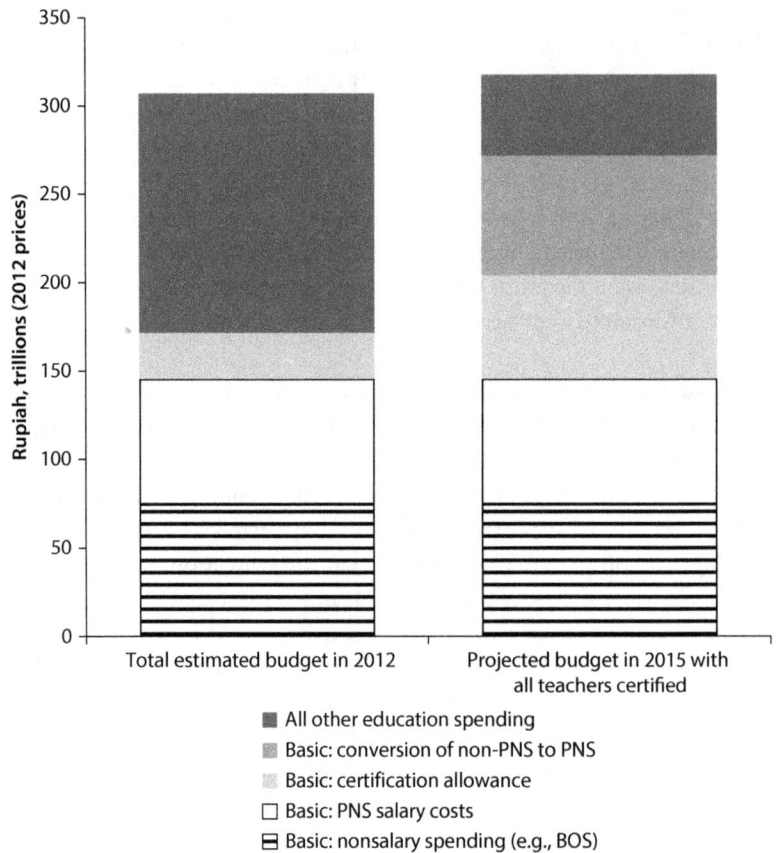

Legend:
- ■ All other education spending
- ▨ Basic: conversion of non-PNS to PNS
- ▧ Basic: certification allowance
- ☐ Basic: PNS salary costs
- ☰ Basic: nonsalary spending (e.g., BOS)

Sources: Budget data and projections from Cerdan-Infantes and Makarova 2013; World Bank 2012a. Salary spending data are based on teacher numbers and salary grade from Ministry of Education and Culture's 2010 teacher database and the 2012 civil service salary scale.

Note: BOS = School Operational Assistance (*Bantuan Operasional Sekolah*). Projections for 2015 assume that the number of teachers is the same as in 2012. Projections of certification costs based on author's calculations of basic pay for all current PNS (civil service) teachers and a monthly Rp 1.5 million allowance for GTY (*Guru Tetap Yayasan*) teachers, who are non-PNS teachers currently eligible to receive a certification allowance. Calculations for conversion of non-PNS teachers assume that non-PNS teachers would be distributed across the pay scale in a similar way to PNS teachers. Conversion cost also includes the increase in the professional allowance from Rp 1.5 million per month to an amount equivalent to the basic pay of newly converted GTY non-PNS teachers.

senior secondary access in this way would be Rp 15 trillion ($1.5 billion), equivalent to 26 percent of the overall cost of the basic education certification program (Cerdan-Infantes and Makarova 2013). It is unclear where these resources will come from, given the costs of the certification program and the limited prospects for education receiving more than 20 percent of the government budget in the near future.

More broadly, the costs of the certification program will slow the shift of spending from basic to postbasic education seen in other rapidly developing middle-income countries. The budget projections show that the share of the budget going to basic education will increase as more teachers become certified. Indonesia already spends a relatively high share of its public education spending on basic education and significantly more than other countries in the region (see figure 6.5). As in these countries, Indonesia will need to start investing more heavily in both preschool and postbasic education if it is to provide the skilled labor force necessary to improve productivity and continue its impressive record of economic growth.

Capping Unsustainable Certification Costs, Finding Savings

Government plans to convert all non-PNS teachers to civil servants are financially unsustainable given current budget projections.[6] Approximately Rp 68 trillion ($5 billion) would be needed to certify and convert all existing non-PNS teachers to civil servants.[7] Taking the certification and conversion of non-PNS

Figure 6.5 Share of Education Spending by Level, Selected East Asian Countries, 2009

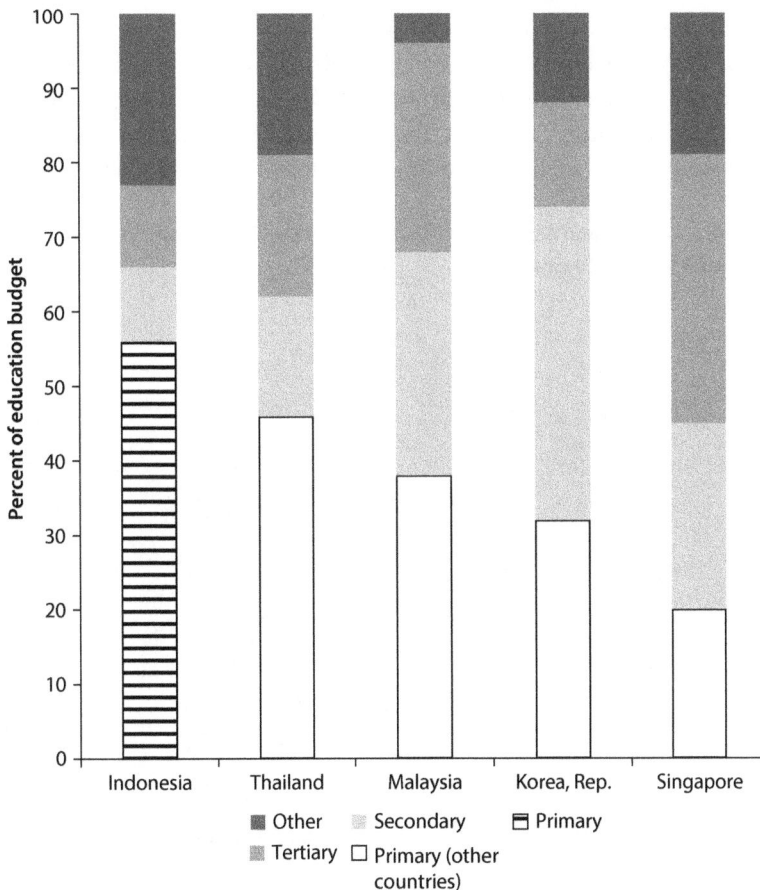

Legend: Other, Secondary, Primary, Tertiary, Primary (other countries)

Source: Cerdan-Infantes and Makarova 2013.

teachers to civil servants of all primary and junior secondary school teachers together would imply that 89 percent of the total education budget in 2015 would need to be devoted to basic education (as previously shown in figure 6.4). Given the commitments outside of basic education, this level of spending is completely unsustainable.

Improving the use of teachers and raising student-teacher ratios hold out the prospect of lessening the budgetary impact of certification. Simple simulations demonstrate the significant savings that could be realized by raising student-teacher ratios. Figure 6.6 shows the overall salary and certification costs for teachers eligible for certification at different student-teacher ratios.

The first bar shows the costs of salaries and professional allowances if all these teachers were certified at current student-teacher ratios. The subsequent bars show the effect of modest increases in the student-teacher ratio on the cost of certifying all teachers. If the student-teacher ratio increased to 22 to 1— Indonesia's level in the early 2000s—the salary and certification costs would be Rp 102 trillion ($10.6 billion) or 21 percent less than the costs estimated at current student-teacher ratios. Comparing this figure with the budget projections outlined earlier in the chapter shows that this increase in the student-teacher ratio would mean that basic education absorbs a slightly smaller share of overall educational resources in 2015. This shift would leave more resources available for other access and quality investments. Clearly, raising student-teacher ratios to these levels requires reducing the overall teaching force in basic education and adjusting staffing standards to improve the efficiency of teacher use.

Figure 6.6 Salary and Certification Costs for Civil Service Teachers in Indonesia under Different Student-Teacher Ratios

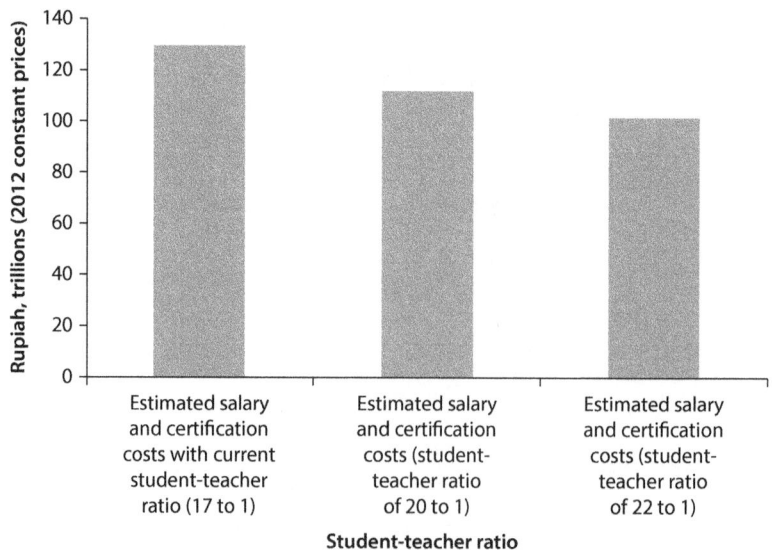

Source: Based on Cerdan-Infantes and Makarova 2013.
Note: The estimates compare the salary and certification costs under different student-teacher ratios. It is assumed that the student population remains the same.

Effects on the Efficiency of Teacher Use

Changes to the staffing standards introduced in the aftermath of the Teacher Law have not addressed the overstaffing issue. Teacher numbers have continued to rise at a faster rate than the student population at the primary level, and student-teacher ratios have declined from 19 to 1 when reforms were introduced in 2005 to around 17 to 1 in 2010 (Cerdan-Infantes and Makarova 2013). At the junior secondary level, student-teacher ratios have risen since the introduction of the teacher reforms, which may be largely due to the faster enrollment expansion in this subsector.

Too Many Teachers, Unequally Distributed

Overall, Indonesia continues to have some of the lowest student-teacher ratios in the world (see figure 6.7). While some other countries have seen student-teacher ratios decline significantly over the past five years, those ratios started out at

Figure 6.7 Student-Teacher Ratios in Basic Education, Selected East Asian and Pacific Countries, 2010

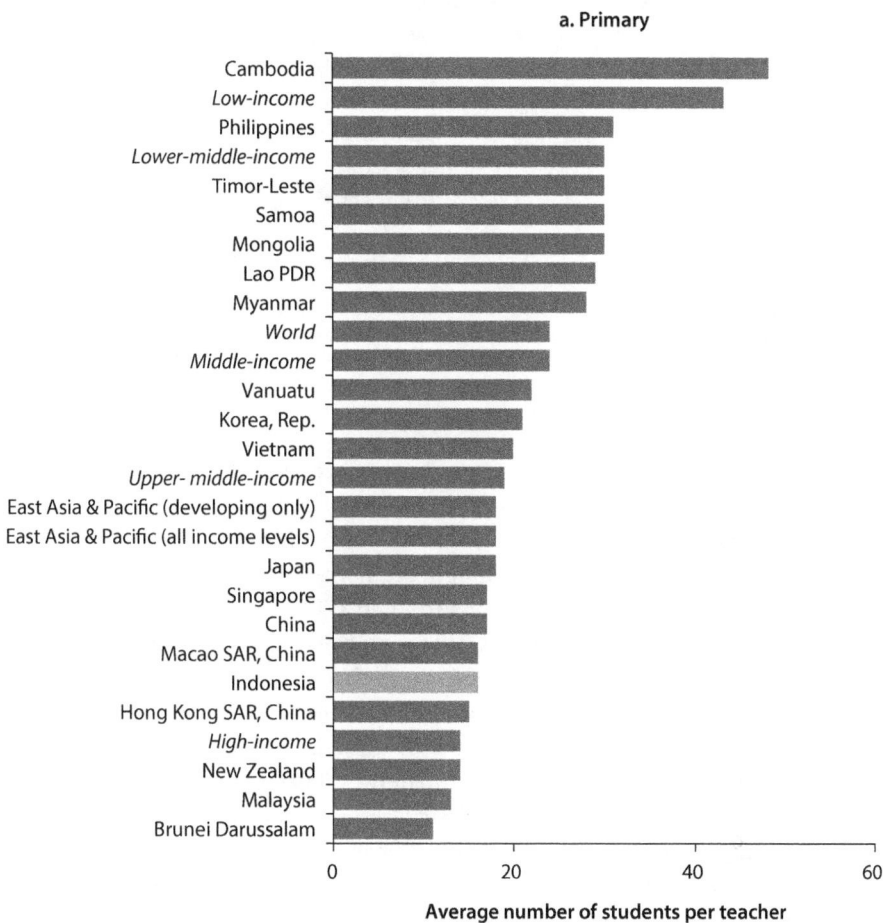

a. Primary

Average number of students per teacher

figure continues next page

Figure 6.7 Student-Teacher Ratios in Basic Education, Selected East Asian and Pacific Countries, 2010 *(continued)*

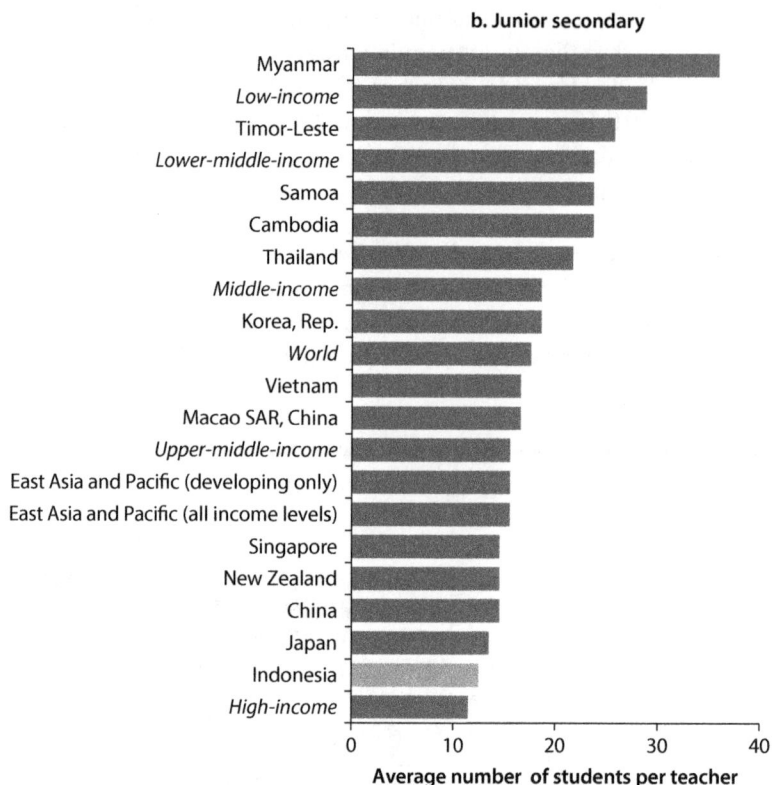

b. Junior secondary

Average number of students per teacher

Myanmar, Low-income, Timor-Leste, Lower-middle-income, Samoa, Cambodia, Thailand, Middle-income, Korea, Rep., World, Vietnam, Macao SAR, China, Upper-middle-income, East Asia and Pacific (developing only), East Asia and Pacific (all income levels), Singapore, New Zealand, China, Japan, Indonesia, High-income

Source: World Bank n.d. EdStats online database, http://go.worldbank.org/ITABCOGIV1.
Note: Data for Malaysia, the Philippines, and Singapore are for 2009. Student-teacher ratios for Indonesia may be different from rates reported from national sources because of adjustments made for international comparability. Country income groupings (e.g., "Low-income") pertain to worldwide country groups by income.

much higher levels and the declines are much more likely to be associated with improvements in quality. For example, between 2007 and 2010, the junior secondary student-teacher ratio in Cambodia declined from 31 to 1 to 24 to 1.

Estimates of the size of the teaching force needed to fulfill the new staffing standards show that there are too many teachers (both civil service teachers and non-PNS) currently in the system. Comparing existing staffing levels with the standards for student-teacher ratios laid out in the latest joint decree on teacher management shows that there is a surplus of approximately 100,000 primary school teachers, equivalent to 7 percent of the current teaching force. At the junior secondary level, there are approximately 30,000 surplus teachers, equivalent to 6 percent of the teaching force.[8] But although there are too many teachers in the system, their unequal distribution means that many schools still have fewer teachers than they need.

Although there are more teachers in the national teaching force than required under existing staffing norms, implementing these standards fully would not lead to significant improvements in teacher efficiency. Despite some gains in efficiency at the junior secondary level, existing staffing standards limit the extent to which student-teacher ratios can rise further. For example, based on 2010 enrollment, fulfillment of the joint decree staffing standards would increase the student-teacher ratio at the primary and junior secondary levels by only one student. These changes are unlikely to improve the efficiency of overall teacher use significantly.

The 24-hour rule for teachers has not had a significant impact on the size of the teaching force so far. A recent study showed that approximately half of all primary and junior secondary school teachers' workloads fell below the 24 period-hour minimum for certification (Ragatz 2010). A much larger proportion of junior secondary school teachers (71 percent) fell below the threshold than primary school teachers (30 percent) (Ragatz 2010). As more teachers seek certification, a greater proportion of teachers will need to teach a minimum of 24 period-hours a week. It is possible that this will reduce the overall need for teachers and address some of the overstaffing issues. Although this result will rely on strong enforcement of the 24-hour rule, it also has the potential to affect learning quality. Evidence suggests that teachers are complying with the law by teaching in more than one school. The increased travel time and burden on teachers of teaching in different schools may have negative effects on learning. The impact evaluation study, however, does not reveal any systematic effects of certification on teaching hours (as shown in chapter 4, figure 4.12).

Reliance on Small Schools Increases Inefficiency

Staffing standards for small schools are a key contributor to the low student-teacher ratios in primary and junior secondary schools. Indonesia is not alone in facing the challenge of providing an adequate learning environment in schools serving relatively few children. In much of Eastern Europe, where population levels are declining, and in countries such as China, where massive urban migration has shrunk enrollment in rural schools, traditional class-based teacher allocations have increased the costs of education provision. Approximately a third of Indonesia's primary schools have fewer than 120 students (see table 6.1). These

Table 6.1 Primary and Junior Secondary School Size in Indonesia, 2010

	Primary	Junior secondary
Average student enrollment per school	173	261
% of schools with fewer than 150 students	48	40
Average students per learning group	16	25
% of schools with fewer than 120 students	34	33
Average students per learning group	13	23
% of schools with fewer than 90 students	19	25
Average students per learning group	10	20

Source: World Bank 2012b.

schools commonly have one learning group for each grade, and under current staffing norms this would require a total of eight teachers: six class-based teachers in addition to sports and religion teachers (and, in some cases, a principal as well). Staffing levels of this kind result in low student-teacher ratios. Schools with fewer than 120 students have a maximum student-teacher ratio of 15 to 1, and for schools with fewer than 90 students, the ratio falls to 11 to 1. Similar issues exist in junior secondary schools because all schools are required to have a subject teacher for each of the 11 curriculum subjects. Staffing small schools at these levels clearly has a downward impact on national student-teacher ratios and the overall efficiency of the education system.

The large number of small schools is commonly explained by the low population density of many areas in Indonesia. Where areas are sparsely populated, the size of schools can be limited because the number of potential students in any school's catchment area can be small. One way of looking at this is to compare the proportion of small schools in a province with its population density (see figure 6.8). This shows that schools tend to be smaller in provinces with sparser populations, but the relationship is weak.[9] For example, 64 percent of all primary schools have fewer than 120 students in East Kalimantan where population density is very low (64 people per square kilometer). However, in South Sumatra, the proportion of small schools is much lower despite only having a slightly higher population density than East Kalimantan (86 people per square kilometer).

However, some of the most densely populated provinces have large numbers of small schools and relatively low student-teacher ratios. For example, 39 percent of the primary schools in East Java have fewer than 120 students despite being densely populated (that is, a population density of 828 people per square

Figure 6.8 Population Density, Proportion of Small Schools, and Number of Primary Teachers in Indonesia, by Province, 2010

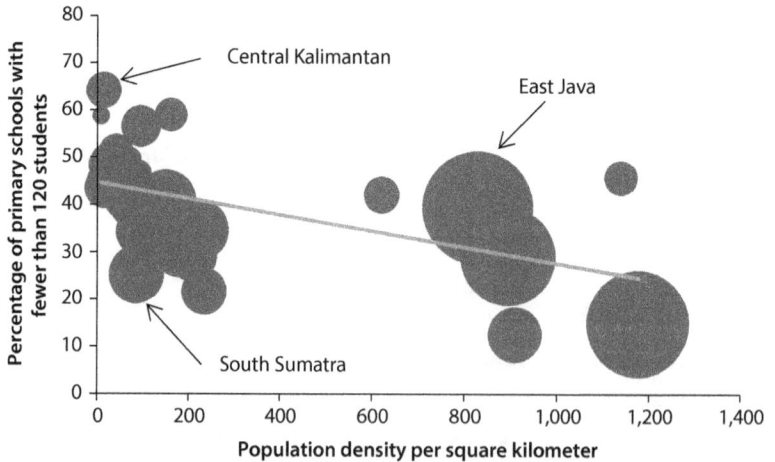

Source: Cerdan-Infantes and Makarova 2013.
Note: Bubble sizes represent the relative numbers of primary school teachers.

kilometer). Given that 14 percent of teachers and 21 percent of all primary school students are located in East Java, raising teacher efficiency by increasing the size of schools in this province could have significant national payoffs.

Additional efforts to address staffing issues in small schools have not been implemented on a national scale. For example, multigrade teaching has been used successfully in other countries to tackle staffing issues in small schools (Little 2006). In Indonesia, multigrade teaching is already practiced in a very small number of primary schools, and training for teachers in this approach is available from a number of sources (World Bank 2010). However, these pilot programs have not been successfully expanded and have not begun to address the significant inefficiencies associated with the staffing of small schools.

At the junior secondary level, dual subject-based teaching also has the potential to improve the efficiency of staffing in small schools. Current staffing norms require junior secondary schools to have one teacher for each subject, and teachers can only be accredited in a single subject. In small schools where class sizes are small, these standards result in low student-teacher ratios. They also make it difficult for teachers to fulfill their commitment to teach 24 period-hours each week. Informally, dual subject teaching takes place, but reforms to preservice education courses' certification criteria to make teaching in more than one subject acceptable have not yet been planned or implemented.

Effects on Composition of Teaching Force

Although recent reforms have failed to tackle significantly the overstaffing of schools, they have affected the composition of the primary school teaching force. Between 2006 and 2010, a large number of teachers hired at the district level were converted to civil servants. Coupled with temporary freezes on recruitment, the number of civil service teachers has remained relatively unchanged since 2006.

Increase in Temporary Contract Teachers

However, the increased hiring of teachers at the school level has meant that total teacher numbers have continued to rise (see figure 6.9). For example, between 2006 and 2010, the number of school-hired temporary primary school teachers (*Guru Tidak Tetap*, or GTT) increased from 175,000 to 475,000; they now represent nearly 30 percent of all primary school teachers. The School Operational Assistance program, introduced in 2005, has contributed to these increases. In 2011, schools used approximately a fifth of the school grants received under the program to hire teachers.

Teacher hiring at the school level is not governed by existing regulations outlining the required qualifications and experience that civil service teachers require. This omission of school-hired teachers circumvents any attempt by central and local governments to achieve a more efficient teaching force. Although there is little evidence of the criteria used for school hiring, it is possible that factors apart from teaching competency are used that result in weaker candidates being employed. On the whole, non-PNS teachers are less

Figure 6.9 Composition of Indonesian Teaching Force after Reforms, 2006–10

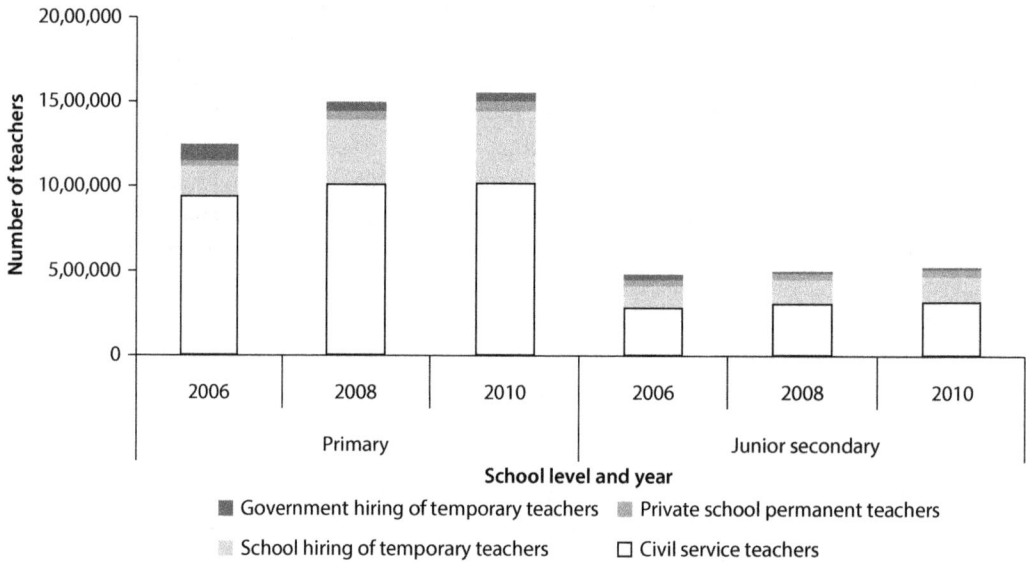

Source: Cerdan-Infantes and Makarova 2013.
Note: PNS = *Pegawai Negeri Sipil* (civil service) teachers. GTY = *Guru Tetap Yayasan*, non-PNS permanent private school teachers (eligible for certification). GTT = *Guru Tidak Tetap*, school-hired temporary teachers (not eligible for certification).

qualified and experienced than civil service teachers. For example, in 2010, 24 percent of primary school non-PNS teachers had qualifications at the four-year degree level or above compared with 29 percent of civil service teachers (NUPTK 2010).

The large number of non-PNS teachers in Indonesian schools is also common in other countries such as Cambodia, China, India, Nepal, Nicaragua, Pakistan, and Sri Lanka (Duthilleul 2005; Fyfe 2007). Contract or temporary teachers have been employed in these countries for a range of reasons. In some countries, they are seen to provide a cheap or cost-effective way of extending access to education. For example, in West Africa, much of the recent expansion in primary school access has been facilitated by the hiring of contract teachers (UNESCO 2009). In other countries, contract teachers have been an effective way of tackling teacher deployment issues by recruiting from the local population in hard-to-reach areas. In India, many states have recruited contract teachers from marginalized communities, thus increasing the teaching force in areas where civil service teachers are generally unwilling to work (Govinda and Josephine 2005). Contract teachers have also been seen as a way of addressing weaknesses in the mechanisms used to hold civil service teachers accountable. In particular, short-term contracts controlled by lower levels of government, the school, or school committees are seen to provide stronger incentives and better monitoring of teacher performance.

International evidence on the impact contract teachers have on teacher performance is mixed. Although the evidence base remains small and concentrated in only a few countries, a review of recent evaluations using randomized, controlled trials and matching methodologies showed that in some countries contract teachers were less often absent than civil service teachers and their students learned more (Bruns, Filmer, and Patrinos 2011). In other countries, contract teachers were more likely to be absent, and their effect on learning was not uniform.

Although comparisons between civil service and contract teachers are illuminating, these two types of teachers are not usually alternatives for each other. Many teachers accept the lower wages and poorer working conditions of contract teaching because it is the first step to securing a civil service job. It is unlikely in these cases that introducing contract teaching on a wider scale would be sustainable over the longer term. A study in India showed that differences in learning outcomes between contract and civil service teachers narrowed as the number of contracts received by the contract teacher increased (Goyal and Pandey 2009).

Mixed Evidence on the Impact of Contract Teachers

In Indonesia, the recruitment of non-PNS teachers has contributed to the poor distribution and overstaffing of the basic education system. The large number of school-hired and temporary non-PNS teachers is only partly driven by filling vacant civil service posts. Schools with shortages of civil service teachers tend to hire more non-PNS teachers, but many small schools with adequate civil service teachers also hire non-PNS teachers from their own funds. For example, in 2010, over 80 percent of primary schools with adequate or surplus numbers of civil service teachers employed non-PNS teachers. Approximately 30 percent of all non-PNS teachers were teaching in these schools. Non-PNS teachers are also not heavily concentrated among the more remote and poorer areas of Indonesia. For example, approximately 6 percent of all non-PNS teachers teach in remote areas of Indonesia compared with 4 percent of civil service teachers.

In a similar way to the international literature, evidence on the impact of non-PNS teachers in Indonesia is mixed. A recent cross-sectional study suggested that the share of non-PNS teachers is positively related to learning outcomes (Chen 2011). However, there does not seem to be a clear difference in absenteeism levels between civil service and non-PNS teachers. On the one hand, a national survey on teacher absenteeism found that non-PNS teachers were more likely to be absent than their civil service counterparts (Usman and Suryadarma 2004). On the other hand, more recent work in the poorer and more remote Papua province shows that non-PNS teachers are less likely to be absent than civil service teachers (UNCEN *et al.* 2012).

The Teacher Law and the requirement for all teachers to have a four-year degree are having a significant impact on non-PNS teachers. Approximately three-quarters of all primary school non-PNS teachers, or 400,000 teachers, will need to upgrade their qualifications to a four-year degree to continue to teach and become eligible for certification. Upgrading is occurring on a massive scale, with approximately 500,000 in-service teachers enrolling in distance learning courses. However, non-PNS teachers are not eligible for the same professional allowances, and this will add to growing pressure from teacher associations for these teachers to become civil servants.

Incentives and Corruption in Civil Service Teacher Recruitment

Despite the slowdown in civil service hiring, with the introduction of decentralization in 2001, the teacher recruitment process for local governments included significant incentives for overhiring civil service teachers. Intergovernmental resource transfers are partly determined by the size of a local government's payroll. Districts with larger numbers of civil servants receive more from the transfer system. It has been estimated that central government transfers cover approximately 75 percent of the salary of an additional civil service teacher. This, in effect, subsidizes local governments' costs for additional teachers and creates incentives for increased hiring.

The process of establishing new civil service teaching posts also contributes to incentives for overhiring. Decisions on the establishment of new posts in each district are made at the central level by the Ministry of Administrative and Bureaucratic Reform (MenPAN) and the Ministry of Finance based on requests from local governments. Quotas are set annually by considering local government requests for additional staff and the current budget situation. The actual process within MenPAN of determining quotas remains unclear (Kluyskens and Firdaus 2009). However, the process usually results in provincial and district governments receiving fewer posts every year than they requested. This creates incentives for local governments to exaggerate their actual needs, knowing that they will only receive a fraction of their initial request.

The political economy of local governance also creates incentives for local governments to seek to raise the number of civil service teachers. A recent symposium held at the Ministry of Education and Culture concluded that the appointment of teachers is "characterized by corruption, lack of transparency, primordial regionalism, and co-opted by the political interests of the ruling authorities" and that "many teachers are not appointed in accordance with the requirements of the minimum standards of teacher competencies" (Ministry of Education and Culture 2012).

A number of studies have shown that it is common for payments to be made to obtain access to civil service jobs. A study conducted in 2004 interviewed 60 civil servants in two districts in Nusa Tenggara Barat and found that payment for jobs was commonplace (Kristiansen and Ramli 2006). Civil servants reported paying Rp 24 million on average in 2004 (Rp 41 million in 2012 prices) to obtain a position—equivalent to about one year's basic pay for a primary or junior secondary teacher.[10] The study also found that payment for posts had increased since decentralization reforms were implemented. Although payment for civil service positions appears to be common, it is not uniform across districts. A 2005/06 study found that in seven of the eight districts surveyed, nongovernment respondents reported the necessity to pay for civil service positions although the amount of the payment varied significantly. In the remaining district, Solok in West Sumatra, no payments were thought to be needed to gain access to the civil service (Von Luebke 2009).

For the individual, paying for a post provides access to a stable income and a number of nonmonetary benefits that are often unavailable outside of the civil service. On the other side of the transaction, payments for civil service positions do not just benefit those allocating the posts. They are frequently part of revenue-generating schemes that support political activity at the local and national levels. Positions are also sometimes allocated as rewards for political support or part of the payoff for broader local political settlements. This has become more commonplace with the election of district regents who then appoint the heads of government offices such as education—who in turn have considerable influence in personnel issues in the district. The upshot of these recruitment practices is that a larger civil service often serves a number of personal and political objectives at the local level.

Recruitment practices can also have consequences for the quality of the national teaching force. Once in the civil service, teachers have the opportunity to recoup payments made to obtain their jobs by, for example, charging informal fees at school or obtaining side payments from school suppliers (Rosser, Joshi, and Edwin 2011). These practices can have negative impacts for education because they divert resources intended for improving access and quality. In addition, where payments are required for positions, it is rare for only the best qualified candidates to gain employment. This can have the effect of reducing the overall quality of the national teaching force.

If existing recruitment processes are left unchanged, some of the longer-term positive effects of the certification program will be reduced. As previous chapters have shown, increased teacher pay is attracting more and perhaps better students into teacher education. However, current recruitment practices imply that merit is only one factor in determining who gets a teaching position, and it is therefore unclear whether the more-able new graduates will enter the profession. Furthermore, the significant increase in the supply of new teachers and the limited projected need for additional teachers are likely to raise the cost of obtaining a civil service teaching post and may deter the abler students from entering the profession.

Effects on Teacher Distribution

Many countries face enormous challenges in allocating teachers across schools in a fair and transparent way (Mulkeen 2009; UNESCO 2009). Frequently, weaknesses in teacher distribution lead to very different learning environments for children in different areas. For example, in many countries, children in remote areas and from poor households often face a double disadvantage in their school careers: school infrastructure tends to be in a poorer state, and the teaching force is less qualified and experienced relative to schools in more affluent areas.

Indonesian Teacher Allocation: Widespread Inequality

The distribution of teachers across schools in Indonesia is unequal and has not improved significantly as a result of reform efforts over the past 10 years. In 2005, a survey using the existing entitlement formula showed that 55 percent of primary schools in Indonesia were overstaffed and 34 percent understaffed (Ragatz 2010). Analysis using data from 2010 and the latest staffing standards show that 30 percent of primary schools remain understaffed, and 59 percent remain overstaffed (World Bank 2012b).

The scale of redistribution necessary to allocate teachers more equally is large. If local governments redistributed existing teachers to fulfill the latest standards, approximately 343,000 primary and junior secondary school teachers (17 percent of the total workforce) would need to be transferred. Most of this redistribution would involve moving teachers within the same districts. However, approximately 66,000 teachers would need to be moved from districts with surplus teachers to deficit districts in the same province (see figure 6.10). After transfers within and across districts, approximately 37,000 teachers could transfer from districts in one province to fill deficits in other provinces to further improve teacher redistribution.

Formal and Informal Mechanisms for Transfers, with Mixed Results

Existing mechanisms that govern cross-border redeployment are not sufficient to deal with the scale of transfer needed to improve the distribution of teachers. Transfers across districts and provinces tend to be done on an ad hoc basis and rely on individual teachers identifying openings in one district or school and each district initially agreeing to a transfer. When transfers are agreed on, the budget for the salaries of transferring teachers is moved to the receiving district or province. It seems unlikely that districts and provinces would be willing to lose a teacher and the associated resources to effect a transfer (Kluyskens and Firdaus

Figure 6.10 Teacher Redistribution Necessary to Comply with Staffing Standards in Indonesian Primary and Junior Secondary Schools, 2010

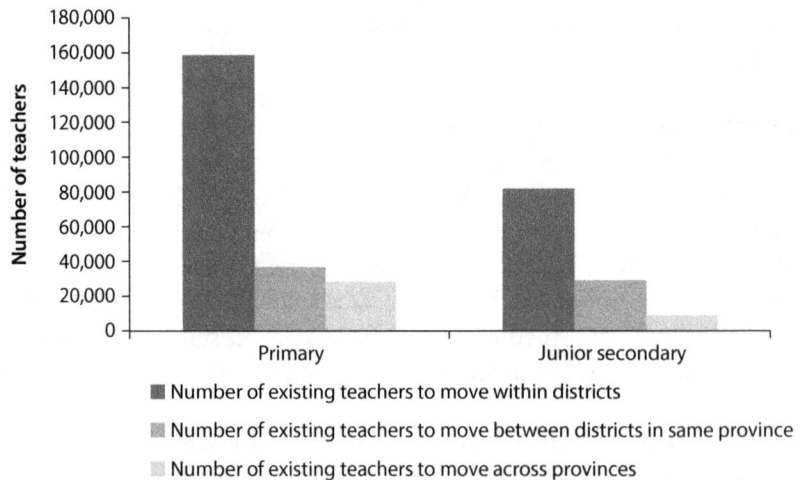

■ Number of existing teachers to move within districts

■ Number of existing teachers to move between districts in same province

■ Number of existing teachers to move across provinces

Sources: World Bank 2012b.
Note: The estimates show the number of teachers currently in schools with excess teachers (according to the joint decree) that could be transferred to take up teaching in schools with staffing deficits. Class-based, sports, and local content teachers are included in the estimates. The estimates include both civil service and non-civil-service teachers. Madrassahs are not included in these estimates.

2009). These relatively informal mechanisms for redistribution are therefore unlikely to be sufficient for the large redistribution required to achieve a more equitable distribution of teachers nationally.

The Teacher Law also introduced a remote area allowance to encourage teachers to teach in remote areas and improve their motivation. In 2012, approximately 53,000 teachers received the allowance. However, many of the teachers who are currently receiving the allowance were already working in remote areas, and so the extent to which it has attracted new teachers to these areas is unclear. In some areas, enlightened local governments have used these allowances to enforce redistribution, without which this remote allowance may not have a major effect on the distribution of teachers.

Despite the limited coverage of incentives of this kind, they have the potential to improve teacher distribution. A 2008 study in four districts showed that in one, absenteeism rates for teachers receiving the allowance were lower, but in the remaining districts, differences were either small or absenteeism was higher for teachers receiving the allowance (SMERU Research Institute 2010). In a more recent study conducted in Papua in 2011, absenteeism rates for teachers receiving incentives for teaching in remote areas were lower compared with other teachers (UNCEN *et al.* 2012). However, the study also noted that the coverage and targeting of the remote area allowance were weak and that this resulted in many teachers not receiving the support they needed to teach in remote areas. These results suggest that incentives introduced as part of the Teacher Law need to be strengthened to maximize their impact on the distribution of teachers.

Recruiting teachers from local communities may also be an effective strategy for improving teacher distribution. Teachers who move to remote and hard-to-reach areas can face significant challenges in finding accommodation, enrolling their children in school, and generally assimilating to local life. These challenges can be reduced if teachers are recruited from the local community. However, the poor state of education in remote areas frequently means that the number of individuals with the requisite qualifications is limited. Some local governments have begun to address these constraints by providing scholarships to local youth to train as teachers on the condition that they return and teach in their own community. A similar program, introduced by the central government, is also supporting the professional development of teachers in remote areas. These initiatives provide an alternative strategy to providing incentives for teachers to move to remote areas.

Differences in the educational qualifications of teachers between provinces and districts still remain significant despite the reforms that have taken place. A teacher's educational background provides only a partial proxy for teaching competency, but data from 2010 show that there are still large disparities across provinces and districts (see figure 6.11). Just over 20 percent of teachers in Kalimantan Barat Province have a four-year degree compared with 60 percent in Jakarta. Although it may be difficult to move existing teachers, it is possible that the distribution can be improved over time by allocating newly qualified teachers to areas and schools with the greatest need, as further discussed in box 6.1.

Figure 6.11 Percentage of Indonesian Teachers with a Four-Year Degree, by Province, 2010

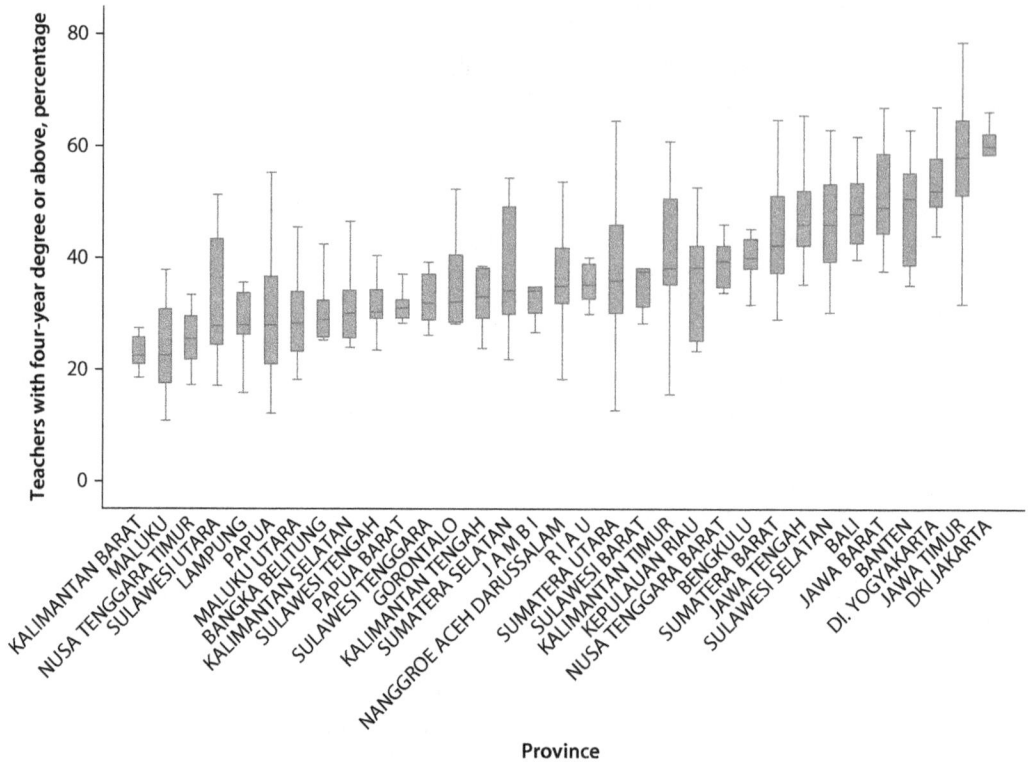

Source: Cerdan-Infantes and Makarova 2013.
Note: Includes all teachers from TK (Kindergarten) to SMU (Senior Secondary). The box plot graph shows the distribution of districts within each province in terms of the percentage of teachers with at least a four-year degree. The box represents the difference between the districts at the 25th and 75th percentiles of the distribution (that is, the interquartile range), and the line within the box represents the value for the median district. The lines (whiskers) above (below) the box show the most extreme value above (below) the 75th (25th) percentile that is within 1.5 times the interquartile range.

Box 6.1 District Initiatives to Improve Teacher Distribution

A successful program was introduced in Gorontalo district in 2006. The local government introduced a policy to employ only those teachers who agreed to be posted to schools that required that particular teacher's skill set. Teachers also agreed, through an eight-year contract with the local government, to be redeployed with the changing staffing needs of schools within the district (Kluyskens, Rawlinson, and Ragatz 2007). This policy allowed new teachers to be deployed to schools with the greatest need while also giving the local education office the flexibility to move teachers according to changing needs.

Conclusions

Large-scale teacher reforms have been introduced over the past decade to improve the quality of teaching in Indonesia. A key component of these reforms has been an increase in pay for certified teachers. While previous chapters have shown that the short-run impact of certification on teacher behavior and student learning has been limited, the current chapter shows that its impact on the education budget has and will continue to be enormous. Failure to address the rapidly rising costs of certification will result in the crowding out of spending in other areas necessary to improve educational quality and further expand access. Therefore, efforts to improve teacher management will be key to tackling the growing wage bill.

Reforms to manage the overstaffing and low student-teacher ratios that characterize the Indonesian education system have been less successful. The chapter has shown that student-teacher ratios—a good indicator of the efficiency of teacher use—are very low in Indonesia compared with other countries. Efforts to improve staffing standards and the introduction of the 24-hour rule have not, up until now, led to significant improvements in these ratios. At the primary level, student-teacher ratios have continued to decline over the decade.

The failure to improve teacher management is only partly connected with how staffing standards have been implemented. Although many schools are not staffed according to current standards, this chapter shows that even if these standards were implemented fully, student-teacher ratios would not increase significantly. A number of structural issues limit the ability of staffing standards to improve efficiency. In particular, standards have yet to tackle staffing issues in the large number of small schools in Indonesia. Potential solutions to staffing small schools—such as multigrade and dual or cluster-based teaching—have not been introduced on a national scale. These structural issues are only likely to intensify as Indonesia continues to urbanize.

The distribution of teachers has also not improved significantly over the past 10 years. Despite increases in the overall number of teachers, many schools still have fewer teachers than they need while others have too many. Clearly, some local governments and schools choose to employ more teachers than the minimum set out in staffing standards. However, this raises serious issues about equity when some urban schools are better staffed than more remote schools in the same district. The finding that better and more qualified teachers tend to teach in urban areas reinforces these inequalities.

The political economy of teacher hiring and distribution is also important in explaining the current situation. The current overstaffing of schools and the low student-teacher ratios are not driven by the lack of a detailed diagnosis of the problem; the issues covered in this chapter have been well documented in studies commissioned prior to the reforms. It is likely that some of the increased teacher hiring in recent years has been the result of the national 20 percent budgetary commitment to education. Local governments and schools, with few alternatives, have hired teachers as a way of fulfilling these spending commitments. At the local level, teacher hiring and transfer decisions are also highly political, and there are many benefits to hiring teachers as well as agreeing to teacher demands to stay in urban and better-connected areas. Addressing these issues will be vital if the efficiency of teacher management is to be improved.

It is important to recognize that improvements to the current distribution of teachers will take time to implement. However, a number of trends present opportunities to improve teacher management over the medium term. Government plans for further expansion of both kindergartens and secondary education will require more teachers, and this provides an opportunity to redeploy existing teachers to teach in these new schools. Reductions in the teaching force resulting from retirement also present opportunities to improve efficiency. In the next five years, approximately 10 percent (150,000 primary and 30,000 junior secondary school teachers) of the teaching force will reach retirement age. This represents a large opportunity to adjust the size of the teaching force without having to resort to the reassignment of teachers across levels.

Education is central to Indonesia's ambitious plans to accelerate economic growth and reduce poverty. If these plans are to be achieved, the education system needs to provide broader access to educational opportunities and improve the quality of existing provision. The government has signaled its commitment to achieving these goals by earmarking 20 percent of the national budget to education. However, significant inefficiencies exist that, left unchecked, will severely constrain future improvements in educational quality and access. Teacher oversupply and the very low student-teacher ratios that result are a key determinant of existing inefficiency. Tackling these inefficiencies through improved teacher management is vital if national goals for education and accelerated economic growth are to be realized.

Notes

1. This data are from NUPTK (2010) and include teachers from kindergarten to senior secondary. It excludes teachers in the madrassah system.

2. Currently school-hired temporary teachers (*Guru Tidak Tetap*, or GTT) are not eligible for the certification program. In 2010 there were approximately 900,000 teachers of this type teaching between kindergarten and senior secondary. These teachers are included in the 1.7 million teachers reported as being noncertified.

3. These estimates assume that the professional allowance associated with certification is equivalent to the basic pay of a civil service teacher and Rp 1.5 million per month for a non-civil-service permanent private school teacher (*Guru Tetap Yayasan*, or GTY).

4. These estimates exclude the certification of madrassah teachers.

5. The projected 2015 figures exclude the conversion of non-civil-service teachers to civil service teachers.

6. Current certification guidelines exclude school-hired contract teachers, who make up approximately 30 percent of the teaching force at the primary and secondary level.

7. This expense includes the increased cost of the professional allowance associated with certification that contract teachers would receive upon conversion.

8. These figures are used to demonstrate the magnitude of the oversupply. They are based on 2010 data for all teachers (both civil service and non-civil-service) and do not take account of subject mismatches. For example, at primary schools, there are approximately 165,000 surplus class-based teachers, but there are shortages of sports teachers that reduce the overall surplus. See Cerdan-Infantes and Makarova (2013) for more details.

9. A similar weak relationship holds when the density and proportion of small schools are analyzed at the district level.

10. The study found that teachers as a subgroup of the civil service paid a similar amount for their posts as the average, based on data from NUPTK (2010) and the 2012 civil service salary scale.

References

BPS (National Statistics Center [*Badan Pusat Statistik*]). 2010. *Indonesian Labor Force Survey (Sakernas)*, Jakarta.

Bruns, B., D. Filmer, and H. A. Patrinos. 2011. *Making Schools Work: New Evidence on Accountability Reforms*. Washington, DC: World Bank.

Cerdan-Infantes, P., and Y. Makarova. 2013. *Spending More or Spending Better: Improving Education Financing in Indonesia*. Jakarta: World Bank.

Chen, D. 2011. "School-Based Management, School Decision-Making and Education Outcomes in Indonesian Primary Schools." Policy Research Working Paper 5809, World Bank, Washington, DC.

Duthilleul, Y. 2005. *Lessons Learnt in the Use of 'Contract' Teachers*. Synthesis report, Paris: United Nations Educational, Scientific, and Cultural Organization (UNESCO), International Institute for Educational Planning.

Fyfe, A. 2007. "The Use of Contract Teachers in Developing Countries: Trends and Impact." Working Paper 252, International Labour Organization, Geneva, Switzerland.

Govinda, R., and Y. Josephine. 2005. "Parateachers in India: A Review." *Contemporary Education Dialogue* 2 (2): 193–224.

Goyal, S., and P. Pandey. 2009. *How Do Government and Private Schools Differ? Findings from Two Large Indian States*. South Asia Human Development Sector Report 30, World Bank, Washingon, DC.

Kluyskens, J., and M. Firdaus. 2009. "Teacher Management: Recruitment, Selection and Data, Probation and Transfer." Backgound paper, Education Sector Assessment workshop for the formulation of the medium-term education sector strategy (RENSTRA) (2009–14), Government of Indonesia.

Kluyskens, J., R. Rawlinson, and A. Ragatz. 2007. "Improving Efficiency and Equity in Teacher Employment and Deployment." Background paper, World Bank, Jakarta.

Kristiansen, S., and M. Ramli. 2006. "Buying an Income: The Market for Civil Service Positions in Indonesia." *Contemporary Southeast Asia* 28 (2): 207–33.

Little, A., ed. 2006. *Education for All and Multigrade Teaching: Challenges and Opportunities*. London: Springer.

Ministry of Education and Culture. 2012. *Recruitment of Teachers in the Future*. Workshop report, Balitbang (Department for Research and Development).

Mulkeen, A. 2009. *Teachers in Anglophone Africa: Issues in Teacher Supply, Training, and Management*. Washington, DC: World Bank.

Ragatz, A. 2010. *Transforming Indonesia's Teaching Force. Volume II: From Pre-service Training to Retirement: Producing and Maintaining a High-quality, Efficient, and Motivated Workforce.* Human Development Series, Jakarta: World Bank.

Rosser, A., A. Joshi, and D. Edwin. 2011. "Power, Politics, and Political Entrepreneurs: Realising Universal Free Basic Education in Indonesia." Working Paper 358, Institute of Development Studies, Brighton, UK.

SMERU Research Institute. 2010. "Remote Area Allowance and Absentee Levels for Teachers in Remote Areas." Policy brief, SMERU Research Institute, Jakarta.

UIS (UNESCO Institute for Statistics). 2010. http://stats.uis.unesco.org. UIS, Montreal, Canada.

UNCEN (Universitas Cenderawash), UNIPA (Universitas Negeri Papua), SMERU (Independent Research Institute of Indonesia), BPS (Badan Pusat Statistik), and UNICEF (United Nations Children's Fund). 2012. *We Like Being Taught: A Study on Teacher Absenteeism in Papua and West Papua.* Research study, UNICEF, Australian AID, and USAID Indonesia, Jakarta.

UNESCO (United Nations Educational, Scientific, and Cultural Organization). 2009. "Universal Primary Education in Africa: The Teacher Challenge." Education sector analysis, UNESCO, Pôle de Dakar, Dakar.

Usman, A. S., and D. Suryadarma. 2004. *When Teachers Are Absent: Where Do They Go and What Is the Impact on Students?* Field report, SMERU Research Institute, Jakarta.

Von Luebke, C. 2009. "The Political Economy of Local Governance Findings from an Indonesian Field Study." *Bulletin of Indonesian Economic Studies* 45 (2): 201–30.

World Bank. 2010. "Investing in Multi-grade Teaching in Indonesia." Policy brief, World Bank, Jakarta.

———. 2012a. *Indonesia Economic Quarterly (IEQ): Maintaining Resilience*, Jakarta.

———. 2012b. "Making Better Use of Teachers: Strengthening Teacher Management to Improve the Efficiency and Equity of Public Spending." Policy brief, World Bank, Jakarta.

———. n.d. EdStats online database. Washington, DC. http://go.worldbank.org /ITABCOGIV1.

CHAPTER 7

Conclusions and Recommendations

The Teacher Law: Taking Measure

> Teachers in Indonesia do not cast themselves in the role of change agent; they do not even audition for the part.

> —Christopher Bjork, *Indonesian Education: Teachers, Schools, and Central Bureaucracy (2005)*

The Indonesian Teacher Law of 2005 was a landmark in many ways. In one sweep of legislation, it confirmed teaching as a "profession" equivalent to other professions, dramatically increasing the income of teachers to be commensurate with, or exceed, that of lawyers or doctors. It attempted to reverse a decades-long decline in the status of teaching and put in place a massive scheme of academic qualification and formal certification that has had an impact on every aspect of the education system, at all levels of government. It mandated a wide range of other reforms focusing on the entire teacher management and development system of the Ministry of Education and Culture.[1] And it committed the government to increasingly large financial outlays to reward professional certification, which may have serious implications for the ability of the education budget to further expand the system or improve its quality.

It is not surprising, therefore, that the law's various stakeholders and supporters have paid so much attention to its impact on the structure, mechanisms, strategies, processes, and ultimate outcomes of the Indonesian education system. The Ministry of Education and Culture itself, of course, is attentive because the effectiveness of the Teacher Law's implementation directly reflects on the efficiency and professionalism of the ministry. The national Parliament, the Ministry of Finance, and the National Planning and Development Board worry about the added value to the education system and its "clients"—the learners—from the large investment now being paid to certified teachers. The teachers' associations, especially the largest and most official (the Teachers' Association of the Republic of Indonesia) are concerned not only about the welfare and status of their individual members but also about the extent to which they have genuinely earned and will remain worthy of the title of "professional." And such worthiness will ultimately be assessed, of course, by the learners themselves, their parents, their future employers, and the larger society.[2]

Implementation of such a reform, however, is a political process that in Indonesia involves almost 3 million teachers (or as one political analyst put it, at least 30 million votes, given the minimal estimate that each teacher can each affect 10 votes from family members). As a result, media coverage of the reform has focused on teachers' rights and welfare (for example, late payment of the professional allowance or administrative charges levied on the allowance by district offices) and has lost sight of the original aim of making teachers (once again) professionals. Elevating the public debate beyond that of solely teacher welfare to that of the quality of schooling for students has been a challenge for the Ministry of Education and Culture. But as empirical evidence surfaced in this regard, it has helped to embolden the ministry to take more stringent measures to ensure that the original intentions of the law are achieved.

This book has documented the interplay in the reform process between the political context and evidence-based policy making and has drawn useful lessons for other emerging nations. The key lesson is that teacher reform is a very long-term and iterative process where compromises appropriate to the political and economic context of the time will likely have to be made. However, over time, with the support of empirical evidence and renewed commitment from the ministry, adjustments to reform efforts can be made, as in Indonesia, that may go a long way toward a much more faithful implementation of the reform's original intentions.

So what has worked, and what has not—and why? Organized around the conceptual framework for teacher reform (figure 7.1, as previously shown in chapter 2), the lessons drawn here resonate with the international literature.

Financial and Political Economy Factors

For a variety of reasons related to the political economy of the time, the mere fact of certification and the consequent doubling of teacher income have not achieved what was expected—better teaching and better learning. Certification was meant to be based on a minimum academic qualification (a four-year degree) and mastery of the teacher's subject and its required pedagogy; the assumption was that this would be translated into different teacher behaviors and better student outcomes. The logic of this process, however, was distorted in several ways:

• The selection of teachers for the early rounds of certification was based largely on seniority rather than merit and thus gave preference either to those whose four-year degrees were already many years old or to the large cohort of teachers employed during the expansion of the system in the 1970s and 1980s with low academic qualification, low motivation, and little training (either then or

Figure 7.1 Conceptual Framework for Quality Education

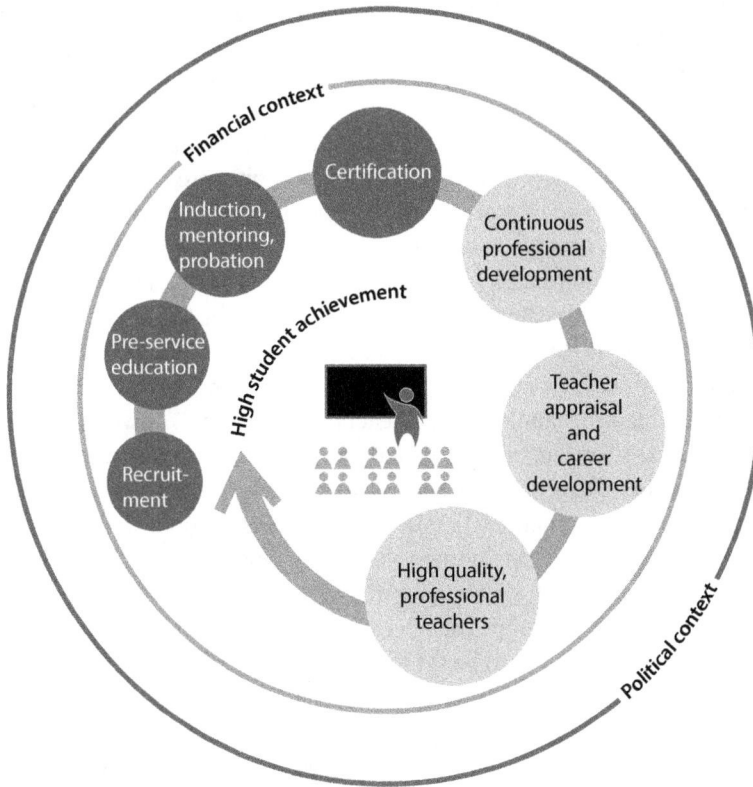

subsequently) who either did not need the four-year degree because of their age and seniority or got the degree in a piecemeal fashion. Many, therefore, began the certification process with low mastery of the required competencies. (Others, anecdotally, also got into the certification queue through political and personal favoritism or outright bribery.)

- Many of these same teachers, as the analysis in chapter 1 showed, had begun their careers in an era when accountability (and loyalty) to the central government and identification with the civil service took precedence over accountability to their students and identification as a member of the teaching profession. Working for decades in such a bureaucratic environment—and the school cultures this engendered—did little to make them able or eager to become agents of change.

- The first method of measuring competency, the portfolio, did little to demonstrate either subject knowledge or pedagogical skill. The questionable manner through which the portfolios were often assembled, and the rather inconsistent way in which they were evaluated, did little to assure that the required competencies had, in fact, been mastered.

- The remedial measure to a failed portfolio—the 90-hour course—was helpful but, given its short length and the fact that it was largely standardized across all teachers rather than responsive to individual needs, could not make up for the low levels of competency of the participating teachers.

The result was that the quality of the certification process as a whole was not as good as originally intended (that is, based on tested mastery of specific skills and knowledge and adapted to the needs of individual teachers) so that there is now virtually no evidence of differences between certified and uncertified teachers in their competencies or in their impact on student learning outcomes.

This result is consistent with the Organisation for Economic Co-operation and Development (OECD) Teaching and Learning International Survey (TALIS) finding that key aspects of teaching and learning that have been shown to improve learning include (a) teachers' content knowledge; (b) teachers' pedagogical knowledge (both general and specific to their subject); (c) teaching practices that focus on clear and well-structured lessons supported by effective classroom management; (d) individualized instruction; and (e) active professional collaboration including classroom observations, team teaching, and constructive feedback (Schleicher 2011).

For countries therefore considering a blanket increase in teacher pay, the bar to gain this increase has to be set to ensure that teachers are tested for competencies known to be necessary for a good teacher and to ensure that low-performing teachers do not remain in the profession. This outcome requires that politicians and senior decision makers take a firmer stand in supporting the efforts of ministries of education to enforce higher standards, implement more effective competency assessment, and redeploy or dismiss teachers who cannot meet the required competencies.

From a financial perspective, Indonesia increased its education budget 120 percent between 2001 and 2009, but significant inequity remains, starting with the inequitable distribution as well as the overall oversupply of teachers.

The costs of extending the certification program to all civil service teachers and other eligible contract or temporary teachers is associated with significant trade-offs. Estimates suggest that spending on teacher compensation will need to absorb a much larger share of the available public education resources. This means that spending in other areas of the education budget will need to be reduced. For example, the certification program is likely to limit resources to (a) increase access to early childhood and postbasic education, and (b) invest in other quality-improving strategies. This book has also shown that converting non-civil-service (*Pegawai Negeri Sipil* [PNS]) teachers to civil servants and certifying them will be unsustainable given current budgetary projections.

To reduce the budgetary impact of the certification program, the inefficiencies associated with teacher hiring and deployment need to be addressed. Indonesia's student-teacher ratios are already low by international standards and, at the primary level, are continuing to fall. This book has shown that even relatively small increases in student-teacher ratios could realize significant budget savings while having limited impact on quality. Serious attention must therefore be paid soon to significantly restricting intake to teacher educational institutions and new hiring at all levels; removing incentives for overhiring at school and district levels; enforcing the policies and bearing the expense of moving teachers from teacher-surplus to teacher-deficit schools and districts; and moving underperforming teachers elsewhere in (or out of) the civil service system. Attention will also need to be paid to staffing standards in small schools, which are a key driver of low student-teacher ratios.

Recruitment Advances and Challenges

It can be argued that the expectation around certification for the senior cohort of existing teachers (that is, given 25 years of teaching, limited preservice education, a school culture that encouraged civil servant obedience rather than pedagogic innovation, and few opportunities for further development) was overoptimistic, especially in the absence of any systematic postcertification follow-up. *But the incentive of both professional status and professional pay is now attracting more (and sometimes better-quality) candidates into teacher education at the expense of other fields.* So although the professional allowance has had little impact on the quality of current teacher competence or student outcomes, it may produce a better cadre of teachers in the future if the rapid growth of low-quality teacher education institutions is controlled, if minimum competency standards are enforced at *all* stages of teacher management and development—and, of course, if qualified graduates have (merit-based) access to a teaching job upon graduation.

Preservice Education

The attraction of certification has led to an increase in the number of teachers who have achieved the required minimum of a four-year degree. This, as opposed to just the fact of certification, can lead to greater mastery by a graduate teacher of relevant subject knowledge, which can then be directly correlated with student achievement: the more the teachers know, the more is transmitted successfully to their students. Likewise, at least in the sample of 8th-grade mathematics studies in the context of the Trends in International Mathematics and Science Study (TIMSS), teachers with mathematics *education* degrees (as opposed to those with pure mathematics degrees) have adequate knowledge of their subject but also demonstrate more useful teaching practices such as investigation and problem solving. This finding supports the Teacher Law in its definition of teacher quality as depending on both subject knowledge and pedagogy. The increase in enrollment for four-year degrees by practicing teachers at the Open University (and at other teacher education institutions with distance learning programs) could be a good sign, therefore, that higher-quality teachers will be entering the certification queue in the future—if the quality of these upgrading four-year programs can be assured.

Teacher Reform in Indonesia • http://dx.doi.org/10.1596/978-0-8213-9829-6

For countries setting new standards for their teaching forces, and depending on the structure of the education system, a four-year degree could be a useful benchmark. However, there has to be careful accreditation of teacher education institutions to ensure they test graduates for subject matter and pedagogical competencies as well as other necessary characteristics of a good teacher. In Singapore, for example, to put the focus on student learning, the National Institute of Education (the sole provider of initial teacher education) cut subjects such as history and philosophy of education from its undergraduate teacher education syllabus because these subjects were not leading to noticeable increases in student learning. More emphasis was instead placed on practical classroom teaching with a strong focus on subject content; for example, mathematics teachers should graduate with the same mathematics content knowledge as straight mathematics graduates. In the Republic of Korea, preservice institutions are rated, and those with an A-rating receive substantial financial bonuses. Courses with a D-rating must reduce their student numbers by 50 percent the following year. In addition, graduates must sit for examinations before they become teachers.

Induction, Mentoring, Probation, and Certification

In many education systems, these stages in a teacher's career are quite distinct. However, in Indonesia their precise sequence in the process of teacher management and development remains unclear—thus their combination here in one critical stage of this process. For practicing teachers who enter the certification queue (with the four-year degree) and then get certified either via a portfolio or (as is currently the case) following the 90-hour training course, there is no induction, mentoring, and probation. They were teachers before certification, and they are (supposedly more "professional") teachers after certification. And there is no postcertification process in place (except regular and routine appraisals)—such as a new round of mentoring and probation or regular recertification—to ensure that they are now acting as professionals or, in other words, teaching better.

New entrants to teacher education institutions must do the following:

- Pass the coursework to obtain the four-year degree (granted by the institution)
- Pass the newly mandated postgraduate, classroom-focused course of professional study (six months for primary school teachers, one year for secondary teachers)
- Gain an authorized teaching post (as opposed to being hired on a school contract)
- Pass a one-year probation (through what is meant to be a systematic process of induction and mentoring)

The last is meant to be based both on the teacher's previous academic record and on the principal's report of the new teacher's competence, efficiency, and effectiveness. The probation is completed when the teacher education institution finally certifies the new teacher—which, if accepted by the ministry, will lead to provision of the professional allowance.

This whole process is largely still intention, although the regulations are in place and the necessary guidelines and formats have been developed and, in some cases, piloted for wider use throughout the system. What is essential here is the combination of institution- and employer-based assessment. Because many teacher educators have had little experience in actual school teaching (especially at the primary level) and often have little competence in the kind of dynamic, interactive, child-centered pedagogy meant to be used in schools, assessment based solely on one's academic, institutional record is simply not adequate. Thus, it is also important that principals and supervisors join in the assessment leading to certification through well-planned induction and mentoring to ensure that new teachers not only have good knowledge of their subject(s) and relevant methodologies but also, even more essentially, have excellent skills in pedagogy. This should be proven through probationary teaching for at least a year with a full load of classroom hours—and perhaps, even evidence of strong dedication to the profession of teaching.

But useful induction processes and good mentoring and appraisal skills on the part of school principals and district supervisors do not just happen by themselves. It is therefore essential in Indonesia—and in other countries undertaking comprehensive teacher reforms—to lay out clearly what a useful process of induction looks like and what kinds of mentoring skills (and training to produce them) are needed by principals and supervisors to ensure that the final certification of teachers (unconditionally and for life in Indonesia) is based on adequate knowledge, skills, and motivation. Shanghai offers one good example of an induction process whereby mentors and mentees regularly observe each other's lessons and observe demonstration lessons together. There, mentoring focuses on core teaching skills, such as diagnosing student learning, and teachers are trained in classroom and lesson observation by colleagues as part of the professional culture.

Continuing Professional Development

The original intention of the Teacher Law was to put in place a framework of effective policies and procedures that would both assure the quality of the process and its products and encourage continuing professional development. Putting in place such a framework is, in fact, essential both for new teachers (by enforcing minimum competency standards at all stages of their management and development) and for older, already certified teachers (by putting in place a postcertification process that can try to assure that many of the new "professionals" gain, maintain, and enhance the competencies they never really mastered in the first place). In other words, it is essential to try to rectify the weaknesses in the implementation process of the Teacher Law by quickly putting in place the essential parts of a quality assurance and professional development framework.

Among these elements, the teacher working groups are already in place and apparently performing effectively. Research has shown that this decades-old but often neglected mechanism is expanding in reach, in the relevance of its activities, and in the improvement of its members' cognitive and pedagogical abilities. It is interesting to note that although this particularly effective method of in-service training was not related to certification and teachers do not receive double income as a result of participation, there has been a significant increase in membership in, and benefits gained from, these groups.

But other parts of this quality assurance framework also need be to put in place—and probably should have been established at the start of the Teacher Law (and the certification process) rather than several years later. These missing elements include the following:

- More rigorously accredited teacher education institutions, charged with both (a) the preservice preparation of candidates as teachers and their certification and (b) the in-service work of continuing professional development
- A cadre of principals selected on merit, specifically trained for their work (both administrative and academic); deployed to where they are needed most; and focused on the essential teacher management and development tasks of early induction, mentoring, probation, and ongoing teacher development
- A cadre of supervisors, likewise chosen on merit and trained for their work, in a post of enhanced responsibility for the system's effective functioning and therefore of a higher status to match this responsibility
- A supportive, nonpoliticized district education office (backed up by a similarly nonpoliticized district regent) with a specific unit focused on continuing professional development, quality assurance, and the unified servicing of all aspects of teacher management and development

Teacher Appraisal and Career Development

What this whole process of teacher management and development ultimately leads to is a systematic teacher appraisal process linked not only to ongoing professional development but also to the regular and accelerated progression and promotion of teachers through the education system. The last is especially important. All teachers should be held accountable through an annual performance appraisal mechanism for the quality of their work, and principals and supervisors must likewise be held accountable through the district authorities for the manner in which this mechanism of quality assurance is applied. Those meeting or exceeding the required standards should be guided through further stages of professional and perhaps administrative training, leading to promotions within the teaching career structure or into more administrative, supervisory positions. In other words, for further quality enhancement, good teachers should not always get promoted *out* of classrooms but rather become master teachers and mentors *for* more classrooms. This kind of career development implies that rather than providing blanket increases for all teachers regardless of performance, the teacher career structure should eventually reward high performers with additional responsibilities and higher salaries that encourage them to remain in teaching.

On the other hand, those unable to maintain the required standards must be compelled to undertake some kind of intensive program of professional improvement (for example, related to subject mastery, pedagogic competence, or both) and then be assessed as to their improvement. Based on the result, decisions need to be made about their future as teachers. The system must divest itself of underperforming teachers (as it is often most eager to do with underperforming students!) who are unable or unwilling to improve their performance—perhaps redeploying them to another part of the civil service or even dismissing them. Either way, it is critical for some form of sanction to be applied to noncompliant personnel.

Specific Recommendations for Indonesia

The above conclusions and recommendations should be relevant to any education system attempting to reform its teacher management and development system. But for Indonesia, given that the reform process still has a long way to go and that there are large numbers of certified as well as uncertified teachers not meeting competency standards, the following specific recommendations are provided.

For New Teachers
- Ensure that the intake of teacher candidates across all teacher education institutions is linked to the likely number of teachers required by the system—by level and subject—when each cohort graduates.
- Ensure that the hiring of new teachers is based on merit. It will do nothing for the credibility of the ministry if bright, motivated new graduates emerge from teacher education with little chance of getting a teaching post—unless, perhaps, they pay for it.
- Ensure that essential competencies in subject matter and pedagogy underlie all aspects of the preservice education program.
- Require that the graduates of these preservice programs pass the competency test (that is, for subject matter and pedagogy) required for certification *at an appropriate passing grade*. Again, the credibility of the ministry is at stake if most of those who pass the test do so with a grade of, say, only 50 percent.
- Ensure that appropriate induction, mentoring, and probation processes are in place at the school level, based on the required competencies, and supervised by the principal and supervisor, preferably so that final certification is based on both the candidate teacher's academic record and classroom performance.

For Teachers Not Yet Certified
- Monitor (a) the methods used for uncertified teachers to apply for entry into a four-year degree program (for example the Open University or HYLITE[3]); (b) the quality of the four-year program (for example, its basis on the essential

competencies for subject matter and pedagogical competencies); and (c) the awarding of the degree (for example, at an appropriate passing grade).

- Establish structured, well-monitored, and supervised in-service training focusing on classroom needs (specifically subject mastery and pedagogical techniques).

For Certified Teachers

- Implement rapidly and effectively the full range of quality assurance and continuing professional development mechanisms to further enhance the competency and professionalism of certified teachers. These mechanisms include the teacher working groups, well-chosen and well-trained principals and supervisors able and willing to monitor and improve the performance of certified teachers, and continuing teacher appraisal linked to further career advancement.
- Encourage or mandate the expenditure of a certain percentage of a teacher's professional allowance for continuing professional development activities.
- Establish some system of ensuring that teachers master the required competencies at ever higher levels of achievement during their careers—for example, putting even newly certified teachers on probation and through a process of further mentoring, requiring some kind of recertification or confirmation of certification every five years (perhaps with a higher passing grade), and so forth.
- Establish and implement procedures for underperforming teachers, including both (a) additional support, supervision, and training; and (b) if needed, redeployment or dismissal.

Teaching as a Vocation and the School as a Learning Community

> Indonesian teachers are rooted in environments that have not historically promoted the behaviors and attitudes that lie at the core of recently adopted education reforms. ... Indonesian civil service culture ... promotes values and behaviors that are fundamentally at odds with the new role of the teacher that the government is currently promoting. The civil service system is structured to reward individuals who display loyalty and obedience (Bjork 2005, 84, 96).

A final lesson is related to teacher development. Even comprehensive, expensive reforms concerning teacher management and development will not work if teachers don't have the intrinsic motivation to be a teacher. Teachers who are passionate about teaching are likely to teach better than those who just want to get paid more or those who follow only the required upgrading programs and certification processes. The Teacher Law has included personality among the four required competencies for teachers. This is important for the teacher recruitment process in Indonesia given the opportunity it now has, with a surplus of teacher applicants, to be more selective in this process and to admit to the profession only those who want to treat teaching as a genuine vocation. Based on international literature (Jensen *et al.* 2012), people change behavior if they have a purpose to believe in, if their role models act consistently, if they have the skills and capacity for the new behavior, and if reinforcement systems such as performance measures are consistent. If the first of these—purpose—is absent, any behavioral change resulting from the other three may well be superficial at best. And for teachers accustomed to seeing themselves as civil servants first and teachers second, enhancing their motivation will take more than the label "professional" and an increase in their income.

This is where the concept of whole-school reform toward a learning community becomes so essential. Any reforms adopted "must facilitate the development of a culture of continuous professional improvement for all teachers and the concept that every school is a 'learning community' with students, teachers, and the wider community enhancing their knowledge and skills through activities generated in the school" (World Bank 2009, 202). In such a learning community, for example, having a good mentor for a new teacher is not enough; what is needed is working in a school with an integrated, collective professional culture. Fullan (2010, 101) quotes Byrk *et al.* (2010) in listing five key factors for such a collective solution: "(1) school leadership (the principal) as driver who works with teachers, students, parents, and the community to build, in turn, four other interrelated focuses and supports—(2) parent and community ties, (3) professional capacity of staff (including focused work orientation), (4) a student-centered learning climate, and (5) instructional focus and guidance."

Fullan goes on to quote a survey done by Yarrow (2009) that resulted in three categories of teachers: (a) the *disheartened* (in the survey, 40 percent), who get little support and are concerned about working conditions and student behavior; (b) the *idealists* (23 percent), who became teachers to help students and think that good teachers can lead all students to learn and that they have had an impact on their students; and (c) the *contented* (37 percent), who report excellent working conditions in better schools and also think they have helped their more-advantaged students to learn. Fullan argues that the task is to "hearten" the disheartened, not through individualistic incentives such as pay for performance but rather through incentives that focus on the collective. He lists 11 (Fullan 2010, 83–84):

- Good salaries
- Decent surroundings
- Positive climate
- Strong induction
- Extensive professional learning
- Opportunity to work with and learn from others
- Supportive, even assertive, leadership about the agenda
- Helpful feedback

Teacher Reform in Indonesia • http://dx.doi.org/10.1596/978-0-8213-9829-6

- Reasonable class size
- Long-term collective agreements (that is, career stability)
- Realizable moral purpose

Other than the incentive of "reasonable class size" (which, in the case of Indonesia, might be unreasonably small), the Teacher Law of 2005 and the comprehensive standards and regulations that have supported it cover most of this list. The salaries and the career stability came first, for quite understandable reasons given the political economy of the time, but this has led now to serious challenges in realizing the rest of the items on the list, including the following:

- How to guarantee "decent surroundings" for all educational institutions when so much of the education budget is going to an oversized and now well-compensated cohort of teachers
- How to ensure that the "learning" is actually both extensive and professional when the pressure is to certify as many teachers as possible in the time mandated by the law
- How to effectively put in place the other postcertification, quality assurance incentives on the list—strong induction, opportunity to work with and learn from others, supportive leadership about the agenda, and getting helpful feedback
- Perhaps most challenging, how to create in schools a "positive climate" and in teachers a "realizable moral purpose" when historically these were not the priorities of the education system

The Government of Indonesia, through its Teacher Law, has undertaken the immense and complicated task of essentially trying to reprofessionalize a deprofessionalized occupation. Whether it succeeds will go a long way toward determining the response of Indonesia to the national and global challenges it is facing in the new century.

Notes

1. Until 2011, the Ministry was called the Ministry of National Education.
2. Anecdotal evidence is mixed in this regard, with some certified teachers reportedly using their allowances to purchase reference books and laptops to support their work and others hiring assistants to teach their classes, going into debt to buy cars, and even losing the respect of parents because they appear to be less professional, despite their higher income, than before certification.
3. HYLITE is the Hybrid Learning for Indonesian Teachers program, further discussed in chapter 3.

References

Bjork, C. 2005. *Indonesian Education: Teachers, Schools, and Central Bureaucracy*. London: Routledge.

Byrk, A., P. B. Sebring, E. Allensworth, S. Luppescu, and J. Q. Easton. 2010. *Organizing Schools for Improvement: Lessons from Chicago.* Chicago: University of Chicago Press.

Fullan, M. 2010. *All Systems Go: The Change Imperative for Whole System Reform.* Thousand Oaks, CA: Corwin.

Jensen, B., A. Hunter, J. Sonnemann, and T. Burns. 2012. *Catching Up: Learning from the Best School Systems in East Asia.* Report 2012-3, Grattan Institute, Melbourne, Australia. (accessed February 27, 2013) http://grattan.edu.au/static/files /assets/00d8aaf4/130_report_learning_from_the_best_detail.pdf.

Schleicher, A. 2011. *Building a High-Quality Teaching Profession: Lessons from around the World.* Paris: Organisation for Economic Co-operation and Development.

World Bank. 2009. "Teacher Certification in Indonesia: A Strategy for Teaching Quality Improvement." Background paper, Ministry of National Education and World Bank, Jakarta.

Yarrow, A. 2009. "State of Mind: America's Teaching Corps." *Education Week* 29 (8): 21–23.

Appendixes

Appendix A

Coefficient and z-statistic data for figure 5.2: Relationship of Lesson Structure Teaching Practices with Student Learning Outcomes.
  Variables shaded gray below were used in creating the figure.

	Base regression	w/teacher variables	Base regression	w/teacher variables	Base regression	w/teacher variables
Mathematics	0.251	0.557				
	1.22	(2.55)**				
Nonmathematics			−0.682	−0.753		
			(−2.43)**	(−3.09)***		
Mathematics organization					0.075	0.065
					0.25	1.05
Student pretest score	0.529	0.541	0.527	0.540	0.530	0.545
	(21.04)***	(20.63)***	(20.99)***	(20.71)***	(21.11)***	(20.86)***
Student age	−0.001	−0.003	−0.001	−0.003	−0.001	−0.003
	−0.18	−0.86	−0.2	−0.9	−0.16	−0.83
Hours homework/week	0.006	0.006	0.005	0.006	0.006	0.006
	(1.69)*	(1.68)*	1.64	1.63	(1.7)*	(1.69)*
Student job hours/week	0.001	0.000	0.001	0.000	0.001	0.000
	0.33	−0.18	0.33	−0.2	0.35	−0.16
Student sports hours/week	0.000	0.001	−0.001	0.001	−0.001	0.001
	−0.18	0.22	−0.2	0.19	−0.18	0.21
Student reads hours week	0.002	0.003	0.003	0.003	0.002	0.003
	0.77	0.99	0.8	1.04	0.78	0.99
Student has dictionary at home	0.008	0.005	0.007	0.004	0.008	0.005
	0.88	0.57	0.84	0.48	0.88	0.58
Student has computer at home	0.007	0.007	0.008	0.007	0.008	0.007
	1.09	1.03	1.11	0.99	1.1	1.04
Student's mom education level	−0.001	−0.001	−0.001	−0.001	−0.001	−0.001
	−0.73	−0.74	−0.72	−0.77	−0.74	−0.77
Student hours tutoring/ week	−0.001	−0.002	−0.001	−0.002	−0.001	−0.002
	−0.8	−1.32	−0.88	−1.49	−0.81	−1.31
Teacher female		0.006		0.002		−0.004
		0.31		0.12		−0.2
Teacher civil servant		−0.005		−0.009		−0.004
		−0.15		−0.31		−0.13
Teacher school-hired		−0.017		−0.017		−0.019
		−0.68		−0.69		−0.73
Teacher math satisfaction level		0.003		−0.006		0.009
		0.2		−0.44		0.61

table continues next page

Teacher Reform in Indonesia • http://dx.doi.org/10.1596/978-0-8213-9829-6

Appendix A *(continued)*

	Base regression	w/teacher variables	Base regression	w/teacher variables	Base regression	w/teacher variables
Teacher attends working group		−0.016		−0.007		−0.007
		−0.83		−0.42		−0.36
Teacher maths education degree		0.026		0.026		0.024
		1.66		(1.78)*		1.55
Teacher experience years		0.002		0.003		0.002
		(2.07)**		(2.39)**		1.67
Teacher 4-year degree		0.052		0.038		0.035
		1.51		1.22		1
Teacher certified		−0.018		−0.014		−0.021
		−0.95		−0.79		−1.09
Teacher assessment score		0.219		0.177		0.185
		(2.24)**		(1.95)*		(1.87)*
Class size (number of students)	0.000	0.000	0.000	0.000	0.000	0.000
	0.17	−0.13	0.23	0.05	0.21	−0.08
School private	0.015	0.020	0.012	0.016	0.017	0.020
	0.73	0.66	0.6	0.54	0.84	0.64
School religious	−0.009	0.016	0.004	0.023	−0.013	0.004
	−0.43	0.78	0.17	1.24	−0.64	0.22
School size (number of students)	0.000	0.000	0.000	0.000	0.000	0.000
	1.52	0.39	1.6	0.56	(1.7)*	0.79
School materials shortage	−0.009	0.009	−0.009	0.009	−0.009	0.008
	−1.16	1.05	−1.18	1.24	−1.12	0.98
School building deficiency	0.007	0.003	0.009	0.004	0.007	0.003
	0.87	0.44	1.12	0.63	0.9	0.42
School library deficiency	−0.012	−0.012	−0.011	−0.012	−0.013	−0.010
	−1.38	−1.43	−1.3	−1.52	−1.41	−1.27
Frequency students skip class	−0.008	−0.015	−0.006	−0.010	−0.006	−0.012
	−0.63	−1.42	−0.46	−1	−0.5	−1.12
Frequency students skip class	−0.025	−0.028	−0.032	−0.038	−0.028	−0.030
	(−1.78)*	(−2.13)**	(−2.34)**	(−3.04)***	(−1.98)**	(−2.27)**
Frequency students late	0.009	0.023	0.012	0.025	0.009	0.021
	1.24	(3.07)***	1.63	(3.58)***	1.17	(2.9)***
Frequency bullying	−0.004	0.004	−0.003	0.003	−0.005	0.001
	−0.25	0.31	−0.25	0.26	−0.39	0.1
Community size	−0.002	0.008	−0.005	0.005	−0.001	0.006
	−0.24	1.11	−0.63	0.72	−0.19	0.76
Community poor (%)	−0.010	−0.016	−0.007	−0.014	−0.008	−0.015
	−1.19	(−2.02)**	−0.88	(−1.83)*	−0.91	(−1.86)*

table continues next page

Appendix A *(continued)*

	Base regression	w/teacher variables	Base regression	w/teacher variables	Base regression	w/teacher variables
Community affluent (%)	−0.008	−0.007	−0.006	−0.008	−0.009	−0.008
	−1.07	−0.9	−0.76	−1.02	−1.23	−1.05
Constant	0.209	−0.012	0.255	0.140	0.227	0.079
	1.54	−0.08	(3.15)***	1.41	(2.66)**	0.78
Random effects parameters						
Level 1: Student level						
estimate	0.0111	0.0109	0.0111	0.0109	0.0111	0.0109
Standard error	0.0004	0.0004	0.0004	0.0004	0.0004	0.0004
Level 2: Classroom level						
estimate	0.0109	0.0109	0.0109	0.0109	0.0109	0.0109
Standard error	0.0006	0.0004	0.0005	0.0003	0.0006	0.0004
Level 3: Region level						
estimate	0.0109	0.0109	0.0109	0.0109	0.0109	0.0109
Standard error	0.0000	0.0000	0.0000	0.0000	0.0000	0.0000

Note: Robust z-statistics in parentheses. Regressions are multi-level models run with MLwIN.
Significance level: * = 10 percent, ** = 5 percent, *** = 1 percent.

Appendix B

Coefficient and z-statistic data for figure 5.4: Relationship of Teaching Approach Practices to Student Learning Outcomes. Variables shaded gray below were used in creating the figure.

	Base regression	w/teacher variables	Base regression	w/teacher variables	Base regression	w/teacher variables	Base regression	w/teacher variables	Base regression	w/teacher variables
Discussion	-0.054 (-1.17)	-0.101 (-1.97)**								
Exposition			-0.068 (-2.01)**	-0.096 (-1.54)						
Investigation					0.223 (2.06)**	0.230 (2.04)**				
Practical work							0.068 (2.15)**	0.054 (1.59)		
Problem solving									0.026 (0.68)	0.040 (0.84)
Student pre-test score	0.530 (21.09)***	0.543 (20.84)***	0.531 (21.2)***	0.544 (20.88)***	0.530 (21.13)***	0.545 (20.96)***	0.530 (21.11)***	0.542 (20.75)***	0.530 (21.09)***	0.544 (20.85)***
Student age	-0.001 (-0.17)	-0.003 (-0.83)	0.000 (-0.11)	-0.003 (-0.78)	0.000 (-0.11)	-0.003 (-0.76)	-0.001 (-0.23)	-0.003 (-0.88)	-0.001 (-0.15)	-0.003 (-0.79)
Hours homework/week	0.006 (1.67)	0.006 (1.64)	0.006 (1.69)*	0.006 (1.7)[a]	0.006 (1.67)	0.006 (1.68)*	0.006 (1.69)*	0.006 (1.68)*	0.006 (1.68)*	0.006 (1.68)*
Student job hours/week	0.001 (0.33)	0.000 (-0.16)	0.001 (0.34)	0.000 (-0.18)	0.001 (0.37)	0.000 (-0.14)	0.001 (0.33)	0.000 (-0.16)	0.001 (0.33)	0.000 (-0.18)
Student sports hours/week	0.000 (-0.16)	0.001 (0.21)	-0.001 (-0.2)	0.001 (0.2)	0.000 (-0.15)	0.001 (0.27)	-0.001 (-0.19)	0.001 (0.2)	0.000 (-0.18)	0.001 (0.21)
Student reads hours week	0.002 (0.76)	0.003 (0.99)	0.002 (0.78)	0.003 (1.00)	0.002 (0.75)	0.003 (0.96)	0.002 (0.78)	0.003 (1.00)	0.002 (0.77)	0.003 (0.99)
Student has dictionary at home	0.007 (0.86)	0.004 (0.52)	0.008 (0.89)	0.005 (0.59)	0.007 (0.87)	0.005 (0.59)	0.007 (0.85)	0.005 (0.56)	0.008 (0.88)	0.005 (0.58)
Student has computer at home	0.007 (1.09)	0.008 (1.08)	0.007 (1.07)	0.007 (1.01)	0.007 (1.10)	0.008 (1.06)	0.007 (1.05)	0.007 (1.02)	0.007 (1.10)	0.007 (1.04)

table continues next page

200

Appendix B *(continued)*

	Base regression	W/teacher variables	Base regression	W/teacher variables	Base regression	W/teacher variables	Base regression	W/teacher variables	Base regression	W/teacher variables
Student's mom education level	-0.001 (-0.75)	-0.001 (-0.77)	-0.001 (-0.73)	-0.001 (-0.74)	-0.001 (-0.70)	-0.001 (-0.74)	-0.001 (-0.73)	-0.001 (-0.73)	-0.001 (-0.74)	-0.001 (-0.77)
Student hours tutoring/week	-0.001 (-0.82)	-0.002 (-1.33)	-0.001 (-0.82)	-0.002 (-1.30)	-0.001 (-0.74)	-0.002 (-1.19)	-0.001 (-0.91)	-0.002 (-1.36)	-0.001 (-0.79)	-0.002 (-1.28)
Teacher female		-0.010 (-0.54)		0.007 (0.41)		-0.003 (-0.2)		0.001 (0.06)		0.001 (0.07)
Teacher civil servant		0.004 (0.11)		-0.009 (-0.27)		0.002 (0.08)		-0.001 (-0.03)		-0.006 (-0.2)
Teacher school-hired		-0.011 (-0.43)		-0.019 (-0.74)		-0.013 (-0.54)		-0.016 (-0.63)		-0.018 (-0.7)
Teacher math satisfaction level		0.010 (0.7)		0.005 (0.32)		0.003 (0.2)		0.010 (0.67)		0.005 (0.35)
Teacher attends working group		-0.014 (-0.77)		-0.017 (-0.9)		-0.011 (-0.63)		-0.015 (-0.79)		-0.014 (-0.72)
Teacher maths education degree		0.033 (2.02)**		0.017 (1.01)		0.020 (1.28)		0.024 (1.56)		0.025 (1.58)
Teacher experience years		0.002 (2.12)**		0.003 (2.21)**		0.003 (2.32)**		0.002 (1.97)**		0.002 (2.02)**
Teacher 4-year degree		0.045 (1.38)		0.050 (1.52)		0.048 (1.53)		0.041 (1.26)		0.048 (1.45)
Teacher certified		-0.025 (-1.28)		-0.019 (-0.97)		-0.022 (-1.17)		-0.018 (-0.94)		-0.022 (-1.12)
Teacher assessment score		0.181 (1.88)*		0.224 (2.34)**		0.145 (1.51)		0.224 (2.3)**		0.201 (2.08)**
Class size (number of students)	0.000 (0.10)	-0.001 (-0.41)	0.001 (0.49)	0.000 (0.13)	0.000 (-0.18)	-0.001 (-0.59)	0.000 (0.29)	0.000 (-0.03)	0.000 (0.23)	0.000 (-0.10)
School private	0.016 (0.80)	0.030 (0.95)	0.010 (0.51)	0.015 (0.49)	0.025 (1.19)	0.037 (1.20)	0.019 (0.92)	0.025 (0.79)	0.014 (0.62)	0.017 (0.53)

table continues next page

Appendix B *(continued)*

	Base regression	w/teacher variables	Base regression	w/teacher variables	Base regression	w/teacher variables	Base regression	w/teacher variables	Base regression	w/teacher variables
School religious	-0.010	0.011	-0.010	0.011	-0.015	-0.001	-0.009	0.011	-0.011	0.011
	-0.51	0.58	-0.51	0.56	-0.76	-0.03	-0.43	0.56	-0.53	0.57
School size (number of students)	0.000	0.000	0.000	0.000	0.000	0.000	0.000	0.000	0.000	0.000
	1.62	0.82	1.28	0.34	(2.13)**	1.47	1.55	0.51	1.45	0.50
School materials shortage	-0.011	0.005	-0.007	0.010	-0.007	0.009	-0.008	0.009	-0.010	0.008
	-1.30	0.61	-0.83	1.26	-0.86	1.13	-1.01	1.08	-1.17	0.96
School building deficiency	0.008	0.002	0.007	0.005	0.004	0.000	0.009	0.004	0.007	0.003
	1.02	0.31	0.95	0.61	0.49	-0.01	1.17	0.52	0.88	0.45
School library deficiency	-0.013	-0.010	-0.011	-0.011	-0.008	-0.005	-0.012	-0.011	-0.013	-0.011
	-1.44	-1.23	-1.23	-1.43	-0.92	-0.64	-1.33	-1.37	-1.42	-1.40
Frequency students skip class	-0.009	-0.016	-0.008	-0.015	-0.012	-0.017	-0.008	-0.014	-0.008	-0.015
	-0.71	-1.53	-0.67	-1.36	-0.97	-1.62	-0.62	-1.32	-0.62	-1.37
Frequency students skip class	-0.025	-0.024	-0.024	-0.029	-0.025	-0.028	-0.027	-0.028	-0.025	-0.027
	(-1.84)*	(-1.88)*	(-1.8)*	(-2.24)**	(-1.82)*	(-2.27)**	(-2.01)**	(-2.16)**	(-1.77)*	(-2.1)*
Frequency students late	0.009	0.020	0.008	0.020	0.009	0.019	0.007	0.020	0.009	0.022
	1.18	(2.69)***	1.11	(2.76)***	1.23	(2.73)***	0.91	(2.62)**	1.24	(3)***
Frequency bullying	-0.005	0.006	-0.002	0.000	-0.007	-0.002	0.001	0.005	-0.005	0.001
	-0.37	0.45	-0.16	0.03	-0.52	-0.15	0.05	0.40	-0.35	0.11
Community size	-0.002	0.007	-0.003	0.007	-0.005	0.003	-0.003	0.007	-0.002	0.008
	-0.29	0.92	-0.39	1.02	-0.64	0.36	-0.37	0.93	-0.20	1.06
Community poor (%)	-0.008	-0.012	-0.016	-0.017	-0.008	-0.012	-0.014	-0.017	-0.010	-0.015
	-0.94	-1.55	(-1.8)*	(-2.21)**	-0.97	-1.57	-1.59	(-2.1)*	-1.17	(-1.92)*
Community affluent (%)	-0.008	-0.005	-0.013	-0.011	-0.011	-0.011	-0.011	-0.008	-0.009	-0.008
	-1.13	-0.66	(-1.71)*	-1.35	-1.43	-1.43	-1.54	-1.01	-1.17	-1.01
Constant	0.255	0.068	0.293	0.120	0.253	0.110	0.248	0.070	0.241	0.076
	(3.07)***	0.67	(3.43)***	1.15	(3.1)***	1.10	(3.04)***	0.69	(2.9)***	0.75

table continues next page

Appendix B *(continued)*

Random effects parameters

	Base regression	w/teacher variables	Base regression	w/teacher variables	Base regression	w/teacher variables	Base regression	w/teacher variables	Base regression	w/teacher variables	Base regression	w/teacher variables
Level 1: Student level estimate	0.0111	0.0109	0.0111	0.0109	0.0111	0.0109	0.0111	0.0109	0.0111	0.0109	0.0111	0.0109
Standard error	0.0004	0.0004	0.0004	0.0004	0.0004	0.0004	0.0004	0.0004	0.0004	0.0004	0.0004	0.0004
Level 2: Classroom level estimate	0.0109	0.0109	0.0109	0.0109	0.0109	0.0109	0.0109	0.0109	0.0109	0.0109	0.0109	0.0109
Standard error	0.0006	0.0004	0.0005	0.0004	0.0005	0.0004	0.0005	0.0004	0.0005	0.0004	0.0006	0.0004
Level 3: Region level estimate	0.0109	0.0109	0.0109	0.0109	0.0109	0.0109	0.0109	0.0109	0.0109	0.0109	0.0109	0.0109
Standard error	0	0	0	0	0	0	0	0	0	0	0	0

Note: Robust z-statistics in parentheses. Regressions are multi-level models run with MLwiN.
Significance level: * = 10 percent, ** = 5 percent, *** = 1 percent.

Appendix C

Coefficient and z-statistic data for figure 5.6: Relationship of Public Interaction Categories to Student Learning Outcomes.

Variables shaded gray below were used in creating the figure.

	Base regression	w/teacher variables	Base regression	w/teacher variables	Base regression	w/teacher variables
Teacher only	−0.064	−0.089				
	−0.94	(−1.89)*				
Teacher and students			0.091	0.153		
			(1.71)*	(2.5)**		
Students only					−0.170	−0.086
					(−2.04)**	−0.99
Student pretest score	0.529	0.542	0.527	0.539	0.527	0.544
	(21.06)***	(20.76)***	(20.9)***	(20.53)***	(20.92)***	(20.82)***
Student age	−0.001	−0.003	−0.001	−0.003	−0.001	−0.003
	−0.18	−0.91	−0.22	−0.92	−0.2	−0.84
Hours homework/week	0.006	0.006	0.006	0.006	0.006	0.006
	(1.69)*	1.67	(1.7)*	(1.71)*	(1.72)*	(1.68)*
Student job hours/week	0.001	0.000	0.001	0.000	0.001	0.000
	0.33	−0.15	0.33	−0.15	0.34	−0.17
Student sports hours/ week	0.000	0.001	0.000	0.001	−0.001	0.001
	−0.18	0.2	−0.17	0.21	−0.21	0.21
Student reads hours week	0.002	0.003	0.002	0.003	0.002	0.003
	0.76	0.96	0.73	0.93	0.76	0.99
Student has dictionary at home	0.008	0.005	0.007	0.005	0.007	0.005
	0.88	0.57	0.87	0.53	0.86	0.59
Student has computer at home	0.007	0.007	0.007	0.007	0.007	0.007
	1.09	1.04	1.05	0.95	1.02	1.04
Student's mom education level	−0.001	−0.001	−0.001	−0.001	−0.001	−0.001
	−0.73	−0.75	−0.78	−0.82	−0.71	−0.75
Student hours tutoring/ week	−0.001	−0.002	−0.001	−0.002	−0.001	−0.002
	−0.81	−1.41	−0.87	−1.41	−0.79	−1.31
Teacher female		0.000		0.000		0.001
		−0.01		−0.02		0.07
Teacher civil servant		−0.003		0.016		−0.006
		−0.1		0.48		−0.17
Teacher school-hired		−0.018		−0.014		−0.018
		−0.69		−0.56		−0.71
Teacher math satisfaction level		0.008		0.008		0.007
		0.51		0.56		0.46

table continues next page

Appendix C *(continued)*

	Base regression	w/teacher variables	Base regression	w/teacher variables	Base regression	w/teacher variables
Teacher attends working group		−0.015		−0.017		−0.012
		−0.81		−0.9		−0.66
Teacher maths education degree		0.028		0.033		0.025
		(1.81)*		(2.08)**		1.59
Teacher experience years		0.002		0.002		0.002
		(1.94)*		(2.07)**		(1.91)*
Teacher 4-year degree		0.037		0.037		0.044
		1.14		1.14		1.33
Teacher certified		−0.018		−0.021		−0.020
		−0.95		−1.1		−1.01
Teacher assessment score		0.227		0.204		0.208
		(2.37)**		(2.17)**		(2.12)**
Class size (number of students)	0.000	−0.001	0.000	−0.001	0.001	0.000
	0.12	−0.52	−0.13	−0.63	0.4	−0.14
School private	0.017	0.024	0.019	0.042	0.013	0.019
	0.79	0.79	0.92	1.31	0.64	0.61
School religious	−0.011	0.009	−0.009	0.012	−0.009	0.010
	−0.53	0.47	−0.42	0.64	−0.46	0.5
School size (number of students)	0.000	0.000	0.000	0.000	0.000	0.000
	1.58	0.87	(1.79)*	0.82	0.81	0.61
School materials shortage	−0.010	0.008	−0.011	0.005	−0.007	0.008
	−1.16	0.95	−1.33	0.6	−0.86	1.02
School building deficiency	0.007	0.005	0.009	0.004	0.005	0.003
	0.88	0.72	1.05	0.56	0.61	0.44
School library deficiency	−0.013	−0.011	−0.012	−0.009	−0.012	−0.011
	−1.4	−1.42	−1.41	−1.17	−1.42	−1.37
Frequency students skip class	−0.007	−0.010	−0.006	−0.010	−0.008	−0.014
	−0.56	−0.95	−0.45	−0.97	−0.64	−1.28
Frequency students skip class	−0.026	−0.029	−0.026	−0.029	−0.030	−0.028
	(−1.84)*	(−2.23)**	(−1.9)*	(−2.27)**	(−2.15)**	(−2.15)**
Frequency students late	0.009	0.023	0.009	0.020	0.007	0.022
	1.22	(3.18)***	1.28	(2.84)***	0.94	(2.94)***
Frequency bullying	−0.005	−0.004	−0.007	0.001	−0.001	0.002
	−0.34	−0.32	−0.52	0.09	−0.05	0.13
Community size	−0.001	0.010	0.000	0.009	0.005	0.008
	−0.17	1.29	−0.03	1.24	0.64	1.01
Community poor (%)	−0.010	−0.015	−0.011	−0.017	−0.012	−0.015
	−1.12	(−1.92)*	−1.24	(−2.22)**	−1.43	(−1.92)*

table continues next page

Appendix C *(continued)*

	Base regression	w/teacher variables	Base regression	w/teacher variables	Base regression	w/teacher variables
Community affluent (%)	−0.009	−0.007	−0.009	−0.009	−0.004	−0.008
	−1.15	−0.94	−1.25	−1.1	−0.48	−0.95
Constant	0.251	0.133	0.254	0.086	0.231	0.078
	(2.77)***	1.25	(3.06)***	0.86	(2.72)***	0.77
Random effects parameters						
Level 1: Student level						
estimate	0.0111	0.0109	0.0111	0.0109	0.0111	0.0109
Standard error	0.0004	0.0004	0.0004	0.0004	0.0004	0.0004
Level 2: Classroom level						
estimate	0.0109	0.0109	0.0109	0.0109	0.0109	0.0109
Standard error	0.0006	0.0004	0.0006	0.0004	0.0006	0.0004
Level 3: Region level						
estimate	0.0109	0.0109	0.0109	0.0109	0.0109	0.0109
Standard error	0.0000	0.0000	0.0000	0.0000	0.0004	0.0000

Note: Robust z-statistics in parentheses. Regressions are multi-level models run with MLwIN.
Significance level: * = 10 percent, ** = 5 percent, *** = 1 percent.

Teacher Reform in Indonesia • http://dx.doi.org/10.1596/978-0-8213-9829-6

Appendix D

Coefficient and z-statistic data for figure 5.10: Relationship of Problem-Solving Approach Categories to Student Learning Outcomes. Variables shaded gray below were used in creating the figure.

	Base regression	w/teacher variables	Base regression	w/teacher variables	Base regression	w/teacher variables	Base regression	w/teacher variables	Base regression	w/teacher variables	Base regression	w/teacher variables
Mathematical language	0.105 1.58	0.115 (2.1)**										
Real world			-0.105 -1.58	-0.115 (-2.1)**								
Routine					-0.114 (-2.01)**	-0.085 -1.48						
Nonroutine							0.114 (2.01)**	0.085 1.48				
Open									0.155 (2.38)**	0.120 (1.98)**		
Closed											-0.155 (-2.38)**	-0.120 (-1.98)**
Student pretest score	0.537 (20.54)***	0.551 (20.22)***	0.537 (20.54)***	0.551 (20.22)***	0.540 (20.64)***	0.549 (20.1)***	0.540 (20.64)***	0.549 (20.1)***	0.537 (21.27)***	0.547 (20.75)***	0.537 (21.27)***	0.547 (20.75)***
Student age	0.001 0.34	-0.001 -0.35	0.001 0.34	-0.001 -0.35	0.001 0.32	-0.001 -0.31	0.001 0.32	-0.001 -0.31	0.000 -0.02	-0.003 -0.68	0.000 -0.02	-0.003 -0.68
Hours homework/week	0.004 1.18	0.004 1.18	0.004 1.18	0.004 1.18	0.004 1.22	0.004 1.17	0.004 1.22	0.004 1.17	0.006 (1.75)*	0.006 (1.72)*	0.006 (1.75)*	0.006 (1.72)*
Student job hours/week	0.003 1.21	0.002 0.71	0.003 1.21	0.002 0.71	0.003 1.13	0.002 0.70	0.003 1.13	0.002 0.70	0.002 0.65	0.000 0.14	0.002 0.65	0.000 0.14
Student sports hours/week	-0.002 -0.58	-0.001 -0.17	-0.002 -0.58	-0.001 -0.17	-0.002 -0.55	0.000 -0.15	-0.002 -0.55	0.000 -0.15	-0.001 -0.41	0.000 0.02	-0.001 -0.41	0.000 0.02

table continues next page

Appendix D *(continued)*

	Base regression	W/teacher variables	Base regression	W/teacher variables	Base regression	W/teacher variables	Base regression	W/teacher variables	Base regression	W/teacher variables
Student reads hours week	0.003 0.90	0.004 1.17	0.003 0.90	0.004 1.17	0.003 0.89	0.004 1.16	0.003 0.89	0.004 1.16	0.003 0.83	0.003 1.06
Student has dictionary at home	0.013 1.38	0.010 1.08	0.013 1.38	0.010 1.08	0.013 1.42	0.009 1.03	0.013 1.42	0.009 1.03	0.008 0.91	0.006 0.66
Student has computer at home	0.010 1.36	0.009 1.21	0.010 1.36	0.009 1.21	0.010 1.37	0.009 1.21	0.010 1.37	0.009 1.21	0.008 1.10	0.008 1.06
Student's mom education level	0.000 -0.38	-0.001 -0.41	0.000 -0.38	-0.001 -0.41	0.000 -0.40	-0.001 -0.42	0.000 -0.40	-0.001 -0.42	-0.001 -0.70	-0.001 -0.78
Student hours tutoring/week	-0.001 -0.51	-0.002 -1.16	-0.001 -0.51	-0.002 -1.16	-0.001 -0.54	-0.002 -1.27	-0.001 -0.54	-0.002 -1.27	-0.001 -0.72	-0.002 -1.30
Teacher female		-0.004 -0.20		-0.004 -0.20		-0.006 -0.29		-0.006 -0.29		0.003 0.17
Teacher civil servant		-0.040 -0.83		-0.040 -0.83		-0.023 -0.47		-0.023 -0.47		-0.006 -0.19
Teacher school-hired		-0.045 -1.50		-0.045 -1.50		-0.037 -1.20		-0.037 -1.20		-0.021 -0.79
Teacher math satisfaction level		0.003 0.19		0.003 0.19		0.009 0.53		0.009 0.53		0.006 0.39
Teacher attends working group		-0.025 -1.26		-0.025 -1.26		-0.024 -1.15		-0.024 -1.15		-0.015 -0.80

table continues next page

Appendix D *(continued)*

	Base regression	w/teacher variables	Base regression	w/teacher variables	Base regression	w/teacher variables
Teacher maths education degree		0.033 (1.71)*		0.027 1.38		0.023 1.42
Teacher experience years		0.003 (2.28)**		0.002 (1.81)*		0.002 (1.73)*
Teacher 4-year degree		0.058 1.65		0.055 1.56		0.044 1.33
Teacher certified		−0.016 −0.70		−0.013 −0.59		−0.014 −0.64
Teacher assessment score		0.152 1.43		0.187 (1.84)*		0.205 (2.12)**
Class size (number of students)	0.001 0.52	0.001 0.44	0.001 0.44	0.001 0.42	0.001 0.77	0.000 0.23
School private	0.008 0.34	−0.015 −0.32	0.016 0.76	0.000 −0.01	0.017 0.85	0.021 0.66
School religious	0.006 0.25	0.030 1.42	0.002 0.09	0.024 1.14	−0.002 −0.08	0.012 0.61
School size (number of students)	0.000 1.05	0.000 −0.19	0.000 0.95	0.000 −0.03	0.000 1.29	0.000 0.32
School materials shortage	−0.012 −1.36	0.002 0.26	−0.010 −1.17	0.003 0.32	−0.010 −1.23	0.007 0.86

table continues next page

Appendix D (continued)

	Base regression	w/teacher variables	Base regression	w/teacher variables	Base regression	w/teacher variables	Base regression	w/teacher variables	Base regression	w/teacher variables	Base regression	w/teacher variables
School building deficiency	0.009	0.004	0.009	0.004	0.009	0.005	0.009	0.005	0.011	0.005	0.011	0.005
	1.08	0.51	1.08	0.51	1.04	0.55	1.04	0.55	1.43	0.64	1.43	0.64
School library deficiency	−0.012	−0.011	−0.012	−0.011	−0.008	−0.009	−0.008	−0.009	−0.010	−0.010	−0.010	−0.010
	−1.21	−1.24	−1.21	−1.24	−0.79	−0.97	−0.79	−0.97	−1.16	−1.24	−1.16	−1.24
Frequency students skip class	−0.014	−0.021	−0.014	−0.021	−0.013	−0.017	−0.013	−0.017	−0.012	−0.015	−0.012	−0.015
	−1.06	(−1.77)*	−1.06	(−1.77)*	−0.99	−1.50	−0.99	−1.50	−0.96	−1.41	−0.96	−1.41
Frequency students skip class	−0.018	−0.016	−0.018	−0.016	−0.021	−0.025	−0.021	−0.025	−0.025	−0.029	−0.025	−0.029
	−1.13	−1.08	−1.13	−1.08	−1.41	−1.57	−1.41	−1.57	(−1.92)*	(−2.22)**	(−1.92)*	(−2.22)**
Frequency students late	0.009	0.024	0.009	0.024	0.008	0.026	0.008	0.026	0.010	0.022	0.010	0.022
	1.20	(3.19)***	1.20	(3.19)***	1.11	(3.39)***	1.11	(3.39)***	1.38	(2.96)***	1.38	(2.96)***
Frequency bullying	0.000	0.009	0.000	0.009	0.004	0.008	0.004	0.008	0.001	0.003	0.001	0.003
	0.01	0.67	0.01	0.67	0.24	0.58	0.24	0.58	0.10	0.23	0.10	0.23
Community size	−0.004	0.004	−0.004	0.004	−0.003	0.003	−0.003	0.003	−0.004	0.008	−0.004	0.008
	−0.51	0.52	−0.51	0.52	−0.32	0.32	−0.32	0.32	−0.51	1.03	−0.51	1.03
Community poor (%)	−0.008	−0.013	−0.008	−0.013	−0.010	−0.014	−0.010	−0.014	−0.012	−0.014	−0.012	−0.014
	−0.84	−1.39	−0.84	−1.39	−1.12	−1.46	−1.12	−1.46	−1.48	(−1.8)*	−1.48	(−1.8)*
Community affluent (%)	−0.005	−0.004	−0.005	−0.004	−0.004	−0.005	−0.004	−0.005	−0.009	−0.007	−0.009	−0.007
	−0.58	−0.46	−0.58	−0.46	−0.52	−0.50	−0.52	−0.50	−1.28	−0.91	−1.28	−0.91
Constant	0.111	0.025	0.186	0.072	0.275	−0.024	0.167	0.048	0.198	0.062	0.352	0.062
	1.11	0.23	(2.03)**	0.66	(2.58)**	−0.19	(1.85)*	0.46	(2.35)**	0.60	(3.36)***	0.48

table continues next page

	Base regression	w/teacher variables	Base regression	w/teacher variables	Base regression	w/teacher variables	Base regression	w/teacher variables	Base regression	w/teacher variables	Base regression	w/teacher variables	Base regression	w/teacher variables	Base regression	w/teacher variables
Random effects parameters																
Level 1: Student level																
estimate	0.0111	0.0109	0.0111	0.0109	0.0111	0.0109	0.0111	0.0109	0.0111	0.0109	0.0111	0.0109	0.0111	0.0109	0.0111	0.0109
Standard error	0.0004	0.0004	0.0004	0.0004	0.0004	0.0004	0.0004	0.0004	0.0004	0.0004	0.0004	0.0004	0.0004	0.0004	0.0004	0.0004
Level 2: Classroom level																
estimate	0.0109	0.0109	0.0109	0.0109	0.0109	0.0109	0.0109	0.0109	0.0109	0.0109	0.0109	0.0109	0.0109	0.0109	0.0109	0.0109
Standard error	0.0006	0.0004	0.0006	0.0004	0.0006	0.0004	0.0006	0.0004	0.0006	0.0004	0.0005	0.0004	0.0005	0.0004	0.0005	0.0004
Level 3: Region level																
estimate	0.0109	0.0109	0.0109	0.0109	0.0109	0.0109	0.0109	0.0109	0.0109	0.0109	0.0109	0.0109	0.0109	0.0109	0.0109	0.0109
Standard error	0.0000	0.0000	0.0000	0.0000	0.0000	0.0000	0.0000	0.0000	0.0000	0.0000	0.0000	0.0000	0.0000	0.0000	0.0000	0.0000

Note: Robust z-statistics in parentheses. Regressions are multi-level models run with MLwiN.
Significance level: * = 10 percent, ** = 5 percent, *** = 1 percent.

Appendix E

Coefficient and t-statistic data for figure 5.11: Differences in Teaching Practices of Certified Teachers vs. Uncertified Teachers.

Variables Shaded gray below were used in creating the figure.

	(1)	(2)	(3)	(4)	(5)	(6)	(7)	(8)	(9)	(10)	(11)	(12)	(13)
Regressions with dependent variable of teachers having obtained certification	Mathematical	Nonmathematical	Mathematical organization	Review	New content	Practice	Assessment	Private (group or seatwork)	Public (whole class)	Public: teacher only	Public: teacher and student	Public: student only	Discussion
Teaching practice variable (listed in columns above)	-1.14	0.956	1.036	0.321	0.032	-0.189	0.313	-0.642	0.642	-0.141	0.361	-0.129	-0.225
	-1.57	0.61	1.34	0.99	0.18	-0.95	0.45	(2.25)**	(2.25)**	-0.53	0.99	-0.41	-0.62
Student age	0.015	0.013	0.011	0.014	0.009	0.009	0.011	0.013	0.013	0.005	0.002	0.011	0.012
	0.82	0.69	0.63	0.78	0.51	0.53	0.64	0.74	0.74	0.29	0.12	0.61	0.69
Hours homework/week	-0.018	-0.02	-0.02	-0.019	-0.022	-0.02	-0.022	-0.014	-0.014	-0.022	-0.02	-0.021	-0.023
	-1.65	(1.99)*	(1.78)*	(1.78)*	(1.99)*	(1.86)*	(2.00)**	-1.49	-1.49	(2.02)**	(1.88)*	(1.92)*	(2.16)**
Student job hours/week	-0.016	-0.018	-0.017	-0.02	-0.019	-0.02	-0.02	-0.016	-0.016	-0.019	-0.018	-0.019	-0.019
	(1.92)*	(2.20)**	(2.01)**	(2.51)**	(2.29)**	(2.38)**	(2.44)**	(2.12)**	(2.12)**	(2.31)**	(2.30)**	(2.27)**	(2.23)**
Student sports hours/week	-0.002	-0.004	-0.002	-0.004	-0.004	-0.004	-0.004	-0.006	-0.006	-0.004	-0.004	-0.003	-0.002
	-0.26	-0.45	-0.25	-0.42	-0.43	-0.46	-0.39	-0.67	-0.67	-0.46	-0.45	-0.38	-0.23
Student reads hours week	0.035	0.035	0.036	0.035	0.035	0.035	0.036	0.03	0.03	0.035	0.034	0.035	0.035
	(2.79)***	(2.83)***	(2.81)***	(2.78)***	(2.82)***	(2.78)***	(2.89)***	(2.73)***	(2.73)***	(2.82)***	(2.76)***	(2.81)***	(2.81)***
Student has dictionary at home	-0.004	-0.007	-0.006	-0.007	-0.008	-0.005	-0.007	0.001	0.001	-0.01	-0.01	-0.007	-0.012
	-0.12	-0.19	-0.16	-0.21	-0.21	-0.13	-0.18	0.02	0.02	-0.27	-0.28	-0.20	-0.34
Student has computer at home	0.034	0.035	0.034	0.028	0.034	0.029	0.034	0.027	0.027	0.037	0.032	0.031	0.037
	1.36	1.37	1.36	1.20	1.36	1.10	1.30	1.08	1.08	1.52	1.19	1.21	1.51
Student's mom education level	0.004	0.004	0.004	0.003	0.004	0.004	0.004	0.003	0.003	0.004	0.003	0.004	0.004
	0.93	0.81	0.86	0.67	0.85	0.95	0.71	0.72	0.72	0.76	0.61	0.72	0.70
Student hours tutoring/week	-0.002	-0.004	-0.003	-0.005	-0.005	-0.005	-0.005	-0.005	-0.005	-0.006	-0.007	-0.004	-0.006
	-0.25	-0.52	-0.48	-0.65	-0.67	-0.71	-0.60	-0.69	-0.69	-0.88	-0.90	-0.59	-0.73
Teacher female	-0.019	0.009	-0.021	-0.017	0.006	-0.002	0.003	0.031	0.031	0.001	-0.011	0.003	-0.014
	-0.18	0.08	-0.19	-0.16	0.05	-0.02	0.03	0.29	0.29	0.01	-0.10	0.03	-0.12
Teacher civil servant	0.268	0.285	0.24	0.255	0.265	0.268	0.228	0.376	0.376	0.226	0.242	0.284	0.259
	1.32	1.25	1.17	1.18	1.21	1.29	0.95	(1.78)*	(1.78)*	0.96	1.15	1.26	1.23
Teacher school-hired	-0.109	-0.093	-0.118	-0.14	-0.096	-0.094	-0.108	-0.069	-0.069	-0.115	-0.117	-0.094	-0.087
	-0.76	-0.63	-0.80	-0.91	-0.63	-0.66	-0.72	-0.48	-0.48	-0.75	-0.80	-0.63	-0.57
Teacher math satisfaction level	0.021	0.027	0.011	0.03	0.02	0.026	0.013	-0.01	-0.01	0.026	0.035	0.018	0.023
	0.28	0.37	0.16	0.41	0.27	0.36	0.19	-0.14	-0.14	0.37	0.49	0.25	0.32

(14)	(15)	(16)	(17)	(18)	(19)	(20)	(21)	(22)	(23)	(24)	(25)	(26)	(27)	(28)
Exposition	Investigation	Practical work	Problem solving	Problem	Nonproblem	Math lanDage	Real world	Routine	Nonroutine	Question and answer	Rhetorical	True-false	Open	Closed
0.207	−0.668	0.008	−0.053	−0.402	0.402	−0.556	0.556	−0.402	0.402	0.006	0.005	−2.246	0.486	−0.486
0.85	−1.27	0.04	−0.18	−0.85	0.85	−1.59	1.59	−0.85	0.85	0.83	0.42	−0.50	1.44	−1.44
0.01	0.007	0.01	0.009	0.012	0.012	0.002	0.002	0.012	0.012	0.009	0.01	0.009	0.005	0.005
0.57	0.38	0.55	0.52	0.64	0.64	0.12	0.12	0.64	0.64	0.50	0.53	0.50	0.27	0.27
−0.021	−0.021	−0.022	−0.022	−0.019	−0.019	−0.023	−0.023	−0.019	−0.019	−0.02	−0.02	−0.019	−0.026	−0.026
(2.01)**	(1.95)*	(1.98)*	(1.99)*	(1.80)*	(1.80)*	(2.20)**	(2.20)**	(1.80)*	(1.80)*	(1.89)*	(1.89)*	(1.91)*	(2.41)**	(2.41)**
−0.018	−0.02	−0.019	−0.019	−0.018	−0.018	−0.021	−0.021	−0.018	−0.018	−0.018	−0.017	−0.017	−0.018	−0.018
(2.25)**	(2.38)**	(2.32)**	(2.29)**	(2.28)**	(2.28)**	(2.78)***	(2.78)***	(2.28)**	(2.28)**	(2.12)**	(2.12)**	(2.05)**	(2.19)**	(2.19)**
−0.002	−0.006	−0.004	−0.004	−0.001	−0.001	0	0	−0.001	−0.001	−0.001	−0.001	0	0.002	0.002
−0.25	−0.73	−0.42	−0.41	−0.06	−0.06	−0.02	−0.02	−0.06	−0.06	−0.12	−0.09	−0.02	0.22	0.22
0.034	0.037	0.036	0.035	0.039	0.039	0.036	0.036	0.039	0.039	0.038	0.039	0.038	0.038	0.038
(2.84)***	(2.96)***	(2.82)***	(2.90)***	(3.23)***	(3.23)***	(2.87)***	(2.87)***	(3.23)***	(3.23)***	(3.14)***	(3.18)***	(3.13)***	(3.10)***	(3.10)***
−0.008	−0.008	−0.008	−0.008	−0.02	−0.02	−0.036	−0.036	−0.02	−0.02	−0.025	−0.026	−0.026	−0.034	−0.034
−0.21	−0.23	−0.23	−0.23	−0.59	−0.59	−0.99	−0.99	−0.59	−0.59	−0.69	−0.72	−0.69	−1.10	−1.10
0.036	0.034	0.035	0.035	0.031	0.031	0.039	0.039	0.031	0.031	0.028	0.03	0.032	0.032	0.032
1.38	1.35	1.37	1.36	1.11	1.11	1.39	1.39	1.11	1.11	1.01	1.06	1.14	1.39	1.39
0.004	0.004	0.004	0.004	0.002	0.002	0.001	0.001	0.002	0.002	0.002	0.002	0.002	0.005	0.005
0.92	0.71	0.79	0.87	0.37	0.37	0.16	0.16	0.37	0.37	0.46	0.43	0.43	0.92	0.92
−0.004	−0.006	−0.005	−0.005	−0.012	−0.012	−0.014	−0.014	−0.012	−0.012	−0.012	−0.012	−0.013	−0.009	−0.009
−0.59	−0.76	−0.66	−0.66	−1.62	−1.62	(1.99)*	(1.99)*	−1.62	−1.62	(1.77)*	(1.80)*	(1.87)*	−1.42	−1.42
0.001	0.013	0.005	0.008	0.061	0.061	0.047	0.047	0.061	0.061	0.043	0.048	0.056	0.028	0.028
0.01	0.12	0.04	0.07	0.55	0.55	0.43	0.43	0.55	0.55	0.40	0.44	0.52	0.27	0.27
0.308	0.253	0.26	0.268	0.309	0.309	0.177	0.177	0.309	0.309	0.333	0.328	0.317	0.295	0.295
1.45	1.18	1.22	1.21	1.30	1.30	0.78	0.78	1.30	1.30	1.43	1.41	1.32	1.24	1.24
−0.084	−0.107	−0.101	−0.1	−0.086	−0.086	−0.057	−0.057	−0.086	−0.086	−0.073	−0.068	−0.045	−0.024	−0.024
−0.56	−0.73	−0.69	−0.68	−0.53	−0.53	−0.38	−0.38	−0.53	−0.53	−0.46	−0.43	−0.29	−0.17	−0.17
0.011	0.028	0.02	0.022	0.042	0.042	0.057	0.057	0.042	0.042	0.067	0.054	0.039	0.035	0.035
0.15	0.38	0.24	0.28	0.56	0.56	0.75	0.75	0.56	0.56	0.71	0.57	0.52	0.53	0.53

table continues next page

Appendix E *(continued)*

	(1)	(2)	(3)	(4)	(5)	(6)	(7)	(8)	(9)	(10)	(11)	(12)	(13)
Regressions with dependent variable of teachers having obtained certification	*Mathematical*	*Nonmathematical*	*Mathematical organization*	*Review*	*New content*	*Practice*	*Assessment*	*Private (group or seatwork)*	*Public (whole class)*	*Public: teacher only*	*Public: teacher and student*	*Public: student only*	*Discussion*
Teacher attends working group	0.072	0.057	0.083	0.07	0.069	0.083	0.077	0.111	0.111	0.064	0.062	0.068	0.06
	0.63	0.48	0.72	0.60	0.58	0.71	0.65	0.92	0.92	0.56	0.55	0.58	0.52
Teacher maths education degree	0.064	0.042	0.068	0.064	0.045	0.037	0.033	0.137	0.137	0.06	0.079	0.047	0.064
	0.58	0.40	0.62	0.58	0.41	0.33	0.29	1.37	1.37	0.58	0.74	0.43	0.59
Teacher experience years	0.018	0.02	0.018	0.02	0.02	0.02	0.02	0.019	0.019	0.02	0.02	0.019	0.02
	(2.57)**	(2.73)***	(2.54)**	(2.70)***	(2.70)***	(2.73)***	(2.70)***	(2.60)**	(2.60)**	(2.76)***	(2.75)***	(2.69)***	(2.72)***
Teacher 4-year degree	0.533	0.569	0.548	0.578	0.575	0.554	0.569	0.552	0.552	0.586	0.574	0.57	0.585
	(3.69)***	(4.01)***	(3.85)***	(4.41)***	(4.18)***	(4.03)***	(4.21)***	(4.15)***	(4.15)***	(4.22)***	(4.36)***	(4.12)***	(4.27)***
Teacher assessment score	−0.226	−0.259	−0.203	−0.285	−0.231	−0.241	−0.257	−0.249	−0.249	−0.212	−0.235	−0.26	−0.215
	−0.50	−0.56	−0.45	−0.61	−0.50	−0.53	−0.56	−0.56	−0.56	−0.44	−0.49	−0.56	−0.46
Student pretest score	−0.005	−0.02	−0.044	−0.039	−0.053	−0.049	−0.058	−0.02	−0.02	−0.056	−0.094	−0.064	−0.068
	−0.02	−0.09	−0.19	−0.17	−0.22	−0.21	−0.24	−0.09	−0.09	−0.24	−0.39	−0.27	−0.28
Class size (number of students)	−0.007	−0.006	−0.008	−0.005	−0.007	−0.007	−0.007	−0.007	−0.007	−0.008	−0.009	−0.007	−0.008
	−0.70	−0.62	−0.77	−0.52	−0.69	−0.64	−0.65	−0.71	−0.71	−0.80	−0.88	−0.64	−0.76
School private	0.097	0.124	0.087	0.105	0.121	0.135	0.081	0.239	0.239	0.101	0.114	0.124	0.106
	0.53	0.62	0.47	0.53	0.61	0.70	0.39	1.23	1.23	0.52	0.62	0.64	0.56
School religious	0.142	0.187	0.185	0.233	0.217	0.214	0.214	0.229	0.229	0.228	0.235	0.217	0.223
	1.04	1.35	1.37	(1.67)*	1.64	1.66	1.56	(1.70)*	(1.70)*	(1.71)*	(1.85)*	1.64	(1.69)*
School size (number of students)	0	0	0	0	0	0	0	0	0	0	0	0	0
	(1.79)*	−1.65	(1.85)*	−1.62	(1.75)*	(1.74)*	(1.75)*	(1.78)*	(1.78)*	(1.80)*	(1.89)*	−1.60	(1.71)*
School materials shortage	0.003	−0.007	−0.001	−0.029	−0.006	0	−0.014	−0.02	−0.02	−0.017	−0.025	−0.009	−0.01
	0.05	−0.11	−0.02	−0.39	−0.08	−0.01	−0.22	−0.30	−0.30	−0.26	−0.42	−0.14	−0.15
School building deficiency	−0.077	−0.065	−0.074	−0.062	−0.065	−0.067	−0.061	−0.084	−0.084	−0.058	−0.063	−0.069	−0.066
	−1.54	−1.32	−1.50	−1.29	−1.33	−1.37	−1.22	(1.76)*	(1.76)*	−1.08	−1.28	−1.30	−1.40
School library deficiency	0.018	0.024	0.017	0.026	0.024	0.024	0.017	0.014	0.014	0.02	0.024	0.027	0.024
	0.31	0.43	0.30	0.45	0.43	0.42	0.29	0.25	0.25	0.34	0.44	0.48	0.42
Frequency students skip class	0.026	0.032	0.02	0.035	0.024	0.019	0.026	0.004	0.004	0.038	0.047	0.023	0.029
	0.33	0.39	0.26	0.43	0.29	0.23	0.32	0.05	0.05	0.48	0.59	0.29	0.36
Frequency students late	−0.062	−0.059	−0.056	−0.056	−0.054	−0.053	−0.052	−0.044	−0.044	−0.052	−0.051	−0.055	−0.054
	(1.70)*	−1.62	−1.59	−1.51	−1.46	−1.42	−1.41	−1.20	−1.20	−1.38	−1.39	−1.49	−1.48
Frequency bullying	0.089	0.097	0.089	0.096	0.098	0.107	0.098	0.142	0.142	0.082	0.095	0.109	0.101
	1.00	1.08	0.99	1.07	1.08	1.21	1.11	1.54	1.54	0.82	1.05	1.16	1.14
Community size	−0.021	−0.01	−0.023	−0.013	−0.012	−0.008	−0.01	0.008	0.008	−0.01	−0.014	−0.016	−0.013
	−0.45	−0.21	−0.48	−0.26	−0.26	−0.16	−0.21	0.17	0.17	−0.21	−0.31	−0.32	−0.28

(14)	(15)	(16)	(17)	(18)	(19)	(20)	(21)	(22)	(23)	(24)	(25)	(26)	(27)	(28)
Exposition	Investigation	Practical work	Problem solving	Problem	Nonproblem	Math lanDage	Real world	Routine	Nonroutine	Question and answer	Rhetorical	True-false	Open	Closed
0.071	0.067	0.067	0.066	0.118	0.118	0.139	0.139	0.118	0.118	0.125	0.13	0.135	0.104	0.104
0.59	0.57	0.57	0.56	0.93	0.93	1.27	1.27	0.93	0.93	1.02	1.06	1.12	0.86	0.86
0.088	0.066	0.047	0.052	0.01	0.01	−0.039	−0.039	0.01	0.01	−0.012	−0.007	0	0.078	0.078
0.80	0.61	0.43	0.49	0.09	0.09	−0.39	−0.39	0.09	0.09	−0.11	−0.07	0.00	0.79	0.79
0.018	0.019	0.02	0.02	0.019	0.019	0.021	0.021	0.019	0.019	0.018	0.018	0.018	0.024	0.024
(2.35)**	(2.49)***	(2.72)***	(2.67)***	(2.38)**	(2.38)**	(3.02)***	(3.02)***	(2.38)**	(2.38)**	(2.39)**	(2.40)**	(2.45)**	(3.29)***	(3.29)***
0.552	0.566	0.578	0.57	0.584	0.584	0.635	0.635	0.584	0.584	0.599	0.6	0.621	0.554	0.554
(3.86)***	(4.20)***	(4.24)***	(3.88)***	(3.83)***	(3.83)***	(4.73)***	(4.73)***	(3.83)***	(3.83)***	(4.14)***	(4.16)***	(3.81)***	(3.79)***	(3.79)***
−0.2	−0.164	−0.235	−0.224	−0.19	−0.19	0.048	0.048	−0.19	−0.19	−0.207	−0.184	−0.12	−0.145	−0.145
−0.44	−0.35	−0.49	−0.49	−0.41	−0.41	0.10	0.10	−0.41	−0.41	−0.44	−0.39	−0.23	−0.33	−0.33
−0.042	−0.02	−0.054	−0.059	0.002	0.002	−0.062	−0.062	0.002	0.002	−0.016	−0.018	−0.013	−0.126	−0.126
−0.18	−0.09	−0.23	−0.26	0.01	0.01	−0.26	−0.26	0.01	0.01	−0.07	−0.08	−0.06	−0.55	−0.55
−0.007	−0.006	−0.007	−0.007	−0.019	−0.019	−0.018	−0.018	−0.019	−0.019	−0.019	−0.019	−0.018	−0.016	−0.016
−0.75	−0.52	−0.67	−0.63	(2.12)**	(2.12)**	(2.14)**	(2.14)**	(2.12)**	(2.12)**	(2.18)**	(2.12)**	(2.06)**	(1.84)*	(1.84)*
0.157	0.081	0.113	0.125	0.133	0.133	0.087	0.087	0.133	0.133	0.142	0.144	0.154	0.131	0.131
0.83	0.42	0.59	0.60	0.59	0.59	0.44	0.44	0.59	0.59	0.66	0.67	0.71	0.60	0.60
0.222	0.239	0.219	0.219	0.195	0.195	0.156	0.156	0.195	0.195	0.184	0.185	0.19	0.194	0.194
1.65	(1.78)*	1.66	1.65	1.28	1.28	1.09	1.09	1.28	1.28	1.24	1.23	1.28	1.49	1.49
0	0	0	0	0.001	0.001	0.001	0.001	0.001	0.001	0.001	0.001	0.001	0.001	0.001
(1.74)*	−1.35	(1.72)*	(1.74)*	(2.76)***	(2.76)***	(3.15)***	(3.15)***	(2.76)***	(2.76)***	(2.78)***	(2.81)***	(2.90)***	(2.35)**	(2.35)**
−0.011	−0.015	−0.01	−0.009	0.011	0.011	0.031	0.031	0.011	0.011	0.007	0.008	0.015	0.007	0.007
−0.17	−0.23	−0.15	−0.14	0.17	0.17	0.52	0.52	0.17	0.17	0.12	0.14	0.23	0.11	0.11
−0.075	−0.052	−0.064	−0.065	−0.088	−0.088	−0.094	−0.094	−0.088	−0.088	−0.082	−0.083	−0.085	−0.089	−0.089
−1.61	−1.03	−1.28	−1.32	(1.75)*	(1.75)*	(1.99)*	(1.99)*	(1.75)*	(1.75)*	−1.67	(1.69)*	(1.74)*	(1.92)*	(1.92)*
0.023	0.014	0.023	0.024	−0.026	−0.026	−0.011	−0.011	−0.026	−0.026	−0.016	−0.02	−0.018	−0.011	−0.011
0.41	0.24	0.41	0.42	−0.48	−0.48	−0.22	−0.22	−0.48	−0.48	−0.30	−0.35	−0.33	−0.21	−0.21
0.019	0.034	0.026	0.025	0.039	0.039	−0.002	−0.002	0.039	0.039	0.018	0.016	0.012	0.052	0.052
0.24	0.42	0.33	0.31	0.48	0.48	−0.03	−0.03	0.48	0.48	0.24	0.21	0.17	0.67	0.67
−0.049	−0.053	−0.054	−0.055	−0.029	−0.029	−0.01	−0.01	−0.029	−0.029	−0.021	−0.022	−0.027	−0.038	−0.038
−1.33	−1.43	−1.44	−1.47	−0.79	−0.79	−0.27	−0.27	−0.79	−0.79	−0.56	−0.60	−0.68	−1.07	−1.07
0.103	0.11	0.097	0.098	0.078	0.078	0.084	0.084	0.078	0.078	0.073	0.075	0.076	0.095	0.095
1.13	1.19	1.08	1.07	0.86	0.86	0.91	0.91	0.86	0.86	0.80	0.81	0.81	1.12	1.12
−0.012	−0.001	−0.013	−0.015	−0.03	−0.03	0.002	0.002	−0.03	−0.03	−0.037	−0.034	−0.026	−0.031	−0.031
−0.25	−0.02	−0.28	−0.30	−0.56	−0.56	0.04	0.04	−0.56	−0.56	−0.70	−0.63	−0.45	−0.58	−0.58

table continues next page

Appendix E *(continued)*

	(1)	(2)	(3)	(4)	(5)	(6)	(7)	(8)	(9)	(10)	(11)	(12)	(13)
Regressions with dependent variable of teachers having obtained certification	*Mathematical*	*Nonmathematical*	*Mathematical organization*	*Review*	*New content*	*Practice*	*Assessment*	*Private (group or seatwork)*	*Public (whole class)*	*Public: teacher only*	*Public: teacher and student*	*Public: student only*	*Discussion*
Community poor (%)	0.015	−0.01	0.015	−0.008	−0.009	−0.008	−0.009	−0.012	−0.012	−0.005	−0.012	−0.013	−0.007
	0.25	−0.17	0.23	−0.13	−0.15	−0.14	−0.15	−0.23	−0.23	−0.08	−0.19	−0.22	−0.11
Community affluent (%)	−0.073	−0.076	−0.074	−0.068	−0.076	−0.071	−0.078	−0.058	−0.058	−0.08	−0.08	−0.074	−0.073
	−1.51	−1.63	−1.49	−1.41	−1.60	−1.46	−1.63	−1.18	−1.18	(1.68)*	−1.65	−1.54	−1.48
Region Java	0.173	0.049	0.149	0.02	0.04	0.028	0.031	0.078	0.078	0.016	0.002	0.047	0.058
	1.11	0.30	0.93	0.12	0.24	0.17	0.20	0.49	0.49	0.09	0.01	0.29	0.34
Region Sumatera	0.225	0.114	0.208	0.081	0.107	0.071	0.093	0.073	0.073	0.1	0.103	0.115	0.13
	1.37	0.68	1.23	0.46	0.63	0.41	0.55	0.45	0.45	0.58	0.62	0.69	0.76
Region Kalimantan	0.122	0.069	0.143	0.075	0.087	0.048	0.076	0.075	0.075	0.088	0.062	0.083	0.094
	0.53	0.27	0.63	0.31	0.36	0.18	0.32	0.34	0.34	0.37	0.27	0.34	0.39
Region Bali/NTT/ NTB	0.097	0.025	0.101	0.013	0.029	−0.005	0.032	0.072	0.072	0.002	−0.036	0.038	0.023
	0.50	0.13	0.52	0.07	0.15	−0.02	0.17	0.37	0.37	0.01	−0.17	0.20	0.12
Constant	0.419	−0.489	−0.563	−0.479	−0.398	−0.373	−0.33	−0.392	−1.033	−0.186	−0.225	−0.36	−0.397
	0.51	−0.76	−0.87	−0.77	−0.59	−0.57	−0.50	−0.65	−1.66	−0.26	−0.35	−0.54	−0.61
Observations	2338	2338	2338	2338	2338	2338	2338	2338	2338	2338	2338	2338	2338
R^2	0.49	0.47	0.49	0.47	0.47	0.48	0.47	0.50	0.50	0.47	0.48	0.47	0.47
Adj. R^2	0.48	0.46	0.48	0.47	0.46	0.47	0.47	0.50	0.50	0.46	0.47	0.46	0.47

Note: Robust t-statistics in parentheses. Regressions run on multiple-imputed data.

Significance level: * = 10 percent, ** = 5 percent, *** = 1 percent.

(14)	(15)	(16)	(17)	(18)	(19)	(20)	(21)	(22)	(23)	(24)	(25)	(26)	(27)	(28)
Exposition	Investigation	Practical work	Problem solving	Problem	Nonproblem	Math lanDage	Real world	Routine	Nonroutine	Question and answer	Rhetorical	True-false	Open	Closed
−0.003	−0.018	−0.009	−0.01	0.043	0.043	0.037	0.037	0.043	0.043	0.034	0.035	0.035	−0.026	−0.026
−0.05	−0.28	−0.15	−0.16	0.73	0.73	0.65	0.65	0.73	0.73	0.58	0.60	0.60	−0.46	−0.46
−0.061	−0.065	−0.077	−0.077	−0.061	−0.061	−0.071	−0.071	−0.061	−0.061	−0.068	−0.07	−0.072	−0.099	−0.099
−1.17	−1.29	−1.61	−1.60	−1.18	−1.18	−1.42	−1.42	−1.18	−1.18	−1.34	−1.39	−1.41	(2.17)**	(2.17)**
0.025	0.039	0.039	0.033	0.018	0.018	0.114	0.114	0.018	0.018	0.015	0.018	0.022	0.002	0.002
0.15	0.24	0.24	0.19	0.10	0.10	0.67	0.67	0.10	0.10	0.08	0.10	0.13	0.01	0.01
0.101	0.104	0.109	0.106	0.159	0.159	0.178	0.178	0.159	0.159	0.151	0.153	0.152	0.138	0.138
0.62	0.64	0.65	0.62	0.97	0.97	1.02	1.02	0.97	0.97	0.90	0.92	0.90	0.84	0.84
0.059	0.082	0.09	0.075	0.363	0.363	0.465	0.465	0.363	0.363	0.363	0.363	0.363	0.078	0.078
0.25	0.34	0.37	0.29	1.38	1.38	(1.86)*	(1.86)*	1.38	1.38	1.37	1.37	1.38	0.36	0.36
0.009	0.025	0.033	0.025	0.164	0.164	0.324	0.324	0.164	0.164	0.154	0.175	0.263	0.065	0.065
0.05	0.13	0.17	0.12	0.83	0.83	1.53	1.53	0.83	0.83	0.74	0.85	1.12	0.35	0.35
−0.553	−0.435	−0.373	−0.359	0.115	−0.287	0.091	−0.465	0.115	−0.287	−0.175	−0.195	−0.285	−0.013	0.473
−0.80	−0.66	−0.56	−0.55	0.15	−0.49	0.16	−0.78	0.15	−0.49	−0.29	−0.32	−0.44	−0.02	0.68
2338	2338	2338	2338	2116	2116	2116	2116	2116	2116	2116	2116	2116	2296	2296
0.48	0.48	0.47	0.47	0.52	0.52	0.55	0.55	0.52	0.52	0.52	0.52	0.52	0.53	0.53
0.47	0.47	0.46	0.46	0.51	0.51	0.54	0.54	0.51	0.51	0.51	0.51	0.51	0.52	0.52

Appendix F

Coefficient and z-statistic data for figure 5.12: Relationship of Teacher Degree to Student Learning Outcomes.

Variables highlighted in brown below were used in creating the figure.

	Base regression	w/teacher variables	Base regression	w/teacher variables	Base regression	w/teacher variables
Degree in mathematics education	0.023 (1.74)*	0.033 (2.48)**				
Degree in pure mathematics			−0.032 (−2.22)**	−0.043 (−2.87)***		
Degree not mathematics					0.005 0.35	−0.002 −0.1
Student pretest score	0.529 (21.05)***	0.543 (20.8)***	0.530 (21.11)***	0.545 (20.98)***	0.529 (21.07)***	0.542 (20.74)***
Student age	−0.001 −0.16	−0.003 −0.82	0.000 −0.14	−0.003 −0.78	−0.001 −0.18	−0.003 −0.88
Hours homework/week	0.006 (1.69)*	0.006 (1.71)*	0.006 (1.68)*	0.006 (1.68)*	0.006 (1.69)*	0.006 (1.71)*
Student job hours/week	0.001 0.38	0.000 −0.13	0.001 0.4	0.000 −0.08	0.001 0.33	0.000 −0.12
Student sports hours/ week	−0.001 −0.23	0.001 0.23	−0.001 −0.22	0.001 0.25	0.000 −0.16	0.001 0.27
Student reads hours week	0.002 0.77	0.003 0.99	0.002 0.76	0.003 1	0.002 0.75	0.003 0.95
Student has dictionary at home	0.007 0.84	0.005 0.59	0.007 0.86	0.005 0.62	0.008 0.91	0.006 0.67
Student has computer at home	0.007 1.08	0.007 1.02	0.008 1.14	0.008 1.08	0.008 1.12	0.008 1.09
Student's mom education level	−0.001 −0.66	−0.001 −0.74	−0.001 −0.63	−0.001 −0.7	−0.001 −0.73	−0.001 −0.8
Student hours tutoring/ week	−0.001 −0.82	−0.002 −1.29	−0.001 −0.8	−0.002 −1.25	−0.001 −0.8	−0.002 −1.3
Teacher female		0.003 0.19		0.007 0.4		0.015 0.84
Teacher civil servant		−0.007 −0.2		−0.010 −0.32		−0.005 −0.15
Teacher school-hired		−0.015 −0.59		−0.015 −0.64		−0.004 −0.15

table continues next page

Appendix F *(continued)*

	Base regression	*w/teacher variables*	*Base regression*	*w/teacher variables*	*Base regression*	*w/teacher variables*
Teacher math satisfaction level		0.007		0.005		0.003
		0.48		0.33		0.21
Teacher attends working group		−0.015		−0.022		−0.004
		−0.8		−1.24		−0.25
Teacher experience years		0.002		0.002		0.001
		1.62		(1.72)*		1.12
Teacher 4-year degree		0.031		0.026		0.040
		1.02		0.9		1.35
Teacher certified						
Teacher assessment score		0.227		0.231		0.249
		(2.4)**		(2.58)**		(2.63)**
Class size (number of students)	0.000	0.000	0.001	0.000	0.000	0.000
	0.32	−0.01	0.4	0.16	0.19	−0.18
School private	0.016	0.018	0.013	0.010	0.013	0.012
	0.79	0.59	0.65	0.34	0.61	0.39
School religious	−0.005	0.007	0.001	0.014	−0.011	0.006
	−0.25	0.39	0.03	0.77	−0.55	0.33
School size (number of students)	0.000	0.000	0.000	0.000	0.000	0.000
	1.03	0.2	1	0.07	1.66	0.49
School materials shortage	−0.008	0.008	−0.010	0.006	−0.010	0.009
	−1.04	0.98	−1.28	0.79	−1.24	1.05
School building deficiency	0.005	0.004	0.005	0.003	0.008	0.009
	0.69	0.51	0.69	0.44	1	1.29
School library deficiency	−0.012	−0.012	−0.011	−0.012	−0.012	−0.012
	−1.4	−1.48	−1.34	−1.52	−1.4	−1.43
Frequency students skip class	−0.008	−0.013	−0.009	−0.014	−0.008	−0.016
	−0.6	−1.23	−0.76	−1.4	−0.66	−1.43
Frequency students skip class	−0.026	−0.029	−0.028	−0.031	−0.029	−0.039
	(−1.87)*	(−2.24)**	(−2.1)**	(−2.56)**	(−2.06)**	(−2.96)***
Frequency students late	0.008	0.022	0.008	0.023	0.009	0.024
	1.07	(3.05)***	1.11	(3.32)***	1.29	(3.33)***
Frequency bullying	0.001	0.001	0.006	0.007	−0.004	−0.003
	0.04	0.1	0.46	0.55	−0.28	−0.25
Community size	0.006	0.008	0.006	0.008	−0.002	0.006
	0.66	1.03	0.69	1.13	−0.31	0.79
Community poor (%)	−0.013	−0.015	−0.017	−0.019	−0.010	−0.014
	−1.51	(−1.88)*	(−1.97)**	(−2.49)**	−1.22	(−1.83)*
Community affluent (%)	−0.005	−0.006	−0.005	−0.006	−0.008	−0.007
	−0.67	−0.76	−0.66	−0.81	−1.15	−0.92

table continues next page

Appendix F *(continued)*

	Base regression	w/teacher variables	Base regression	w/teacher variables	Base regression	w/teacher variables
Constant	0.200	0.092	0.232	0.141	0.249	0.104
	(2.36)**	0.9	(2.81)***	1.43	(3.02)***	1.02
Random effects parameters						
Level 1: Student level						
estimate	0.011	0.011	0.011	0.011	0.011	0.011
Standard error	0.000	0.000	0.000	0.000	0.000	0.000
Level 2: Classroom level						
estimate	0.011	0.011	0.011	0.011	0.011	0.011
Standard error	0.001	0.000	0.001	0.000	0.001	0.000
Level 3: Region level						
estimate	0.011	0.011	0.011	0.011	0.011	0.011
Standard error	0.000	–	0.000	–	–	–

Note: Robust z-statistics in parentheses. Regressions are multi-level models run with MLwIN.
Significance level: * = 10 percent, ** = 5 percent, *** = 1 percent.

Appendix G

Coefficient and t-statistic data for figure 5.13: Practices of Teachers with Mathematics Education Degrees vs. Those with Pure Mathematics or Nonmathematics Degrees.

Variables shaded gray below were used in creating the figure.

	(1)	(2)	(3)	(4)	(5)	(6)	(7)	(8)	(9)	(10)	(11)	(12)	(13)
Regressions with dependent variable of teacher having a degree in mathematics education	Mathematical	Nonmathematical	Mathematical organization	Review	New content	Practice	Assessment	Private (group or seatwork)	Public (whole class)	Public teacher only	Public teacher and student	Public student only	Discussion
Teaching practice variable (listed in columns above)	0.624	1.322	−0.846	−0.557	0.147	−0.158	0.795	0.856	−0.856	0.442	−0.711	−0.024	0.642
	0.86	0.64	−1.12	−1.53	0.75	−0.68	(2.13)**	(3.42)***	(3.42)***	(2.28)*	(2.30)**	−0.07	(2.33)**
Student age	−0.042	−0.035	−0.04	−0.046	−0.042	−0.039	−0.035	−0.04	−0.04	−0.024	−0.022	−0.039	−0.043
	(1.97)*	(1.73)*	(1.96)*	(2.28)**	(2.02)**	(1.84)*	−1.65	(1.88)*	(1.88)*	−1.20	−1.08	(1.78)*	(2.07)**
Hours homework/week	0.013	0.017	0.014	0.01	0.015	0.016	0.013	0.005	0.005	0.015	0.011	0.015	0.019
	1.44	(1.91)*	1.50	1.14	1.57	1.66	1.48	0.56	0.56	1.59	1.19	1.62	(2.09)**
Student job hours/week	−0.001	0.001	−0.001	0.003	0.001	0	−0.003	−0.002	−0.002	0	0	0	−0.001
	−0.10	0.11	−0.09	0.34	0.11	−0.04	−0.31	−0.27	−0.27	−0.01	−0.01	−0.03	−0.06
Student sports hours/week	0.003	0.003	0.002	0.004	0.003	0.003	0.004	0.006	0.006	0.005	0.004	0.004	−0.002
	0.35	0.40	0.28	0.43	0.39	0.40	0.53	0.87	0.87	0.66	0.48	0.45	−0.27
Student reads hours week	−0.005	−0.005	−0.005	−0.004	−0.005	−0.004	−0.003	0.001	0.001	−0.003	−0.001	−0.004	−0.004
	−0.49	−0.47	−0.53	−0.41	−0.47	−0.44	−0.27	0.11	0.11	−0.29	−0.14	−0.43	−0.43
Student has dictionary at home	0.038	0.042	0.038	0.038	0.042	0.043	0.042	0.025	0.025	0.044	0.041	0.04	0.049
	0.87	0.95	0.88	0.87	0.96	1.00	1.00	0.62	0.62	1.05	0.94	0.92	1.21
Student has computer at home	−0.016	−0.016	−0.016	−0.004	−0.017	−0.02	−0.017	−0.007	−0.007	−0.023	−0.01	−0.016	−0.022
	−0.59	−0.54	−0.58	−0.16	−0.61	−0.77	−0.60	−0.25	−0.25	−0.84	−0.36	−0.64	−0.82
Student's mom education level	−0.008	−0.008	−0.008	−0.007	−0.007	−0.007	−0.008	−0.007	−0.007	−0.008	−0.006	−0.008	−0.007
	(2.25)**	(2.05)**	(2.19)**	(1.95)*	(1.94)*	(1.97)*	(2.19)**	(2.13)**	(2.13)**	(2.11)**	(1.72)*	(2.13)**	(1.87)*
Student hours tutoring/week	0.002	0.006	0.003	0.004	0.004	0.004	0.005	0.004	0.004	0.009	0.007	0.004	0.005
	0.37	0.91	0.44	0.62	0.55	0.58	0.82	0.66	0.66	1.32	1.14	0.69	0.80
Teacher female	0.061	0.054	0.069	0.085	0.054	0.043	0.043	0.007	0.007	0.06	0.076	0.049	0.1
	0.70	0.63	0.79	0.94	0.61	0.49	0.48	0.08	0.08	0.69	0.94	0.56	1.20
Teacher civil servant	−0.082	−0.037	−0.062	−0.067	−0.05	−0.065	−0.15	−0.241	−0.241	0.031	−0.04	−0.069	−0.07
	−0.61	−0.27	−0.45	−0.52	−0.33	−0.44	−0.98	(1.94)*	(1.94)*	0.21	−0.28	−0.45	−0.50
Teacher school-hired	−0.02	−0.015	−0.01	0.044	0	−0.021	−0.045	−0.058	−0.058	0.019	0.009	−0.025	−0.065
	−0.14	−0.10	−0.07	0.30	0.00	−0.14	−0.30	−0.43	−0.43	0.12	0.06	−0.17	−0.42
Teacher math satisfaction level	0.055	0.068	0.061	0.036	0.059	0.062	0.04	0.087	0.087	0.032	0.02	0.056	0.043
	0.72	0.83	0.81	0.47	0.77	0.81	0.54	1.26	1.26	0.44	0.28	0.73	0.55
Teacher attends working group	0.136	0.126	0.124	0.131	0.146	0.153	0.162	0.06	0.06	0.144	0.141	0.141	0.155
	1.34	1.14	1.21	1.25	1.39	1.41	1.50	0.66	0.66	1.41	1.40	1.35	1.57
Teacher experience years	−0.003	−0.003	−0.002	−0.003	−0.003	−0.003	−0.002	−0.003	−0.003	−0.004	−0.004	−0.003	−0.003
	−0.40	−0.51	−0.38	−0.46	−0.43	−0.41	−0.39	−0.46	−0.46	−0.73	−0.62	−0.49	−0.56
Teacher 4-year degree	0.304	0.279	0.3	0.275	0.277	0.275	0.264	0.243	0.243	0.25	0.264	0.291	0.251
	(2.04)**	(1.87)*	(1.98)*	(1.81)*	(1.80)*	(1.79)*	(1.75)*	(1.77)*	(1.77)*	1.63	(1.79)*	(1.90)*	(1.85)*
Teacher certified	0.062	0.039	0.065	0.059	0.042	0.035	0.03	0.121	0.121	0.055	0.071	0.044	0.058
	0.57	0.39	0.61	0.57	0.40	0.32	0.28	1.25	1.25	0.56	0.72	0.42	0.57

(14)	(15)	(16)	(17)	(18)	(19)	(20)	(21)	(22)	(23)	(24)	(25)	(26)	(27)	(28)
Exposition	Investigation	Practical work	Problem solving	Problem	Nonproblem	Math lanDage	Real world	Routine	Nonroutine	Question and answer	Rhetorical	True-false	Open	Closed
−0.702	1.196	0.028	0.38	0.686	−0.686	−0.286	0.286	0.686	−0.686	0.012	0.019	2.795	1.029	−1.029
(4.52)***	(2.39)**	0.09	(2.19)**	1.11	−1.11	−1.6	1.6	1.11	−1.11	(2.04)**	(2.13)**	0.86	(2.59)**	(2.59)**
−0.035	−0.033	−0.04	−0.032	−0.014	−0.014	−0.016	−0.016	−0.014	−0.014	−0.014	−0.014	−0.011	−0.03	−0.03
(1.69)*	−1.54	(1.92)*	−1.48	−0.66	−0.66	−0.73	−0.73	−0.66	−0.66	−0.65	−0.66	−0.50	−1.41	−1.41
0.012	0.013	0.015	0.013	0.019	0.019	0.018	0.018	0.019	0.019	0.021	0.021	0.02	0.017	0.017
1.22	1.45	1.65	1.41	(2.25)**	(2.25)**	(2.08)**	(2.08)**	(2.25)**	(2.25)**	(2.37)**	(2.35)**	(2.33)**	(1.85)*	(1.85)*
−0.004	0.002	0	0	0.004	0.004	0	0	0.004	0.004	0.002	0.002	0.002	0.001	0.001
−0.47	0.26	−0.02	−0.03	0.51	0.51	−0.03	−0.03	0.51	0.51	0.19	0.19	0.26	0.14	0.14
−0.002	0.008	0.004	0.003	−0.001	−0.001	0	0	−0.001	−0.001	−0.001	−0.001	−0.002	0.002	0.002
−0.27	1.00	0.44	0.35	−0.11	−0.11	−0.05	−0.05	−0.11	−0.11	−0.16	−0.14	−0.22	0.22	0.22
−0.001	−0.007	−0.004	−0.001	−0.009	−0.009	−0.008	−0.008	−0.009	−0.009	−0.01	−0.01	−0.008	−0.008	−0.008
−0.10	−0.75	−0.43	−0.13	−0.98	−0.98	−0.88	−0.88	−0.98	−0.98	−1.05	−1.07	−0.84	−0.77	−0.77
0.034	0.039	0.04	0.041	0.032	0.032	0.038	0.038	0.032	0.032	0.047	0.048	0.042	0.037	0.037
1.03	0.85	0.90	1.01	0.71	0.71	0.83	0.83	0.71	0.71	1.05	1.06	0.95	0.90	0.90
−0.019	−0.014	−0.016	−0.016	0.004	0.004	0.01	0.01	0.004	0.004	0	0	0.004	−0.019	−0.019
−0.71	−0.51	−0.56	−0.56	0.12	0.12	0.30	0.30	0.12	0.12	−0.01	0.00	0.11	−0.67	−0.67
−0.009	−0.007	−0.008	−0.011	−0.011	−0.011	−0.011	−0.011	−0.011	−0.011	−0.01	−0.01	−0.011	−0.007	−0.007
(2.61)**	(2.03)**	(2.09)**	(2.87)***	(2.83)***	(2.83)***	(2.92)***	(2.92)***	(2.83)***	(2.83)***	(2.70)***	(2.67)***	(2.90)***	(2.00)**	(2.00)**
0.002	0.005	0.004	0.003	0.005	0.005	0.006	0.006	0.005	0.005	0.008	0.008	0.007	0.008	0.008
0.25	0.80	0.60	0.50	0.86	0.86	0.88	0.88	0.86	0.86	1.15	1.16	1.07	1.25	1.25
0.054	0.033	0.049	0.024	0.087	0.087	0.105	0.105	0.087	0.087	0.092	0.095	0.101	0.036	0.036
0.63	0.37	0.56	0.27	0.99	0.99	1.22	1.22	0.99	0.99	1.04	1.07	1.14	0.40	0.40
−0.236	−0.062	−0.077	−0.128	−0.041	−0.041	−0.134	−0.134	−0.041	−0.041	−0.056	−0.063	−0.058	−0.152	−0.152
−1.62	−0.46	−0.57	−0.90	−0.35	−0.35	−1.03	−1.03	−0.35	−0.35	−0.47	−0.53	−0.47	−1.01	−1.01
−0.079	−0.013	−0.027	−0.033	0.091	0.091	0.049	0.049	0.091	0.091	0.028	0.026	0.029	−0.068	−0.068
−0.56	−0.09	−0.18	−0.23	0.59	0.59	0.32	0.32	0.59	0.59	0.18	0.17	0.19	−0.47	−0.47
0.075	0.038	0.06	0.035	−0.001	−0.001	0.01	0.01	−0.001	−0.001	0.049	0.048	0.003	0.052	0.052
1.03	0.48	0.69	0.43	−0.01	−0.01	0.14	0.14	−0.01	−0.01	0.58	0.57	0.04	0.73	0.73
0.107	0.136	0.139	0.145	0.184	0.184	0.164	0.164	0.184	0.184	0.14	0.138	0.159	0.111	0.111
1.12	1.30	1.30	1.44	(1.87)*	(1.87)*	(1.68)*	(1.68)*	(1.87)*	(1.87)*	1.35	1.32	1.59	1.07	1.07
0.001	−0.002	−0.003	−0.003	−0.009	−0.009	−0.005	−0.005	−0.009	−0.009	−0.008	−0.008	−0.008	−0.003	−0.003
0.26	−0.28	−0.48	−0.47	−1.61	−1.61	−0.90	−0.90	−1.61	−1.61	−1.44	−1.43	−1.47	−0.56	−0.56
0.32	0.294	0.291	0.343	0.357	0.357	0.381	0.381	0.357	0.357	0.347	0.349	0.317	0.256	0.256
(2.80)***	(1.97)*	(1.95)*	(2.47)**	(2.48)**	(2.48)**	(2.55)**	(2.55)**	(2.48)**	(2.48)**	(2.38)**	(2.40)**	(2.00)**	(1.79)*	(1.79)*
0.072	0.061	0.045	0.047	0.009	0.009	−0.037	−0.037	0.009	0.009	−0.01	−0.006	0	0.079	0.079
0.77	0.60	0.43	0.48	0.10	0.10	−0.39	−0.39	0.10	0.10	−0.11	−0.07	0.00	0.78	0.78

table continues next page

Appendix G *(continued)*

	(1)	(2)	(3)	(4)	(5)	(6)	(7)	(8)	(9)	(10)	(11)	(12)	(13)
Regressions with dependent variable of teacher having a degree in mathematics education	*Mathematical*	*Nonmathematical*	*Mathematical organization*	*Review*	*New content*	*Practice*	*Assessment*	*Private (group or seatwork)*	*Public (whole class)*	*Public: teacher only*	*Public: teacher and student*	*Public: student only*	*Discussion*
Teacher assessment score	0.206	0.176	0.183	0.291	0.236	0.203	0.149	0.219	0.219	0.124	0.199	0.205	0.141
	0.61	0.51	0.55	0.84	0.68	0.59	0.44	0.75	0.75	0.37	0.61	0.60	0.40
Student pretest score	−0.076	−0.007	−0.056	−0.072	−0.052	−0.048	−0.064	−0.084	−0.084	−0.038	0.036	−0.053	−0.003
	−0.37	−0.03	−0.28	−0.37	−0.26	−0.24	−0.31	−0.45	−0.45	−0.20	0.21	−0.27	−0.02
Class size (number of students)	−0.005	−0.005	−0.004	−0.008	−0.006	−0.005	−0.005	−0.004	−0.004	−0.001	−0.001	−0.005	−0.003
	−0.57	−0.51	−0.49	−0.90	−0.68	−0.59	−0.55	−0.52	−0.52	−0.15	−0.10	−0.60	−0.38
School private	−0.134	−0.126	−0.121	−0.126	−0.106	−0.123	−0.218	−0.302	−0.302	−0.101	−0.138	−0.14	−0.118
	−0.98	−0.91	−0.88	−0.93	−0.72	−0.86	−1.42	(2.18)**	(2.18)**	−0.73	−0.99	−1.01	−0.85
School religious	−0.256	−0.339	−0.268	−0.315	−0.302	−0.297	−0.297	−0.291	−0.291	−0.314	−0.314	−0.297	−0.296
	(1.88)*	(2.43)**	(2.06)**	(2.28)**	(2.28)**	(2.29)**	(2.41)**	(2.33)**	(2.33)**	(2.38)**	(2.38)**	(2.30)**	(2.31)**
School size (number of students)	0	0	0	0	0	0	0	0	0	0	0	0	0
	(1.83)*	(1.76)*	(1.74)*	(2.05)**	(1.89)*	(1.88)*	(1.99)**	(1.72)*	(1.72)*	−1.04	−1.29	(1.76)*	(1.95)*
School materials shortage	0.017	0.027	0.016	0.056	0.042	0.032	0.013	0.035	0.035	0.045	0.053	0.024	0.022
	0.38	0.62	0.39	1.26	0.88	0.72	0.28	0.88	0.88	0.98	1.10	0.54	0.49
School building deficiency	0.146	0.135	0.146	0.132	0.133	0.134	0.139	0.154	0.154	0.117	0.13	0.138	0.139
	(3.15)***	(3.02)***	(3.17)***	(3.01)***	(2.90)***	(2.91)***	(3.11)***	(3.89)***	(3.89)***	(2.53)**	(2.95)***	(3.00)***	(3.16)***
School library deficiency	−0.046	−0.048	−0.044	−0.052	−0.046	−0.048	−0.064	−0.032	−0.032	−0.035	−0.049	−0.048	−0.048
	−0.87	−0.91	−0.83	−1.06	−0.91	−0.93	−1.19	−0.73	−0.73	−0.69	−0.95	−0.92	−0.91
Frequency students skip class	−0.062	−0.054	−0.057	−0.076	−0.07	−0.067	−0.061	−0.027	−0.027	−0.096	−0.1	−0.063	−0.067
	−0.62	−0.52	−0.57	−0.78	−0.71	−0.67	−0.62	−0.30	−0.30	−0.94	−0.96	−0.62	−0.72
Frequency students late	0.081	0.069	0.078	0.079	0.076	0.076	0.079	0.058	0.058	0.066	0.066	0.076	0.073
	(1.91)*	1.63	(1.88)*	(2.16)**	(1.95)*	(1.88)*	(1.94)*	(1.99)*	(1.99)*	1.50	1.41	(1.84)*	(1.75)*
Frequency bullying	−0.169	−0.171	−0.167	−0.169	−0.164	−0.162	−0.162	−0.221	−0.221	−0.122	−0.162	−0.171	−0.18
	(2.09)**	(2.13)**	(2.07)**	(2.12)**	(2.09)**	(2.02)**	(2.03)**	(2.85)***	(2.85)***	−1.40	(2.01)**	(2.04)**	(2.33)**
Community size	−0.121	−0.123	−0.116	−0.124	−0.124	−0.122	−0.116	−0.138	−0.138	−0.131	−0.116	−0.128	−0.12
	(2.49)**	(2.73)***	(2.44)**	(2.64)**	(2.61)**	(2.58)**	(2.42)**	(2.98)***	(2.98)***	(2.90)***	(2.58)**	(2.67)***	(2.63)**
Community poor (%)	0.132	0.143	0.124	0.14	0.145	0.145	0.14	0.133	0.133	0.127	0.142	0.145	0.133
	(1.93)*	(2.24)**	(1.77)*	(2.13)**	(2.23)**	(2.25)**	(2.23)**	(2.00)**	(2.00)**	(1.94)*	(2.42)**	(2.19)**	(2.12)**
Community affluent (%)	−0.01	−0.009	−0.01	−0.023	−0.008	−0.005	−0.013	−0.026	−0.026	0.004	0.001	−0.009	−0.019
	−0.19	−0.16	−0.18	−0.42	−0.15	−0.09	−0.26	−0.51	−0.51	0.08	0.02	−0.17	−0.37
Region of Java	−0.207	−0.118	−0.222	−0.097	−0.129	−0.142	−0.147	−0.172	−0.172	−0.057	−0.054	−0.132	−0.184
	−1.32	−0.96	−1.43	−0.75	−1.06	−1.15	−1.22	−1.36	−1.36	−0.39	−0.37	−1.04	−1.33
Region of Sumatera	0.148	0.221	0.128	0.255	0.204	0.183	0.168	0.227	0.227	0.233	0.21	0.217	0.142
	0.84	1.44	0.74	(1.75)*	1.33	1.13	1.12	1.56	1.56	1.37	1.24	1.41	0.86
Region of Kalimantan	0.263	0.252	0.235	0.302	0.263	0.247	0.238	0.263	0.263	0.28	0.321	0.283	0.26
	1.43	1.48	1.22	(2.03)**	1.57	1.37	1.45	(1.81)*	(1.81)*	1.66	(1.89)*	1.65	1.50
Region of Bali, NTT and NTB	0.062	0.085	0.041	0.129	0.077	0.065	0.091	0.031	0.031	0.194	0.228	0.099	0.123
	0.34	0.46	0.22	0.72	0.41	0.35	0.48	0.15	0.15	1.05	1.32	0.53	0.66

	(14)	(15)	(16)	(17)	(18)	(19)	(20)	(21)	(22)	(23)	(24)	(25)	(26)	(27)	(28)
	Exposition	Investigation	Practical work	Problem solving	Problem	Nonproblem	Math lanDage	Real world	Routine	Nonroutine	Question and answer	Rhetorical	True-false	Open	Closed
	0.064	0.077	0.217	0.111	0.369	0.369	0.431	0.431	0.369	0.369	0.25	0.257	0.275	0.176	0.176
	0.22	0.22	0.62	0.34	1.08	1.08	1.29	1.29	1.08	1.08	0.70	0.72	0.77	0.54	0.54
	−0.078	−0.106	−0.057	−0.002	0.138	0.138	0.153	0.153	0.138	0.138	0.183	0.183	0.17	0	0
	−0.40	−0.52	−0.30	−0.01	0.87	0.87	0.93	0.93	0.87	0.87	1.10	1.10	1.01	0.00	0.00
	−0.003	−0.008	−0.005	−0.007	−0.004	−0.004	−0.005	−0.005	−0.004	−0.004	−0.006	−0.006	−0.005	0.003	0.003
	−0.43	−0.90	−0.60	−0.91	−0.51	−0.51	−0.58	−0.58	−0.51	−0.51	−0.73	−0.73	−0.59	0.25	0.25
	−0.275	−0.083	−0.145	−0.221	−0.15	−0.15	−0.199	−0.199	−0.15	−0.15	−0.182	−0.184	−0.184	−0.214	−0.214
	(1.85)*	−0.59	−1.05	−1.42	−1.17	−1.17	−1.54	−1.54	−1.17	−1.17	−1.45	−1.47	−1.42	−1.48	−1.48
	−0.273	−0.326	−0.296	−0.29	−0.193	−0.193	−0.182	−0.182	−0.193	−0.193	−0.173	−0.173	−0.183	−0.262	−0.262
	(2.21)**	(2.46)**	(2.27)**	(2.39)**	−1.43	−1.43	−1.36	−1.36	−1.43	−1.43	−1.33	−1.33	−1.41	(1.97)*	(1.97)*
	0	0.001	0	0	0	0	0.001	0.001	0	0	0	0	0	0	0
	(1.74)*	(2.46)**	(1.94)*	(1.85)*	(2.67)***	(2.67)***	(2.72)***	(2.72)***	(2.67)***	(2.67)***	(2.40)**	(2.37)**	(2.56)**	−1.48	−1.48
	0.024	0.032	0.024	0.018	0.031	0.031	0.044	0.044	0.031	0.031	0.029	0.029	0.027	0.009	0.009
	0.56	0.74	0.54	0.40	0.67	0.67	0.98	0.98	0.67	0.67	0.64	0.65	0.58	0.22	0.22
	0.16	0.115	0.14	0.146	0.128	0.128	0.113	0.113	0.128	0.128	0.126	0.127	0.124	0.157	0.157
	(4.12)***	(2.36)**	(2.96)***	(3.35)***	(2.61)**	(2.61)**	(2.24)**	(2.24)**	(2.61)**	(2.61)**	(2.54)**	(2.55)**	(2.49)**	(3.39)***	(3.39)***
	−0.041	−0.031	−0.049	−0.053	−0.044	−0.044	−0.046	−0.046	−0.044	−0.044	−0.039	−0.039	−0.057	−0.046	−0.046
	−0.87	−0.56	−0.94	−1.02	−0.96	−0.96	−0.95	−0.95	−0.96	−0.96	−0.82	−0.81	−1.18	−0.93	−0.93
	−0.031	−0.074	−0.061	−0.051	−0.174	−0.174	−0.138	−0.138	−0.174	−0.174	−0.123	−0.123	−0.13	−0.052	−0.052
	−0.34	−0.77	−0.61	−0.51	(1.77)*	(1.77)*	−1.53	−1.53	(1.77)*	(1.77)*	−1.27	−1.28	−1.38	−0.51	−0.51
	0.048	0.072	0.075	0.077	0.065	0.065	0.06	0.06	0.065	0.065	0.058	0.058	0.059	0.074	0.074
	1.44	(1.72)*	(1.80)*	(1.86)*	1.61	1.61	1.41	1.41	1.61	1.61	1.39	1.38	1.36	(1.79)*	(1.79)*
	−0.176	−0.194	−0.172	−0.182	−0.149	−0.149	−0.14	−0.14	−0.149	−0.149	−0.153	−0.155	−0.148	−0.155	−0.155
	(2.21)**	(2.52)**	(2.15)**	(2.24)**	(1.74)*	(1.74)*	(1.68)*	(1.68)*	(1.74)*	(1.74)*	(1.76)*	(1.77)*	(1.71)*	(1.93)*	(1.93)*
	−0.111	−0.144	−0.128	−0.108	−0.089	−0.089	−0.071	−0.071	−0.089	−0.089	−0.098	−0.096	−0.095	−0.134	−0.134
	(2.40)**	(3.03)***	(2.82)***	(2.32)**	(1.96)*	(1.96)*	−1.49	−1.49	(1.96)*	(1.96)*	(2.09)**	(2.07)**	(1.96)*	(2.75)***	(2.75)***
	0.106	0.157	0.145	0.149	0.174	0.174	0.188	0.188	0.174	0.174	0.182	0.182	0.192	0.146	0.146
	1.63	(2.70)***	(2.38)**	(2.41)**	(3.16)***	(3.16)***	(3.54)***	(3.54)***	(3.16)***	(3.16)***	(3.47)***	(3.45)***	(3.59)***	(2.33)**	(2.33)**
	−0.057	−0.028	−0.01	−0.008	0.007	0.007	0.024	0.024	0.007	0.007	0.033	0.033	0.025	−0.008	−0.008
	−1.17	−0.51	−0.20	−0.16	0.13	0.13	0.48	0.48	0.13	0.13	0.65	0.66	0.51	−0.14	−0.14
	−0.069	−0.13	−0.132	−0.087	−0.088	−0.088	−0.044	−0.044	−0.088	−0.088	−0.104	−0.103	−0.096	−0.133	−0.133
	−0.64	−0.99	−1.06	−0.72	−0.69	−0.69	−0.39	−0.39	−0.69	−0.69	−0.83	−0.82	−0.77	−1.10	−1.10
	0.206	0.215	0.218	0.224	0.158	0.158	0.184	0.184	0.158	0.158	0.16	0.159	0.175	0.215	0.215
	1.56	1.35	1.43	1.48	0.97	0.97	1.27	1.27	0.97	0.97	0.99	0.98	1.09	1.41	1.41
	0.35	0.29	0.28	0.393	0.266	0.266	0.332	0.332	0.266	0.266	0.268	0.262	0.272	0.312	0.312
	(2.38)**	(1.67)*	1.55	(2.17)**	1.13	1.13	1.39	1.39	1.13	1.13	1.15	1.11	1.12	(1.89)*	(1.89)*
	0.167	0.109	0.095	0.158	0.38	0.38	0.415	0.415	0.38	0.38	0.275	0.286	0.254	−0.006	−0.006
	0.89	0.56	0.51	0.84	(2.17)**	(2.17)**	(2.59)**	(2.59)**	(2.17)**	(2.17)**	1.45	1.53	1.18	−0.03	−0.03

table continues next page

Appendix G *(continued)*

Regressions with dependent variable of teacher having a degree in mathematics education	(1) Mathematical	(2) Nonmathematical	(3) Mathematical organization	(4) Review	(5) New content	(6) Practice	(7) Assessment	(8) Private (group or seatwork)	(9) Public (whole class)	(10) Public: teacher only	(11) Public: teacher and student	(12) Public: student only	(13) Discussion
Constant	0.237	0.502	0.821	0.841	0.545	0.66	0.75	0.643	1.499	0.065	0.348	0.672	0.715
	0.29	0.88	1.39	1.47	0.86	1.11	1.24	1.13	(2.73)***	0.11	0.64	1.12	1.25
Observations	2338	2338	2338	2338	2338	2338	2338	2338	2338	2338	2338	2338	2338
R^2	0.45	0.45	0.45	0.46	0.45	0.45	0.46	0.51	0.51	0.47	0.48	0.44	0.47
Adj. R^2	0.44	0.44	0.45	0.45	0.44	0.44	0.45	0.51	0.51	0.46	0.47	0.44	0.46

Note: Robust t-statistics in parentheses. Regressions run on multiple-imputed data.

Significance level: * = 10 percent, ** = 5 percent, *** = 1 percent.

(14)	(15)	(16)	(17)	(18)	(19)	(20)	(21)	(22)	(23)	(24)	(25)	(26)	(27)	(28)
Exposition	Investigation	Practical work	Problem solving	Problem	Nonproblem	Math lanDage	Real world	Routine	Nonroutine	Question and answer	Rhetorical	True-false	Open	Closed
1.2	0.766	0.667	0.555	−0.56	0.126	0.147	−0.14	−0.56	0.126	0.067	0.067	0.087	0.38	1.409
(2.07)**	1.24	1.09	0.96	−0.71	0.22	0.26	−0.24	−0.71	0.22	0.12	0.12	0.14	0.66	(1.95)*
2338	2338	2338	2338	2116	2116	2116	2116	2116	2116	2116	2116	2116	2296	2296
0.52	0.46	0.44	0.46	0.49	0.49	0.49	0.49	0.49	0.49	0.49	0.49	0.48	0.46	0.46
0.51	0.46	0.44	0.45	0.48	0.48	0.48	0.48	0.48	0.48	0.48	0.48	0.47	0.45	0.45

Appendix H

Coefficient and z-statistic data for figure 5.14: Relationship between Teacher Knowledge and Student Learning.

Variables shaded gray below were used in creating the figure.

	Base regression	w/teacher variables	Base regression	w/teacher variables	Base regression	w/teacher variables
Overall teacher assessment score	0.200 (3.74)***	0.172 (3.05)***				
Subject matter assessment			0.159 (3.75)***	0.142 (3.22)***		
Pedagogy assessment					0.132 (2.19)**	0.132 (2.02)**
Student pretest score	0.530 (20.58)***	0.544 (20.84)***	0.530 (20.52)***	0.543 (20.82)***	0.534 (20.74)***	0.546 (20.97)***
Student age	−0.001 −0.35	−0.003 −0.85	−0.001 −0.33	−0.003 −0.84	−0.001 −0.33	−0.003 −0.85
Hours homework/week	0.006 (1.77)*	0.006 1.67	0.006 (1.78)*	0.006 (1.69)*	0.006 (1.77)*	0.006 (1.68)*
Student job hours/ week	0.001 0.21	0.000 −0.17	0.000 0.17	0.000 −0.17	0.001 0.21	0.000 −0.19
Student sports hours/ week	−0.001 −0.25	0.001 0.2	−0.001 −0.23	0.001 0.22	−0.001 −0.24	0.001 0.22
Student reads hours week	0.003 0.83	0.003 0.96	0.003 0.85	0.003 0.99	0.003 0.78	0.003 0.93
Student has dictionary at home	0.006 0.75	0.005 0.57	0.007 0.77	0.005 0.59	0.006 0.74	0.005 0.57
Student has computer at home	0.008 1.07	0.007 1.03	0.008 1.08	0.007 1.03	0.007 1.02	0.007 1
Student's mom education level	−0.001 −0.64	−0.001 −0.77	−0.001 −0.61	−0.001 −0.75	−0.001 −0.72	−0.001 −0.83
Student hours tutoring/ week	−0.002 −1.12	−0.002 −1.33	−0.002 −1.12	−0.002 −1.3	−0.002 −1.19	−0.002 −1.41
Teacher female		−0.003 −0.18		0.002 0.09		−0.012 −0.73
Teacher civil servant		−0.007 −0.21		−0.004 −0.12		−0.001 −0.04
Teacher school-hired		−0.020 −0.77		−0.018 −0.7		−0.028 −1.09

table continues next page

Appendix H *(continued)*

	Base regression	w/teacher variables	Base regression	w/teacher variables	Base regression	w/teacher variables
Teacher math satisfaction level		0.007		0.007		0.008
		0.46		0.47		0.53
Teacher attends working group		−0.008		−0.013		−0.008
		−0.45		−0.72		−0.43
Teacher maths education degree		0.026		0.025		0.029
		1.62		1.6		(1.77)*
Teacher experience years		0.002		0.002		0.002
		(1.93)*		(1.92)*		(1.87)*
Teacher 4-year degree		0.040		0.045		0.039
		1.23		1.39		1.15
Teacher certified		−0.024		−0.020		−0.029
		−1.3		−1.07		−1.5
Class size (number of students)	0.000	0.000	0.000	0.000	0.000	0.000
	−0.22	−0.17	−0.13	−0.11	0.01	−0.02
School private	0.024	0.019	0.021	0.021	0.020	0.021
	1.19	0.6	1.09	0.66	0.96	0.64
School religious	−0.013	0.009	−0.015	0.010	−0.011	0.006
	−0.66	0.49	−0.77	0.52	−0.53	0.32
School size (number of students)	0.000	0.000	0.000	0.000	0.000	0.000
	(2)**	0.81	(1.89)*	0.6	(1.96)**	0.96
School materials shortage	0.003	0.006	0.005	0.008	−0.004	0.000
	0.39	0.83	0.57	1.02	−0.5	0.06
School building deficiency	0.005	0.003	0.005	0.003	0.006	0.003
	0.7	0.43	0.6	0.41	0.77	0.36
School library deficiency	−0.015	−0.010	−0.015	−0.011	−0.013	−0.008
	(−1.78)*	−1.28	(−1.82)*	−1.36	−1.54	−1.01
Frequency students skip class	−0.009	−0.015	−0.008	−0.014	−0.008	−0.013
	−0.74	−1.35	−0.65	−1.32	−0.66	−1.18
Frequency students skip class	−0.021	−0.027	−0.023	−0.028	−0.020	−0.025
	−1.64	(−2.06)**	(−1.79)*	(−2.18)**	−1.49	(−1.87)*
Frequency students late	0.016	0.022	0.015	0.022	0.016	0.021
	(2.27)**	(3.07)***	(2.06)**	(3.02)***	(2.09)**	(2.79)***
Frequency bullying	−0.007	0.004	−0.008	0.003	−0.005	0.007
	−0.51	0.35	−0.64	0.21	−0.34	0.52
Community size	0.003	0.006	0.004	0.007	−0.002	0.002
	0.41	0.81	0.58	1.02	−0.26	0.22

table continues next page

Appendix H *(continued)*

	Base regression	*w/teacher variables*	*Base regression*	*w/teacher variables*	*Base regression*	*w/teacher variables*
Community poor (%)	−0.009	−0.016	−0.009	−0.016	−0.011	−0.017
	−1.05	(−2.01)**	−1.04	(−1.96)**	−1.31	(−2.11)**
Community affluent (%)	−0.002	−0.008	−0.002	−0.008	−0.006	−0.011
	−0.21	−1.06	−0.23	−0.97	−0.76	−1.34
Constant	0.098	0.089	0.107	0.079	0.172	0.144
	1.07	0.88	1.17	0.78	(1.94)*	1.45
Random effects parameters						
Level 1: Student level						
estimate	0.0111	0.0109	0.0111	0.0109	0.0111	0.0109
Standard error	0.0004	0.0004	0.0004	0.0004	0.0004	0.0004
Level 2: Classroom level						
estimate	0.0109	0.0109	0.0109	0.0109	0.0109	0.0109
Standard error	0.0005	0.0004	0.0005	0.0004	0.0005	0.0004
Level 3: Region level						
estimate	0.0109	0.0109	0.0109	0.0109	0.0109	0.0109
Standard error	0.0000	0.0000	0.0000	0.0000	0.0000	0.0000

Note: Robust z-statistics in parentheses. Regressions are multi-level models run with MLwIN.
Significance level: * = 10 percent, ** = 5 percent, *** = 1 percent.

Appendix I

Coefficient and t-statistic data for figure 5.15: Relationship between Teaching Practices and Teacher Knowledge (Assessment Score Percentage).

Variables shaded gray below were used in creating the figure.

	(1)	(2)	(3)	(4)	(5)	(6)	(7)	(8)	(9)	(10)	(11)	(12)	(13)
Regressions with dependent variable of teacher assessment score (percentage)	Mathematical	Nonmathematical	Mathematical organization	Review	New content	Practice	Assessment	Private (group or seatwork)	Public (whole class)	Public: teacher only	Public: teacher and student	Public: student only	Discussion
Teaching practice variable (listed in columns above)	0.008	0.453	−0.08	0.125	−0.035	−0.008	0.095	−0.022	0.022	0.064	0.003	−0.113	0.062
	0.04	0.92	−0.39	1.23	−0.77	−0.14	0.68	−0.27	0.27	0.85	0.03	−1.21	0.72
Student age	−0.003	−0.001	−0.003	−0.001	−0.002	−0.003	−0.002	−0.002	−0.002	−0.001	−0.003	−0.001	−0.003
	−0.52	−0.24	−0.52	−0.15	−0.36	−0.50	−0.43	−0.46	−0.46	−0.12	−0.49	−0.28	−0.62
Hours homework/week	0.003	0.003	0.003	0.003	0.003	0.003	0.002	0.003	0.003	0.003	0.003	0.003	0.003
	1.06	1.28	1.01	1.46	0.99	1.05	0.98	1.13	1.13	1.04	1.02	1.26	1.21
Student job hours/week	−0.003	−0.002	−0.003	−0.003	−0.003	−0.003	−0.003	−0.003	−0.003	−0.003	−0.003	−0.003	−0.003
	−1.10	−0.98	−1.14	−1.33	−1.14	−1.11	−1.25	−1.07	−1.07	−1.10	−1.09	−1.12	−1.13
Student sports hours/week	0	0	0	0	0	0	0	0	0	0	0	0	−0.001
	−0.06	−0.11	−0.10	−0.06	0.00	−0.06	−0.01	−0.09	−0.09	−0.05	−0.05	−0.10	−0.28
Student reads hours week	0.002	0.002	0.002	0.002	0.002	0.002	0.002	0.002	0.002	0.002	0.002	0.002	0.002
	0.94	0.86	0.90	0.92	0.98	0.94	1.05	0.93	0.93	1.02	0.93	0.89	0.94
Student has dictionary at home	−0.004	−0.003	−0.004	−0.004	−0.004	−0.004	−0.003	−0.004	−0.004	−0.003	−0.004	−0.003	−0.003
	−0.42	−0.35	−0.43	−0.41	−0.46	−0.40	−0.37	−0.38	−0.38	−0.32	−0.42	−0.33	−0.30
Student has computer at home	0.005	0.005	0.004	0.002	0.005	0.004	0.004	0.004	0.004	0.003	0.004	0.002	0.004
	0.61	0.59	0.60	0.27	0.67	0.57	0.59	0.58	0.58	0.44	0.61	0.21	0.52
Student's mom education level	0.001	0.001	0.001	0.001	0.001	0.001	0.001	0.001	0.001	0.001	0.001	0.001	0.001
	0.85	0.91	0.83	0.69	0.68	0.86	0.79	0.83	0.83	0.82	0.84	0.67	0.90
Student hours tutoring/week	−0.003	−0.003	−0.003	−0.003	−0.003	−0.003	−0.003	−0.003	−0.003	−0.003	−0.003	−0.003	−0.003
	−1.49	−1.13	−1.49	−1.39	−1.37	−1.44	−1.36	−1.43	−1.43	−1.27	−1.45	−1.26	−1.40
Teacher female	−0.051	−0.048	−0.049	−0.058	−0.052	−0.051	−0.051	−0.05	−0.05	−0.048	−0.051	−0.051	−0.045
	(1.95)*	(1.82)*	(1.89)*	(2.16)**	(1.95)*	(1.90)*	(1.93)*	(1.85)*	(1.85)*	(1.74)*	(1.79)*	(1.94)*	−1.56
Teacher civil servant	0.106	0.117	0.107	0.103	0.1	0.107	0.096	0.111	0.111	0.12	0.106	0.126	0.106
	(2.48)**	(2.77)***	(2.49)**	(2.31)**	(2.16)**	(2.44)**	(1.96)*	(2.40)**	(2.40)**	(2.57)**	(2.44)**	(2.65)***	(2.46)**
Teacher school-hired	−0.053	−0.048	−0.051	−0.067	−0.059	−0.052	−0.055	−0.052	−0.052	−0.046	−0.053	−0.046	−0.056
	−1.24	−1.16	−1.21	−1.46	−1.34	−1.24	−1.27	−1.21	−1.21	−1.06	−1.23	−1.08	−1.31
Teacher math satisfaction level	−0.001	0.003	−0.001	0.003	−0.002	−0.001	−0.003	−0.002	−0.002	−0.004	−0.001	−0.002	−0.002
	−0.05	0.13	−0.02	0.15	−0.08	−0.03	−0.13	−0.09	−0.09	−0.21	−0.04	−0.07	−0.10
Teacher attends working group	0.015	0.009	0.013	0.016	0.013	0.015	0.018	0.016	0.016	0.016	0.015	0.015	0.017
	0.52	0.33	0.46	0.55	0.47	0.55	0.60	0.55	0.55	0.56	0.52	0.54	0.58
Teacher maths education degree	0.016	0.013	0.014	0.023	0.018	0.016	0.012	0.019	0.019	0.01	0.016	0.015	0.011
	0.61	0.51	0.55	0.84	0.68	0.59	0.44	0.73	0.73	0.37	0.61	0.60	0.40
Teacher experience years	−0.003	−0.003	−0.003	−0.003	−0.003	−0.003	−0.003	−0.003	−0.003	−0.003	−0.003	−0.003	−0.003
	(2.00)**	(2.03)**	(1.97)*	(2.03)**	(2.02)**	(2.03)**	(1.94)*	(2.03)**	(2.03)**	(2.12)**	(2.01)**	(2.12)**	(2.05)**

(14)	(15)	(16)	(17)	(18)	(19)	(20)	(21)	(22)	(23)	(24)	(25)	(26)	(27)	(28)
Exposition	Investigation	Practical work	Problem solving	Problem	Nonproblem	Math lanDage	Real world	Routine	Nonroutine	Question and answer	Rhetorical	True-false	Open	Closed
−0.051	0.325	−0.092	0.079	−0.12	0.12	0.135	−0.135	−0.12	0.12	0.005	0.007	3.145	0.016	−0.016
−0.82	(2.76)***	−1.57	1.24	−1.11	1.11	(2.22)**	(2.22)**	−1.11	1.11	(2.50)**	(2.38)**	(3.66)***	1.94	−1.94
−0.003	−0.001	−0.001	−0.001	−0.002	−0.002	−0.001	−0.001	−0.002	−0.002	−0.003	−0.003	−0.001	−0.002	−0.002
−0.50	−0.20	−0.26	−0.25	−0.37	−0.37	−0.11	−0.11	−0.37	−0.37	−0.59	−0.60	−0.19	−0.44	−0.44
0.003	0.002	0.003	0.002	0.004	0.004	0.004	0.004	0.004	0.004	0.003	0.003	0.003	0.003	0.003
1.03	0.90	1.14	0.94	1.36	1.36	(1.75)*	(1.75)*	1.36	1.36	1.34	1.32	1.05	1.14	1.14
−0.003	−0.002	−0.002	−0.003	−0.003	−0.003	−0.001	−0.001	−0.003	−0.003	−0.003	−0.003	−0.003	−0.003	−0.003
−1.24	−0.89	−0.92	−1.13	−1.28	−1.28	−0.62	−0.62	−1.28	−1.28	−1.22	−1.22	−1.16	−1.08	−1.08
0	0.001	0	0	0	0	0	0	0	0	0	0	−0.001	0	0
−0.20	0.53	−0.03	−0.11	−0.12	−0.12	−0.05	−0.05	−0.12	−0.12	0.00	−0.04	−0.39	−0.16	−0.16
0.002	0.001	0.002	0.003	0.002	0.002	0.002	0.002	0.002	0.002	0.001	0.001	0.002	0.002	0.002
1.04	0.54	0.96	1.24	0.83	0.83	0.78	0.78	0.83	0.83	0.48	0.49	1.13	0.83	0.83
−0.004	−0.004	−0.002	−0.003	0.004	0.004	0.005	0.005	0.004	0.004	0.004	0.004	0	−0.003	−0.003
−0.42	−0.38	−0.19	−0.39	0.43	0.43	0.50	0.50	0.43	0.43	0.35	0.36	−0.01	−0.31	−0.31
0.004	0.005	0.004	0.004	−0.001	−0.001	−0.004	−0.004	−0.001	−0.001	−0.004	−0.003	−0.003	0.004	0.004
0.56	0.61	0.56	0.61	−0.19	−0.19	−0.56	−0.56	−0.19	−0.19	−0.48	−0.44	−0.35	0.59	0.59
0.001	0.001	0.001	0.001	0.001	0.001	0.001	0.001	0.001	0.001	0.001	0.001	0	0.001	0.001
0.72	0.88	0.66	0.43	0.44	0.44	0.58	0.58	0.44	0.44	0.63	0.64	−0.17	0.80	0.80
−0.003	−0.003	−0.003	−0.003	−0.004	−0.004	−0.003	−0.003	−0.004	−0.004	−0.003	−0.003	−0.003	−0.003	−0.003
−1.44	−1.29	−1.34	−1.49	−1.42	−1.42	−1.46	−1.46	−1.42	−1.42	−1.35	−1.36	−1.32	−1.37	−1.37
−0.05	−0.053	−0.05	−0.055	−0.044	−0.044	−0.045	−0.045	−0.044	−0.044	−0.051	−0.05	−0.052	−0.052	−0.052
(1.89)*	(1.99)*	(1.89)*	(2.03)**	−1.51	−1.51	−1.56	−1.56	−1.51	−1.51	(1.83)*	(1.78)*	(1.79)*	(1.93)*	(1.93)*
0.093	0.105	0.113	0.093	0.102	0.102	0.133	0.133	0.102	0.102	0.11	0.107	0.114	0.103	0.103
(2.05)**	(2.34)**	(2.56)**	(2.01)**	(2.44)**	(2.44)**	(3.06)***	(3.06)***	(2.44)**	(2.44)**	(2.74)***	(2.67)***	(2.77)***	(2.20)**	(2.20)**
−0.056	−0.047	−0.05	−0.053	−0.081	−0.081	−0.071	−0.071	−0.081	−0.081	−0.08	−0.081	−0.092	−0.055	−0.055
−1.30	−1.13	−1.22	−1.28	(1.68)*	(1.68)*	−1.54	−1.54	(1.68)*	(1.68)*	(1.77)*	(1.78)*	(1.87)*	−1.28	−1.28
0.001	−0.006	−0.012	−0.005	−0.01	−0.01	−0.014	−0.014	−0.01	−0.01	0.01	0.008	−0.007	−0.002	−0.002
0.04	−0.26	−0.54	−0.23	−0.41	−0.41	−0.58	−0.58	−0.41	−0.41	0.38	0.31	−0.28	−0.09	−0.09
0.014	0.014	0.021	0.016	0.013	0.013	0.013	0.013	0.013	0.013	0.01	0.009	0.016	0.013	0.013
0.48	0.50	0.74	0.58	0.43	0.43	0.48	0.48	0.43	0.43	0.35	0.34	0.56	0.45	0.45
0.006	0.006	0.016	0.009	0.033	0.033	0.036	0.036	0.033	0.033	0.021	0.022	0.023	0.014	0.014
0.22	0.22	0.62	0.34	1.08	1.08	1.32	1.32	1.08	1.08	0.71	0.73	0.77	0.54	0.54
−0.003	−0.003	−0.004	−0.003	−0.003	−0.003	−0.005	−0.005	−0.003	−0.003	−0.004	−0.004	−0.004	−0.003	−0.003
(1.71)*	(1.71)*	(2.22)**	(1.87)*	(2.00)**	(2.00)**	(2.77)***	(2.77)***	(2.00)**	(2.00)**	(2.27)**	(2.24)**	(2.39)**	(1.98)*	(1.98)*

table continues next page

Appendix I (continued)

	(1)	(2)	(3)	(4)	(5)	(6)	(7)	(8)	(9)	(10)	(11)	(12)	(13)
Regressions with dependent variable of teacher assessment score (percentage)	Mathematical	Nonmathematical	Mathematical organization	Review	New content	Practice	Assessment	Private (group or seatwork)	Public (whole class)	Public teacher only	Public teacher and student	Public student only	Discussion
Teacher 4-year degree	−0.02	−0.023	−0.019	−0.017	−0.017	−0.021	−0.022	−0.019	−0.019	−0.024	−0.02	−0.025	−0.022
	−0.43	−0.52	−0.41	−0.39	−0.37	−0.45	−0.49	−0.43	−0.43	−0.52	−0.43	−0.58	−0.47
Teacher is certified	−0.017	−0.019	−0.015	−0.02	−0.017	−0.018	−0.019	−0.019	−0.019	−0.015	−0.017	−0.018	−0.016
	−0.51	−0.57	−0.46	−0.62	−0.51	−0.54	−0.58	−0.56	−0.56	−0.45	−0.51	−0.57	−0.46
Student pretest score	0.13	0.144	0.13	0.133	0.13	0.13	0.128	0.131	0.131	0.131	0.13	0.117	0.134
	$(2.78)^{***}$	$(2.98)^{***}$	$(2.77)^{***}$	$(2.89)^{***}$	$(2.78)^{***}$	$(2.85)^{***}$	$(2.72)^{***}$	$(2.85)^{***}$	$(2.85)^{***}$	$(2.85)^{***}$	$(2.71)^{***}$	$(2.65)^{***}$	$(2.90)^{***}$
Class size (number of students)	0.001	0.001	0.001	0.001	0.001	0.001	0.001	0.001	0.001	0.001	0.001	0.001	0.001
	0.36	0.56	0.42	0.67	0.44	0.37	0.40	0.35	0.35	0.60	0.33	0.51	0.46
School private	0.026	0.031	0.028	0.023	0.017	0.027	0.016	0.03	0.03	0.031	0.026	0.035	0.027
	0.55	0.67	0.58	0.47	0.35	0.58	0.30	0.61	0.61	0.65	0.55	0.73	0.58
School religious	−0.011	−0.026	−0.009	−0.005	−0.009	−0.011	−0.012	−0.01	−0.01	−0.015	−0.011	−0.012	−0.012
	−0.30	−0.78	−0.25	−0.13	−0.26	−0.32	−0.35	−0.29	−0.29	−0.42	−0.31	−0.34	−0.35
School size (number of students)	0	0	0	0	0	0	0	0	0	0	0	0	0
	−0.45	−0.58	−0.48	−0.62	−0.47	−0.45	−0.38	−0.45	−0.45	−0.72	−0.43	−0.76	−0.41
School materials shortage	−0.036	−0.035	−0.037	−0.043	−0.041	−0.036	−0.037	−0.037	−0.037	−0.033	−0.036	−0.035	−0.036
	$(2.59)^{**}$	$(2.59)^{**}$	$(2.64)^{**}$	$(3.20)^{***}$	$(2.80)^{***}$	$(2.48)^{**}$	$(2.68)^{***}$	$(2.66)^{***}$	$(2.66)^{***}$	$(2.20)^{**}$	$(2.54)^{**}$	$(2.50)^{**}$	$(2.67)^{***}$
School building deficiency	−0.006	−0.007	−0.005	−0.005	−0.005	−0.006	−0.005	−0.007	−0.007	−0.008	−0.006	−0.01	−0.005
	−0.41	−0.46	−0.35	−0.35	−0.32	−0.42	−0.35	−0.47	−0.47	−0.55	−0.41	−0.67	−0.36
School library deficiency	0.002	0.002	0.002	0.003	0.001	0.002	0	0.002	0.002	0.004	0.002	0.005	0.002
	0.17	0.20	0.20	0.25	0.11	0.17	−0.01	0.14	0.14	0.31	0.17	0.42	0.16
Frequency students skip class	−0.015	−0.012	−0.014	−0.011	−0.013	−0.015	−0.015	−0.016	−0.016	−0.02	−0.015	−0.017	−0.016
	−0.77	−0.60	−0.74	−0.54	−0.65	−0.78	−0.77	−0.79	−0.79	−0.98	−0.73	−0.89	−0.82
Frequency students late	−0.015	−0.017	−0.015	−0.016	−0.015	−0.015	−0.014	−0.015	−0.015	−0.016	−0.015	−0.015	−0.015
	−1.21	−1.34	−1.19	−1.22	−1.26	−1.19	−1.16	−1.22	−1.22	−1.27	−1.21	−1.24	−1.21
Frequency bullying	0.012	0.012	0.013	0.012	0.01	0.013	0.013	0.014	0.014	0.019	0.012	0.023	0.011
	0.54	0.54	0.55	0.53	0.44	0.55	0.57	0.61	0.61	0.75	0.53	0.97	0.47
Community size	0	0.001	0.001	0	−0.001	0	0.001	0.001	0.001	−0.001	0	−0.003	0
	−0.01	0.11	0.07	−0.01	−0.05	−0.02	0.07	0.06	0.06	−0.10	0.00	−0.22	−0.02
Community poor (%)	0.005	0.004	0.003	0.005	0.005	0.005	0.005	0.005	0.005	0.003	0.005	0.001	0.004
	0.32	0.28	0.20	0.38	0.34	0.35	0.34	0.33	0.33	0.21	0.34	0.04	0.30
Community affluent (%)	−0.005	−0.005	−0.005	−0.002	−0.005	−0.005	−0.006	−0.005	−0.005	−0.003	−0.005	−0.003	−0.006
	−0.35	−0.34	−0.35	−0.12	−0.36	−0.33	−0.38	−0.32	−0.32	−0.22	−0.35	−0.22	−0.41
Region Java	0.117	0.122	0.109	0.109	0.116	0.118	0.115	0.119	0.119	0.127	0.118	0.123	0.112
	$(1.79)^{*}$	$(2.03)^{**}$	1.62	$(1.79)^{*}$	$(2.01)^{**}$	$(1.98)^{*}$	$(1.97)^{*}$	$(1.98)^{*}$	$(1.98)^{*}$	$(2.21)^{**}$	$(1.98)^{*}$	$(2.26)^{**}$	$(1.90)^{*}$
Region Sumatera	0.035	0.038	0.027	0.024	0.037	0.034	0.03	0.034	0.034	0.039	0.035	0.04	0.029
	0.52	0.60	0.40	0.40	0.61	0.54	0.49	0.56	0.56	0.67	0.58	0.72	0.48
Region Kalimantan	−0.009	−0.02	−0.013	−0.015	−0.004	−0.011	−0.013	−0.01	−0.01	−0.008	−0.009	−0.016	−0.01
	−0.10	−0.20	−0.14	−0.16	−0.05	−0.11	−0.14	−0.10	−0.10	−0.08	−0.10	−0.17	−0.11
Region Bali/NTT/NTB	0.079	0.074	0.074	0.07	0.084	0.078	0.078	0.081	0.081	0.093	0.079	0.082	0.082
	1.00	0.98	0.91	0.90	1.05	0.98	1.00	1.05	1.05	1.24	0.97	1.18	1.07

(14)	(15)	(16)	(17)	(18)	(19)	(20)	(21)	(22)	(23)	(24)	(25)	(26)	(27)	(28)
Exposition	Investigation	Practical work	Problem solving	Problem	Nonproblem	Math lanDage	Real world	Routine	Nonroutine	Question and answer	Rhetorical	True-false	Open	Closed
−0.015	−0.016	−0.017	−0.007	−0.033	−0.033	−0.047	−0.047	−0.033	−0.033	−0.027	−0.026	−0.061	−0.022	−0.022
−0.32	−0.35	−0.36	−0.15	−0.78	−0.78	−1.05	−1.05	−0.78	−0.78	−0.65	−0.63	−1.46	−0.47	−0.47
−0.015	−0.012	−0.017	−0.016	−0.015	−0.015	0.004	0.004	−0.015	−0.015	−0.016	−0.014	−0.009	−0.012	−0.012
−0.44	−0.35	−0.50	−0.50	−0.41	−0.41	0.10	0.10	−0.41	−0.41	−0.45	−0.40	−0.23	−0.33	−0.33
0.127	0.11	0.145	0.138	0.142	0.142	0.14	0.14	0.142	0.142	0.135	0.135	0.119	0.135	0.135
(2.77)***	(2.47)**	(3.08)***	(2.93)***	(2.95)***	(2.95)***	(2.96)***	(2.96)***	(2.95)***	(2.95)***	(2.95)***	(2.94)***	(2.73)***	(2.92)***	(2.92)***
0.001	0	0	0	0.001	0.001	0.001	0.001	0.001	0.001	0	0	0	0.001	0.001
0.41	−0.03	−0.03	−0.11	0.43	0.43	0.50	0.50	0.43	0.43	−0.12	−0.15	−0.19	0.53	0.53
0.015	0.04	0.032	0.008	0.045	0.045	0.059	0.059	0.045	0.045	0.044	0.044	0.036	0.024	0.024
0.30	0.82	0.67	0.17	1.00	1.00	1.34	1.34	1.00	1.00	1.04	1.03	0.82	0.49	0.49
−0.012	−0.021	−0.014	−0.012	−0.03	−0.03	−0.028	−0.028	−0.03	−0.03	−0.032	−0.032	−0.039	−0.011	−0.011
−0.35	−0.59	−0.40	−0.33	−0.87	−0.87	−0.84	−0.84	−0.87	−0.87	−0.95	−0.95	−1.24	−0.31	−0.31
0	0	0	0	0	0	0	0	0	0	0	0	0	0	0
−0.45	−0.10	−0.25	−0.46	−0.63	−0.63	−0.84	−0.84	−0.63	−0.63	−0.73	−0.75	−0.42	−0.57	−0.57
−0.036	−0.032	−0.037	−0.037	−0.038	−0.038	−0.042	−0.042	−0.038	−0.038	−0.039	−0.039	−0.043	−0.037	−0.037
(2.60)**	(2.35)**	(2.73)***	(2.67)***	(2.66)***	(2.66)***	(3.06)***	(3.06)***	(2.66)***	(2.66)***	(2.71)***	(2.71)***	(2.96)***	(2.65)***	(2.65)***
−0.003	−0.011	−0.009	−0.003	−0.007	−0.007	−0.002	−0.002	−0.007	−0.007	−0.004	−0.004	−0.005	−0.005	−0.005
−0.20	−0.74	−0.59	−0.24	−0.45	−0.45	−0.15	−0.15	−0.45	−0.45	−0.26	−0.25	−0.29	−0.29	−0.29
0.002	0.006	0.002	0.001	0.012	0.012	0.01	0.01	0.012	0.012	0.017	0.017	0.006	0.003	0.003
0.18	0.55	0.14	0.07	0.95	0.95	0.81	0.81	0.95	0.95	1.39	1.39	0.46	0.27	0.27
−0.013	−0.018	−0.017	−0.013	−0.005	−0.005	−0.008	−0.008	−0.005	−0.005	−0.009	−0.009	−0.01	−0.016	−0.016
−0.69	−0.97	−0.90	−0.66	−0.22	−0.22	−0.42	−0.42	−0.22	−0.22	−0.44	−0.45	−0.47	−0.81	−0.81
−0.016	−0.015	−0.011	−0.014	−0.012	−0.012	−0.013	−0.013	−0.012	−0.012	−0.009	−0.009	−0.005	−0.015	−0.015
−1.28	−1.20	−0.99	−1.18	−1.08	−1.08	−1.15	−1.15	−1.08	−1.08	−0.75	−0.79	−0.43	−1.25	−1.25
0.01	0.005	0.008	0.009	0.012	0.012	0.008	0.008	0.012	0.012	0.008	0.008	0.012	0.012	0.012
0.46	0.20	0.34	0.40	0.50	0.50	0.34	0.34	0.50	0.50	0.36	0.34	0.50	0.51	0.51
0	−0.006	0.003	0.003	−0.004	−0.004	−0.012	−0.012	−0.004	−0.004	−0.008	−0.007	−0.011	0.001	0.001
−0.01	−0.46	0.22	0.27	−0.29	−0.29	−0.91	−0.91	−0.29	−0.29	−0.66	−0.57	−0.94	0.07	0.07
0.003	0.009	0.009	0.006	0.007	0.007	0.004	0.004	0.007	0.007	0.003	0.003	0.008	0.005	0.005
0.24	0.63	0.65	0.45	0.45	0.45	0.28	0.28	0.45	0.45	0.20	0.19	0.50	0.40	0.40
−0.009	−0.01	−0.001	−0.005	−0.003	−0.003	−0.005	−0.005	−0.003	−0.003	−0.003	−0.003	−0.006	−0.004	−0.004
−0.57	−0.69	−0.08	−0.33	−0.18	−0.18	−0.36	−0.36	−0.18	−0.18	−0.19	−0.19	−0.42	−0.25	−0.25
0.12	0.114	0.111	0.125	0.119	0.119	0.092	0.092	0.119	0.119	0.113	0.114	0.111	0.119	0.119
(2.04)**	(1.94)***	(2.14)**	(2.25)**	(2.00)**	(2.00)**	(1.71)***	(1.71)***	(2.00)**	(2.00)**	(1.93)***	(1.95)***	(1.87)***	(1.98)***	(1.98)***
0.037	0.036	0.027	0.038	0.045	0.045	0.034	0.034	0.045	0.045	0.039	0.039	0.046	0.033	0.033
0.58	0.59	0.52	0.65	0.73	0.73	0.66	0.66	0.73	0.73	0.66	0.66	0.76	0.55	0.55
−0.001	−0.005	0.005	0.016	0.099	0.099	0.064	0.064	0.099	0.099	0.096	0.094	0.094	−0.009	−0.009
−0.02	−0.05	0.06	0.17	0.74	0.74	0.51	0.51	0.74	0.74	0.71	0.70	0.73	−0.09	−0.09
0.085	0.081	0.087	0.091	0.03	0.03	0	0	0.03	0.03	0.009	0.016	−0.067	0.077	0.077
1.08	1.04	1.17	1.15	0.32	0.32	0.00	0.00	0.32	0.32	0.10	0.16	−0.82	1.00	1.00

table continues next page

Appendix I *(continued)*

Regressions with dependent variable of teacher assessment score (percentage)	(1) *Mathematical*	(2) *Nonmathematical*	(3) *Mathematical organization*	(4) *Review*	(5) *New content*	(6) *Practice*	(7) *Assessment*	(8) *Private (group or seatwork)*	(9) *Public (whole class)*	(10) *Public: teacher only*	(11) *Public: teacher and student*	(12) *Public: student only*	(13) *Discussion*
Constant	0.537	0.481	0.557	0.489	0.568	0.542	0.552	0.541	0.519	0.454	0.544	0.542	0.547
	(2.72)***	(3.12)***	(3.80)***	(3.28)***	(3.82)***	(3.78)***	(3.80)***	(3.76)***	(3.06)***	(2.48)**	(3.68)***	(3.85)***	(3.91)***
Observations	2338	2338	2338	2338	2338	2338	2338	2338	2338	2338	2338	2338	2338
R^2	0.457	0.463	0.458	0.468	0.461	0.458	0.461	0.458	0.458	0.462	0.457	0.467	0.46
Adj. R^2	0.449	0.455	0.45	0.459	0.452	0.449	0.453	0.45	0.45	0.454	0.449	0.458	0.452

Note: Robust t-statistics in parentheses. Regressions run on multiple-imputed data.

Significance level: * = 10 percent, ** = 5 percent, *** = 1 percent.

(14)	(15)	(16)	(17)	(18)	(19)	(20)	(21)	(22)	(23)	(24)	(25)	(26)	(27)	(28)
Exposition	Investigation	Practical work	Problem solving	Problem	Nonproblem	Math lanDage	Real world	Routine	Nonroutine	Question and answer	Rhetorical	True-false	Open	Closed
0.583	0.557	0.537	0.513	0.615	0.495	0.426	0.561	0.615	0.495	0.534	0.534	0.589	0.526	0.509
(3.78)***	(3.98)***	(3.85)***	(3.74)***	(3.78)***	(3.46)***	(2.99)***	(4.22)***	(3.78)***	(3.46)***	(3.97)***	(3.95)***	(4.16)***	(3.63)***	(2.48)**
2338	2338	2338	2338	2116	2116	2116	2116	2116	2116	2116	2116	2116	2296	2296
0.462	0.476	0.471	0.467	0.451	0.451	0.475	0.475	0.451	0.451	0.464	0.461	0.481	0.458	0.458
0.453	0.467	0.462	0.459	0.442	0.442	0.466	0.466	0.442	0.442	0.454	0.451	0.471	0.449	0.449

www.ingramcontent.com/pod-product-compliance
Lightning Source LLC
Chambersburg PA
CBHW081500200326
41518CB00015B/2326